Ps 1. 2. 23. 32. 51. 42.

Psalms

Volume 1

Allan Harman's commentary is the fruit of a lifetime's study of the Psalter and provides a well-informed, reliable guide to the vast literature on the subject. The extensive introduction is itself worth its weight in gold while the Scripture text is opened up in a clear, careful and devout way.

Philip H Eveson,
*Former principal of London Theological Seminary
and lecturer in Old Testament exegesis, theology and preaching*

Harman's Commentary on the Psalms is a solid exposition of the Psalms. The focus is on the original meaning of the psalms with clear explanations of the message of each psalm through an analysis of structure, key words, and the flow of the psalm. And yet, the meaning of the psalms for God's people today is also emphasized by showing important connections to the New Testament. The reader will discover the rich treasures in the Psalms through the use of this commentary.

Richard P. Belcher, Jr.
*Professor of Old Testament,
Reformed Theological Seminary, Charlotte, North Carolina*

Allan Harman writes as a Christian scholar, with academic precision and devotional warmth. The unique character of this commentary is undoubtedly due to the method of its preparation (revealed in the author's "Foreword"). After completing careful exegesis of each Psalm, Allan brought the fruits of his study into the service of family worship in his own home. The result is a commentary that is both academically solid and devotionally rich. This commentary will be a worthy resource for the pastor and student in the study as well as the layman seeking personal edification.

Michael LeFebvre
Pastor, Christ Church Reformed Presbyterian Church, Indianapolis, Indiana

Psalms

Volume 1
Psalms 1-72

A Mentor Commentary

Allan Harman

MENTOR

To Mairi

Allan Harman is Research Professor of Old Testament at the Presbyterian Theological College in Melbourne, Australia. He has taught graduate courses at Ontario Theological Seminary, Toronto and Reformed Theological Seminary, Jackson, Mississippi.

Copyright © Allan Harman 2011

ISBN 978-1-84550-737-4

(Volume 2 ISBN 978-1-84550-738-1)

10 9 8 7 6 5 4 3 2 1

Published in 2011
in the
Mentor Imprint
by
Christian Focus Publications,
Geanies House, Fearn, Tain,
Ross-shire, IV20 1TW, Great Britain
www.christianfocus.com

Cover design by Daniel van Straaten
Printed and bound by MPG Books, UK

All rights reserved. No part of this publication may be reproduced, stored in a retrieval system, or transmitted, in any form, by any means, electronic, mechanical, photocopying, recording or otherwise without the prior permission of the publisher or a license permitting restricted copying. In the U.K. such licenses are issued by the Copyright Licensing Agency, Saffron House, 6-10 Kirby Street, London, EC1 8TS www.cla.co.uk.

Contents

Abbreviations 7
Glossary 9
Notes on Hebrew 11
Foreword 15
Approaching the Psalms 17
Suggestions for Further Reading 95

BOOK 1
Psalm 1 97
Psalm 2 101
Psalm 3 109
Psalm 4 113
Psalm 5 117
Psalm 6 121
Psalm 7 125
Psalm 8 131
Psalm 9 135
Psalm 10 145
Psalm 11 153
Psalm 12 157
Psalm 13 161
Psalm 14 165
Psalm 15 169
Psalm 16 173
Psalm 17 179
Psalm 18 185
Psalm 19 201
Psalm 20 207
Psalm 21 211
Psalm 22 215
Psalm 23 225
Psalm 24 229
Psalm 25 233
Psalm 26 241
Psalm 27 245
Psalm 28 251
Psalm 29 255
Psalm 30 261
Psalm 31 265
Psalm 32 275
Psalm 33 281
Psalm 34 287
Psalm 35 295
Psalm 36 303

Psalm 37	309
Psalm 38	321
Psalm 39	329
Psalm 40	335
Psalm 41	343

BOOK 2

Psalm 42-43	349
Psalm 44	357
Psalm 45	365
Psalm 46	371
Psalm 47	375
Psalm 48	379
Psalm 49	383
Psalm 50	389
Psalm 51	397
Psalm 52	407
Psalm 53	413
Psalm 54	415
Psalm 55	419
Psalm 56	427
Psalm 57	433
Psalm 58	437
Psalm 59	441
Psalm 60	447
Psalm 61	451
Psalm 62	457
Psalm 63	463
Psalm 64	469
Psalm 65	475
Psalm 66	481
Psalm 67	487
Psalm 68	491
Psalm 69	505
Psalm 70	517
Psalm 71	521
Psalm 72	529

Abbreviations

ASV	*American Standard Version.*
AV	*Authorised (King James) Version.*
BASOR	*Bulletin of the American Schools of Oriental Research.*
BBR	*Bulletin for Biblical Research.*
BDB	Brown, Driver, and Briggs, eds., *A Hebrew and English Lexicon of the Old Testament.* (Oxford: Clarendon Press, 1975 reprint).
BHS	*Biblia Hebraica Stuttgartensia* (Stuttgart: Deutsche Bibelstiftung, 1967/77).
Bib	*Biblica.*
BS	*Bibliotheca Sacra.*
c.	Latin, around, about.
CJT	*Canadian Journal of Theology.*
CHAL	*A Concise Hebrew and Aramaic Lexicon of the Old Testament* (Grand Rapids: Eerdmans, 1988).
DCH	*Dictionary of Classical Hebrew*, ed. David J.A. Clines, 7 vols. (Sheffield: Sheffield Academic Press, 1993-)
DIHG~S	J. C. L. Gibson, *Davidson's Introductory Hebrew Grammar~Syntax*, 4th ed. (Edinburgh: T. & T. Clark, 1994).
DOTT	*Documents from Old Testament Times.*
EBC	*Expositor's Bible Commentary.*
ESV	*English Standard Version.* Wheaton: Good News Publishers, 2001.
EQ	*Evangelical Quarterly.*
ET	*Expository Times.*
GKC	*Gesenius' Hebrew Grammar*, 2nd ed., Gesenius, Kautzsch, Cowley eds. (Oxford: Clarendon Press), 1966.
HALOT	*The Hebrew and Aramaic Lexicon of the Old Testament* (Leiden: Brill, 2000).
Heb.	Hebrew.
IBHS	*An Introduction to Biblical Hebrew Syntax*, Bruce K. Waltke and M. O'Connor (Winona Lake: Eisenbrauns, 1990).
IBS	*Irish Biblical Studies.*
IDB	*Interpreter's Dictionary of the Bible*, 4 vols. (Nashville: Abingdon Press, 1962).
ISBE	*International Standard Bible Encyclopaedia.* 4 vols. (Grand Rapids: Eerdmans, 1979).
JANES	*Journal of the Ancient Near Eastern Society.*
JB	*Jerusalem Bible.*
JBL	*Journal of Biblical Literature.*
JETS	*Journal of the Evangelical Theological Society.*
JNSL	*Journal of North West Semitic Languages.*
JSOT	*Journal for the Study of the Old Testament.*

JSS	*Journal of Semitic Studies.*
JTS	*Journal of Theological Studies.*
lit.	literally.
LXX	The Septuagint, the oldest and most important Greek translation of the Old Testament made in Egypt about 250 BC.
mg.	margin.
MT	Massoretic text, the Hebrew text of the Old Testament that became recognised as authoritative after the fall of Jerusalem in 70 AD.
NASB	*New American Standard Bible*: Updated Edition. Anaheim, CA: Foundation Publications, 1997.
NEB	*The New English Bible.* New York: Oxford University Press, 1976.
NICOT	*New International Commentary on the Old Testament.*
NIDOTTE	*New International Dictionary of Old Testament Theology and Exegesis,* ed. Willem A. VanGemeren, 5 vols. (Grand Rapids: Zondervan, 1997).
NIV	*New International Version.* Colorado Springs: International Bible Society, 1984.
NKJV	*New King James Version.* Nashville: Thomas Nelson, 1982.
NLT	*New Living Translation.* Wheaton: Tyndale House, 1996.
NRSV	*New Revised Standard Version.* Nashville: Thomas Nelson, 1989.
OTS	*Oudtestamentische Studiën.*
part.	participle.
pass.	passive.
PEQ	*Palestine Exploration Quarterly.*
PTR	*Princeton Theological Review.*
REB	*The Revised English Bible.* Oxford University Press, 1989.
RSV	*Revised Standard Version.*
RTR	*Reformed Theological Review.*
RV	*Revised Version.*
SJT	*Scottish Journal of Theology.*
TB	*Tyndale Bulletin.*
TS	*Theological Studies.*
TDOT	*Theological Dictionary of the Old Testament,* 15 vols. (Grand Rapids: Zondervan, 1997).
TWOT	*Theological Wordbook of the Old Testament,* 2 vols. (Chicago: Moody Press, 1980).
VT	*Vetus Testamentum.*
WTJ	*Westminster Theological Journal.*
×	The number of occurrences of a word in a particular verse or section is marked by this multiplication sign, e.g. 2×.
ZAW	*Zeitschrift für die alttestamentliche Wissenschaft.*
ZPEB	*Zondervan Pictorial Encyclopedia of the Bible,* 5 vols. (Grand Rapids: Zondervan Publishing House, 1975).

GLOSSARY

acrostic
: In an acrostic poem the first letter of each verse or stanza follows an alphabetic sequence.

Dead Sea Scrolls
: About 800 scrolls containing all or part of Old Testament books discovered at or near Qumran, on the north-western side of the Dead Sea.

fixed pair
: The term 'fixed pair' refers to words that regularly occur in parallel expressions in Hebrew, e.g., head/skull, earth/dust, mouth/lip.

ellipsis (or, gapping)
: This occurs when a normal element of a sentence is missing and has to be understood from the context.

hapax legomenon
: A word occurring only once (pl. *hapax legomena*).

hendiadys
: lit. 'one through two [words]', the presentation of one idea by two expressions, e.g., 'with might and main'.

homonym
: A word having the same sound as another, but with a different meaning and origin. In the text, these Hebrew words are marked by the addition of a Roman numeral as listed in the *Dictionary of Classical Hebrew*, e.g., *rav* II.

inclusio
: A literary device by which a repeated theme both introduces and concludes a passage, so marking it as a separate section.

K^{e}tiv
: A massoretic marginal note to the Hebrew text meaning 'that which is written' (see also Q^{e}re).

maqqef
: A short horizontal stroke linking two Hebrew words.

Massoretes	Groups of Jewish scholars (AD 600-1000) who produced the final form of the OT text, adding the vocalisation, accents, and various notations.
Q^{e}re	A massoretic marginal note to the Hebrew text meaning 'that which is to be read' (in place of 'that which is written', the K^{e}tiv).
Qumran	See above, 'Dead Sea Scrolls'.
targum	An Aramaic translation or paraphrase of some part of the Old Testament. They were oral at first but were later written. The earliest examples (found at Qumran) are from the second century BC.
theophany	A visible appearance of God.
Vulgate	The Latin version of the Bible produced by Jerome in the period AD 380-405, which became the official Bible of the Roman Catholic Church at the Council of Trent in 1546.

Notes on Hebrew

Verbal Themes

Qal	Qal
Ni.	Nif'al
Pi.	Pi'el
Pu.	Pu'al
Hi.	Hif'il
Ho.	Hof'al
Hitp.	Hitpa'el

Grammatical Expressions

absol. inf.	Absolute infinitive: a verbal form normally placed before another form of the verb in order to emphasise it.
cognate accusative	The use of a noun as the object of a verb which comes from the same root, e.g., 'They dreaded [with] dread' (Ps. 14:5).
coh.	cohortative: indirect imperative forms in the 1st person singular and plural, e.g., 'Let me (us) send'.
constr.	construct: a noun, usually in a shortened form, placed before another noun and with a close semantic relation to it, covering all the nuances of the English *of*.
enclitic *mem*	A final *mem* added to words in poetry. This is a rare survival of an archaic form that has no obvious function.
imper.	imperative
imperfect	A verbal conjugation in Hebrew that identifies a situation as fluid or in motion.
inf.	infinitive

interrogative marker	The use of h^a prefixed to a sentence to change it into a question.
jussive	3rd person forms of the indirect imperative, e.g., 'Let him (them) send'.
m.	masculine
part.	participle
pass.	passive
perfect	A verbal conjugation in Hebrew that identifies a situation as static or at rest.
pers.	person
pl.	plural
s.	singular
vav consecutive	The use of the conjunction *vav* ('and') and a verbal form to indicate a simple action that has arisen out of something that has gone before.

Transliteration of Consonants

alef	ʾ
bet	b/v
gimel	g
dalet	d
he	h
vav	v
zayin	z
chet	ch (as in German *ich*, or Scottish *loch*)
tet	t
yod	y
kaf	k
lamed	l
mem	m
nun	n

samek	s
ayin	ʿ
peh	p/f
tsadeh	ts
qof	q
resh	r
sin	s
shin	sh
taw	t

Note:

1. Long vowels are marked with a circumflex, e.g. *â, ê, î, ô, û*.
2. Hebrew words are normally accented on the final syllable. However, there is a group of nouns in which the stress is placed on the first of a pair of vowels, resulting in next-to-last syllable stress. This is marked by the use of an acute, e.g. *régel* (foot). The acute is also used with a small number of other nouns that do not have the stress on the final syllable, e.g. *shâmáyim* (heavens).

13

Foreword

To be able to work twice through the Psalms in preparing commentaries has been a special privilege for me. I thank Christian Focus Publications for the invitation to enlarge my earlier commentary (published in 1998). I have expanded the exegesis, and in doing so I have maintained my method as a commentator that I have explained in the foreword to *Isaiah: A Covenant to be Kept for the Sake of the Church* (Fearn: Christian Focus Publications, 2005). My aim has been to explain the Hebrew text without entering into debate with others. Footnotes have been added to expand on some matters requiring further detail, or to direct the reader's attention to sources of grammatical or lexicographical information. While I have referred to Hebrew quite often, I hope I have done it in a way that still makes it easy for those without a knowledge of the language to feel at home in using this commentary.

It has been encouraging to hear from those who have used my earlier volume and to know that it has served the purpose for which it was written. In the years since its publication I have read widely on the Psalms, and I thank those who have contributed to my thinking, even though there is no express acknowledgement of them in the text.

Once more I have to thank my wife Mairi, who has either read the manuscript, or listened to me reading it, as we worked through the Psalter in our evening devotions. She has partnered me in the work of the Gospel and her help and encouragement continues to be integral to my writing ministry.

Allan M. Harman

Approaching the Psalms

1. SINGING GOD'S PRAISE

1.1 Introducing God's Songs

Songs of praise to God do not only occur in the Book of Psalms. Scattered through various books of the Old Testament are songs sung by the believing community of Israel. The list includes songs such as:

- The Song of the Sea (Exod. 15:1-18) which was composed to celebrate the LORD's deliverance of his people from their bondage in Egypt, and recorded following their dramatic passage through the sea.
- The Song of Moses (Deut. 32:1-43) which was taught to the children of Israel by Moses as a review and a farewell.
- The Song of Deborah and Barak (Judg. 5:1-31) in which they give thanks for the righteous and protective acts of the Lord which had just been manifested in their midst (Judg. 4).
- The Song of Hannah (1 Sam. 2:1-10), a song of thanksgiving with a recognition that life and death come from the Lord.
- 2 Samuel 22:2-51 (appearing also as Ps. 18), a song of joy by David in God as his rock and deliverer.
- Hezekiah's Song (Isa. 38:9-20), composed after his recovery from illness, and in which he sings of God's faithfulness to him (vv. 18-19).

These and various other songs have many similarities with the Book of Psalms. Their language is the same, and they use the same kind of style. In singing both *to* God and *about* him, they do so in a way we quickly recognise as being like the psalmists. It helps to look at some general features of these songs of praise before we come specifically to the Psalter.

1.2 Singing Doxologies

Praise is addressed to God primarily because it is a special way of extolling who he is and what he does. Often we think of using what we call 'doxologies' at the beginning or end of a service of worship. However, every hymn addressed to God is really a doxology, for in using it we are proclaiming to God what we know of his person and work. Thus we say to God: 'You are the one whose glory is over all the earth' (Ps. 108:5), or 'You are my King and my God, who decrees victories for Jacob. Through you we push back our enemies; through your name we trample our foes' (Ps. 44:4-5).

Singing in this way in front of others, or joining with them in communal songs of praise, also involves an element of confession. In addressing God in words or song we are telling others what we know of him, and also confessing that he is the God whom we have come to honour and trust. Singing the Lord's songs then can be an acknowledgment of an allegiance to him.

1.3 Praise and the Wonderful Deeds of the LORD

The songs of praise in the Old Testament focus attention on what God has done. They are often long recitals of the great deeds of God. This is particularly so of the 'historical psalms' such as 78, 105, 106, and 136, while in many other psalms there are references to historical incidents. The psalmist, in Psalm 77, speaks of calling to mind the deeds of the LORD and remembering God's wonders of old (vv. 11-12). The use of the word 'wonder' is important in psalms like this, because it translates a Hebrew word which has the idea that it is something that only God can do. Telling out the 'wonders of the LORD' means to proclaim the great things God has done for the salvation of his people.

1.4 Praise and Commitment to God's Covenant

The praises of Israel have to be seen in the wider context of Israel's commitment to the LORD. There was a bond or covenant between God and Israel, and they were solemnly pledged to be the Lord's people. In all their worship they acknowledged the relationship, and numerous features of their life were said to be 'to the LORD' (e.g. the Passover, Exod. 12:11, 27, 48; the Sabbath, Exod. 16:23; the year of Jubilee, Deut. 15:2; the Nazirite, Num. 6:2). In singing to the LORD the people were in a verbal way paying their tribute to their great king and Saviour. It was another way of reaffirming the oath they had taken to him. This comes out strikingly in David's words, 'The LORD lives, blessed be my Rock' (Ps. 18:46). It is clear from Jeremiah 5:2 that the phrase 'as the LORD lives' was part of an oath formula. Here it appears in conjunction with a doxology to God.

Another way to see this same commitment is in regard to God's law. There are psalms such as Psalm 119 in which there is constant reference to God's word, or statutes, or testimonies. In other words, the praise of God's law is once again submission to God's covenant requirements.[1] From the same perspective we can see that the laments, especially of a communal nature, are saying that the people have departed from God's covenant pattern for them.

1.5 Praise and Promise for the Future

Believers are able to sing contemporaneously with glorified believers in heaven. There is a union between saints on earth and saints in heaven (Heb. 12:22-24). They sing a song on earth that echoes that of saints above. Believers still living have access to the heavenly Zion of which they have become citizens. They are 'Blest inhabitants of Zion, Washed in the Redeemer's blood' (John Newton, 'Glorious things of thee are spoken'), and so can sing in unison with the great company in heaven of redeemed sinners and angels who together sing praise to the Lamb who was slain (Rev. 5:12-13; 7:9-12).

---

[1] A valuable discussion on 'The Concept of the Word of God as Seen in Psalm 119' can be found in John P. Milton, *The Psalms* (Rock Island, Illinois: Augustana Book Concern, 1954), pp. 99-127.

Having learned of the grace of God in salvation, Old Testament psalmists also realised that it had implications for the future. The kingdom of God had not come to full expression. The Gentiles were hardly yet touched with the blessings of God, but they would yet experience the blessing of the Lord (Ps. 67). There are songs which express longing for the extension of God's kingdom, so that Messiah will reign from the River (i.e. the Euphrates) to the uttermost ends of the earth (Ps. 72:11), and all ends of the earth will turn to the Lord, and all families of the nations will bow down before Him (Ps. 22:27).

The fact that God has often intervened in human history and does great and wonderful things encourages his people to sing of coming events. Believers have the confidence that the LORD will keep them and ultimately bring them into his glory (Ps. 73:24). At the end the LORD will come to judge the world in righteousness (Ps. 96:13). He has established a throne from which he will judge the world (Ps. 9:8), but he will vindicate his own people (Ps. 135:14).

2. THE USE OF POETRY

2.1 Poetry and Music

Jewish and Christian worship make extensive use of religious poetry. Such poetry involves two distinct features:

(a) It is a style of writing that is different from the normal style of narrative prose. For example, compare the account of God's covenant with David as recorded in 2 Samuel 7 with the poetical expression of it in Psalm 89; or Genesis 1 with Psalm 8. The same ideas can be conveyed in prose and poetry, but poetry contains music in words and this attracts us and is more memorable.

(b) This religious poetry is not only *said*, but it is *sung*, and such singing forms an important part of religious expression. Naturally we do not have examples directly from biblical times but there are many examples of synagogue music. Some of these are carried over into Christian worship, as, for example, the tune Leoni sung to the hymn, 'The God of Abraham Praise'.

Music, like language, has its origin in the fact that man is a creature of God, and in making music man is imitating God himself. He has been created in God's image, and his ability to use both words and music is a result of his being a unique image bearer. Music is not given for pure entertainment but as a thing of beauty that directs attention to God's works of creation (creativity) and providence (order). When music and religious poetry are brought together in harmony there is a special appeal to the human mind and emotions. In itself music is not identical to language but it has some of the same abilities as poetical language to appeal to the imagination and to touch human emotions.

Creativity in language and music are brought together in psalmody and hymnody. A message is conveyed in both words and music which combine to produce an effect upon the hearer, which in turn heightens religious understanding and experience.

2.2 Characteristics of Poetry

The poetry of the Old Testament shares some features with Western poetry, but in other respects it is quite different. Some of the features in common are:

(a) The normal patterns of word order can be varied in poetry. The impact of normal word order is important as we can often predict what the end of a sentence will be. However, an unusual pattern has the effect of pressing on our attention the idea being presented.

(b) The language of poetry is often much more conservative than popular speech, and unusual words are frequently used. Some words are even invented to fit a particular context. We have only to glance at an older hymn book (and some modern ones) to see examples which would be very strange in ordinary conversation: 'inly', 'Bethlem', 'sage', 'Christly', 'illuming', 'wert', 'cloys', 'lays', 'supernal', 'pent', 'till moons shall *wax* ...', 'riven', 'assuage', 'transport of delight'. It also retains words that have dropped out of everyday use, and thereby fossilises them in poetic form. For example, in modern Scripture in song you will still find words like 'thee', 'thine', 'thou', 'realm', 'diadem', and many others.

(c) It uses many features of style such as playing on the initial sound in words (alliteration) or sound in other syllables (assonance). Poetry also uses similes (in which there is a comparison) and metaphors (in which something is said to be something else, e.g. the LORD is a rock). Metaphors are very important because they ensure that our minds are involved because we have to work out the meanings of the words of the poem. They also appeal to our imagination which is attracted by the total idea. Moreover, metaphors often touch our emotions for they appeal to our senses. Hence, because they combine an idea with a feeling, they express much more to us than the bare idea expressed without a metaphor.

(d) There is no sharp dividing line between prose and poetry, for sometimes elevated prose will contain features which are normally characteristic of poetry. There are distinctive characteristics of both prose and poetry, and many examples of literature share features from both. The distinction between poetry and prose may be one of degree, rather than an absolute division. For Old Testament poetry this can be illustrated by the following diagram:

Parallelism
Figurative language
Non-predictable word order

↘↘↘

Prose ←——————————————→ Poetry

↖↖↖

Narrative sequence
Non-figurative language
Predictable word order

2.3 The Distinctiveness of Old Testament Poetry

Other features of Old Testament poetry are quite different because they are part of Hebrew and therefore of Near Eastern poetic style. The most important feature of Old Testament poetry is the use of phrases in a parallel way. Thus the psalmist says:

> The eyes of the LORD are on the righteous,
> and his ears are attentive to their cry (Ps. 34:15).

There is a correspondence between the two phrases which may be similar as in this one, or which may express opposites as in Psalm 1:6:

> For the LORD watches over the way of the righteous,
> but the way of the wicked will perish.

Perhaps the most common pattern is where the second phrase adds something more to the expression. The poet introduces an idea, and then focuses more specifically on it in the following phrase. We can express this by calling the two phrases A and B. The pattern is:

> A, and what's more,
>   B.

For example, Psalm 6 commences with the words:

> O LORD, do not rebuke me in your anger
> or discipline me in your wrath.

The psalm opens with a plea to God not to speak words of rebuke to him (A), but then in the second part of the verse (B), the psalmist asks that no action ('discipline') will be taken against him. The phrases are clearly not identical, but show a progression of thought.

Hebrew poetry also uses a range of devices to draw attention to the ideas. These include features that are very stilted if we attempt to bring them over into English translations. For example, many poems in the Old Testament use acrostics, in which the letters of the alphabet appear in order at the beginning of lines. This can be done where a single line follows (Ps. 34) or where several lines follow (Pss. 9-10), or as in Psalm 119, in which every line of the twenty-two sections starts with the appropriate letter of the Hebrew alphabet.[2] This explains why in English translations of this psalm the Hebrew letters are actually printed in the text (see also the NIV footnote). For native Hebrew speakers these devices would attract attention and make an appeal to the reader or listener. Also, they may have been useful for memorisation. They can be likened to embroidery, which takes so many hours to do, but the result is a beautiful piece of work that attracts and delights.[3]

2.4 Sung Praise in Old Testament Worship

From earliest times music was employed (Gen. 4:21) and songs of praise feature in the Pentateuch (Exod. 15:1-18, 21; Deut. 32) and the early historical books (Judg. 5; 1 Sam. 2). Music and religious poetry are inseparably connected from the time of David onwards. When the ark of the covenant was brought to Jerusalem David instructed the leaders of the Levites to appoint singers of joyful songs, who were to be accompanied with lyres, harps and cymbals (1 Chron. 15:16). For service in the house of God he appointed the sons of Asaph, Heman, and Jeduthun to a ministry of singing (1 Chron. 25:1ff.; singing is called 'prophesying' in the Hebrew of this passage). On the day in which the ark was brought to Jerusalem David committed to Asaph and his associates a song which is a combination of several psalms (cf. 1 Chron. 16:8-36 with Pss. 105:1-15; 96; 106:1, 47-48), and to this song the people responded with 'Amen, Hallelujah'. Over 80 per cent of the

---

[2] Cf. the attempt by Edward H. Sugden, *The Psalms of David: Translated into English Verse in accordance with the Metres and Strophic Structure of the Hebrew* (Melbourne: MacMillan & Co., 1924), to reproduce the alphabetic patterns in his translations.

[3] For readers who want to carry on further reflection on this subject, an excellent and stimulating starting point is the discussion by Leland Ryken, '"I Have Used Similitudes": The Poetry of the Bible', *BS* (1990), pp. 259-69.

Psalms come from the period of David or later, and over 40 per cent are attributed to David himself. There was song in the temple especially when sacrifices were being offered, and at times the people responded with refrains (2 Chron. 7:3; Ezra 3:11).

2.5 Printing Biblical Poetry

Translation and printing of biblical poetry involves difficulties, as the effort to reproduce in English the complexities of a totally different type of poetry forces many choices to be made. The older translations, such as the Authorised Version, simply printed the Psalms in the same way as the prose passages. Recent translations (e.g. NIV, ESV) have attempted to print the poetic parts of the Bible in a different way to prose. This alerts the reader to the fact that the translators consider these passages are poetical. While they have not necessarily carried over many aspects of Hebrew poetry, yet at least the form in which they are printed prepares the reader for dealing with poetry, not prose. Poems have formal qualities (cf. the reference above to alphabetical psalms) and sometimes these can be brought out in a way that catches the reader's eye. Consider this rendering of Psalm 117 by the Elizabethan poetess, Mary Sidney Herbert (1561-1621):

P raise him that aye
R emains the same:
A ll tongues display
I ehovah's fame,
S ing all that share
T his earthly ball:
H is mercies are
E xposed to all
L ike as the word
O nce he doth give,
R olled in record,
D oth time outlive.

While the poems of the Old Testament are part of divinely inspired Scripture, yet human activity is entailed both in the composition as well as in the translation and printing.[4] Continued effort has to be devoted to translation *and* format so that as much as possible of the original Hebrew poems are conveyed in modern printed English.[5] Communication of the content of the Psalms to generation after generation requires constant endeavour to accurately translate and intelligently convey its message to modern readers and listeners.[6]

3. INTRODUCING THE PSALTER

3.1 The Titles

The Hebrew Bible simply calls the Book of Psalms in Hebrew *t^ehillîm*, 'Praises'. The Greek translation of the Old Testament (commonly referred to as the LXX), produced by about 200 BC, called them 'Psalmoi', and it is from this word that ultimately we get our English word 'Psalms'. In the New Testament the collection of Psalms is called 'the Book of Psalms' (Luke 20:42; Acts 1:20) and from that expression we get our general descriptive title for the book. One early manuscript of the LXX translation has the title 'Psalterion'. This was the word used

---

[4] This was stated clearly by B. B. Warfield in his discussion, 'The Divine and the Human in the Bible', *Selected Shorter Writings of Benjamin B. Warfield*, ed. John E. Meeter (Phillipsburg: Presbyterian and Reformed, 1973), 2, p. 547: 'The whole of Scripture is the product of divine activities which enter it, however, not by superseding the activities of the human authors, but confluently with them; so that the Scriptures are the joint product of divine and human activities, both of which penetrate them at every point, working harmoniously together to the production of a writing which is not divine here and human there, but at once divine and human in every part, every word, every particular.' See also the discussion on this and other points in D. G. Hart, 'The Divine and the Human in the Seminary Curriculum,' *WTJ* 65 (2003), pp. 36-41.

[5] While alphabetic poetry cannot be imitated in translation (apart from noting the twenty-two sections in Psalm 119), yet other features can be shown, e.g. some chiastic patterns, or the refrains in psalms such as 42-43, 46, and 99.

[6] Further helpful discussions are by Keith R. Crim, 'Translating the Poetry of the Bible', *BT* (January 1972), pp. 102-09; and, William A. Smalley, 'Restructuring Translations of the Psalms as Poetry', in Matthew Black and William A. Smalley, edd., *On Language, Culture, and Religion: In Honor of Eugene A. Nida* (The Hague: Moulton, 1974), pp. 337-71.

for an instrument like a zither, and from this Greek word we get another English title for the Psalms, 'the Psalter'. Many of the individual psalms have titles given to them. These titles may not have originally been part of the psalms, but they are certainly very early. This is shown by the way in which songs outside the Book of Psalms have titles, such as David's psalms of thanksgiving (2 Sam. 22:1), Hezekiah's song (Isa. 38:9) and Habakkuk's psalm (Hab. 3:1, 19b). Also, the fact that the translators of the Old Testament into Greek had difficulties with the titles when they came to translate them suggests their antiquity. The titles can be grouped according to the type of information they contain. Some merely designate the type of psalm in question (e.g. hymn or song, 32, 83, 145), while others contain musical information (e.g., 4 and 5) or an indication of special use (e.g. 30, 'For the dedication of the Temple'; 92, 'For the Sabbath Day'). Many of the titles relate to a person or groups of people (e.g. David, 3; Solomon, 72; Moses, 90) or give information relating the particular psalm to a historical situation particularly with reference to David (e.g. 18, 56, 60, and 63).[7]

3.2 Difficulties in Approaching the Psalms

The greatest difficulty we face is our familiarity with the Book of Psalms. For many Christian people the Psalms, or particular well-loved psalms, are the parts of the Bible that they know best. In many branches of the Christian tradition the Psalms are said or sung in a distinctive and traditional manner. Thus in Anglican churches usually the Psalms are read or chanted. In Reformed churches, originating either on the Continent or in Scotland, the Psalms for long formed either the major part of sung praise or in many cases the exclusive content of praise. Others are known because they are now part of the paraphrased poetry of a hymn book. Simply because they

---

[7] For full listings of the titles, see W. VanGemeren, 'The Psalms', *The Expositor's Bible Commentary* (Grand Rapids: Zondervan, 1991), 5, pp. 33-39; or, C. Hassell Bullock, *Encountering the Psalms: A Literary and Theological Introduction* (Grand Rapids: Baker Academic, 2001), pp. 24-30. An excellent discussion on the antiquity of the titles can be found in Roger T. Beckwith, 'The Early History of the Psalter', *TB* 46.1 (May 1995), pp. 10-17.

are used so much does not necessarily mean that they are understood better than other parts of the Bible. A fresh look at the Psalms will bring us to a deeper appreciation of their content and meaning.

The Psalter is also a difficult book to study because it has an accumulation of problems that we do not face in the same way elsewhere in the Old Testament. For example, when we come to another book of the Old Testament, such as a historical book like Joshua, or a prophetical book like Ezekiel, we are able to put it in a distinct historical setting. When we are faced with the Psalter we have a tremendous range of historical settings, so that each psalm has to be interpreted individually. Moreover, we are not just dealing with one type of literature in the Psalms. While we can go to historical, prophetical, and poetical parts of the Old Testament in general, in the Psalter we have all these represented and more. For the Psalter, though, the absence of historical context for a particular psalm makes our task harder as we try to date the period from which it came, to see if the historical background helps us to interpret it better.

3.3 The Creed of Israel

The Book of Psalms brings together the faith of Israel into one book. The format in which it appears is new, but not the content. All the themes of the book are held together by the fact that it is the confession of Israel, for it is Israel's creed, sung not signed. That is to say, it expresses for us what believers in Israel of old knew and felt about the Lord in whom they trusted. It is a word from the heart, not the formal expression of a carefully composed creedal statement to which they could have added their signature. The unity that it possesses is the unity which that faith gives to the whole book.

The Psalter is also important because it is virtually a theology of the Old Testament. Even without the other books that make up our Old Testament we could produce from the Psalms all the essential material from which we could write the theology. It contains long historical psalms which recount the history of God's people, while other psalms, as we know either by their titles or their contents, show us how the church in the Old Testament times reacted to particular situations. Their faith was on trial, and the songs they sang expressed their deepest religious convictions.

The theology of the Psalms, moreover, is popular theology. That is to say, it is not the theology or philosophy of a group of expert theologians discussing matters and formulating their conclusions in a very abstract way. The concreteness of the Psalms strikes us as we read them, as well as how down-to-earth they are. They display how life in response to God was lived in ancient Israel, and how believers 'through each perplexing path of life' ('O God of Bethel', Scottish Paraphrase 2) put their trust in him. When we read other parts of the Old Testament we have to balance them with the underlying ideas about God contained in the Psalter, for it gives us what people were thinking and feeling in relation to their religious experiences. This is also another reason why the Psalms appeal to the broad Christian community. While many Christians feel they need special help to understand, for example, the Book of Leviticus, they are able to approach and appropriate the Psalms for themselves.

As we will see later, the groupings of Psalms may well reflect some aspects of theological significance. That is to say, the way in which the Psalms are brought together in the one bundle, may well have significance in that psalms with similar meanings are often placed in close proximity. Psalms 3 and 4 have similarities and are placed together, while Psalms 9 and 10 may well have originally been a single composition, for together they form in Hebrew a single acrostic poem. Other psalms, such as Psalms 42 and 43 and Psalms 142 and 143, are also brought together because of common themes.

It is also important to see the first two psalms as setting the pattern for the whole book. Psalm 1 contains the basic distinction between the righteous and the wicked and speaks of the blessedness or happiness of the person who delights in the LORD and his law (vv. 1-4). Jesus, in the Sermon on the Mount, also uses the idea of blessedness, when he expounds the same basic principles even more fully and carries on the teaching concerning the two ways (Matt. 5–7). The second psalm carries on the theme of the two ways by emphasising how nations set themselves against the LORD and his anointed, which came to pass at the crucifixion (see the quotation from this psalm in Acts 4:25-26). Both psalms refer to 'the way' (1:1; 2:12). The anointed king of Psalm 2 transcends any of David's successors, and the presentation of this figure points to Jesus as the appointed Son and Servant (see Matt. 3:17; 17:5; 2 Pet. 1:17).

3.4 The Prayer Book of the Bible

At times the Book of Psalms has been called the prayer book of the Bible. Although this suggests that all the psalms are addressed to God, there are some which are not (e.g., 1, 2, 32, 45, etc.). It is better to think of the Psalms as showing us the true nature of prayer, and how believers can respond to the great saving acts of God. To what God does in an objective way, his people give their subjective response in the meditation and prayers of the Psalter.

The Psalms help us to understand the true nature of prayer because of their main characteristics.

(a) When men pray to God using human words, the prayer can only be the response to God's words to them. Thus when the psalmists are praying to God, they are praying back to him what he had spoken. They also appeal to God to remember the word that he has given (Ps. 119:49). The whole principle of meditation rests upon the fact that God has both spoken and acted.

(b) The focus of attention is God himself. This holds true even when the psalmists are praying concerning their own needs. So many of the psalms are declarations of God's gracious character, and they are therefore basically songs of praise. It is not surprising, therefore, that the Jews called the whole book *tᵉhillîm* ('praises'). The very act of prayer to God is a recognition of who he is, and in coming to him in this way we are proclaiming that we acknowledge that he is precisely who he claims to be.

(c) The Psalms also teach us that a mark of true prayer is humility before God. The descriptions we have of human sin and guilt in the Psalms are not accidental. Rather, these descriptions go to the very heart of prayer with the recognition that we have no right to stand our ground before a holy God (Ps. 24:3), for none living is righteous in his sight (Ps. 143:2). We are reminded that those who pray come as humble servants, waiting till the LORD shows mercy (Ps. 123:2). The constant references in the Psalms to the need for God's intervention are another aspect of the psalmists' humility before him. They know that in need or in deliverance the glory is to be given to God's name on account of his love and faithfulness (Ps. 115:1).

4. THE PSALMS AND SPIRITUAL LIFE

4.1 The Psalms — The Most Comprehensive Book of the Old Testament

The Book of Psalms is very different from every other Old Testament book. To use the illustration of Athanasius (AD c. 295-373), all the other books are like gardens that grow only one kind of fruit. However, the Book of Psalms, in addition to growing its own special fruit, also grows some from all the other gardens. Thus it includes history and prophecy as well as praise and prayer. As Luther expressed it: 'You may rightly call the Psalter a Bible in miniature.'

There is no other Old Testament book that has such a historical range. Psalm 90 is attributed to Moses, while the bulk of the book comes from the period of David and Solomon. There are psalms such as Psalm 74, 79, and 80 which are clearly written after the destruction of Jerusalem, and in them the psalmists recount something of the destruction of Jerusalem (74:3-8; 79:1-4; 80:4-6, 8-16) and appeal to God to again visit his people and restore them. Psalm 137 pictures the exiles being mocked in their captivity in Babylon, while Psalm 126 rejoices in what the LORD has done in restoring the people to their own land.

In the Psalms we have a representative sample of the faith of Israel over centuries. This helps us to see how enduring was the commitment of the people to the LORD, and how their trust in him sustained them during periods of testing. Clearly too the psalmists saw the responsibility of parents and elders to pass on the faith to coming generations. They wanted succeeding generations not only to know about the great deeds of the LORD, but also to put their trust in him for themselves (78:7). Generations yet unborn had to be told about the LORD and his righteousness, so that they too would serve him (22:30-31). Children were encouraged to learn of the fear of the LORD and to know that his eyes were on the righteous (34:11-16).

4.2 The Psalms – The Most Personal Book of the Old Testament

The Psalter is markedly different from the rest of the Old Testament in other ways as well. The human authors normally write in the third person about events, even those concerning themselves. We see this illustrated by the way in which Moses reports the conflict between himself and Aaron and Miriam (Num. 12:1-16), or in the manner in which Amos speaks in the third person in connection with his own conflict with Jeroboam and Amaziah (Amos 7:10-17). There are brief biographical elements in some of the prophets such as Isaiah (6:1-13) and Jeremiah (1:4-19), but in the main the Old Testament is written in the third person.

However, the Psalter uses the first person throughout. It speaks of 'I' or 'we', which points out straight away that they are expressions of personal religious life. The Psalms are not abstract writing about theology, or anything approaching a philosophical discussion of religious themes. They are really an expression of the knowledge about God and his ways that is rooted in personal experience of a vital relationship with him. If knowledge of God was revealed for all in Israel to profit from it, then that knowledge should be grasped and used by all. The Psalms articulate that theology for ancient Israel, and so we see in them the popular religious feeling of redeemed sinners.

Another amazing feature of the Psalms is that they portray all the varied experiences and emotions of the human heart, with all its ups and downs. They describe real life in which the psalmists bare their souls for others to see and express their deepest emotions and longings. We not only see them at the heights of joy, but they express their honest feelings of despair and doubt.

4.3 Identification with the Psalmist

The Psalms also provoke a response in us because of our similar spiritual experiences. They are in themselves a response to God and truths concerning him. They stimulate us as we pass through similar experiences and find that we can identify with the psalmists in their days. Their words become our words, and we find that we can take over their expression of religious faith and use it as if it were our own.

This also means that the Psalms serve as a mirror of the soul. Calvin expressed it like this: 'I am in the habit of calling this book, not inappropriately, "The Anatomy of all the parts of the soul," for not an affection will no one find in himself, an image of which is not reflected in this mirror'.[8] Here Calvin is echoing the words of Athanasius who said: 'It seems to me, moreover, that because the Psalms thus serve him who sings them as a mirror, wherein he sees himself and his own soul, he cannot help but render them in such a manner that their words go home with equal force to those who hear him sing, and stir them also to a like reaction.' The Psalms both serve as a suitable means for us to express our own feelings, and also stimulate us further as we crystallise our thoughts regarding

---

[8] This comes in Calvin's Preface to his commentary on the *Psalms: A Commentary on the Psalms of David* (Oxford: D. A. Talboys, 1840), I, p. vi. James A. De Young further elaborates on the impact of the Psalms on Calvin in his article, '"An Anatomy of All Parts of the Soul": Insights into Calvin's Spirituality from His Psalms Commentary', in W. H. Neusner, ed., *Calvinus Sacrae Scripturae Professor: Calvin as Confessor of Holy Scripture* (Grand Rapids: Eerdmans, 1994), pp. 1-14. I have discussed the broader question of the place of the Psalms for life in the Reformed community in 'The Psalms and Reformed Spirituality', *RTR* 53, 2 (1994), pp. 53-62.

God's dealings with us. In this way, the Psalms not only speak to us, but they also speak for us.

The variety of experiences described by the psalmists also meets us in our needs. Whatever the situation in which we are, we can turn to the Psalms knowing that something appropriate for us will be found there. This is why Martin Luther gained such comfort in the Psalms during his own spiritual agony, for he discovered in them his own innermost feelings. If Luther was mad, then so was the psalmist; if Luther was hungry and thirsty for God, then so was the psalmist! He said that in the Psalms 'everyone, in whatever state he is, finds words that fit his case and suit him exactly, as though they were put there for his sake alone ... Then he becomes sure that he is in the communion of saints.'

The emotional element of poetry and song enables us to express with power and feeling our response to God in the words of the Psalms. The Psalms are directed towards the emotions of men and women, because they are the expressions of human beings as they passed through crises in their lives. One of the ways in which we can classify the Psalms is by the emotion expressed in them. Thus we can think of songs of joy, or cries of despair, or laments of abandonment, or the calm peace of confident trust. Emotions are grounded in our faith, and thus our present relationship with God will affect our emotions. The Psalms help us to see how Old Testament believers wrestled with their emotional response to situations, and how their changed understanding of God and his ways impelled them to action.

4.4 The Faith of the Psalmists

We must not make any distinction between the faith of Old Testament believers and believers in the New Testament period in respect to trust in God and his word. The same principle applies even to us today. When the New Testament writers wish to illustrate the nature of faith they appeal to Old Testament examples (Rom. 4; Gal. 3; Heb. 11; James 2). Those believers are part of the great cloud of witnesses whose testimony should stimulate us to run with patience looking unto Jesus (Heb. 12:2). While they did not have the fullness of New Testament revelation, yet they responded to what God had revealed up to their day, and they believed it.

When we turn to the Psalms we see frequent expressions of trust in the LORD. Those whose trust is in him display an entire self-commitment to him, coupled with obedience to his word and commands. A wide variety of language is used to describe this relationship. The people of God are said to act in certain ways including 'believe', 'trust', 'take refuge in', 'rely upon', 'wait for', and 'wait patiently for'. Some of these expressions are used in contrast to putting trust in substitutes like military weapons, princes, idols, or even man himself (44:6; 146:3; 135:15-18; 52:7). The words of Psalm 62:8 express the basic message of the Psalms regarding faith: 'Trust in him at all times, O people.'

In all their experiences the psalmists were relying on the character of God as he had made himself known. There was no special word of revelation to help them in their time of need. Because there was no personal message they had to rely simply on God's love and mercy revealed previously. In times of great perplexity, it was knowledge of God's existing revelation which broke through and brought light into a dark situation. Thus in Psalm 73 the psalmist was in turmoil about the prosperity of the wicked until he came into God's house and then understood their end (73:16-17). In the Book of Psalms faith is like faith elsewhere in the Bible; it is reliance on God and his character as revealed in earlier periods of the Old Testament.

5. DEVELOPMENT OF THE PSALTER

5.1 The Groupings

Clearly the Psalms have been arranged in some order, but certainly this is not chronological. While we do have psalms from the period of the exile or later (such as 126 or 137) coming towards the end of the Psalter, they do not come at the very end. The most that can be said is that the psalms of David appear predominantly in the first half of the Psalter, though just after a song of the exile (137) a psalm of David follows (138). Neither is the arrangement by author or by content, though some sections do bring together psalms by a particular author or link by theme. However, this is not done consistently throughout the whole book. What is apparent is that, whereas the Psalms have been brought together into a complete book, there are actually five separate books that make the whole. Jewish tradition accepted that the division into five was in imitation of the five books of Moses (Genesis to Deuteronomy), with Psalter readings linked to the appropriate Pentateuchal passages for reading in the synagague.[9] This division can be set out in a table like this:

The Complete Psalter

Book 1	Psalms 1-41
Book 2	Psalms 42-72
Book 3	Psalms 73-89
Book 4	Psalms 90-106
Book 5	Psalms 107-150

Each of these divisions ends with a doxology. Thus the first book ends with the words of Psalm 41:13:

> Praise be to the LORD, the God of Israel,
>   from everlasting to everlasting.
>   Amen and Amen.

Similar doxologies occur at the end of Books 2, 3, 4 (72:18-19; 89:52; 106:48). There is no doxology of that kind to end the final book, but the whole of Psalm 150 is a doxology, which fittingly concludes the whole Psalter with the call: 'Let everything that has breath praise the LORD. Praise the LORD.'

This division is old, because the Greek translation (LXX) contains it. The doxology that ends the fourth book is also quoted in 1 Chronicles 16:36 in connection with the ark of the covenant being brought into Jerusalem.

---

[9] *Midrash Tehillim* on Psalm 1:5.

5.2 The Development of the Psalter[10]

The gradual development of the Psalter is shown by several facts:

(a) In addition to the doxology at the end of the third book there is also a note, 'This concludes the prayers of David son of Jesse' (72:20). As psalms of David do come later than this (cf. 108-110, 138-145) it seems that Psalm 72 must have been the ending of an earlier collection later incorporated in the present Psalter.

(b) There are various psalms or portions that are repeated in the Psalter. They are:

Psalm 14	=	Psalm 53
Psalm 40:13-17	=	Psalm 70
Psalm 57:7-11	=	Psalm 108:1-5
Psalm 60:5-12	=	Psalm 108:6-13

Duplication is not unknown in the prophetical books where the same passage can occur in two different prophets (cf. Isaiah 2:2-4 with Micah 4:1-3) but very rare within the same book. Here it suggests that collections of psalms were in use prior to the present full Psalter.

(c) Within the Psalter there are clearly defined blocks of material, which appear to have been collected together prior to their being brought into the full Psalter. There are various smaller groups but the main subsidiary collections can be seen from the following table:

Groups of Songs within the Psalter

| Davidic Collections | 3-41; 51-72; 138-145 |
| Korahite Collections | 42-49; 84-85; 87-88 |

---

[10] For a fine survey of the information relating to this topic, see R. Dean Anderson, 'The Division and the Order of the Psalms', *WTJ* 56 (1994), pp. 219-41. Leslie McFall, 'The Evidence for a Logical Arrangement of the Psalter', *WTJ* 62 (2000), 223-56, is an extremely detailed discussion with valuable charts. He argues that the present shape of the Psalter is a result of a hierarchical order of sorting, according to authorship, the use of divine names, placing of psalms according to genre, and grouping according to the continuity of thought.

Elohistic Collection (using the name Elohim in reference to God)	42-83
Asaphite Collection	73-83
Kingship Psalms	93-100
Praise Psalms	103-107
Songs of Ascent (used on pilgrimage to Jerusalem or on return from exile)	120-134
Hallelujah Psalms (beginning or ending with 'Hallelujah')	104-106; 111-118; 146-150

(d) The use of the names for God in the Psalter also suggests stages in development. Psalms 1-41 (Book 1) mainly use the covenant name *Yahweh* (taken into English as 'Jehovah'), with *Elohîm* only occurring rarely. In Psalms 42-72 (Book 2) the main word for God is *Elohîm*, while in Book 4 only *Yahweh* is used. The preference for one name for God over another comes out very clearly in the duplicate psalms. Whereas Psalm 14 uses the name *Yahweh*, its duplicate, Psalm 53, has *Elohîm* instead (there are some other minor alterations as well).[11] The Jews felt great reverence for the name Yahweh and did not even pronounce it, substituting the word 'Lord' instead, and this usage carried over into the New Testament.

(e) Certain facts, however, suggest that there was an earlier division into three books, two of which were later subdivided to create the present five. The difference in size among the five books has often been noted, with two of them being much shorter than the other three. Books 3 and 4 only have seventeen psalms each, whereas Book 2

---

[11] Discussions in regard to literary features in the Psalms must also take into account the use of divine names, and some implications for the connection between the books that comprise the Psalter may follow. See Ronald Youngblood, 'Divine Names in the Book of Psalms: Literary Structures and Number Patterns', *JANES* 19 (1989), pp. 171-181; Gerald H. Wilson, 'The Use of Royal Psalms at the "Seams" of the Hebrew Psalter', *JSOT* 35 (1986), p. 87. For a convenient tabulation of the usage of divine names in the Psalter, see L. McFall, 'A Logical Arrangement of the Psalter', pp. 248-49.

has thirty-one, Book 1 has forty-one, and Book 5 has the largest number, forty-four. The contents, the use of the divine names, and the psalm titles point to this threefold division, with Book 1 having forty-one psalms, Books 2-3 having forty-eight, and Books 4-5 having sixty-one. This explanation helps to solve other difficulties, including the odd separation of the Hallelujah psalms between Books 4 and 5. The present situation, with three of these psalms coming in Book 4 (104-106) but the majority in Book 5 (111-13, 115-17, 135, 146-150) is explicable if they all originally came in the same book.[12]

Clearly the Psalter is a collection of songs which was brought together over centuries, and finally some time after the return from Exile were put into its present form. It has often been called 'the hymn book of the second temple', that is to say, the book used for song in the restored temple in Jerusalem (completed in 516 BC) and which remained in use until the destruction of Jerusalem in AD 70. While definitive proof of this is lacking, the evidence certainly points to the use of the Psalter in the Jewish observances before and after Christ, and the continuing use of the Psalms in early Christian worship (Matt. 26:30; 1 Cor. 14:26; James 5:13). The Psalter should not be compared to the building of a magnificent palace, but rather to the development over centuries of a cathedral. It bears the marks of various styles, distinctive development in stages, and yet an overall beauty as a whole book of the Bible.

There is another movement in the Psalter and that is towards a climax of praise. With all the varied moods of the human heart being apparent in earlier songs, it is clear that towards the end of the Psalter the exultant joy of God's people come to the fore. The final songs (Pss. 144-150) are all ones of joyous praise that culminate in the call: 'Let everything that has breath praise the LORD. Praise the LORD' (Ps. 150:6). The emphasis on praise towards the end of the Psalter seems deliberate, and this movement may well be the reason why the whole book was called *tᵉhillîm, songs of praise*.

---

[12] For full discussion of this argument for an original three books, see Roger T. Beckwith, 'The Early History of the Psalter'.

5.3 The Message of the Five Books

While it is certainly possible to interpret individual psalms, or trace their use in Old Testament worship, or their use in the New Testament, yet the question remains: 'Is there a point behind the whole Psalter?' Or, to state the question another way: 'What place does the Psalter as a whole have within Old Testament biblical theology?'

Older commentators discussed the structure of the Psalter and the reasons behind its development.[13] In more recent times the debate on this matter has been vigorous, though no consensus has been reached.[14] It has been noted that there is a progression from lament to praise in the Psalter, with its final form emphasising that the LORD is king.[15] This progression from obedience to God's Word (Ps. 1) to universal praise of him (Ps. 150) has been proposed as the main theme of the Psalms,[16] though the stress on the Davidic covenant has also been proposed as the main theme.[17] Another view that has been advanced is that eschatology dominates the Psalter, not

---

[13] For examples, see E. W. Hengstenberg, *Commentary on the Psalms* (Edinburgh: T. & T. Clark, 1869), III, Appendix, pp. i-liv; F. Delitzsch, *Psalms* (Edinburgh: T. & T. Clark, 1871), I, pp. 19-30; J. J. S. Perowne, *The Book of Psalms; A New Translation, with Introductions and Notes Explanatory and Critical*, 6th ed. (London: George Bell & Sons, 1886), I, pp. 70-83; A. F. Kirkpatrick, *The Book of Psalms* (Cambridge: CUP, 1903), pp. xiii-xviii, l-lix.

[14] The recent discussion was provoked by the work of Gerald H. Wilson, *The Editing of the Hebrew Psalter* (Chico, CA: Scholars Press, 1985). He gives a summary of his position in 'The Structure of the Psalter,' in *Interpreting the Psalms: Issues and Approaches*, edd. Philip S. Johnston and David G. Firth (Leicester: Apollos, 2005), pp. 229-46. His other contributions on this topic are listed in his volume *Psalms 1* (The NIV Application Commentary, Grand Rapids:, Zondervan, 2002), p. 88. For help in orientation to the debate regarding the structure of the Psalter, see the article by David M. Howard Jr.; 'Recent Trends in Psalms Study', in David W. Baker, and Bill T. Arnold, edd., *The Face of Old Testament Studies: A Survey of Contemporary Approaches* (Leicester: Apollos, 1999), pp. 329-44; and his abbreviated, but more recent discussion, in *Interpreting the Psalms*, pp. 23-29.

[15] This is G. H. Wilson's position, ibid., p. 249.

[16] For this view, see Walter Brueggemann, 'Bounded by Obedience and Praise: The Psalms as Canon', *JSOT* 50 (1991), pp. 63-92.

[17] J. H. Walton, building on Wilson's work, has suggested this in his discussion, 'Psalms: A Cantata about the Davidic Covenant', *JETS* 34 (1991), pp. 21-31.

only in that this dominates the content, but that it is part of the purposeful shaping of the arrangement of the 150 psalms.[18]

While various single themes have been proposed, none of them seem to be satisfactory explanations of the evidence. All hypotheses depend upon the selection of psalms around which a proposed common theme is based.[19] While evident connections between adjacent psalms exist, and even between books (the so-called 'seams' connecting them to each other), yet no evidence points to a systematic ordering of the entire content of the Psalter. This means that we should not try and state a single overarching theme but rather recognise that the Psalter reflects the breadth of theological reflection in Israel.[20]

5.4 The Numbering of the Psalms and Verses

The decision to make the Psalter comprise 150 songs seems to have been deliberate, and this number is confirmed both by the LXX and the major psalms scroll from cave 11 at Qumran. The latter contains an idealised note relating to David's songs, which says that he wrote 3,600 psalms and 450 songs. These numbers are divisible by 150, and 3,600 is 150 multiplied by 24, the number of courses of Levites appointed to sing the psalms at the temple (1 Chron. 25:9–31).[21]

While the verse enumeration does not affect our understanding of the Psalms, it does affect our use of the Bible and also commentaries on the text. There is a difference

---

[18] For this approach, see David Mitchell, *The Message of the Psalter: An Eschatological Programme to the Book of Psalms* (Sheffield: JSOT, 1997). Mitchell also interacts with the views of Gerald H. Wilson in his essay, 'Lord, Remember David: G. H. Wilson and the Message of the Psalter', *VT* LVI (2006), pp. 526-47.

[19] This is the conclusion of S. Jonathan Murphy, 'Is the Psalter a Book with a Single Message?' *BS* 165 (2008), pp. 283-93.

[20] For discussions that demonstrate the breadth of the theology embraced within the Psalter, see Robert B. Chisholm, Jr, 'A Theology of the Psalms', in Roy B. Zuck, ed., *A Biblical Theology of the Old Testament* (Chicago: Moody Press, 1991), pp. 257-304; and, Paul R. House, 'The God Who Rules (Psalms)', in his book, *Old Testament Theology* (Downers Grove: IVP, 1998), pp. 402-23.

[21] R. T. Beckwith, 'The Early History of the Psalter', p. 22. The other Qumran manuscripts of the Psalms have variations in content and order, but it must be remembered that the Qumran sect was not within mainstream Judaism, and some of its manuscripts were assembled as part of a liturgical manual.

between the numbering of verses in the printed Hebrew Bible and most English versions. The reason for this is that in the Hebrew Bibles the titles of the Psalms are often regarded as a verse, and therefore the numbering of what we regard as the first verse will be v. 2. This means that for many psalms the Hebrew text shows one more verse than corresponding English versions. Quite a few commentaries, especially those working from the Hebrew text, follow this system.

There is also a difference in the numbering of the Psalms themselves. The explanation for this lies in differences between the Hebrew Bible and the way in which the Psalms have come over into English. The Greek Bible subdivided two of the psalms (116 and 147) and twice joined two of them together (9/10 and 114/115). The Greek Bible also contains an additional psalm (151) that has never been reckoned by others as part of the Psalter. It is specifically noted that this psalm is 'outside of the number'.[22] The table below shows the two systems of numbering the psalms.

The Numbering of the Psalms

Hebrew and Protestant Bibles	Greek and Roman Catholic Bibles
1-8	1-8
9	9
10	
11-113	10-112
114	113
115	
	114
116	115
117-146	116-145
	146
147	147
148-150	148-150
	151 (Greek)

---

[22] The full inscription in the LXX is: 'This psalm is a genuine one of David, though outside the number (*exôthen tou arithmou*), when he fought alone with Goliad.'

6. THE PSALMS AND GOD'S COVENANT

6.1 God and Covenant

The Bible speaks of God's relationship with his people as being a covenant. This relationship is the concept that gives unity to the whole of the biblical revelation. A covenant is a bond between God and man, and it is given by a sovereign God as an expression of his grace. In a formal way he expresses the relationship that exists between himself and his people. The central core of the covenant is that God promises, 'I will be your God and you shall be my people.' There is a progressive unfolding of this covenant throughout the Old Testament in various stages. The arrangement entered into by God at creation (Gen. 1-2) is reaffirmed after the flood (Gen. 6:18; 9:1-7). The call of Abraham is followed by a formal covenant arrangement (Gen. 12, 15, 17) which is supplemented by the covenant at Sinai (Exod. 20–23) following the Exodus from Egypt. After the introduction of kingship there is a special covenant in which the Davidic family is chosen (2 Sam. 7). Finally the Old Testament speaks about a new covenant which will come to pass (Jer. 31:31-34; and see Hebrews 8:7-13; 10:11-16).

From archaeological discoveries we know that God used a form of covenant that was familiar to the people. Kings who conquered another nation forced them to enter into a covenant bond, in which they pledged themselves to serve him as their overlord. Many of the expressions used in the Old Testament of the covenant relationships can be paralleled from extra-biblical sources. The treaties or covenants from these sources follow a formalised pattern that has many similarities to the biblical covenants. The language they employed in connection with them and various aspects of the ceremony of entering into a covenant or of enforcing one have their counterpart in the Old Testament.

6.2 Covenant in the Psalms

The word 'covenant' is not common in the Psalms, occurring only twenty-one times (25:10, 14; 44:17; 50:5, 16; 55:20; 74:20;

78:10, 37; 83:5 (NIV, 'alliance'); 89:3, 28, 34, 39; 103:18; 105:8, 10; 106:45; 111:5, 9; 132:12).[23] This is very similar to its use in the prophetical books of the Old Testament where it does not appear frequently. However, in both there are many other indications of the presence of the whole idea of covenant that underlies all the expressions of religious faith and feeling.

The Psalms contain many references to the earlier parts of the Old Testament and especially to the relationships between God and the patriarchs and with the people of Israel after they had been redeemed from Egypt. There is also reference to the covenant with David which is set out in 2 Samuel 7. A summary of the references is as follows:

Covenant with Abraham	105:1-22
Exodus and the Sinai Covenant	50:4-6, 16; 66:5-12; 78:12-53; 80:8-11; 81:1-16; 86:5; 99:7; 103:7; 105:23-4; 106:1-33; 114; 135:4, 8-9
Covenant with David	78:65-72; 89:1-52; 132:1-18

A series of other expressions also draws attention to the covenant relationship. Many of these expressions echo passages from the Pentateuch which speak of God and his people. Attention can be focussed on a few of these terms.

(a) Israel is often spoken of as the people of God (29:11; 81:11; 100:3). They were the inheritance of the Lord and often this phrase is used in conjunction with reference to them as God's people (28:9; 78:62, 71; 94:5; 106:4–5). The phrase, 'I will be your God and you shall be my people,' is echoed in passages like Psalm 95:7 which declares: 'for he is our God and we are the people of his pasture, the flock under his care.'

---

[23] For covenantal language in the Psalter, the best listing I have found is in the unpublished Cambridge Ph.D. thesis of J. A. Thompson, *The Vocabulary of Covenant in the Old Testament* (1963). Parts of his research appeared in his booklet, *The Ancient Near Eastern Treaties and the Old Testament* (London: Tyndale Press, 1964), and in his commentary, *Deuteronomy: An Introduction and Commentary* (London: Inter-Varsity Press, 1974).

(b) The fact that God had chosen Israel to be his covenant people is emphasised in the Psalter. The word 'choose' is first used in Deuteronomy to describe Israel as God's choice (Deut. 7:6). The Psalms use it when recalling the wonder of God's election of Israel, and link it with other words that also point to the same sovereign choice. For example, 33:12 speaks of Israel being chosen as God's inheritance, while 135:4 says that he chose Israel as his 'special possession' ($s^e gull\hat{a}h$). This latter word is a rare one, being used to denote the utterly special position that Israel occupied before God (Exod. 19:5; Deut. 7:6; 14:2; Mal. 3:17).

(c) A variety of other terms associated with the covenant also make their appearance in the Psalter. The repeated use of the word 'servant' recalls how this expression is used of an inferior submitting to a great king. Thus King Ahaz sent word to the king of Assyria and said: 'I am your servant and your son' (2 Kings 16:7). Reference is also made to the oath by which the covenant was sworn, and to such features as the ark of the covenant. There is constant reference to God's faithfulness, which is not just expressing trust in God's character in general but in the specific form in which he revealed it in the covenant relationship. He was the God who even in the Ten Words declared that he would show his 'steadfast love to the thousandth generation of those who love him and who keep his commandments' (Exod. 20:6; Deut. 5:10).

6.3 The Covenant Relationship

The Psalms are not just individual expressions of religious understanding but rather they are distinctly expressions of faith which came out of a community of faith. The sphere from which the songs of Israel came was the covenant community, bound in common allegiance to the Lord. Some of the Psalms are clearly communal because they use the first person plural ('we', 'our'), but even the majority, which use the first person singular ('I', 'my'), stem from a common commitment to the God of Israel.

The Psalms also show how vital the covenant relationship was, for the various songs put into poetry the depth of such a relationship with God. The faith of the psalmists is built upon God's word to his people, not upon individual personal promises from God. Knowledge of God's character and his works provided the common basis upon which individuals could live. The singers knew that God was concerned with their personal lives and with the good of each one of his covenant children. Psalm 84 puts it like this: 'For the LORD God is a sun and a shield; the LORD bestows favour and honour; no good things does he withhold from those whose walk is blameless. O LORD Almighty, blessed is the man who trusts in you' (vv. 11-12; notice the connection with passages such as Gen. 15:1; 17:1). It is not surprising that they wanted to sing and rejoice in this relationship, for those who feared the LORD lacked no good thing (Ps. 34:9).

The central feature is God's kingship over his people. As covenant servants the people had to reaffirm in various ways their allegiance to the LORD. They paid their tribute of praise to him in extolling his creation or his great acts of redemption. In speaking of the majesty of his person they were offering spiritual sacrifices of praise to their king. When they sang of the beauties of God's law, this was another affirmation of the manner in which they were submitting to his claims upon them. The Psalter, therefore, served the broad purpose of reminding the people that they were God's people, the people who made up his flock (Ps. 100:4). It also assisted them in maintaining a right relationship with him.

God's presence with his people in their history and also with them as individuals is reaffirmed in the Psalms. The long historical psalms in particular are recitals of the ways in which God's power had been shown in the life of Israel. At important times Israel had to repeat summaries of what God had done for her (see the declaration at the time of bringing the firstfruits [Deut. 26:3-10] and at the time of covenant renewal [Josh. 24:16-18]).

Finally, the Psalter emphasises the grace of God in forgiving and restoring an erring covenant people. Thus one psalmist can say to God: 'You were to Israel a forgiving God, though you punished their misdeeds' (Ps. 99:8). This was simply a re-affirmation of the declaration that God had made of himself when he proclaimed his own name to Moses on the occasion of the second giving of the tablets of stone (Exod. 34:6-7). David says that 'all the ways of the LORD are loving and faithful for those who keep the demands of his covenant'. Then on the basis of God's covenant he pleads: 'For the sake of your name, O LORD, forgive my iniquity, though it is great' (Ps. 25:10-11). A covenant God was true to his word of promise and would forgive and restore.

7. SPECIAL TYPES OF PSALMS

7.1 Identifying Types

In English we have various types of literature, just as we have various types of spoken language. To illustrate the latter first of all, we know that there are different styles in keeping with different occasions. Thus when a bridegroom stands up to speak at his wedding we can often predict the style his speech will take and some of the standard expressions that will be used. There is an expected format to the speech and we are almost disappointed if it does not occur. Other types of speeches to think about could be a politician conceding an election defeat or a speech presenting a gift to a fellow-employee on his retirement.

The same thing holds true concerning written English. We adopt a particular style depending on the complete set of circumstances that has led to our writing. A letter written to one's mother will be quite different from a formal letter to one's solicitors concerning some property matter. The form in which a newspaper report on a traffic accident is written will be quite different from the style of the same paper's editorial. A variety of situations demand a known and predictable style.

We very quickly identify particular forms of writing, and subconsciously read them with that in mind. This is important because our mental approach to the form will often determine our attitude to the text. If, for example, we recognise a particular piece as a novel, we know we can read it quickly and even miss out some parts without affecting the flow of the story. However, if we try that with other pieces of writing, for example, a set of instructions on how to construct an unassembled piece of furniture, we could run into great difficulty and create problems for ourselves.

So it is when we come to the Psalms. There are various types of psalms and we have to recognise the differences. Look at these three quotations from successive psalms:

> O LORD my God, I take refuge in you;
>> save and deliver me from all who pursue me,
> or they will tear me like a lion and rip me in pieces with
>> no one to rescue me (Ps. 7:1-2).

> O LORD, our Lord,
>> how majestic is your name in all the earth!
>> You have set your glory above the heavens (Ps. 8:1).

> I will praise you, O Lord,
>> with all my heart;
> I will tell of all your wonders.
> I will be glad and rejoice in you;
>> I will sing praise to your name,
>>> O Most High (Ps. 9:1-2).

They are all quite different and are indicative of different styles. The first is from a lament in which an individual is asking God for protection as he faces false accusations from his enemies. The second comes from a hymn of praise, and particularly one that is praising God for his creation. The third example is from a hymn in which there is mention of rejoicing and exaltation of God's name. As we note the different types of psalms it helps us to recognise other psalms of a similar nature and to read them accordingly.

There are several benefits to be gained by looking at the psalms in this way. It means above all else that we are viewing them as whole units, rather than just individual verses. That is to say, we are considering them as a total piece of literary composition and reading them in that light. We come to them knowing that they are not like a telephone directory, in which there is no necessary connection between successive entries. Any connection that might appear is quite accidental, not by design. In the Psalms, however, the connection is there simply because each psalm is a poem which holds together as a unit, and therefore we must interpret it in that way. To extract a single verse and isolate it from its context in the psalm is to distort the meaning. Thus a phrase such as 'I will fear no evil' (Ps. 23:4) should not be taken out of that psalm and used as an isolated encouragement. Its meaning can only be seen in the light of the whole psalm and the certainty of God's care as a shepherd of his people. Similarly the opening verse of Psalm 89, 'I will sing of the LORD's great love forever; with my mouth I will make your faithfulness known throughout all generations', is not an isolated promise concerning God's faithfulness. It comes in a psalm that is putting into poetry the covenant which God made with David (see 2 Sam. 7). To extract the one verse and apply its teaching without reference to the setting in the psalm is to teach contrary to the express message of the psalm itself. This principle of interpreting a verse within the unit of which it forms a part applies, of course, to the whole of the Bible.

This type of approach also lets us ask questions regarding the function of any particular song. From the books of Chronicles we know that particular songs were appropriate to special occasions such as the bringing of the ark of the covenant into Jerusalem (1 Chron. 16:7-36, and cf. Pss. 96; 105:1-5; and 106:1, 47, 48), or for use at the dedication of the temple (2 Chron. 5-7 and especially cf. 5:13 and 7:3, 6 with Ps. 136). If we can find out something about the function that a particular psalm fulfilled, we will be helped to understand it better. Sometimes this may be apparent from within the psalm itself, or the title may show how the psalm was used. Clearly the Psalms were meant for singing, and many were used in appropriate settings during the religious life of the people. We can compare this to the way in which modern Christian hymn books not only list hymns according to content but also show the appropriate hymns for particular occasions (e.g. Easter,

Pentecost, Christmas, Baptism, the Lord's Supper, Harvest Thanksgiving).

A word of warning is also needed. This method of listing psalms according to type should be used as a valuable tool to help our understanding but should not be pressed to an extreme. There is the constant danger that a psalm will be classified according to a specific type, and in so doing its individual distinctiveness may be overlooked. The characteristics of a particular psalm have to be taken seriously so that common features of a group do not cause us to overlook important variations. Any classification has to be fluid, and certain groups of psalms overlap in their characteristics. An outline of some of the major Psalm types follows.

7.2 Hymns

A hymn is a song that extols the glory and greatness of God. Many psalms come into this category, for the Psalter contains a great number of songs of joy in the LORD. Typical examples are 92, 103, 113, and 117. Songs other than those in the Psalter also come into this category. The Song of Moses and the Song of Miriam (Exod. 15:1-18, 21) are good examples, as are Hannah's Song (1 Sam. 2:1-10) and Hezekiah's Song (Isa. 38:10-20).

Nearly all of them share some common features, including initial and concluding calls to worship and reasons why God is to be praised. It is this latter feature that takes the greatest space, for the psalmists draw attention to the concrete things that God has done and which call forth a response of praise.

The hymns have a definite structure like this:

A. Introduction: Call to Worship

Usually the hymn commences with a call to worship in the form of an imperative in the second person plural. Sometimes it can be a form in which the person calls upon his own soul to praise the LORD, such as in 103 and 104, 'Praise the LORD, O my soul.'

B. Main Section: The Reasons for Praise

Often this section is introduced by a clause beginning with the word 'for', followed by the explanation of the motives behind the praise. Sometimes this is disguised in English translation for the Hebrew word which is normally used (*kî*) can be translated by more than one English word (e.g., in 8:3 it is translated by 'when': *when I look up into the heavens ...*). If this 'for' is omitted in the Hebrew, there will be other words which serve the same function, such as can be seen in 103:3-5 or 104:2-4.

C. Call to Worship: A Repetition of the Opening Call

Frequently the same sort of call resounds again at the end of the song.

A good example of the hymn is Psalm 117, the shortest song in the book.

> A. Praise the LORD, all you nations;
>   Extol him, all you peoples.
>
> B. For great is his love towards us
>   and the faithfulness of the LORD endures for ever.
>
> C. Praise the LORD.

Martin Luther wrote a long commentary on this shortest of all psalms because he thought that these two verses were basic to our understanding of the love of God. They stress the covenant love of the LORD to his people and the missionary vision of reaching out to the nations.

Three major topics provide the motive for praise of the LORD in these psalms. First, there is a group of psalms (66:1-12; 100; 114; 149) that praise God for the fact that he created (or redeemed) Israel. They have much in common with songs outside the Psalter such as Exodus 15:1-8, Deuteronomy 32:1-43, Habakkuk 3:2-19, and Isaiah 52:7-10. Secondly, another group of psalms sing the praise of God as creator of the world, either in a brief form such as in Psalm 8, or much more extensively as in Psalm 104. In this latter psalm even the order of Genesis 1 is preserved as the psalmist describes poetically the wonder of God's creation (104:2-4 = Gen. 1:6-8; 104:5-9 = Gen. 1:9-10; 104:10-13 = implied in Gen. 1:6-10; 104:19-23 = Gen. 1:14-18; 104:24-26 = Gen. 1:20-22; 104:27-30 = Gen. 1:24-30). Thirdly, the final group of hymns sing of God as the creator and covenant God who is the ruler of history (33; 103; 113; 117; 145; 146; 147; 150).

7.3 Laments

Laments form the largest group of psalms in the Psalter. They are cries of distress, either by an individual (e.g. 3, 7, 13, 17, 26) or by the community as a whole (e.g. 12, 44, 60, 74). Enemies are mentioned but rarely are they identified clearly. The term 'laments', however, is rather misleading, as it suggests that these psalms are full of sadness and are completely pessimistic in spirit. That is not altogether true as many of them contain strong affirmations of trust in the LORD. Other terms such as 'complaint', 'confidence in distress', or 'appeal for help' may be closer to the mark in describing them, because they are appeals to God to come and intervene in particular situations and to bring his deliverance. In this way they are songs of praise, however muted, because the psalmists know of God's power to help. Some of them, after pleading for help, contain both an expression of confidence in God's power to aid and a concluding song of praise.

As with other types of psalms, the lamentations have similarities with various parts of the Old Testament outside the Psalter. Job even cursed the day he was born and wonders why it was that he did not perish at birth (Job 3:1-26). The Book of Jeremiah contains several long laments by the prophet (11:18–12:6; 15:10-21; 17:14-18; 18:19-23; 20:7-13; 20:14-18).

The question arises as to why so many psalms are of this kind, as they far outnumber any other type of psalm. What they emphasise is the reality of religious experience, and the fact that believers do not always have periods of great joy. In this way these psalms are so realistic of the experiences of God's people. They pass through times when events overwhelm them, as they are not immune to the changing situations of human life. Suffering is a part of human life, and the Psalms both show us how believers suffered and also how they reacted.[24]

There is a considerable amount of individual variation, depending upon the particular situation of the psalmist. The psalms that have been designated as the penitential psalms since the early Christian centuries are also included in this grouping (6, 32, 38, 51, 102, 130, 143). The following features are characteristic of this type of psalm, though not all may necessarily be present or there may be variation in order:

A. Address to God
This can be very brief or at other times expanded into a longer form.

B. Complaint
The form of complaint varies depending on whether it is a song of the community, who mainly complain about famine or attack by enemies, or an individual complaining from sickness or from fear. The penitential psalms refer to the psalmist's awareness of sin and his plea for forgiveness.

C. Confession of Trust
In the midst of complaints the psalmists often express confidence in God as the one who can help, and frequently they introduce this with words like 'but' or 'nevertheless'.

D. Petition
Appeal is made to God to come and help in the particular situation that the psalmist is facing. At times reasons are given why this should happen.

E. Words of Assurance
The psalmist expresses certainty that his prayer is heard and that God will come to his aid.

---

[24] I have amplified this point in *Suffering in the Psalms* (Han Sang Dong Memorial Lecture, Kosin University, Pusan, 1998).

F. Vow of Praise
In the confidence that God has heard, the psalmist pledges himself to call on God's name and to tell what God has done for him.

A good example is Psalm 13, which has this pattern:

    A.   How long, O Lord? Will you forget me for ever?
              How long will you hide your face from me? (v. 1)

    B.   How long must I wrestle with my thoughts
              and every day have sorrow in my heart?
              How long will my enemy triumph over me? (v. 2)

    C.   But I trust in your unfailing love;
              my heart rejoices in your salvation (v. 5).

    D.   Look on me and answer, O Lord my God.
              Give light to my eyes, or I will sleep in death;
        my enemy will say, 'I have overcome him,'
              and my foes will rejoice when I fall (v. 3–4).

    E.   I will sing to the Lord, for he has been good to me (v. 6).

The setting of some of these psalms of complaint suggests that they may have been said or sung at the temple in conjunction with some form of sacrificial offering. When Hannah prayed in the tabernacle in Shiloh, Eli watched her praying and accused her of drunkenness. In reply she spoke of how she was pouring out her heart before God. She said: 'I have been praying here out of my great anguish and grief.' Eli then responded: 'Go in peace, and may the God of Israel grant what you have asked of him' (1 Sam. 1:9-17). It may have been customary to give such a benediction in response to similar complaints, including many of the complaints recorded in the Psalter. There is often an abrupt change in mood in the psalm, with the indication in some that a similar declaration by the Lord's servant has been made. Thus Psalm 85 has a series of petitions by the psalmist followed by the words:

> I will listen to what God the LORD will say;
>> he promises peace to his people, his saints –
>> but let them not return to folly (85:8).

An assurance like that could well have been made to the psalmist by the person, like Eli, ministering at the altar, and this may explain the more joyful note at the end of the psalm.

7.4 Thanksgiving Psalms

When they respond to God's answer to a cry of need, the psalmists extol him for the answered prayer. The psalms in this group (such as 18, 32, 34) are characterised by praise of the LORD and a testimony to God's goodness, often in the form of a description of God's salvation.

There is a close connection between the thanksgiving psalms and both the psalms of lamentation and the hymns of praise. The lamentations often have a concluding song of praise. In comparison with them the thanksgiving psalms expand that type of song considerably. There is also the difference that in the complaints the song of praise is in *anticipation* of the deliverance of the LORD, while in the thanksgiving psalms the praise is for the deliverance that has *already come*.

The comparison with the hymns is also helpful to see the essential difference between them and the thanksgiving psalms. There are two ways in which God is praised in the psalms. He is praised in general terms simply for what he is in himself or as he is manifested in his creation. On the other hand, he is praised for specific acts of deliverance. In the first case the praise is describing something wonderful about God, while in the second case there is a declaration of what he has done.

Like the laments, the songs of thanksgiving come in two forms. There are several which are a form of thanksgiving by the whole community. The most specific is 124, which rejoices in a deliverance that God brought to his people. Other community thanksgiving songs are 65, 67, 75, 107, and 136. The more common form, however, is the individual song of thanksgiving in which an individual gives a testimony to what the LORD has done in his life. These are typical examples:

> You have granted him the desire of his heart,
> and have not withheld the request of his lips (21:2).
>
> O LORD, you brought me up from the grave;
> you spared me from going down into the pit (30:3).
>
> He put a new song in my mouth,
> a hymn of praise to our God (40:3).
>
> Come and listen, all you who fear God;
> let me tell you what he has done for me (66:16).

The pattern that the individual thanksgivings take is as follows:

A. Address to God
There is direct address to God, frequently brief but sometimes more extended.

B. Description of the Psalmist's Experiences
Usually this includes an account of the trouble which the psalmist faced, an indication of his cry for help, and then finally the deliverance which God has provided for him.

C. Testimony to the LORD
The psalm finishes with a proclamation of the goodness of the LORD. There may also be other features such as a request for future help.

Psalm 116 provides an excellent illustration of this pattern:

A. Address to God
The psalmist calls to the LORD (vv. 1-2), and gives the reason why he is praising him (notice the clause beginning with *for*).

B. Description of the Psalmist's Experiences

Verse 3 gives the circumstances that the psalmist faced, followed by his cry for help (v. 4). As he thinks over what has happened he expresses his confidence in the LORD, who is gracious and righteous (vv. 5-7).

C. Testimony to the LORD

The psalmist rejoices in what God has done for him.

> For you, O LORD, have delivered my soul from death,
>   my eyes from tears,
>   my feet from stumbling,
> that I may walk before the LORD
>   in the land of the living (vv. 8-9).

The psalm ends with the psalmist pledging himself to the LORD and making his vows in the presence of the congregation (referred to in verses 14 and 18). He is the LORD's servant (v. 16), and he ends his song with a 'Hallelujah' (v. 19).

Since the Psalms are so personal in their authorship, clearly there is blessing in our personal appropriation of them.

7.5 Wisdom Psalms

Within the Old Testament there are several books that collectively are often called 'the Wisdom books'. They include Job, Proverbs, and Ecclesiastes, and are so-called because their main emphasis is not on the great facts of God's redemption, but with the practical outworking of life that is lived in the fear of the LORD. This phrase, 'the fear of the LORD', occurs both in the Book of Proverbs and in the Psalms (e.g., Prov. 1:7; 8:13; 14:26; 15:33; Pss. 19:9; 34:11; 111:10). It does not describe the abject fear of a slave before a master, but rather the devotion of a loving heart towards one's sovereign LORD. The wisdom literature shows how such a fear displays itself in practical life, so that it is really 'godliness in working clothes'.

Much of the wisdom literature appears in the form of proverbs. These proverbs are marked out by the following characteristics:

(a) Proverbs are brief, usually consisting of fewer than twenty-five words. The best proverbs are often the shortest, such as 'like father, like son'. The brevity comes from a desire to put the wisdom saying into as short a form as possible, and also as an aid to memorisation. Sometimes there is a repetition of a word or sound which is a further help to the memory.

(b) Proverbs use figurative language. They are dealing with truth, but they put it in a form that is easy to grasp and retain. They take an experience from everyday life and use it to teach a lesson. Because they paint pictures the vividness of the proverb is retained in spite of repeated use.

(c) Proverbs have many different applications. They do not refer to just one situation in life. Rather, their general nature enables them to be applied in a variety of situations. Thus the proverb, 'like father, like son' may be applied to a relationship between a teacher and a pupil, or even between a mother and a daughter.

(d) Proverbs express general truths. They are not promises of God that apply without exception. Rather, they are generalisations based on human experience, and there may well be exceptions to the general truths contained in them.

There are several psalms that fit into the general pattern of the wisdom literature, while parts of other psalms reflect something of the same approach to life or share in matters of style and form. Among the former are 37, 49, and 73, while psalms such as 25, 34, 78, 111, 112, 127, and 128 have features that resemble wisdom literature. Of these Psalm 78 starts with the words:

> O my people, hear my teaching;
> > listen to the words of my mouth.
> I will open my mouth in parables, I will utter things hidden
> > from of old (Ps. 78:1-2).

Several features in this opening are typical of wisdom literature, such as the call to hear and the words 'teaching', 'parables' and 'hidden things'.

In contrast to other types of psalms, these wisdom psalms do not display a structure that remains constant to them all.

Rather, they are distinguished by characteristics that mark them out as distinctive. These characteristics include:
   (a) the knowledge that the fear of the LORD is the beginning of wisdom
   (b) a concern for the practical issues of life
   (c) a clear distinction between the two ways which face us in life, so that a clear distinction is drawn between the righteous and the wicked
   (d) a struggle with the problem of why the wicked seem to prosper as compared with the righteous
   (e) hints that the final solution lies in the life to come.

The first of the major wisdom psalms is Psalm 37, whose eleventh verse ('But the meek will inherit the land and enjoy great peace') was picked up by Christ and appears as the third beatitude (Matt. 5:5). The psalm is an acrostic, with each second verse commencing with another letter of the Hebrew alphabet. The teaching of this psalm has come over into English through John Wesley's translation of Paul Gerhardt's hymn 'Put thou thy trust in God' (Gerhardt's hymn 'Befehl du deine Wege' is also an acrostic, with each of its twelve verses commencing with a successive word from Psalm 37:5, 'Commit your way to the LORD ...'). The psalm points to the source of true wisdom and blessedness and encourages readers to follow the way of the LORD.

The second of these psalms which are strongly in the wisdom type is Psalm 73. It presents teaching very similar to Job and Ecclesiastes and it is clearly a teaching poem. When faced with the arrogance of the wicked and their prosperity, the psalmist did not understand the situation until he went into the sanctuary of God. There in the temple he realised what was to be their ultimate outcome (vv. 16-17).

7.6 Psalms of Trust

The Psalms are full of expressions of confidence in the God of Israel, though many do not clarify with certainty the precise situation that provoked the expression of trust. Some of them are the songs of an individual (e.g. 4, 11, 16, 23, 27, 62, 73, and 91); others are communal in nature (e.g. 90, 115, 123, 125, and 126). This group of psalms share in specific ways several features in common:[25]

(a) while their structure is not the same they share a common content

(b) in the face of enemies there is calm trust in the LORD

(c) their declarations have a ring of certainty about them, and in none of them is this feature omitted

(d) they use a variety of metaphors to describe God ('refuge', 'rock', 'shepherd', 'help').

7.7 Kingship Psalms

There is a group of psalms which all speak of God as king (29, 47, 93, 95-99). These psalms (with which some others may be associated (e.g. 24, 110) have among their characteristics:

a) the assertion that the LORD ('Yahweh') reigns

b) that this rule was from of old

c) that this rule is not only over Israel but over the whole world

d) in Zion, the God of Israel is extolled as universal king.

Some of the terms used of Israel's God are borrowed from the common Semitic background. Thus, he is called 'the Great King' (48:2), a term that was appropriated by human kings in the ancient Near East (cf. its use in reference to the king of Assyria in 2 Kings 18:19//Isa. 36:4). This use is accompanied by assertions of the ways in which God is superior to human rulers. Their kingdoms were limited earthly ones; his kingdom is universal and eternal (see section 10. The Kingship of God, for fuller discussion).

8. PSALMS OF REMEMBRANCE

8.1 Israel's Historical Faith

Another special group of psalms require more extended discussion. The faith of Israel was rooted in the events of

---

[25] Excellent tables depicting the characteristics of both types of psalms of trust are given by C. Hassell Bullock, *Encountering the Psalms*, pp. 167, 169.

Old Testament history. God acted in the world and especially he redeemed his people from their bondage and slavery in Egypt. It was a real world to which God came and the events were calendar events in human history. Thus the happenings in the Old Testament are not fictitious accounts composed to teach a certain message, but the record of actual events. There are serious consequences for any professing Christian to maintain that these events were fictitious. If we accept that the historical confession of Israel's faith does not have its roots in history, then we deprive the Christian faith of its foundation.

Israel expressed her faith over and over again in the Old Testament and in doing so recounted the historical developments of the nation. Some of these opportunities were provided in the annual ceremonies, especially the Passover. In this annual commemoration the children of Israel were reminded of the origin of the nation at the momentous time of the Exodus. When their children asked them, 'What does this ceremony mean to you?' they were to reply: 'It is the Passover sacrifice to the LORD, who passed over the houses of the Israelites in Egypt and spared our homes when he struck down the Egyptians' (Exod. 12:25-27). This was one way in which parents were to teach their children the historical facts that were the basis for the Passover. This was developed over the centuries into the Passover Haggadah that is still used to the present day. Jewish people still confess in the Passover ceremony that not only their forefathers *but they themselves* were brought out of Egypt.

> "It was not alone our fathers whom the Holy One, blessed be He, redeemed, but also us whom He redeemed with them, as it is said, 'And us He brought out thence that He might lead us to, and give us, the land which He swore to our fathers.'"

Similar communal aspects of a confession of faith occur in the declaration required in the presentation of the firstfruits. When Israel came into Canaan at the time of presenting the firstfruits, a man had to confess that his father (Jacob) was a wandering Aramean who had gone down into Egypt and become a great nation. The confession continued:

"But the Egyptians ill-treated us and made us suffer, putting us to hard labour. Then we cried out to the LORD, the God of our fathers, and the LORD heard our voice and saw the misery, toil and oppression. So the LORD brought us out of Egypt with a mighty hand and a stretched out arm, with great terror and with miraculous signs and wonders. He brought us to this place and gave us this land, a land flowing with milk and honey; and now I bring the firstfruits of the soil that you, O LORD, have given me" (Deut. 26:6-10).

This confession was not a private one, for it was performed by all Israelites as they brought the firstfruits to the sanctuary. It was, therefore, a very public acknowledgment and reminder of the great events of the Exodus from Egypt. Moreover, the Israelite had to make the confession not just for himself but for others as well. He identified himself as part of the total community of Israel ('the Egyptians ill-treated *us*', '*we* cried out', 'the LORD heard *our* voice', 'he brought *us*'). The central intent of it was to bring praise to the God of Israel who had done such wonderful things for his people. It sets a pattern of recounting the distress of the people but then extolling the great deeds of the LORD.

It is important to note that the people even sang their history at the command of the LORD himself. Moses was told to write down a song that the LORD would give him, and to teach it to the people. They were to sing this song so that it might be a witness against them. Moses did as he was instructed (Deut. 31:19, 22). In this act he was joined by Joshua, so that the outgoing leader of the people was acting in conjunction with the incoming leader (Deut. 32:44). It was really the covenant commitment expressed in the form of a song, with the warning that the departure from God's requirements would result in his judgments coming upon the nation. The importance of the song of Moses is highlighted by the way in which, in Revelation 15:3-4, 'the song of Moses the servant of God' is linked with 'the song of the Lamb'.

8.2 The Purpose of the Historical Psalms
There are a group of psalms (especially 78, 105, 106, 114, 135, 136) which are essentially story-telling psalms. The story is

not like those in English that begin with 'Once upon a time', for these songs are proclaiming the great deeds of the LORD. They are story-telling in the sense that they are narrative psalms which recount the history of Israel.

Just as the confession on the occasion of the presenting of the firstfruits was intended to be praise of God, so also with the narrative psalms. They were intended to teach the people the events of their history and to point them to the significance of those events so that they would praise the LORD. This is especially true of psalms such as 105 and 106 which both end with a song of praise to the LORD.

Within them there is a pattern of declaring the distress in which God's people were found at particular times, and then of proclaiming the deliverance which God afforded them.

> But he brought his people out like a flock;
> > he led them like sheep through the desert. (Ps. 78:52)
>
> For he remembered his holy promise
> > given to his servant Abraham.
> He brought out his people with rejoicing,
> > his chosen ones with shouts of joy. (Ps. 105:42-43)

The historical songs of Israel were clearly to magnify the deeds of the Lord and remind the people whenever they were used that their God alone was the deliverer of his people. Because many of them recount numerous historical incidents, they are generally much longer than most psalms (with the exception of Psalm 119).

8.3 The Stories of the Lord
The main historical psalms are these:

Psalm 78: A summary of the history of Israel that recounts the story from the Exodus until the time of David and the choice of Jerusalem.

Psalm 105: An account of Israel's history from the Exodus till the occupation of Canaan and surrounding territory.

Psalm 106: Another narrative of Israel's history, but carrying the story further on to tell of the sins of the people after they came into Canaan.

Psalm 135: A song which includes references to God as creator, and one whose power was shown in Egypt and in giving Israel the land of Canaan as an inheritance.

Psalm 136: Another song which refers to creation, and then recounts the history of Israel in antiphonal form.

The narrative style is also displayed in many more psalms, which are not totally given over to historical remembrance. Using the Pentateuch (Genesis to Deuteronomy) as a guide, we can reconstruct from the Psalms the history from the time of Abraham up till the time of occupation of Canaan and later. The events include:

Israel, the offspring of Abraham	105:6
Israel went into Egypt	105:16-25
God delivered from their oppression	77:15; 81:6
He inflicted plagues on Egypt	78:44-51; 105:27-36; 135:8-9; 136:10
He led them through the sea	77:16-20; 78:13, 53; 114:3, 5
He guided them in the wilderness	68:7-10; 78:14-16; 105:39-42; 106:13-33; 114:8
Canaan was their heritage	44:2; 47:4; 60:7-8; 135:10-12; 136:17-22.

However, what is different about these references and the major story-telling psalms is that in the latter there is a chronological record of the events of Israel's history.

8.4 The Faithfulness of God

The historical psalms hark back to the great salvation of God seen in the redemption from Egypt. They record his great deeds in order that his people might have their faith strengthened, and that the record of past deliverance would serve as a model of hope for the believing community. Just as God had acted in this way before, so would he act again to save his people.

Ultimately this idea of hope for the future is based on the faithfulness of God. The fundamental theme of Israel's praise in this group of psalms is the fact that God is utterly faithful to his word of promise. There is frequent mention of the fact that God has remembered his covenant:

He remembered that they were but flesh,
 a passing breeze that does not return (Ps. 78:39).

For he remembered his holy promise
 given to his servant Abraham (Ps. 105:42).

For their sake he remembered his covenant
 and out of his great love he relented (Ps. 106:45).

He remembered us in our low estate (Ps. 136:23).

God's relationship with his covenant people is characterised by his utter steadfastness. He has spoken a word and he will perform it. There was no variableness with him, but complete integrity towards his people. The New Testament reinforces this Old Testament teaching. As Christians we will be kept 'strong to the end', so that we 'will be blameless on the day of the Lord Jesus Christ. God, who has called you into fellowship with his Son Jesus Christ our Lord, is faithful' (1 Cor. 1:8-9).

9. GOD IN THE PSALMS

9.1 Reverence in Worship

Any teaching of the Psalter has to be considered in relation to the fact that they are songs of worship. The presentation of teaching about God and his ways is given in the context of worship of him. Thus all the Psalms are God-centred because they are prayers *to* him or songs *about* him. Our response in studying the Psalms should be one of worship, and our love to him should be deepened through understanding better their message. 'How is my love for God is kindled by the Psalms,' exclaimed Augustine.

The Book of Psalms is a tremendous testimony to the living God, and its use throughout centuries by the Christian church has had a far greater influence than is often realised. In the liturgies of the Christian church the language of the Psalter features very prominently, and the thought of the Psalter has been influential either through its direct use or through hymnology based on Psalter passages. Much of our Christian understanding of God and our relationship with him is based on the Psalter.

In their focus on God the Psalms show us how vital he was in the life of Israel. Our knowledge of that relationship comes largely from the Psalms and when God's attributes are being set forth, it is in the context of prayer and praise. We should not think, though, that the type of understanding of God revealed in the Psalms was universal in Israel. The fact that the prophets had to direct condemnatory speeches against the people shows a different picture.

9.2 The Majestic God

The Psalms are full of praise of God, and this praise takes two forms. In some passages the psalmists simply declare God's praise, but in many of them they describe who the LORD is and what he has done. Thus the opening and closing of Psalm 103 voices praise to God:

> Praise the LORD, O my soul;
>   all my inmost being, praise his holy name. (v. 1)
> Praise the LORD, all his works everywhere in his dominion.
>   Praise the LORD, O my soul. (v. 22)

In between these two exclamations of praise is the main body of the psalm, which contains descriptions of God and his works like this:

> who forgives all my sins
>   and heals all my diseases;
> who redeems my life from the pit
>   and crowns me with love and compassion;
> who satisfies my desires with good things,
>   so that my youth is renewed like the eagle's. (vv. 3-5)

The language of praise is accompanied by content, which tells us things about the God who was being worshipped. The Psalms are not empty liturgy but are full of words that direct attention to the glorious person of the living God.

The picture that the Psalms present of God is that of a sovereign God before whom all must come in worship. The greatness of God is stressed in various ways including the use of a distinctive name. He is said to be *Elyon*, the Most High. This word occurs almost only in poetical passages in the Old Testament, and most of these are in the Psalms (eighteen occurrences out of thirty). At times it is used in parallelism with *Elohîm* ('God') or *Shaddai* ('the Almighty'), but other times by itself. Psalm 47, one of the songs of the sons of Korah, provides a good example of its usage:

> Clap your hands, all you nations;
>   Shout to God with cries of joy.
> How awesome is the Lord Most High,
>   the great King over all the earth! (vv. 1-2)

God's character is stressed at times in contrast to the heathen gods, who are only lifeless idols. When the nations say, 'Where is their God?', Israel can reply, 'Our God is in heaven, and he does whatsoever pleases him' (115:1-3). The response which is called for when one is confronted with the greatness of God is to bow down in worship before him (96:6-7).

But though God is so high, yet he stoops to make himself known to men. 'He made known his ways to Moses, his deeds to the people of Israel' (103:7). The same psalm goes on to liken God to a father who has compassion on his children, and who knows their frailty (vv. 13-16). In him David also found a substitute father and mother (27:10). The picture of God presented in the Psalms is of one involved in the life of his children so that he is a shepherd for them (23:1; 80:1); or like a bird who protects her young under her wings (91:1, 4); or a judge who dispenses justice (50:4, 6); or a warrior who is a shield to them (18:1). The great wonder is that the God who calls the stars by name is the same God who heals the broken-hearted and binds up their wounds (147:3-4).

9.3 God the Creator

The doctrine of creation as set out in Genesis 1 is reaffirmed in the Psalter. God had only to speak the word and the world came into being:

> By the word of the LORD the heavens were made,
>   their starry host by the breath of his mouth ...
> For he spoke, and it came to be;
>   he commanded, and it stood firm. (33:6, 9)

Genesis 1 is turned into a prayer in Psalm 8, and man's role as vice-regent is again set forth. All of creation has been placed under him, and God has made him ruler over everything which has been created (8:5-10). Psalm 104 comprises a long song in praise of creation, in which there are many echoes of Genesis 1.

Throughout the Psalter the creation is depicted as God's handiwork, not something divine in itself or originating by itself. Hence there is no worship of nature, only worship of the creator. He is the God who has shown his power in the creation of the world. The inference is drawn from this that because God is so powerful, then he will care for his own. There is a formula in use in the Psalms that joins together the thought of the Lord as the maker of heaven and earth with the idea of blessing for his people. This formula may well go back very early in the Old Testament, for Melchizedek blessed Abram saying, 'Blessed be Abram by God Most High, Creator of heaven and earth' (Gen. 14:19). By the right of creation the Lord controls the world, and is therefore able to bring blessing and protection to Israel (115:12-15; 121:2; 124:8; 134:3; 146:5-6).

There are also hymns of praise to God as the creator who sustains all his creatures, animals as well as mankind. A group of psalms (104:24-30; 136:25; 145:12-16) speak of God as opening his hand to provide for the needs of his creatures, and they even speak of his 'steadfast love' for them. This term occurs so often of God's covenant love for his own people, but it can be applied to his gracious concern for all his creatures (33:5; 119:64; 136:25). This usage of covenant terminology may surprise us, yet God made a covenant not just with Noah but with all living creatures (Gen. 9:9-16). The scope of God's concern is as extensive as his creation in its entirety.

9.4 The Compassionate God

Special attention needs to be given to this aspect. The very fact that the psalmists come in prayer to God is a recognition of their need of him and his forgiving grace. They come because they know of his righteousness, and how they have offended against him. David, in his cry for mercy in Psalm 51, recognises that his sins against Uriah and Bathsheba were horrendous in the sight of God, and includes them in his utmost confession to the Holy One of Israel: 'Against you, you only, have I sinned and done what is evil in your sight' (51:4). Repeatedly the psalmists confess the sinfulness of man in the strongest terms. Men are sinful right from their mother's womb (51:5; 58:3), and all their actions are corrupt and vile (14:1). In the New Testament, when Paul comes to convince his readers of the universal sinfulness of men, he does so by citing from six psalms and one passage from Isaiah (Rom. 3:10-18), and even his conclusion in that passage echoes a psalm: 'Therefore no one will be declared righteous in his sight by observing the law' (Rom. 3:20; cf. Ps. 143:2b).

The Psalms do not only paint the extent of sin. They also point to the grace of God shown in the forgiveness of sins. There is a group of psalms that Luther once called 'the Pauline Psalms' (32, 51, 103, 130, 143) because they teach the same truths which Paul has in his epistles. He said of these psalms: 'They all teach that the forgiveness of sins comes, without the law and without works, to the man who believes ... and when David sings, "There is forgiveness with you, that you may be feared," this is just what Paul says, "God has concluded them all in unbelief, that he might have mercy upon all" (Rom. 11.32). Thus no man may boast of his own righteousness. That word, 'That you may be feared', dusts away all merit, and teaches us to uncover our heads before God, and confess, *it is mere forgiveness, not merit at all; remission, not satisfaction.* We are brought into a relationship with God in which we enjoy the forgiveness of sins solely by the free grace of God. The teaching that we are forgiven by faith alone is one which is imbedded in the Psalms: 'Blessed are they whose transgressions are forgiven, whose sins are covered. Blessed is the man whose sin the Lord will never count against him' (Rom. 4:7-8, quoting Ps. 32:1-2). God will not despise a broken and a contrite heart (51:17), and those who come to him will find that their cry for mercy will be answered by his declaration of forgiveness (130:1-4).

The God who forgives sin is the one who works in the hearts of the penitent. Many of the Psalms reveal the profound spiritual experiences through which the writers went and they lay the foundation for truths that the New Testament develops more fully. Profound sorrow for sin accompanied confession to God (38:18), and there is a recognition of the need for a profound spiritual change. Psalm 51 highlights this in the case of David, who pleaded for a clean heart and an internal change by the work of the Holy Spirit (v. 10). This experience is described more fully in the New Testament in terms of the new birth (John 3:5, 6; 2 Cor. 5:17; Gal. 6:15). Those who experienced it could sing for joy because God gives his forgiven children a new song to sing, 'a hymn of praise to our God' (Ps. 40:3).

10. THE KINGSHIP OF GOD

10.1 The Idea of Kingship

The idea of God's kingship is central to the Bible. It appears from the beginning of Genesis, even though the actual words 'king' and 'kingdom' do not appear till later. The basic idea underlying the Bible's presentation of the relationship between God and humans is that the creator God is a sovereign who exercises his rule over his world and over his human creatures in particular. The kingdom of God is concerned with God's people, in God's place, and under God's rule. Living under God's covenant rule, they were directed in their response to God by the various commandments he gave them. As loyal servants they yielded obedience to him as their master.

At the time of the Exodus from Egypt the children of Israel were brought into a formal relationship with God and with one another by the formation of the nation of Israel. At Mount Sinai God entered into a covenant with them, which regulated the life of the nation. By this covenant God set the conditions under which his people would live. He initiated the covenant and he was sovereign in the relationship.

As noted earlier, the pattern that the covenant at Sinai takes has been shown to be similar to other covenants in the ancient Near East. Countries, especially when one had been conquered by another, had to enter into a political treaty which noted their subservience. The king of the more powerful country (the conqueror) initiated a new relationship with the less powerful (the conquered). The great king set out his demands on his new subjects, and in turn promised to defend them if they were attacked. In the Book of Exodus God is the great king who establishes a new form of covenant relationship with his people Israel.

When God redeemed his people from Egypt, Moses and the people sang a song extolling his triumph. The song tells of the LORD's power over Pharaoh (15:1-7), the sea (15:8-12), and the nations generally (15:13-18). The LORD is a mighty warrior who saves (v. 2), destroys the enemy (v. 6), does wonders (v. 11), guides his redeemed people (v. 13), and who reigns for ever and ever (v. 18). This last verse is important because it speaks of the eternal reign of the LORD: *The LORD will reign for ever and ever.* The fitting outcome of the victor's conquest is that he rules his people. How that takes place is spelled out in detail later in Exodus. The people have become a royal priesthood and a holy nation (19:6). Everyone in Israel was to be a priest to God, while the nation as a whole was to be consecrated to God. The detailed laws that follow in Exodus and Leviticus show how the king desired his subjects to live under his authority. Specific details were given of the structures in life which were to regulate their lives. The kingdom of God from the period of Moses can be set out in the following diagram:

```
                    God as King
                         |
          ┌──────────────┴──────────┐
          |                  ┌──────────────────┐
          |                  │ Davidic kings    │
          |                  │ as Vice-regents  │
          |                  └──────────────────┘
 ┌─────────────────────┐
 │ Israel as God's kingdom │
 │                         │
 │   A priestly kingdom    │
 │      Exodus 19:6        │
 └─────────────────────┘
          |
 ┌────────┼────────────────┐
```

Family	Judicial	Spiritual
Authority	Authority	Authority
Parents	Elders	Levites
Wider family	Judges	Priests
		Prophets

This form of government, which is often called 'a theocracy', continued until the appointment of the first king of Israel in the person of Saul. When David succeeded Saul, God entered into a special covenant with David, adopting the Davidic family and appointing them as his vice-regents. During the period of the monarchy God was still the ultimate king, but the Davidic kings were to display his rule among men, and they were also to point to the coming of Jesus as the final king.

10.2 The LORD's Kingship in the Psalms

It is hardly surprising that the central fact of Israel's faith, that the LORD was their king, should be so prominent in the songs of the people. They proclaim him as their own Lord and call upon others to acknowledge him also (96:10).

The Psalms speak of God as the one who is king forever and ever (10:16). He is seated on his heavenly throne (11:4; 29:10) and as the creator is clearly the 'king from of old' (74:12). Thus he is rightly king over all the earth (47:2, 7) and all nations are to be told, 'The LORD reigns' (96:10).

But more particularly he is the king of Israel, and many of the psalms which speak in this way of him link his kingship with Zion (Jerusalem). Zion is called 'the city of the Great King' (48:2) and the declaration is made that he is 'great in Zion' (99:2). It is striking the number of times that God is called 'the Great King' or reference is made to his greatness. Several psalms proclaiming his kingship are grouped together in the Psalter (93, 95–100). These psalms use the expression, 'The LORD reigns' (or, 'is king'). This recalls the shout that went up when Absalom assumed the kingship: 'Absalom reigns in Hebron' (2 Sam. 15:10). When used of the LORD this acclamation has something of a dynamic ring about it, rather like the triumphant Easter hymn, 'Jesus Christ is risen today, Alleluia!'

God is also the king who made Israel his own flock, and he calls them 'my people' (50:7, 81:8, 11). He created Israel, and the people can say, 'We are his people, the sheep of his pasture' (100:3). The LORD chose 'Jacob to be his own, Israel to be his treasured possession' (135:4, and cf. Exod. 19:6).

Some psalms also fix attention on the final outcome of human history, when the Lord will be seen to be king of all nations. He will come to judge 'the world in righteousness and the peoples in his truth' (96:13). Because he reigns, even the distant isles can be called upon to rejoice (97:1). It is as if the psalmist is picturing the result after the final judgment when God's universal dominion will be established.

10.3 The Davidic Kingship

There are also many psalms that speak of the kingship of the line of David. They show how the covenant with David (2 Sam. 7) was understood in Israel. If we follow the titles of the psalms, David himself calls God 'my king' (5:3), and recognises that his own authority came from God. Two of the psalms (89 and 132) are expositions of the covenant that God made with David (2 Sam. 7), and they show the special place that the Davidic kingship occupied in Israel. David himself grasped the significance of God's promise affecting the future and destiny of the human race.[26] In psalms such as 18, 20, and 21 David acknowledges that his strength comes from God and that his victories are really God's victories.

The king also speaks of the people as not his own, but as God's people. He can appeal to God in these terms for them: 'Save your people and bless your inheritance; be their shepherd and carry them for ever' (28:9). The evildoers are described as crushing 'your people, O LORD; they oppress your inheritance' (94:5).

This attitude of the king also helps us to explain some of the difficult passages in the Psalter in which there is appeal to God to destroy the enemies. The contexts make it clear that the enemies were not primarily personal enemies but really they were enemies of God. Thus in Psalm 5 David prays for his enemies to be banished for their sins, and he gives as the reason, 'for they have rebelled *against you*' (5:10; for a fuller discussion of these passages, see section 12 on the imprecatory psalms in this introduction).

10.4 Our Response to the Kingship of God

Two important aspects come out of the Psalter in relation to the impact that the teaching about God as king should have upon us.

First, our response should be one of worship. Repeatedly in the kingship psalms the thought of worship appears, especially because God is not only king, but is also a holy God.

> Come, let us bow down in worship,
>   let us kneel before the LORD. (95:6)

> Ascribe to the LORD the glory due to his name;
>   bring an offering and come into his courts.

---

[26] The significance of David's words in 2 Samuel 7:18-21 is brought out by Walter Kaiser in 'The Blessing of David: The Charter for Humanity', in John H. Skilton, ed., *The Law and the Prophets: Old Testament Studies in Honor of Oswald T. Allis* (Nutley, NJ: Presbyterian and Reformed Publishing Co., 1974), pp. 298-318; and, W. J. Dumbrell, *Covenant and Creation: An Old Testament Covenantal Theology* (Exeter: Paternoster Press, 1984), pp. 151-52.

> Worship the LORD in the splendour of his holiness;
> tremble before him, all the earth.
> Say among the nations, 'The LORD reigns' (96:8-10).
>
> Exalt the LORD our God and worship at his footstool; he is holy.
> Exalt the LORD our God and worship at his holy mountain,
> for the LORD our God is holy (99:5, 9).

In a similar way the message of Revelation 19 concludes with the mighty shout: 'Hallelujah! For our Lord God Almighty reigns. Let us rejoice and be glad and give him glory!' John in response to this fell at the angelic messenger's feet, but the angel said: 'Do not do it! Worship God!' (Rev. 19:6-10). A knowledge of God as king should bring us to his footstool in worship.

Secondly, the thought of the kingship of God should be a stimulus to us in regard to missionary work. The Psalms present to us a picture of the nations of the world being subject to our God. God is so great that the nations must come and worship before him. This picture is not just a vision of the future, but something that stirs the psalmists with a real missionary urge. They call upon the world at large to come and worship the LORD (57:8-11; 66:1-4; 67:2-5; 96:3, 7-13; 99:2-3; 100:1-3; 108:3; 113:3-4; 117:1-2; 145:21). There is an eagerness about their longing to see all nations bowing before the king and being subject to his rule. The vision of the ultimate kingdom of God impels them with a real missionary spirit.

11. GOD'S LAW IN THE PSALMS

11.1 A Sovereign and His Laws
The laws of the Old Testament are not abstract moral laws, but the requirements of a covenant God. They are the personal demands of a personal, sovereign God upon his subjects. God spoke his law on Mount Sinai and then it was given in written form, both as the tablets of stone and also as the book of the covenant (Exod. 24:7) and the Book of Deuteronomy (Deut. 31:9). The personal character of the law is emphasised by the exhortations that occur so often, encouraging Israel

to keep the law and to be holy because the LORD was holy (Lev. 20:26).

The way in which the law was given to Israel places stress on the fact that it was given to a redeemed people. They had been brought out of slavery in Egypt by the LORD, who had shown great favour and grace to them in their need. There could be no thought that salvation was going to be based on their obedience to God's law. Even at Mount Sinai the people had sinned against him and provoked him to anger. They had not, and could not have, merited God's favour (Deut. 7:7-8; 9:4-6).

Israel was taught that God's covenant was unchangeable. The promises to the patriarchs, Abraham, Isaac, and Jacob could not be broken (see, for example, Exodus 3:15-17). This meant also that the basic requirements of the covenant, God's law, were also unchangeable. The psalmists say that God remembered his covenant (105:42; 106:45). Moreover he brought his people into the land of Canaan so 'that they might keep his precepts and observe his laws' (105:45).

To enforce his law upon the people, God promised blessings if they obeyed. Following an initial experience of God's grace when they were redeemed from slavery, further obedience would result in greater experience of God's grace. God's choice of Israel came first, and then as the people obeyed God a fuller appropriation of the blessings of salvation would become theirs.

The opposite truth was that curses were expressed against the people if they were unfaithful to God's covenant (for the curses, see especially Leviticus 26 and Deuteronomy 28). The Psalms reflect both these aspects, since blessings are pronounced on those who walk in the way of the LORD (1:1; 119:1), and often judgments are expressed against those who have gone their own way (14:3).

11.2 God's Law in the Psalms

We saw earlier that the Psalter came out of the covenant community. Hence it is quite understandable that a community that sang about God as their great king would also sing about his law. In Psalm 81 God challenges his people to listen to his warning, and says:

> You shall have no foreign god among you;
>   you shall not bow down to an alien god.
> I am the LORD your God, who brought you up out of Egypt
> (vv. 9-10).

These words, of course, are taken from, or echo, the opening of the Decalogue, and contain parts of the preface and the first two commandments (Exod. 20:2-4). They are used to reassert the claims which the Redeemer God had upon his people. They had to own him as their God, and not yield obedience or worship to any other.

There is a group of psalms that concentrate on God's law, and they focus particular attention on the blessings that come to those who obey them. They make God's law the object of thanks and praise, and they teach us especially the blessings of the law. Three of them in particular stand out because of their emphasis of walking in the way of God's law.

(a) Psalm 1 sets the pattern for the whole Psalter, as we have already seen (section 3.3). It opens with the word of blessing on those whose delight is in the law of the Lord. The contrast with the wicked is brought out in a very striking way:

[positive]	1. Blessed is the man who does not walk ...
	Rather ...
	Result
[negative]	2. Not so the wicked! ...
	Rather ...
	Result
	3. Summary
	For the LORD ...

(b) The thought of this psalm is extended in Psalm 19, which first of all refers to the declaration of God's glory in his creation (vv. 1-6) before it goes on to speak of the preciousness of God's law. The language used about the law is deliberate and most revealing. A variety of nouns is employed to describe God's revealed will ('law', 'testimony', 'precepts', 'commandments', and 'ordinances'). The adjectives used in reference to them highlight the nature of God's law ('perfect', 'sure', 'right', 'pure', 'clean', 'true'), while the succession of verbs (e.g. 'reviving', 'making wise', 'giving joy', 'giving light', 'enduring') tell of the impact which God's law has upon his children.

(c) The high point of praise of the law comes in Psalm 119, which is the longest song in the Book. It is an acrostic psalm divided into twenty-two sections, with every verse in each section beginning with the same letter of the Hebrew alphabet. This is not a sudden outpouring of the heart such as other psalms are, for it is not the sort of poem which could be composed quickly. The psalm is a beautiful work of art singing the praise of God's law, for every verse but three (vv. 84, 121, 122) contains a virtual synonym for 'law' ('word', 'statutes', 'testimonies', etc.). The psalmist rings the changes on these words to portray how wonderful God's law is, and to show yet again how it serves as a lamp to the feet and as a light to the path (119:105).

11.3 The Response to God's Law

God's law was clearly precious to the psalmists. This contrasts with the modern view of law which may respect God's demands and try to obey them but hardly thinks of them as exhilarating. But that is precisely the way believers in the Old Testament period considered God's laws.

> The ordinances of the LORD are sure
>   and altogether righteous.
> They are more precious than gold,
>   than much pure gold;
> they are sweeter than honey,
>   than honey from the comb. (19:9-10)

> How sweet are your promises to my taste,
>   sweeter than honey to my mouth! (119:103)

> Because I love your commands
>   more than gold, more than pure gold,
> and because I consider all your precepts right,
>   I hate every wrong path. (119:127-128)

God's law directed the ways of his people. At the time of renewing the covenant just before entry into the land of Canaan Moses said: 'What other nation is so great as to have such righteous decrees and laws as this body of laws which I am setting before you today? ... Teach them to your children and to their children after them' (Deut. 4:8-9). Thus the psalmists can ask for God to teach his way (25:4-5; 119:33) and also make mention of God's command to teach succeeding generations (78:5-8). In pleading for forgiveness David promised that if this was granted he would then 'teach transgressors your ways, and sinners will turn back to you' (51:13).

God's law was the object of meditation. As the children of Israel went into the promised land, they did so with Joshua's words ringing in their ears: 'Do not let this Book of the Law depart from your mouth; meditate upon it day and night, so that you may be careful to do everything written in it' (Josh.1:8). The Psalms show us how the people had taken this command to heart and practised it.

> Blessed is the man
> whose delight is in the law of the LORD
> and on his law he meditates day and night. (1:2)
>
> I will remember the deeds of the LORD;
> yes, I will remember your miracles of long ago.
> I will meditate on all your works
> and consider all your mighty deeds. (77:11-12)
>
> I meditate on your precepts and consider your ways. (119:15)

Meditation, according to the Psalter, consists of three things. It is firstly grounded in the *truth* of God. God has spoken in his word, and that word is to be hidden in the heart (119:1). Meditation stimulates thought about his word and heightens the meaning of a passage. Secondly, meditation is a response to the *love* of God. Faith in God is evidence of a personal relationship with him, and love to him is stimulated by meditation upon his word. Thirdly, meditation is really an aspect of *praise* of God. It is worship of the living God and consists of adoration of God and his works. In meditating on his word our attention is directed to God himself.[27]

12. THE PROBLEM SONGS

12.1 Introduction

One group of psalms stands out above all others because of the difficulties they have created for Christian people. These psalms are often called 'the imprecatory psalms'. The word *imprecation* comes from a Latin word *imprecatio*, which describes calling down harm on someone. Thus the English word is used in this connection to describe the psalms in which curses are expressed on others. Often it is not a whole psalm in question but only some verses from it.[28] The psalms in which these passages mainly occur are 55, 59, 69, 79, 109, and 137.

The problem which they present is of reconciling the curses and prayers for destruction of the wicked with the teaching of the New Testament. For some the problem is so acute that they assert that no New Testament Christian can use or approve of the imprecations in the psalms. This kind of judgment is often made without realising the full picture that has to be taken into consideration.

There are some facts we have to remember before we look at the solutions to the problem.

Firstly, this is not just a pressing problem for those who use the Psalter as a song book in worship. It is just as real a problem for those who merely want to read the Psalms in private devotions or in public worship.

Secondly, the fact that there are other portions of the Bible which contain similar curses must be borne in mind. These occur in passages such as Jeremiah 15:5; 17:18; 18:21-23; 20:12; Nehemiah 6:14 and 13:29. They also occur in New Testament

---

[27] A very helpful introduction to meditation is Edmund Clowney, *Christian Meditation* (Nutley, NJ: Craig Press, 1978).

[28] The total number of verses containing imprecations is around a hundred, and these are spread over thirty-two psalms. A listing of the passages is given in John N. Day, 'The Imprecatory Psalms and Christian Ethics', *BS* 159 (2002), pp. 166-86.

passages such as Acts 8:20; 2 Timothy 4:14; Galatians 1:9; 5:12; and Revelation 6:10.

Thirdly, Christ quoted freely from the Psalms. He used the messianic psalms most frequently, but then quoted most often from the psalms with curses in them. Thus in his lament over Jerusalem he referred to dashing the little ones to the ground, taking the words from Psalm 137:9 (in the LXX version). He also repeatedly used Psalm 69 (see John 2:17; 15:25). The fact that these psalms were endorsed and appropriated by our Lord does not explain their difficulty, but it should warn us not to judge them rashly.

Fourthly, some of these psalms are expressly referred to in the New Testament as having been given by inspiration as the psalmists spoke under the guidance of the Holy Spirit. In the case of Psalm 109 the apostle Peter quoted from it and said 'which the Holy Spirit spoke long ago through the mouth of David concerning Judas' (Acts 1:16).

12.2 Suggested Solutions

Various solutions to the problem have been proposed, and some of these can be reviewed.

An obvious solution which some have adopted is simply to leave these psalms alone and to pretend they are not there. This is done by avoiding any use or recognition of them. This presents us with the problem that the curses often come in psalms with other wonderful sayings, to which we wish to cling. Also, these psalms and many others were part and parcel of our Lord's use of the Old Testament. The problem has to be faced, not avoided.

It has been claimed that the Psalter belongs to the Old Testament dispensation, not the New Testament dispensation of grace, and therefore it teaches a lower morality than the New Testament with its injunction to love one's enemies (Matt. 5:44-45). But this would make Scripture contradict itself, for the Old Testament does not teach hatred towards one's enemies (Exod. 23:4, 5; Lev. 19:17, 18). Also, when Paul was condemning the sin of a revengeful spirit, he does so by quoting in Romans 12:18-20 from two Old Testament passages (Deut. 32:35; Prov. 25:21, 22).

Others have suggested that these psalms merely predict the doom of the wicked but are not to be understood as desiring their destruction. While there is an element of truth in this explanation, yet it does not explain many of the cases which go far beyond mere prediction. They ask God to carry out the destruction of the wicked (see, for example, 55:9 and 59:12-13).

Another view has been that the curses are to be understood in a figurative or spiritual sense. Thus the enemies spoken of are really temptations, and when we use these psalms we are praying that our temptations may be put to death or removed from us. But the persons spoken about give every appearance of having been real persons, not just some desires or emotions we may have.

Some have the idea that the imprecations are cries stemming from personal vindictiveness and they are seeking personal vengeance. Such utterances were wrong, but because of the circumstances in which the psalmists were placed they may to some extent be excused for speaking such curses. This theory does not fit the facts, as they show that in David's history there is no such spirit of vindictiveness. The real answer is deeper.

12.3 The Curses of the Covenant

Earlier we saw that the Psalms have to be placed in their true setting within God's covenant. It is striking that the cursing psalms strongly emphasise the relationship between Israel and the LORD. They stress the kingship of God over his people, and appeal to the God who is enthroned for ever to hear the cry of his people and to afflict their enemies (55:19). The relationship to God is stressed by use of the term 'servant' (69:17; 109:28) and also by the claim of the community to be God's people (79:13).

In almost all the imprecatory psalms the context is one of judgment. The appeal is to God to act as judge, and to be the vindicator of his people. In Psalm 109, for example, there is explicit reference to blessing and cursing (109:17-19, 28). This seems to be a clear allusion back to Genesis 12:3:

'I will bless those who bless you, and whoever curses you I will curse, and all peoples on earth will be blessed through you.' Psalm 137 is different because there is no reference to a judicial procedure. However, two passages from the prophets (Hos. 13:16; Isa. 13:16) provide the background for the curse in this imprecatory psalm. The psalmist speaks a word of cursing against the arch-enemy of Israel, Babylon, in language which is clearly reminiscent of these two prophets. In particular Isaiah 13:16 had already prophesied the downfall of Babylon. This link between prophets and psalmists should also serve as a reminder that there is a prophetic dimension to the Psalter. Just as the prophets deliver divine oracles, so do the psalmists.[29] The New Testament confirms this conjunction by referring to David as a prophet (Acts 2:30), and also understanding passages from the Psalms as prophecies concerning Jesus.[30]

The imprecatory psalms also show that the enemies were indeed God's enemies, not just the enemies of the psalmists. Thus Psalm 5 calls on God to declare the wicked guilty because, he says, 'they have rebelled against *you*' (5:10). Similarly Psalm 79 asks God to repay 'the reproaches they have hurled at *you*, O Lord' (v. 12). Even Psalm 137 must be understood to imply that the enemies are the enemies of the Lord. It is Babylon as the opponent of Israel who is in view. Just as Jeremiah cried: 'Do to her as she has done to others' (Jer. 50:15), so the psalmist was asking for divine visitation on her.

The concept of cursing was central to the whole idea of covenant, both within and without the Bible. In the extra-biblical treaties a person entering into a treaty was obliged to treat the other party's enemies as his enemies. The principle was, as one Hittite treaty puts it, 'with my friend you shall be friend, and with my enemy you shall

---

[29] These oracles are found in 2:6-9; 12:5; 46:10; 50:5-23; 60:6-8; 68:22-23; 81:6-16; 82:2-7; 89:3-4, 19-37; 90:3; 91:14-16; 95:8-11; 105:15; 110:1, 4; and 132:11-18.

[30] For a very helpful discussion on these aspects, see Alex Luc, 'Interpreting the Curses in the Psalms', *JETS* 42/3 (September 1999), pp. 400-05.

be enemy'.[31] In the Old Testament itself the word 'curse' could be employed as a virtual synonym for 'covenant' (Deut. 29:14, 18).[32] When the prophets speak judgment against Israel, they echo the curses of the covenant from passages such as Leviticus 26 and Deuteronomy 27 and 28. Rebels, whether within the covenant nation or outside, came under the same curses. In this respect the curses in the Psalter are typical of the covenantal approach of the Old Testament both in regard to relationships between men and relationships between God and humanity.

Finally, we should remember that the Bible consistently marks a sharp distinction between those who are for God and those who are against him. There is a final judgment day coming when the Son of Man will separate the sheep from the goats (Matt. 25:31-33). The picture the New Testament gives us of heaven is that nothing sinful or unclean will ever enter it (Rev. 21:27). As elsewhere in the Bible, the psalmists are looking at life from the perspective that is going to prevail at the last day. In appealing for God's vindication they are virtually asking for God's final judgment to be advanced in time and made a reality here and now.[33]

13. A CHRISTIAN READING OF THE PSALMS

13.1 An Open Song Book

The Psalter grew up over a long period of time. In its early development it was an open songbook of God's people, in

---

[31] J. B. Pritchard, ed., *Ancient Near Eastern Texts Relating to the Old Testament*, 3rd ed. (Princeton: Princeton University Press, 1991), p. 204.

[32] *DCH*, 1, pp. 272-73, gives as one of the meanings of *'âlâh*, 'covenant stipulation' or 'sometimes perh. used collectively, **'covenant'**, citing Deut. 29:11, 13, 18 [Eng. enumeration 12, 14, 19]. Both 'oath' and 'covenant' are listed as synonyms. This lies behind the decision of the NIV translators to use 'oath' in these verses.

[33] I have discussed more fully the imprecatory psalms in 'The Continuity of the Covenant Curses in the Imprecations of the Psalms', *RTR* 54, 2 (1995), pp. 65-72. For wider discussions, including Christian use of the imprecations, see J. Carl Laney, 'A Fresh Look at the Imprecatory Psalms,' *BS* 138 (January-March 1981), pp. 35-45; reprinted in *The Bib Sac Reader: Commemorating Fifty Years of Publication of Dallas Theological Seminary 1934-1983* (Chicago: Moody Press, 1983), pp. 115-125; Alex Luc, 'Interpreting the Curses of the Psalms'; John N. Day, 'The Imprecatory Psalms and Christian Ethics'.

the sense that it was being added to by the addition of new psalms. Moreover, it was in constant use by individuals and the collective group of believers as it was growing. There must have been many other songs which were composed, but these we have were especially written under the influence of the Holy Spirit and brought together as the special songbook of the Old Testament church.

The Psalter is an open songbook in another sense as well. While the Psalms come out of the individual experiences of their authors, yet they often lack precise indications which would enable us to say exactly what those experiences were. Thus to say that the Lord has delivered our eyes from tears does not specify anything more than that the Lord has removed our sorrow or grief. It does not tell us the details of the experience which caused such sorrow. This is in marked contrast to other Old Testament songs such as the Song of the Sea (Exod. 15) or the Song of Deborah (Judg. 5). The lack of specific details is important, however, as it enables us to identify all the more closely with the Psalms. Because they are general in character we can use them so readily and apply them to our own specific need.

The New Testament sets a pattern of use of the Psalms for Christians in that it appropriates them and uses them for believers passing through similar experiences. Their pastoral use and application were realised, and when in trouble New Testament Christians found comfort in them. Thus when Paul is describing his deliverance on the occasion of his preliminary hearing he says he 'was delivered from the lion's mouth' (2 Tim. 4:17). This is an apparent reference to Psalm 22:21, and may indicate that he had used that lament in prayer at the time of his hearing. In the letter of the Hebrews the writer quotes a word from the Psalms that had relevance for his experience and for his readers: 'The Lord is my helper; I will not be afraid. What can man do to me?' (Heb. 13:6; cf. Ps. 118:6). These and many other quotations and allusions are applied on the principle given by Paul in Romans 15:4: 'For everything that was written in the past was written to teach us, so that through endurance and the encouragement of the

Scriptures we might have hope.' He has just quoted from a psalm (69:9) and his readers are encouraged to place their trust in the Lord, for the Old Testament Scriptures gave ample evidence of his faithfulness.

13.2 The Psalms and the New Testament

We cannot read the Psalms today as believers in the Old Testament read them, for we live *after* the coming of Christ. Jesus himself was brought up in a Jewish environment in which the Psalms were extensively used. Augustine said of Jesus, *iste cantator psalmorum*, 'He, the singer of the psalms.' On occasions of pilgrimage to Jerusalem (Luke 2:41-51), such as at the Passover, he would have been part of the community who sang from the Psalter. During the washing of his feet he quoted from Psalm 41:10 (John 13:18), while on the Cross he used several phrases from the Psalms ('My God, My God, why have you forsaken me?', Ps. 22:1; 'It is done', cf. Ps. 22:31 ['he has done it']; 'Father, into your hands I commend my spirit', Ps. 31:5).

Moreover, Jesus is the focus of both Old and New Testaments, and in his own ministry he gave indications of how we are to understand the Old Testament (including the Psalms) in reference to himself. Twice following his resurrection he spoke of how the Old Testament pointed to himself as the promised Messiah. To Cleopas and his friend he began with Moses and all the prophets and 'explained to them what was said in all the Scriptures concerning himself' (Luke 24:27). Then to the assembled disciples in Jerusalem Jesus appeared and said: 'Everything must be fulfilled that is written about me in the Law of Moses, the Prophets and the Psalms' (Luke 24:44). Clearly Jesus expounded the Psalms to the disciples and explained them in terms of his own coming and work.

Jesus' use of the Psalms also explains the extensive use of the Psalms throughout the New Testament. There are about 360 quotations from the Old Testament in the New, and of these about one-third are from the Book of Psalms. Many appear in the early sermons of the apostles as recorded in the

Book of Acts. Peter uses Psalms 110 and 16 in his speech on the day of Pentecost (Acts 2:25-28, 34), while in his speech to the rulers he quotes Psalm 118:22 (Acts 4:11). When Paul spoke in the synagogue at Pisidian Antioch he quoted from Psalm 2 and like Peter also used Psalm 16 (Acts 13:33-35). Clearly the apostles preached and taught on the basis of the instruction that they had received, and Jesus had assured them that the Holy Spirit would bring to their remembrance the things he had spoken (John 14:26). Hence the meaning and intent of Jesus' words, including his use of passages from the Psalms and other Old Testament books, is developed in the New Testament writings. The New Testament epistles are replete with quotations and allusions to the Psalms.[34]

13.3 Messianic Element[35]

What Jesus himself and his apostles saw in the Psalms his followers also wish to see. In our discussion on the messianic element in the Psalms we must be guided by the way in which the New Testament uses and applies specific psalms. Some writers have taken the position that there are no psalms that directly prophesy of the Messiah. This would be strange as messianic prophecies occur in many other places in the Old Testament, and the closest parallel to many psalms are the eschatological parts of the prophetical books.[36] It is also difficult to uphold this

---

[34] I have examined the Pauline usage in 'Aspects of Paul's Use of the Psalm', *WTJ* 32, 1 (1969), pp. 1-23.

[35] The comments on individual psalms should be consulted for exegesis of particular passages that contain messianic teaching. Further, and fuller, discussion of the messianic element in the Psalter can be found in Derek Kidner, *Psalms 1–72: An Introduction and Commentary on Books I and II of the Psalms* (London: Inter-Varsity Press, 1973), pp. 18-25. See also David Starling, 'The Messianic Hope in the Psalms', *RTR* 58, 3 (1999), pp. 121-34.

[36] This is the point made explicitly by Geerhardus Vos: 'So far as the content [of the Psalter] objectively considered is concerned, the difference from prophecy is not perhaps sufficiently pronounced to justify separate treatment. The general scheme is in both essentially the same'. 'Eschatology of the Psalter', Appendix to *The Pauline Eschatology* (Grand Rapids: Eerdmans, 1972), pp. 331-32. The discussion first appeared in the *PTR 18* (1920), pp. 1-43.

position when we consider the words of quite a few of the Psalms, for they speak of a king in a way which goes far beyond anything that a king in David's line could ever be.[37] The inadequacies of human kings helped to create expectation of a far greater ruler to come.

It is probably best to view the messianic psalms under several categories. Most of the messianic psalms take their starting point from the promise to David in 2 Samuel 7, which involved both a direct promise to David and the prospect of a continuing royal dynasty. A significant group comprises those that refer to this promise, yet speaks of the enduring nature of David's kingdom in such a way as points to the ultimate messianic kingdom. Psalms 89 and 132 expound 2 Samuel 7, while many other psalms, including 18, 21, and 61, celebrate the grace that God showed to David and family. The past deliverances of David formed the basis on which he looked ahead so confidently to the exaltation of the Lord among the nations (Ps. 18:46-50).

Another group of psalms comprises those which are directly related to the coming of the Messiah. While a song like Psalm 2 may be couched in language that echoes 2 Samuel 7, yet the words used point with distinctiveness to the one in whom the promise would find its final fulfilment. The king spoken about is both the Lord's *anointed* and also his *son*. The way in which Paul used this psalm in his speech in Pisidian Antioch confirms this understanding of Psalm 2 (Acts 13:32-33). From the vision of David and his kingdom, the eye was directed to a greater son of David who would ultimately be lord of all, having the ends of the earth as his possession (Ps. 2:8). Psalm 110 points to a promised son of David who would have priesthood, not by ancestry, but by divine appointment (110:5).

Other psalms take their starting point from Solomon's kingdom, and yet point far beyond it. Thus while a psalm

---

[37] Cf. the comments made by Franz Delitzsch on Psalm 22: 'In Ps. xxii., however, David descends, with his complaint, into a depth that lies beyond the depth of his affliction, and rises, with his hopes, to a height that lies far beyond the height of the reward of his affliction'. *Commentary on the Psalms* I, p. 306.

such as Psalm 45 was probably composed on the occasion of a royal wedding, yet the eyes of the inspired psalmist were suddenly lifted up to see the glory of the messianic ruler who is even called 'God' (v. 6). Psalm 72 presents us with the true prince of peace whose kingdom is going to far transcend the limits of the Davidic/Solomonic empire. His kingdom is going to extend from the River (i.e., the Euphrates) outwards! This same reference to Messiah's rule occurs in another messianic passage in Zechariah 9:10.

The final group of messianic psalms are those which are typically messianic. That is to say, their primary reference is not to Jesus, but he is the one who fulfils the descriptions which they give. They are psalms of righteous people; he is the *only* righteous one. The idea of a righteous person undergoing suffering and putting his trust in God is fully realised in the life and ministry of Jesus. These psalms include 6, 16, 22, 35, 40, 41, 69, 70, 71, 102, and 109. In this sense many of the Psalms (or perhaps all) are messianic. Some of this group of psalms had in view not only David but also his descendants (102, 109), and in this way a link is formed with the psalms specifically based on 2 Samuel 7.

14. USING THE PSALMS TODAY

14.1 The Psalms and Spiritual Life

As we have seen in earlier discussion, the Book of Psalms serves two great purposes, which can be expressed in these statements:

The Psalms speak *to us*.
The Psalms speak *for us*.

Each of these aspects is important and has practical consequences for us today. The Psalter came from God and it leads to God. We receive blessing as we read and use the Psalms and as we are instructed by them. They speak *to* our hearts and minister spiritual truths to our minds and consciences. But they also speak *for* us, as we utilise them in praise and prayer as if we were their author. They come out of real life situations and because they are facing the variety of human needs, we are able to respond to God by using their words as our own.

14.2 Personal Devotions

Christians today need the richness of the Psalter to aid them in their spiritual life. It is *the* devotional book of the Bible, and as such continues to be our devotional book and our guide. In using it we are ministered to by the thoughts and prayers it contains, and in turn we mouth our praise and adoration of God and our petitions in its words. Very often the Book of Psalms has been published along with the New Testament so that Christians can have ready access to it for their devotional use.

The Christian church right down throughout the centuries has found spiritual nourishment in the Book of Psalms. It was common in the early church for the whole Psalter to be memorised by those who were seeking to become pastors. Jerome (*c.* 347–420) tells that in his time it was common to hear the Psalms being sung in the fields and in the gardens. The same phenomenon occurred at the time of the Reformation, when the Psalms again became so prominent in the life of the church. The Reformation movement is the reason why the reading and chanting of the Psalms became customary in Anglican churches, while metrical Psalters became central in the worship of Dutch and Scottish churches. The Psalms should fill a central place, not only in the life of individuals, but also in the collective worship of the church.

The word of Christ must dwell in us richly. Paul, in writing to the Colossian Christians, says: 'Let the peace of Christ rule in your hearts, since as members of one body you were called to peace. And be thankful. Let the word of Christ dwell in you richly as you teach and admonish one another with all wisdom, and as you sing psalms, hymns and spiritual songs with gratitude in your hearts to God' (Col. 3:15–16). The various types of Christian songs, including psalms, are regarded as 'Christ's word'. It is to take up its abode in our hearts and it is to be used as we teach and admonish each other. That indwelling word builds us up in our faith and it counsels us, and it also forms part of our praise and thanksgiving to God (Col. 3:15–17).

14.3 Praise[38]

The Psalms have been and can be used in various ways in our worship. Chanting of prose psalms has a long history, though it is frequently associated with Anglican worship. It has the advantage of allowing the words to be dominant, and it usually only requires a restricted number of chants to be known. Many in our cultural setting prefer a greater variety of tunes to be used in worship than is normally the case with chanting.

'Scripture in Song' is a modern phenomenon, whereby small passages of Scripture are set to music. This has meant that many Christian people are singing portions of psalms, and it is good to hear this use of God's Word. The disadvantage is that the selections are taken out of their context in the Psalms, and often they are interpreted by users of 'Scripture in Song' in a way that is not supported by the context in the particular psalm. We need to remember that the Psalms are poetic pieces *as a whole*, and that simply to select a verse or two can distort their essential message.

The Reformation, which in significant respects brought a revolution in worship, in other ways continued the practices of the pre-Reformation church though in a new form. The use of the Psalms not only continued but took on a new role as their use was popularised in the Reformation movement. Luther wrote in 1523: 'I plan after the example of the prophets and ancient fathers of the Church to make German psalms for the people, that is to say, spiritual songs, so that the Word of God may dwell among the people by means of song also.' To this he added that the words were to be 'all quite plain and common, such as the common people may understand, yet pure and skilfully handled.' Calvin also regarded music as a gift of God and encouraged the use of the full Psalter, and he himself attempted to translate some of them into French,

---

[38] A modern survey of the use of the Psalms in Christian worship can be found in John D. Witvliet, *The Biblical Psalms in Christian Worship: A Brief Introduction and Guide to Resources* (Grand Rapids: Eerdmans, 2007), pp. 45-134.

though the work of Clement Marot (1497-1544) and Theodore Beza (1519-1605) was much more extensive and influential. Wherever the Protestant Reformation reached, the Psalms were used in worship, and they became so popular that even Roman Catholics were known to sing them. This tradition of Psalm singing continues to this day.[39] The Scottish Metrical Psalter of 1650 has been widely used, and has often been used alongside modern revisions or alternative versions. The Irish Presbyterian Church undertook a light revision and added twenty-seven additional versions in 1880. The United Presbyterian Church of North America produced complete Psalters in 1871 and 1912 which have been widely used, especially in the United States. *The Book of Psalms with Music* (1950) and *The Book of Psalms for Singing* (1973) of the Reformed Presbyterian Church of North America have also been extensively used. The Presbyterian Church of America produced the *Trinity Psalter* (1994) with metrical settings of all 150 Psalms. In Australia, *The Complete Book of Psalms for Singing* (Presbyterian Church of Eastern Australia, Melbourne, 1991), was intentionally a version of *all* the Psalms, and not just a selection of songs *from* the Psalms. Similarly the Free Church of Scotland has issued a complete new Psalter which is being used quite widely. In modern English Anglicanism there has been renewed interest in the Psalter and *Psalm Praise* (1973) and the later *Psalms for Today* and *Songs from the Psalms* are representative of this approach. The variety of versions available testifies to the abiding character of the Psalter as *the* songbook of the Church and one which has helped to give vitality to the worship of Christians in many countries and situations.

The Psalter has also been most influential in serving as a model for the church's hymnology, and often individual psalms have been used extensively as the basis of many hymns. There are hymns from the Reformation period such as Luther's 'A mighty fortress is our God' (based on Psalm 46), but it is especially from the period of Isaac Watts (1674–1748)

---

[39] For a good, though not complete, list of resources for metrical psalmody, see Witvliet, *ibid.*, pp. 106-14.

and Charles Wesley (1707-1788) that the attempt was made to use the content of the Psalms but to infuse distinctively New Testament teaching into them. Watts in particular carried this too far, but some of his hymns based on psalms remain in constant use today (e.g. 'Jesus shall reign' from Psalm 72, and 'O God our help in ages past' from Psalm 90). Wesley makes no claim that his hymns are translations of psalms, but rather they are Christian hymns based on the Psalms, just as he based other hymns on other parts of the Bible or on Christian writings. Thus his hymn 'O for a heart to praise my God' uses the ideas of Psalm 51, while 'Jesu, mighty to deliver' is Psalm 70 expanded as a Christian song of praise. Many other hymns clearly reflect the influence and pattern of the Psalter, and this is good for the Church.

14.4 Preaching

As part of God's Word, the Psalms are to be preached. They form a section of Holy Scripture that is not duplicated elsewhere. No other part presents so vividly the varied emotions of the human heart, and they show how believers in the Old Testament time put their trust in their covenant God even in times of deep distress. This being so, it is a contradiction to preach in a passionless way on passages from the Psalter, for we must respond to the feelings expressed in them and mediate their teaching to the experiential needs of Christians today. The Psalms are part of the things 'written for our instruction, that through endurance and through the encouragement of the Scriptures we might have hope' (Rom. 15:4). They form an important part of the Scriptures that were God-breathed, and accordingly 'profitable for teaching, for reproof, for correction, and for training in righteousness, that the man of God may be competent, equipped for every good work' (2 Tim. 3:16-17). The Psalms were very important in the ministry of Jesus and his apostles, and they should be in our ministries as well.[40]

---

[40] I have developed this whole subject in 'Preaching from the Psalms' in *Preaching the Word: Essays in Honour of Professor Tom Wilkinson*, ed. Stewart Gill (*RTR* Supplement 3; Melbourne, 2009), pp. 30-41.

14.5 Epilogue

Study of the Psalms should never be an end in itself. The purpose should be to direct us back to the Psalms with fuller understanding and greater interest. The use of them should be a vital part of our spiritual growth, as we use them to pray to God and as they speak to us. In turn that study should provoke us to use them all the more in praise to God and adoration of him and his works. Our song should be like the one which ends the Psalter:

> Praise the Lord . . .
> Let everything that has breath
>   praise the Lord.
> Praise the Lord. (Ps. 150:1, 6)

Suggestions for Further Reading

Commentaries
J. A. Alexander, *The Psalms Translated and Explained* (Darlington: Evangelical Press, 1975).
J. M. Boice, *Psalms*, 3 vols (Grand Rapids: Baker Books, 1994, 1996, 1998).
John Calvin, *Commentary on the Psalms* (Grand Rapids: Baker Book House, 1979).
P. C. Craigie, *Psalms 1–50*, 2nd ed, with 2004 Supplement by Marvin Tate (Waco: Word, 2004).
Geoffrey W. Grogan, *Psalms*, The Two Horizons Commentary (Grand Rapids: Eerdmans, 2008).
E. W. Hengstenberg, *Commentary on the Psalms*, 3 vols (Edinburgh: T. & T. Clark, 1869).
Walter C. Kaiser, *The Journey Isn't Over: The Pilgrim Psalms* [Pss. 120-134] *for Life's Challenges and Joys* (Grand Rapids: Baker Book House, 1993).
F. D. Kidner, *Psalms: An Introduction and Commentary*, 2 vols (London: Inter-Varsity Press, 1973).
H. C. Leupold, *Exposition of the Psalms* (Grand Rapids: Baker Book House, 1969).
J. J. Stewart Perowne, *The Psalms*, 2 vols (London: George Bell and Sons, 1886).
O. Palmer Robertson, *Psalms in Congregational Celebration* (Darlington: Evangelical Press, 1995).
W. VanGemeren, 'The Psalms', in *The Expositor's Bible Commentary* (Grand Rapids: Zondervan 1991), vol. 5, pp. 3-880.
E. J. Young, *The Way Everlasting: A Study in Psalm 139* (Edinburgh: Banner of Truth Trust, 1997).

General
James E. Adams, *War Psalms of the Prince of Peace: Lessons from the Imprecatory Psalms* (Nutley, NJ: Presbyterian and Reformed, 1991).
R. Dean Anderson, Jr., 'The Division and Order of the Psalms', *Westminster Theological Journal* 56,2 (Fall, 1994), pp. 219-41.

J. Calvin Beisner, *Psalms of Promise: Celebrating the Majesty and Faithfulness of God*, 2nd ed. (Nutley, NJ: Presbyterian and Reformed, 1994).

C. Hassell Bullock, *Encountering the Book of Psalms: A Literary and Theological Introduction* (Grand Rapids: Baker Academic, 2001).

C. Hassell Bullock, *An Introduction to the Old Testament Poetic Books* (Chicago: Moody Press, 1988), 'The Book of Psalms', pp. 111-45.

Robert B. Chisholm, Jr., 'A Theology of the Psalms', Roy B. Zuck, ed., *A Biblical Theology of the Old Testament* (Chicago: Moody Press, 1991), pp. 257-304.

Raymond B. Dillard and Tremper Longman III, *An Introduction to the Old Testament* (Grand Rapids: Zondervan, 1994), 'Psalms', pp. 211-34.

Geoffrey W. Grogan, *Prayer, Praise and Prophecy* (Fearn: Mentor, 2001).

Philip S. Johnston and David G. Firth, edd., *Interpreting the Psalms: Issues and Approaches* (Leicester: Apollos, 2005).

Tremper Longman III, *How to Read the Psalms* (Downers Grove: Intervarsity Press, 1988).

J. B. Payne, 'Book of Psalms', *Zondervan Pictorial Bible Encyclopedia*, vol. 4, pp. 934-47.

N. H. Ridderbos and P. C. Craigie, 'Psalms' in *The International Standard Bible Encyclopedia*, fully revised, vol. 3, pp. 1029-40.

Harry Upritchard, *A Son Promised: Christ in the Psalms* (Darlington: Evangelical Press, 1994).

Bruce K. Waltke, 'A Canonical Approach to the Psalms', in *Tradition and Testament: Essays in Honor of Charles Lee Feinberg*, edd. Paul Feinberg and John Feinberg (Chicago: Moody Press, 1981).

Bruce K. Waltke, 'Psalms, Theology of', in *New International Dictionary of Old Testament Theology and Exegesis*, vol. 4, pp. 1100–1115.

John D. Witvliet, *The Biblical Psalms in Christian Worship: A Brief Introduction and Guide to Resources* (Grand Rapids: Eerdmans, 2007).

Book 1
Psalm 1

The manner in which the Book of Psalms opens is important. The first two psalms are keys to the whole Psalter because they are not strictly prayers but declarations. The first prayer is actually Psalm 3. Taken together, Psalms 1 and 2 help us understand the whole book, and their interconnection is shown by a chiastic structure in that Psalm 1 opens with the idea of blessing (*ash^{e}rê hâ'îsh*, 'Blessed is the man') while Psalm 2 closes with it (*ash^{e}rê kol-chôsê bô*, 'Blessed are all who take refuge in him'). A link also exists in thought between the righteous person of Psalm 1 and the messianic king in Psalm 2. The king in Israel had to have a copy of the 'law' for himself (*tôrâh*, Deut. 17:18), and hence he should have been the one in Israel who exemplified most clearly the character of the righteous, delighting in the law and being guided by his daily meditation upon it (Ps. 1:2).[1] The absence of a superscription before Psalm 2 also points to a connection between the two.[2]

The opening and closing of the Psalter are also important (see Introduction, for a discussion of the structure of the Psalter). It opens here in Psalm 1 with a call for obedient service,

---

[1] Some manuscript evidence exists pointing to the fact that Psalms 1 and 2 were regarded as a single psalm. While the majority of Greek manuscripts in Acts 13:33 quote from Ps. 2 and refer to it as 'the second psalm', yet the Western text calls it 'the first psalm'. The early church fathers, Justin Martyr (AD c. 100-165) and Origen (AD c.185-254), both knew them as a single entity.

[2] The only other psalms in Book 1 without a superscription are Psalms 10 and 33. For fuller discussion on the links between Psalms 1 and 2, and their role as the opening of the whole psalter, see P. D. Miller, 'The Beginning of the Psalter', in J. Clinton McCann, ed., *The Shape and Shaping of the Psalter* (Sheffield: JSOT Supplement Series 159, 1993), pp. 83-92.

while it closes in Psalm 150 with a call for universal praise.[3] It commences with the challenge of walking diligently in the ways of the LORD, while it closes with universal adoration of him. This first key starts by contrasting the two ways in which people can go. As the opening song of the whole collection it is intended to challenge readers as to their commitment to the LORD and to his law. It points to two 'ways', just as Jesus did in the Sermon on the Mount (Matt. 7:13-14).

1. Near to God (vv. 1-3)

The book opens with a pronouncement of blessing. **Blessed is the man.** In Hebrew there are two words for blessing, one used by God when he is expressing a benediction (*bâruch*), and the other used here (*'ash⁰rê*) by men when referring to other men. To merit the word **blessed** used here, man has to do something, or, as in this case, not do something, for which he can be commended. Here the character of the blessed man is defined by three negative terms — **who does not walk in the counsel of the wicked or stand in the way of sinners or sit in the seat of the mockers** (*v. 1*). With mounting emphasis the psalmist describes the character of those whose trust is in the LORD. They do not look to ungodly men as a source of wisdom; their path is not that taken by sinners; their company is not with those who mock God or who are self-satisfied and proud.

On the contrary, the blessed man is marked out because **his delight is in law of the LORD, and on his law he meditates day and night** (*v. 2*). God's instruction forms the basis of his conduct and the treasure of his heart. The word 'law' (*tôrâh*) does not mean a list of rules and the appropriate punishments, but the fullness of God's 'teaching' for his children. This instruction, which included the history of God's dealings with his people, was to be passed on from generation to generation (see Ps. 78:1-8). In the Old Testament the references to God's *tôrâh* are almost universally positive,

---

[3] See the discussion by W. Brueggeman *JSOT* 50 (1991), 'Bounded by Obedience and Praise', pp. 63-91.

so that it is to be both obeyed and loved (Ps. 119:97, 113, 163, 165). It was to be the object of reverence and devotion. The Hebrew word translated 'meditates' (*hâgâh*) implies something more than silent reflection. It means to whisper or to murmur, a use that may point to the fact that reading was usually done aloud in biblical times. It also seems to be taking up and using in a new context the words of God to Joshua: 'Do not let this Book of the Law depart from your mouth; meditate upon it day and night, so that you may be careful to do everything written in it. Then you will be prosperous and successful' (Josh. 1:8).[4]

He is like a tree planted by streams of water, which yields its fruit in season and whose leaf does not wither. Whatever he does prospers (*v. 3*). The result of such meditation is that the blessed man is like a transplanted tree, set alongside an irrigation canal.[5] The thought of being transplanted recalls the imagery of God transplanting a little vine from Egypt into Canaan, where it became a great tree (Ps. 80:8-16). It may also reflect the situation prevailing when the whole Psalter was brought to completion, soon after the experience in exile, in which they knew so much about the irrigation canals of Babylon. In its well-watered position the tree brings forth its fruit, and its bountiful location ensures that it will not fade. So it is with the believing child of God who endures to the end (Phil. 1:6) and who brings forth fruits of righteousness (Gal. 5:16-26).

---

[4] The command, 'meditate upon it day and night' (*v^ehâgîtâ bô yômâm vâlay^elâh*) in Josh. 1:8, is replaced by a statement in Ps. 1:2, 'and on his law he meditates day and night' (*ûv^etôrâtô yehgeh yômâm vâlay^elâh*). The comparison is also closer than the NIV suggests as 'then you will be prosperous' is really 'then your way shall prosper', which in Hebrew contains the words 'way' (*dérek*) and 'shall prosper' (*yatslîach*), both occurring in Ps. 1. See verses 1 and 3.

[5] The Hebrew verb used (*shâtal*) can mean either 'plant' or 'transplant'. All its ten occurrences in the Old Testament are metaphorical and all relate either to Israel or the righteous Israelite. What God [trans]plants thrives for ever. Jer. 17:8 contains almost the same phrase as Ps. 1:3, declaring that the 'blessed man' 'will be like a tree planted by the water', though the application is different. Here it is that such a person will bring forth fruit, whereas in Jer. 17 it is that the tree will put forth roots towards the water.

2. Far from God *(vv. 4-6)*

How different are those whose trust is not in the Lord! The lines of demarcation between God's children and the children of the world are clearly drawn. **Not so the wicked! They are like chaff that the wind blows away** *(v. 4)*. The contrast is clear.[6] Instead of being like a living tree, the wicked are as unstable as chaff. They are without root and without fruit. **Therefore the wicked will not stand in the judgment, nor sinners in the assembly of the righteous** *(v. 5)*. Such people will not be able to stand their ground at God's judgment seat, neither have they any right to be among God's people. The combination of the Hebrew verb 'rise' *(qûm)* with the noun 'judgment' *(mishpât)* points to God's final judgment. Their experience will be one of exclusion from the company of God's people on earth, and exclusion from the presence of God in eternity.

The final verse of the psalm sums up the contrast. **For the Lord watches over the way of the righteous, but the way of the wicked will perish** *(v. 6)*. The way of the righteous is overseen constantly by the Lord, whereas the way of the ungodly has no future. It is going to perish utterly. This is a poetic form of the challenge of Moses to the children of Israel in Deuteronomy 30:11-20. By implication the psalmist echoes Moses' command: 'Now choose life, so that you and your children may live.'

---

[6] The contrast is marked by the words 'not so' (*'al kên*), which when appearing at the beginning of a sentence, signify emphasis, or, as here, contrast.

Psalm 2

Psalm 2, like Psalm 1, is a key to the Book of Psalms, and it is linked to the first by two words, 'plot' (in Ps. 1:2 translated as 'meditate') and 'blessed'. Here in this psalm the focus is on the ungodly and specifically on the Gentile nations who reject the LORD's rule. The only solution to their situation is to accept the rule of God's chosen Messiah, and then they will know the blessedness of trusting in him (v. 12). Just as Psalm 1 begins with the word 'blessed' (v. 1), so Psalm 2 ends with this word. It is possible that these two psalms were in fact regarded as one.[1] This psalm is structured around four clearly defined stanzas (cf. the division of Isa. 52:13–53:12 into five stanzas).

1. Rebellious Nations (vv. 1-3)

Why do the nations rage and the peoples plot in vain? The kings of the earth take their stand and the rulers gather together against the LORD and his Anointed One (vv. 1-2).[2] The opening **why?** is not so much indicating the seeking of information as an expression of astonishment that the Gentile nations would act in this way. **In vain** translates a Hebrew noun (rîq) that means 'emptiness' or worthlessness'.[3]

---

[1] See f.n. 1 on Psalm 1.
[2] The Hebrew verbal aspects in these verses (perf./imperf., imperf./perf.) appear to be used almost interchangeably. For a fine discussion on the question of tense in Hebrew, see P. C. Craigie, *Psalms 1-50: Second Edition with 2004 Supplement by Marvin Tate*, 'Excursus II: The Translation of Tenses in Hebrew Poetry' (Word Biblical Commentary; Waco: Word, 2004), pp. 110-13.
[3] The word rîq here is not a Hebrew adverb but a noun forming an accusative of relation.

Whereas the godly meditate on God's word (Ps. 1:2), the ungodly rulers of the Gentile nations meditate in the sense of pondering over plots that they can make, but their plans have no real substance to them. Isaiah presents a similar picture of the turmoil among nations in the Assyrian period, and also has the assurance that God is able to intervene with his devastating rebuke (Isa. 17:12-14). The word 'anointed' (*mâshîach*) is the Hebrew word from which we get the English word 'messiah'. It can be used for any anointed servant of God, including Cyrus of Persia (Isa. 45:1), or can even be applied to the Antichrist (Dan. 9:25, 26).[4] The expression of rebellion mounts to a climax with the words **against the LORD and his Anointed One**. Ultimately the hostility that the nations show is directed against God himself, and not only against him, but also against his chosen servant, whose appointment is spoken of later in this psalm (*vv. 6-9*). What these kings and rulers did not realise is that their plans are useless in God's sight.

When they take their stand and gather together they make a declaration of their independence: '**Let us break their chains,' they say, 'and throw off their fetters'** (*v. 3*). Sinful men never want to walk within the limitations that God places on his creatures. In their arrogance they proclaim their supposed freedom, and they claim to be master of their own destinies. Their spirit is typified in Ernest Henley's poem, *Invictus*:

> It matters not how strait the gate,
> > How charged with punishments the scroll.
> I am the master of my fate;
> > I am the captain of my soul.

The suffix on the words 'chains' and 'fetters' is a poetic form (-*mô*) that can be substituted for many of the regular forms. Here the context favours translating '*his* chains' and '*his* fetters'.[5] The nations are set against the LORD, and hence they desire to be loosed from any restraint he places upon them.

---

[4] For a discussion of the Hebrew *mâshîach* in Daniel 9, see my commentary on *Daniel* (Darlington: Evangelical Press, 2007), pp. 239-44.

[5] See *GKC* §91 b, f.

2. Divine Rule (vv. 4-6)

In contrast to the feverish activity described in verse 1, the LORD is able to view the plottings of men from his heavenly throne. **The One enthroned in heaven laughs; the LORD scoffs at them** (v. 4). The description of God and his kingship uses a common expression for his heavenly rule. He 'dwells in the heavens' (*yôshêv bashshâmayim*; cf. also Pss. 29:10; 113:5), whereas for his temporary manifestations a different verb is used (*shâkan*; cf. the description of him sitting 'between the cherubim', 1 Sam. 4:4; 2 Sam. 6:2; 2 Kings 19:15; Ps. 99:1). He does not laugh to ridicule them, but because he views their planning from his sovereign security, and because he knows that *his* day is coming (Ps. 37:13, *kî yâvo' yômô*), the day of his final judgment. Almost the same expression as here involving the two verbs 'to laugh' and 'to mock' (*sâchaq, lâ'ag*) occurs also in Psalm 59:8.

Then he rebukes them in his anger and terrifies them in his wrath, saying, 'I have installed[6] my King on Zion, my holy hill' (vv. 5-6). When the LORD does speak, it will be in anger for he will terrify them. The thought is stated in a typical pattern of chiastic parallelism: 'speak in anger/in wrath terrify.' By far the most occurrences of the verb 'terrify' (*bâhal*) occur in contexts like this involving the idea of divine judgment. The NIV inserts the word 'saying' to smooth out the translation. In Hebrew it is simply 'and I', or better, 'yet I' (*va'ᵃnî*). The declaration he makes concerns the place of his king, against whom the heathen rulers have been plotting. Kingship in Israel was an institution that God had given for his people (see Deut. 17:14-20). God's displeasure at the people's request for a king (1 Sam. 8:5) was not because the concept was wrong in itself but because of the type of king being envisioned, and the reasons for making the request were a denial of the covenantal relationship with him (for the introduction of kingship, see 1 Sam. 8-12). From the

---

[6] The use of the Hebrew verb *nâsak* is interesting, for it is not the usual verb for anointing. It is employed most often in reference to pouring out a libation, and here it may continue to have that basic meaning: 'consecrate [with a libation]', (*DCH*, V, p. 699), or, 'I have poured out (my libation in the consecration of) my king' (*NIDOTTE*, 3, p. 114).

time that David captured the fortress of Zion (2 Sam. 5:7) it became the centre of both religious and political life in Israel, and there was never any question thereafter for devout Israelites as to where worship was to be offered at the tabernacle/temple. Jeroboam's attempt after the division of the kingdom to have the people worship at Dan and Bethel was a deliberate strategy to stop them worshipping at Zion, God's holy hill (1 Kings 12:26-27).[7] Each Davidic ruler typified the coming of the final messianic king who is spoken of here.

3. God's Declaration to His Son (vv. 7-9)

The third stanza commences with the messianic king speaking of his own appointment. The references to the LORD's anointed in verse 2 and the one called 'my king' in verse 6 are now taken a step further, as New Testament references to this passage confirm. The anointed king declares: '**I will proclaim the decree of the LORD: He said to me, "You are my Son; today I have become your Father"**' (v. 7). Elsewhere in the Psalms the LORD's decree refers to the establishment of his orderly rule in the universe (Ps. 148:6). Here it is used of a sovereign appointment of his son.[8] The words are echoed at Jesus' baptism (Matt. 3:17) and at the transfiguration (Matt. 17:5). Paul also uses the words in reference to the resurrection (Acts 13:33). Jesus later entered another stage of his sonship when through the Spirit of holiness he was 'declared with power to be the Son of God by his resurrection from the dead' (Rom. 1:4).

Ask of me, and I will make the nations your inheritance, the ends of the earth your possession. You will rule them[9]

---

[7] The term 'mountain of God' is used exclusively of Mt Sinai, whereas the term here, 'holy mountain', always refers to Zion (see Pss. 3:4; 43:3; 87:1-2; Isa. 27:13; Zech. 8:3). For discussion of the theology of Zion, see *NIDOTTE*, 4, pp. 1314-21.

[8] The Hebrew expression is unusual: 'I will proclaim to (*'el*) the decree of the LORD.' See the prepositional usage with this noun in *DCH*, III, pp. 301-02 and the translation, 'I will proclaim *concerning* the LORD's decree.'

[9] The MT has *tᵉroʾêm*, 'you will break them'. The LXX reading is *poimaneis* = *tirʿêm*, 'you will shepherd them'. The Hebrew manuscript evidence is uniformly in favour of the former, and it also best suits the context.

with an iron sceptre; you will dash them to pieces like pottery (*vv. 8-9*). The command to ask of the LORD was given to Solomon at Gibeon (1 Kings 3:5), but now it is said to a far greater than Solomon. Just as the kingly rule in Psalm 72 extends to the ends of the earth, so here also. Messiah's rule is one that ensures that the nations become his inheritance and the ends of the earth his possession. Rebellious kings ('them' in verse 9) have already been mentioned in verse 2. They will find that his sceptre is not just a symbolic staff, but an iron sceptre which is able to shatter them in pieces. The word 'sceptre' (*shêvet*) can denote both an instrument of punishment and a mark of authority, and so here the two ideas of smiting and ruling are brought into conjunction.

4. A Call to Allegiance (*vv. 10-12*)

A sovereign call now goes to these kings. **Therefore, you kings, be wise; be warned, you rulers of the earth** (*v. 10*). It opens with a Hebrew expression that often denotes a new stage in an argument, though continuing the same subject matter (*v^e attâh*, lit., 'and now'). Earthly rulers can only find blessing for themselves and their subjects when they are subservient to the claims of God's messiah. The implication is that the wisdom and the warning come from the LORD, a point made explicitly in the wisdom books of the Old Testament with repeated use of these two verbs.

Serve the LORD with fear and rejoice with trembling (*v. 11*), is the call that goes to them. They must become his vassals (for so the word *serve* implies). The expression 'rejoice' with trembling may seem odd because it combines two seemingly opposite emotions, but no really satisfactory alternative translations have emerged. Furthermore, the rulers have to **Kiss the Son, lest he be angry and you be destroyed in your way, for his wrath can flare up in a moment. Blessed are all who take refuge in him** (*v. 12*). The word used here in the Hebrew text for son is not the usual word (*ben*), but an Aramaic form (*bar*). Clearly the early versions had difficulty with this verse, and rendered *bar* with words suggesting they understood it to be *bor* ('pure') or *bad* ('clean'). However, *bar* as 'son' is attested in the Old Testament.[10] Numerous suggestions have been made for emending the text, but the traditional MT text is strongly attested and should be maintained. Three explanatory comments should be made. First, Aramaic was the common language for much of the ancient Near East over many centuries, and it was spoken from about the ninth century BC. Hence, the Davidic/Solomonic empire would have had Aramaic speakers within it. Secondly, the use of the usual Hebrew word would have resulted in an awkward conjunction of *ben pen*, and so to avoid the dissonance *bar pen* may have been used instead.[11] Thirdly, the choice of the Aramaic word may have been done deliberately to bring greater force to the message to Gentile kings, who presumably would have been Aramaic speakers.[12] To 'kiss' was a sign of homage and submission (cf. 1 Sam. 10:1; 1 Kings 19:18; Hosea 13:2) and it is appropriate that such a word is used to call for an act of homage before the LORD's anointed king. The 'son' seems to be the subject of the next verb. If rulers do not submit to his claims, then his anger will burn against them and they will be destroyed. Just as the first Psalm commenced with the concept of blessing, so this second Psalm finishes on the same reassuring note. All who take refuge in the LORD will find true blessing and satisfaction in him. The expression used here, 'all who take refuge in him' (*kol-chôsê wô*),[13] points on the one hand to the insecurity of those who are depending on their own power, but on the other hand to the security of those whose trust is in the LORD. He is the only refuge from the storm of God's anger.

In addition to the quotations of this psalm in the New Testament already noted above, it is important to realise how often it is alluded to in the Book of Revelation (see e.g.,

---

[10] *DCH*, II, p. 257.

[11] This was first suggested by Delitzsch in his *Commentary on the Psalms*, I. p. 98.

[12] As proposed by P. C. Craigie, *Psalms 1-50*, p. 64. Craigie's whole note on the crux is worth consulting. For another good note on it, see Willem VanGemeren, 'Psalms', p. 72.

[13] Grammatically, these three words taken together are the equivalent of a single noun. See *IBHS*, p. 155.

2:27; 12:5; 19:15). Christians see in Psalm 2 the picture of the messianic king who is ruling now in the world, and who is going to rule until he subdues all other rulers, and delivers the kingdom to the Father (1 Cor. 15:24). The Book of Revelation shows us the ultimate picture of Christ ruling with an iron sceptre, and bearing the name 'King of Kings, and Lord of Lords' (Rev. 19:15-16).

Psalm 3

A psalm of David. When he fled from his son Absalom.

For the context of this psalm, we have to look back to the account in 2 Samuel 15-18 in reference to Absalom's conspiracy against his father David. Absalom had plotted the rebellion and won over the hearts of many in the country (2 Sam. 15:1-6). When the rebellion became known to David he fled, and the historical narrative gives a graphic picture of the king weeping as he went up the Mount of Olives, barefooted and with his head uncovered (2 Sam. 15:30).[1] Here David makes his appeal to God. This is the first of a collection of Davidic psalms that constitute Psalms 3-41.[2]

1. A Forlorn Cry (vv. 1-2)

O LORD, how many are my foes! How many rise up against me! Many are saying of me, 'God will not deliver him.' Selah (vv. 1-2). This is the first prayer of the Book of Psalms, and the threefold mention of 'many' attracts attention straight away. David feels the pressure that has been put on him by his numerous opponents, and cries out to his covenantal God. The verb 'rise up' can be used of rebellions or of the enemies who arise against Israel (see Deut. 28:7), but it also has a wider

---

[1] The NIV has 'his [David's] head was covered'. Two homonyms may well have existed, one meaning 'cover' and the other 'uncover'. Ezek. 24:17, 23 suggest that uncovering the head was an appropriate action when mourning, and the context in 2 Sam. 17 supports this. See R. P Gordon, *1 & 2 Samuel: A Commentary* (Exeter: Paternoster Press, 1986), p. 271.

[2] Other psalms attributed to David, or are linked by the title to some aspect of David's life, are Pss. 51-65, 68-70 (Book 2); Ps. 86 (Book 3); Pss. 101 and 103 (Book 4); Pss. 108-10, 122, 124, 131, 138-145 (Book 5). See the discussion on the structure of the Psalter in the Introduction.

connotation of any opposition coming against someone. Here the context suggests enemies within Israel. Not only did David recognise the extent of opposition against him, but he also knew that numerous others were talking *about* him. What they were saying touched the very honour of God himself, for they were claiming that there was no salvation with God. 'Selah', which appears seventy-one times in the Psalter (and three times in Hab. 3), comes in here for the first time. It generally occurs in psalms that are divided into three sections, and always comes at the end of a section, sometimes of all three. It is a technical term that probably denotes louder musical accompaniment, or alternatively, simply identifies the end of a stanza without any indication being given of what was said or sung in the interval between stanzas.[3]

2. Certain Protection (*vv. 3-4*)

In spite of the opposition against him, David knew how sure was the LORD's protection. But [on the contrary] **you are a shield around me, O LORD, my Glorious One, who lifts up my head. To the LORD I cry aloud, and he answers me from his holy hill.** *Selah* (*vv. 3-4*). The opening words of this section are a marked contrast to what the enemies have been saying. The LORD is indeed the protector, for he is David's shield (*mâgên*). The expression goes back to Genesis 15:1, where God reassures Abraham that he will safeguard him from danger. In the context there the military metaphor is plain, especially as in 14:20 mention has been made by Melchizedek that the LORD had delivered Abram (*miggên*). 'Shield' is often used in the Psalms along with another term descriptive of God's power: 'my strength and my shield' (Ps. 28:7); 'our help and our shield' (Ps. 33:20); 'a sun and a shield' (Ps. 84:11). He knew that his 'Glorious One' (see Pss. 4:2; 106:20 for the similar use of this title; Rom. 1:23, '[they] exchanged the glory of the immortal God for images made to look like mortal man' draws upon this

---

[3] See the discussion by N. H. Snaith, 'Selah', *VT* 2 (1952), pp. 43-56. Snaith draws attention to 1 Chron. 16:41 and proposes that *selah* marked the break where the Levites came in with the words: 'Give thanks to the LORD for he is good, for his mercy endures for ever'. A good discussion can also be found in P. C. Craigie, *Psalms 1-50*, pp. 76-7, 'Excursus I, The Meaning of SELAH (סלה) in the Psalms'.

OT usage) would lift him up out of the dust. 'To lift up the head' denotes placing someone in a position of honour, and it is a term rich in theological meaning for it speaks of the redemptive presence of God. David's cry was constantly to the LORD, and he had received repeated answers. These had come from God's holy hill, mount Zion, to which site David had brought the ark of the LORD (see comment on 2:6). The bringing of the ark to it, and the subsequent building of the temple, brought to fulfilment what had been foreshadowed long before in the Song of the Sea. The intention was expressed that God would bring his people in 'and plant them on the mountain of your inheritance – the place, O LORD, you made for your dwelling, the sanctuary, O LORD, your hands established' (Exod. 15:17).

3. Sure Deliverance (*vv. 5-8*)

Quiet sleep was possible for David because his salvation was from the LORD. **I lie down and sleep; I wake again, because the LORD sustains me** (*v. 5*). Moreover, the fact that Absalom had so many followers was not the point. Because the LORD was his shield, David could rest securely at night, and the support he received meant that 'God's hand is his pillow'.[4] The verb 'sustains' (*sâmak*) is often used in the Psalms with God as the subject. He is the one who upholds the righteous (cf., in addition to this verse, Pss. 37:17, 24; 119:116; 145:14).

I will not fear the tens of thousands, drawn up against me on every side (*v. 6*). We know from the historical record that the majority of the people had followed Absalom (2 Sam. 15:13; 17:11; 18:7), but David makes a confident appeal to his protector. The reference to 'the tens of thousands' is an assertion of God's ability to deliver in the face of innumerable enemies.

It is not only the enemies who arise (see v. 1), but also the LORD. **Arise, O LORD! Deliver me, O my God! Strike all my enemies on the jaw; break the teeth of the wicked** (*v. 7*). This is a typical anthropomorphic expression (one describing God in human terms), calling on him to bring help quickly as he had done in the past. The word 'arise' (*qûm*) is used in military contexts in which the idea of anticipated victory by the LORD is present (cf. Judg. 7:15). It

---

[4] F. Delitzsch, *Psalms*, I, p. 107.

is a neutral term in English, but in Hebrew it conveys the idea that God's saving power is going to be demonstrated. Moses used it whenever the ark of the covenant was being moved (Num. 10:35), for Israel's battles were in reality part of the LORD's holy war. When the imperative 'arise' is used here and elsewhere in the Psalms it points to a confident expectation of victory (cf. 7:6; 9:19; 17:13).[5] The outcome of the appeal to God is expressed in metaphorical terms of 'smiting' the cheekbone and 'breaking' the teeth of the enemies. These parallel expressions are descriptive of complete victory. The use of these two verbs (*nâkâh*, Hi., *shâvar*, Pi.) may be significant, for the former is used of God's destruction of the living creatures by the flood (Gen. 8:21), and of his smiting Egypt as he rescued his people (Exod. 3:20; 12:12, 29). The latter conveys the concept of intense breaking of something, so that 'smashing to smithereens'[6] the teeth of the wicked represents the removal of all power. Though the verbs 'strike' and 'break' are strictly perfect forms in the Hebrew text, yet here the context demands that they be treated as supplicatory, and hence English imperatives are in order.[7] The conclusion of the psalm is a confident expression of trust on and hope in the LORD.

From the LORD comes deliverance. May your blessing be on your people. *Selah* (*v. 8*). The word 'deliverance' in Hebrew is *yᵉshûʻa*, from which the word 'Jesus' comes. David knew that this was not only a personal truth, but one that applied to all the people. Hence he prays for the LORD's blessing to be granted to the nation as a whole. Personal problems did not outweigh his spiritual vision for the people. A psalm that commenced with mention of overwhelming opposition ends on the note of victory achieved by the LORD. When that happens, it achieves blessing for his people.

---

[5] J. T. Willis, 'Qûmâh YHWH', *JNSL* 16 (1990), pp. 207-21 suggests that the use of this imperative in military contexts means 'swing into action', a colloquial translation but an effective one.

[6] The translation is that of Victor Hamilton, *TWOT*, II, p. 901.

[7] For discussion on the so-called 'precatory perfect', see *IBHS*, pp. 494-95, and *DIHG~S*, pp. 69-70. The first editions of NIV translated these verbs as English past tenses ('you struck down', 'you have broken'), but this was corrected in the 1984 edition. The usage is most common in Psalms and Lamentations, and rare elsewhere.

Psalm 4

For the director of music. With stringed instruments.
A psalm of David.

There are various connections between Psalms 3 and 4. Jointly they give us morning and evening prayers, even to the extent of repeated key words as the following table shows:

3:1 LORD, how many are my *foes* (*tsâr*)	4:1b from my *distress* (*tsâr*)
3:2 *Many* (*rabbîm*) are *saying* (*'omᵉrîm*) of me	4:6 *Many* (*rabbîm*) are *saying* (*'omᵉrîm*)
3:3b my *Glorious One* (*kewôdî*)	4:2b my *glory* (*kewôdî*)
3:4 To the LORD I *cry aloud* (*qârâ'*) and he *answers* (*'ânâh*) me	4:1a *Answer* (*'ânâh*) me when *I call* (*qârâ'*) to you
	4:3b The LORD hears when I *call* (*qârâ'*) to him.
3:5 I *lie down* (*shâkav*) and *sleep* (*shânâh*)	4:8a I will *lie down* (*shâkav*) and *sleep* (*shânâh*)
	4:4a on your *beds* (*mishkâv*)

1. A Cry in Need (*v. 1*)
David appeals to his righteous God, i.e., the God who does right, and who keeps his covenantal word. **Answer me when I call to you, O my righteous God. Give me relief from my distress; be merciful to me and hear my prayer** (*v. 1*). Whenever he calls, he wants God to respond. This response is not something that God is obliged to give, but it is an expression of his grace (cf. Ps. 69:16, 'out of the goodness of your love'). He desires relief by having his distress removed far from him.

113

There is the recognition of his need for undeserved grace in order that God may hear and answer his prayer.

2. A Description of His Enemies (*vv. 2-6*)
How long, O men, will you turn my glory into shame? How long will you love delusions and seek false gods? *Selah* **Know that the Lord has set apart the godly for himself; the Lord will hear when I call to him** (*vv. 2-3*). Now David speaks to his enemies and accuses them of forsaking the true God and seeking after false gods. 'Glory' is here a title for God as in Psalm 106:20. To turn glory to shame (*kᵉlimmâh*) denotes an entire change in condition so that honour is replaced by disgrace.[1] The action of men is ever the same, for, as Paul says, sinful men always want to exchange the glory of the immortal God for man-made images (Rom. 1:21-23). Moreover, such turning from the living God means that love for him is replaced by love for what is but empty show, while the people have been searching for substitute 'gods' that ultimately prove to be false.[2] But godly ones, like David, are set apart by the Lord, who discriminates between them and those who seek other gods. Anyone who shows covenantal commitment (*chésed*) is a godly one (*châsîd*), and can assuredly say that God will answer one's prayers. It is frequently asserted in the Psalms that God hears the cries of his people and responds to them (cf. Pss. 6:9; 22:24; 61:5; 116:1).

The enemies are then encouraged to consider their evil deeds. **In your anger do not sin; when you are on your beds, search your hearts and be silent** (*v. 4*). The Hebrew verb rendered by 'in your anger' conveys the idea of trembling. David wants his enemies to be deeply moved before the Lord, and not to continue in their sin. Rather, they should heed his words and in the quietness of the night reflect upon their ways. Paul uses this verse in Ephesians 4:26, following exactly

---

[1] The English word 'calumny' may well derive from the Hebrew word *kᵉlimmâh*.

[2] Though Jerry Shepherd, *NIDOTTE*, 4, p. 1107, is critical of the NIV rendering 'false gods', yet the context points to things of shame being loved and sought. Hence the NIV rendering is close to the mark.

the LXX rendering. He is urging the 'new man' (Eph. 4:24) not to sin if anger is present.[3] **Selah** adds emphasis to this call.
Offer right sacrifices and trust in the LORD (*v. 5*). They need to be like the righteous and put their trust in the LORD. Those who do that will also bring the proper and appropriate offerings to the sanctuary. The phrase 'right sacrifices' is first used in Deuteronomy 33:19, and here it probably notes that they would need to make an offering for their past sin.
Many are asking, 'Who can show us any good?' Let the light of your face shine upon us, O LORD (*v. 6*). Spectators, who had seen all that had happened to David, now speak. They desire to share in blessing, and pray for themselves in terms of the Aaronic benediction, merging two of its expressions (Num. 6:24-26; cf. also Pss. 31:16; 80:3, 7, 19). The translation 'let the light of your face shine on us' obscures the fact that in the MT text the clause commences with an imperative *nᵉsâh*, often taken to be from the common verb *nâsâ'*. However, two of the consonants are different, and it is possible that it may be an emphatic form of the verb *nûs*, 'to flee', giving a rendering like the NEB, 'the light of your presence has fled from us'.[4] This is the only occurrence in the Old Testament of the phrase 'the light of your face'. 'Light' is predicated of God in the Old Testament, and he gives it to individuals ('the LORD is my light', Ps. 27:1) and to the nation of Israel ('the light of Israel', Isa. 10:17). 'Light' is virtually equivalent to 'salvation' or 'deliverance'.

3. An Evening Prayer (*vv. 7-8*)
You have filled my heart with greater joy than when their grain and new wine abound. I will lie down and sleep in peace, for you alone, O LORD, make me dwell in safety (*vv. 7-8*). God provides for his servants, like David, joy in

---

[3] For the interpretation of Eph. 4:26, see Peter T. O'Brien, *The Letter to the Ephesians* (Pillar New Testament Commentary: Leicester: Apollos, 1999), pp. 339-40.

[4] For other possible solutions to the problem, see *DCH*, V, p. 759. The conjunction of the verb 'show' in the preceding clause with the idea of light probably points to something like the traditional rendering, though the LXX renders the verb by the Greek verb *sêmeioô*, 'to mark' or 'note'.

the midst of distress. His enemies could have their festive occasions at harvest, but God-given joy was something far greater. Christians are called to rejoice in sufferings (1 Pet. 4:13), and believing in Christ brings 'inexpressible and glorious joy' (1 Pet. 1:8). Peaceful sleep comes because God is his protector. The emphasis at the end of verse 8 is definitely on the LORD: 'Indeed, it is you LORD, you alone ...' The contrast with the false gods of verse 2 is plain. Only in the LORD is there safety.

Psalm 5

For the director of music. For Flutes. A psalm of David.

This psalm is clearly an appeal for help, but no precise indication is given of the circumstances that lay behind it. Throughout the psalm, in almost every verse, there is mention of the words which the psalmist was addressing to God, and also some indication of the evil with which he was contending. It begins with the address to God, and ends with acclamation of him.

1. A Cry to the King (*vv. 1-3*)
Give ear to my words, O Lord, consider my sighing. Listen to my cry for help, my King and my God, for to you I pray (*vv. 1-2*). Now there is an urgent appeal to God, though the psalmist had for long been sighing in his affliction. The word for 'sighing' (Hebrew *hâgîg*) only appears here and in Psalm 39:3 in the Psalter. It is connected with the word for 'murmuring' or 'meditating' (see Pss. 1:2; 2:1), which at times appears in association with verbs like 'cry out' (*zâʿaq*, Jer. 48:31) or 'wail' (*yâlal*, Hi., Isa. 16:7). There is both inaudible prayer to God as well as direct and loud appeals. However, there is confidence in the psalmist's approach, as he is coming to his king and his God. From the time of the Exodus onwards God was regarded as the king of Israel (see Exod. 15:18), and in particular the Davidic kingship was intended as a reflection of the divine rule. Recognition of God as king was not just communal; individual believers saw themselves as his subjects and could address him directly as 'my king'.

Morning by morning, O Lord, you hear my voice; morning by morning I lay my requests before you and wait

in expectation (*v. 3*). Just as there were morning sacrifices, so prayers were directed to the LORD at that time. This was part of the threefold pattern of daily prayer (cf. Dan. 6:10). The language of sacrifice is carried over here, for 'lay my requests' represents the verb used of laying in order the wood (Lev. 1:7) or the victim for sacrifice (Lev. 1:8; 6:12). The psalmist then waits expectantly for God's answer.

2. God and Evildoers (*vv. 4-8*)
You are not a God who takes pleasure in evil; with you the wicked cannot dwell (*v. 4*). Emphasis in the Hebrew text comes on the negative assertion, 'But *not a God taking delight are you* ...' God does not delight in wickedness, and with him is no haven for wicked men because his holiness is to them a consuming fire (Isa. 33:14). Those coming to his holy hill must receive righteousness from God (cf. Pss. 15:1-5 and 24:1-6).

The arrogant cannot stand in your presence; you hate all who do wrong. You destroy those who tell lies; bloodthirsty and deceitful men the LORD abhors (*vv. 5-6*). Those who reject the wisdom of the LORD and live by their own folly cannot stand their ground before him. Here the wicked are characterised as liars, murderers, and deceivers. God's attitude towards them is one of abhorrence and hate, and their ultimate destiny is destruction. Those who have these characteristics will never abide in God's holy presence (Rev. 22:12-15).

But I, by your great mercy, will come into your house; in reverence will I bow down toward your holy temple. Lead me, O LORD, in your righteousness because of my enemies – make straight your way before me (*vv. 7-8*). The opening words of verse 7 provide a contrast with the commencement of verse 4. The psalmist is not shut out from God's presence or God's house. He goes there on one ground only—God's abundant covenantal love to him, and he can enter therefore into the holy place. The Epistle to the Hebrews points to the fact that because Jesus has gone before us into heaven we have an anchor for the soul in the inner sanctuary of God (Heb. 6:19-20). The psalmist prays for assistance from the LORD that he might walk in 'paths of righteousness' (cf. Ps. 23:3) and along a straight way. That is to say, he wants to walk according to the LORD's commands and the precepts he has given. This prayer is made because he does not wish to give his enemies cause to gloat over any deviation from the prescribed way.[1]

3. God and Judgment (*vv. 9-10*)

Not a word from their mouth can be trusted; their heart is filled with destruction. Their throat is an open grave; with their tongue they speak deceit (*v. 9*). After reference to the character of the holy God and the righteous worshipper comes the character of the evildoer. Here the concentration falls on the sins of the tongue (cf. James 3:6-12), and Paul uses the words of the second part of verse 9 as he sets out the universal sinfulness of the human race in his list of quotations from the Old Testament in Romans 3 (see *v.* 13a). The psalmist is accusing his enemies of treachery because there is no sincerity or truth in their speech. 'Throat' is not so much the organ for swallowing as the organ of speech as in Psalms 115:7 and 149:6. This agrees with the context where the emphasis is on speech, with the mouth as the instrument of speech, of the heart as its source, and of the tongue. The comparison with an open grave reflects on the corruption that comes to expression in speech.[2]

Declare them guilty, O God! Let their intrigues be their downfall. Banish them for their many sins, for they have rebelled against you (*v. 10*). The expression 'declare them guilty' is one word in Hebrew. It comes from the root *'âsham*, which is used of the sacrifice for sins of inadvertence. Here

---

[1] The word 'enemy' (*shôrêr*) is not the usual Hebrew word. It only occurs six times, all in the Psalms (in addition to this verse, see 27:11; 54:5; 56:2; 59:10; 92:11). Ps. 27:11 contains the closest parallel to this verse, for it is a prayer for guidance in right living and the exact phrase, 'because of my enemies' (*lᵉmaʿ an shôrᵉrây*) occurs in both. The NIV is inconsistent in its translation of this word, using 'enemy' here and synonyms twice ('oppressor', 27:11; 'adversary', 92:11) but using 'slanderer' three times (54:5; 56:2; 59:10). For the argument for using 'slanderer' consistently, see M. Dahood, *Psalms II: 51-100* (New York: Doubleday & Co., 1974), pp. 25-26.

[2] The same combination, 'an open grave' (*qéver pâtûach*), occurs in Jer. 5:16.

it means 'make guilty' or even 'punish'. Guilt must lead to atonement, or alternatively to destruction. The wicked may think they are so clever in their plotting, but they can be caught out by their own secret scheming. The desired punishment is banishment, using the same verb (*nâdach*, Hi.) that is used in Deuteronomy 30:1 of banishment from Canaan. Covenantal overtones may well be present. That David was not asking for personal vengeance is made clear by the closing words of verse 10: 'they have rebelled *against you*.' As a loyal covenantal servant he asks God to exercise his judgment on his rebel subjects. For fuller discussion of the psalms of cursing, see the Introduction.

4. Protection and Joy (*vv. 11-12*)

But let all who take refuge in you be glad; let them ever sing for joy. Spread your protection over them, that those who love your name may rejoice in you (*v. 11*). The character of God's people as those who take refuge in the LORD is illustrated in this very psalm by David's own trustful attitude. Those who live under God's protection can sing for joy because he provides the screen that overshadows them. Probably the idea is that of the mother bird protecting her young with her wings (cf. Ps. 91:4). Another description of the righteous is that they love God's name, i.e. his character. He had revealed himself as the redeemer of Israel, and the sanctuary of which the psalmist had already spoken (v. 7) was the place where God had made his name dwell (Deut. 12:5).

For surely, O LORD, you bless the righteous; you surround them with your favour as with a shield (*v. 12*). The idea of protection is carried on from the preceding verse. God surrounds his people with a protective shield so that they are safe from the enemy. Moreover, it remains true that blessing from the LORD is the portion of his believing children. It is something that comes through his grace (cf. verse 4 and comment).

Psalm 6

For the director of music. With stringed instruments. According to sheminith. A psalm of David.

Though an individual composition, yet this psalm was intended for corporate singing. The term *sheminith* in the title is difficult, as the literal meaning is 'an eighth'. If this means an octave, then it is possible that the term indicates that it should be accompanied at a lower octave, in keeping with the solemn note of the psalm, or sung by the male voices. While it has been suggested that it could refer to an instrument with eight strings, the fact that it occurs in 1 Chronicles 15:21 along with the verb 'to play on a stringed instrument' (*nâtsach* Pi.) points to it as referring to the range of voice.[1] This psalm is a complaint to God, and exhibits not only appeal to him but also confidence in the midst of distress. It should be compared to other similar appeals in the Psalter and to Hezekiah's prayer after his illness (Isa. 38:10-20). Traditionally, this psalm was the first of the seven penitential psalms (Pss. 6, 32, 38, 51, 102, 130, 143), a collection known to Augustine, and mentioned by Cassiodorus (AD c. 584).

1. A Cry to a Gracious God (*vv. 1-3*)

O LORD, do not rebuke me in your anger or discipline me in your wrath. Be merciful to me, LORD, for I am faint; O LORD, heal me, for my bones are in agony. My soul is in anguish. How long, O LORD, how long? (*vv. 1-3*). Each section of the psalm opens with an imperative, and the first two follow on with a question. The psalmist does not confess any sin here, as compared with Psalm 38, which opens with almost the same

---

[1] See *DCH*, V, p. 736. *Sheminith* also occurs in the title of Ps. 12.

words. Hence the opening request may mean: 'Don't be angry with my raising this matter with you in prayer'. However, he is very conscious that he has brought himself under God's wrath, and he goes on to plead for God's intervention in his case. He desires mercy for he is languishing. Death stares him in the face, and he knows that it is God alone who can deliver him. The full extent of his trouble is disclosed by the reference to both bones and soul. In body and spirit he is greatly troubled. This is not a reference to two distinct entities but is rather a way in which the psalmist refers to himself (cf. the use of 'soul' and 'body' in Pss. 31:9; 63:1). While the prophets often speak of healing in the sense of restoration of the nation, in the Psalms, as here, the use of the verb (*râfâ'*) relates to literal, physical healing. The unfinished question 'how long?' appears about thirty times in the Bible, and of these about sixteen are in the psalms. It is very characteristic of the laments. The NIV translation repeats the expression 'how long', but this is unnecessary and the Hebrew text only has it once. In his distress he breaks off in the midst of the sentence, and the conclusion is implied from the preceding verse: 'O LORD, how long until *you have mercy and heal me*?' During his last painful illness, Calvin uttered no word of complaint, but raising his eyes heavenward he would say in Latin, '*Usquequo Domine*' ('Lord, how long?')

2. His Need Described (*vv. 4-7*)

Turn, O LORD, and deliver me; save me because of your unfailing love (*v. 4*). His appeal is that he feels that God has been absent from him (a frequent experience of distressed believers), and he wants him to turn from his anger. The verb used here for 'turn' or 'return' (*shûv*) is often used in the sense of God turning (or not turning) from his anger.[2] The 'how long?' of the previous verse now becomes an urgent request for deliverance. The basis of his call is God's unfailing covenantal love.

---

[2] The negative form occurs eight times in Amos 1-2, 'do not return [it].' While many translations assume that 'it' is punishment, a more likely explanation is that 'it' is God's anger. See *NIDOTTE*, 4, p. 58.

No one remembers you when he is dead. Who praises you from the grave? (*v. 5*) This verse finds its parallel (or perhaps its echo) in Hezekiah's prayer (Isa. 38:18). It is the living who are the testimony to God's power and grace, not those who are already dead. The Hebrew word translated 'grave' is *sh^e'ôl*. Its translation raises theological as well as linguistic questions. Some versions prefer to simply transliterate the Hebrew word ('Sheol'), but it is better to decide what it means and render accordingly. The context here points to some word that will parallel 'dead', and 'grave' is appropriate.[3]

I am worn out from groaning; all night long I flood my bed with weeping and drench my couch with tears. My eyes grow weak with sorrow; they fail because of all my foes (*vv. 6-7*). At the very centre of the psalm a thematic line describes the psalmist's condition: 'I am worn out from groaning.'[4] The distressing condition is not specified. All we know is that the night hours were particularly difficult for him. Because of physical illness and also the sense of separation from God he wept so copiously that it seemed as if he flooded his bed with tears. No hesitation was felt in the ancient Near East to expressing sorrow and grief by tears and groaning. Moses' eyes had not failed even near his death (Deut. 34:7), but David's eyes failed because of his grief and also because of his enemies. His friends may well have forsaken him at this time, and so appear as if they were enemies.

3. A Prayer Heard (*vv. 8-10*)
Away from me, all you who do evil, for the LORD has heard my weeping. The LORD has heard my cry for mercy; the LORD

---

[3] For an excellent general discussion on the translation of *sh^e'ôl* and explanation of the position adopted by the NIV translators, see R. Laird Harris, 'Why Hebrew Sh^e'ôl Was Translated "Grave"', *The Making of a Contemporary Translation: New International Version*, ed. Kenneth Barker (London: Hodder & Stoughton, 1987), pp. 75-92. Every time the NIV renders the Hebrew *sh^e'ôl* by 'grave' a footnote is inserted, thus enabling readers to judge the suitability of the word in the biblical context.

[4] This same device of placing a key line in the centre of a psalm can also be seen in other psalms. See, for example, 8:4; 23:4; 42:8; 48:8; 71:14; 76:7; 97:7; 141:5.

accepts my prayer. May all my enemies be ashamed and dismayed; may they turn back in sudden disgrace (*vv. 8-10*). The sudden change in tone is surprising. This may indicate either that the psalmist reached an understanding of God's help, or that a priest ministered a word of encouragement, such as Eli gave to Hannah (1 Sam. 1:17). Probably the former is the case, and twice he says that God has heard him. This leads on to the triumphant declaration in verse 9. The tenses are important here: the Lord *has heard* my cry, the Lord *will accept* my prayer. The final verse has a lot of music in the Hebrew text, in that there is repetition of words and sounds. This helps to reinforce the message.[5] Presumably the evildoers and his enemies are the same people, and he longs to see them put to shame. Early in the psalm his bones and soul had been 'disturbed' (vv. 2-3). Now he uses the same verb of his enemies in verse 10 ('dismayed'), while his desire for them is expressed ('turn back') by using the same verb he has used earlier of God's seeming return to him ('turn', verse 4). He knows that when he is restored, then his enemies will be put to shame.

---

[5] The NIV obscures some of the repetition by rendering the same verb (*yēvoshû*) by two different English verbs, 'ashamed' and 'in disgrace'. NKJV is better: 'Let all my enemies be ashamed ... and be ashamed suddenly'.

Psalm 7

A shiggaion of David, which he sang to the LORD
concerning Cush, a Benjamite

In the midst of distress David calls on the LORD. Though his situation is serious, yet at the end of the psalm he is singing praise to his God. The precise details of the incident(s) concerning Cush are unrecorded in the biblical history. We do know, however, that David faced many problems from the Benjamites (see 1 Sam. 24, 26; 2 Sam. 16:5; 20:1), and since Cush was from Benjamin it may be that he was a supporter of Saul. David protests his innocence in the face of false accusations and asks God to arise to help him. *Shiggaion* in the title is only used here in the Psalter, though the plural form occurs in Habakkuk 3:1 (*shigyonôt*). It probably was a word meaning 'a lamentation', though because of its infrequency it cannot be defined with precision. The vocabulary of the psalm stresses the appeal to the heavenly king and judge. The word 'righteousness' (*tsédek*) occurs twice (vv. 8, 17) while 'righteous [person]' (*tsâdîk*) occurs three times (vv. 9 twice, 11). The verb 'to judge' (*shâfat*) or derivatives are used three times (vv. 6, 8, 11), while 'execute justice' (*dîn*) is also employed (v. 8). This vocabulary points to a situation in which David is appealing for divine intervention so that he can be delivered from his enemies.

1. God – A Safe Refuge (*vv. 1-2*)

O LORD my God, I take refuge in you; save and deliver me from all who pursue me, or they will tear me like a lion and rip me to pieces with no-one to rescue me (*vv. 1-2*). David starts with a confident assertion of his hope. He appeals to his God, saying, 'In you [alone] I take refuge.' While the verb 'to take refuge' (*châsâh*) can be used literally of shelter from natural elements (Job 24:8; Isa. 4:6; 25:4), yet its most common use is figurative as here. In the midst of all their troubles, God's children know where their help is to be found, and they turn to the LORD. They can confidently sing:

> All my hope on God is founded;
> He doth still my trust renew.
> Me through change and chance He guideth,
> Only God and only true.
> God unknown,
> He alone
> Calls my heart to be His own.
> (Joachim Neander 1650-1680)

Though David's problem seems to have been slander, he feels that he is being torn apart like a lion's victim. The verb 'pursue' points to the intensity of the attacks on David, so that it is virtually equivalent to 'persecute'. Hence he asks for salvation from his God, for if that does not come, there will be no other salvation ('deliver' and 'to rescue' in these verses are from the same Hebrew verb, *nâtsal*).[1]

2. God — A Just Vindicator (*vv. 3-9*)

O LORD my God, if I have done this and there is guilt on my hands — if I have done evil to him who is at peace with me or without cause have robbed my foe — then let my enemy pursue and overtake me; let him trample my life to the ground and make me sleep in the dust. Selah (*vv. 3-5*). Again, David addresses God in the same terms as in verse 1 ('O LORD my God') before proceeding to express a self-cursing oath. We meet protestations of innocence like this on the part of psalmists quite often (cf. e.g. Pss. 17:3; 18:20-24; 26:1). These should not be taken as claims to sinlessness. Rather they testify to a practical and relevant life of

---

[1] The final phrase, 'no one to rescue me', is the translation of an idiomatic expression in Hebrew (*v^e 'ên matstsîl*) in which the conjunction and a negative particle precede a participle. The negative virtually becomes an adverb, and with the participle forms a compound expression, 'without deliverer'. For further discussion, see *GKC* § 150 *l* and *NIDOTTE*, 4, pp. 1034-35.

obedience as over against their wicked oppressors. They affirm that their lifestyle shows devotion to God, and therefore they are worthy recipients of his protection. The threefold repetition of 'if' (Hebrew *'im*; NIV renders 'if ... and ... if') stresses in a cumulative way the protestation of innocence against the charges. The main accusation seems to have been that he has not been faithful to a covenantal partner ('him who is at peace with me', 'my ally').[2] If that was true, he invites death, with his enemy permitted to pursue[3] him and crush him to the dust.[4]

Arise, O LORD, in your anger; rise up against the rage of my enemies. Awake, my God, decree justice. Let the assembled peoples gather around you. Rule over them from on high; let the LORD judge the peoples (*vv. 6-8a*). Following Moses' example (Num. 10:35), David requests God to take action against his foes, using three synonymous expressions, 'arise', 'rise up', and 'awake'. He follows with another plea, wanting God to intervene in his case and administer his just laws.[5] These terms relate both to military and judicial action. He pictures a judgment scene in which God has gathered the nations on earth before him, and then from on high he carries out his judgment. The psalmist is happy to rest in that judgment. The same verb (*dîn*) is used similarly of righteous

---

[2] I think that Craigie is correct in taking 'him who is at peace with me' (*shôl^emî*) as 'my ally', following a view already found in BDB, p. 1023. However, Craigie has to accept emendation of the second clause of verse 5 to obtain his translation of 'and rescued *his adversary* empty-handed', though no manuscript evidence can be cited. See, P. C. Craigie, *Psalms 1-50*, p. 98.

[3] The MT has a very odd vocalisation of this verb, *yiradof*, which is neither the Qal nor the Piel form of the verb. Probably the explanation in GKC § 63 *n*, that it is simply a form derived from the regular Qal form *yirdof*, is the best one.

[4] The psalmist refers to himself in these verses using three different nouns: 'my soul', 'my life', 'my glory'. The first two are common, but the use of 'glory' is unusual. However, because of the usage here and in passages such as Gen. 49:6 and Ps. 30:12, it is correct to note that this is a form of self-reference in the Old Testament. For further discussion, see C. John Collins in *NIDOTTE*, 2, p. 583, and also the entry in *DCH*, IV, p. 353.

[5] The verb 'decree' (*tsivvîtâ*) is strictly perfect in form, but it is one of a number of cases restricted to Hebrew poetry in which a perfect occurs but 'where the translation as though it were a juss. or an imper. is either demanded or makes better sense': *DIHG~S*, p. 69, §60 (c).

divine action against the nations in Psalms 9:8 and 96:10. The NIV rendering 'rule' involves an emendation of the MT (a change from *shûvâh*, 'return' to *shêvâh*, 'sit [enthroned]'). The fact that the song of the ark in Numbers 10:35-36 contains both the imperatives 'arise' (*qûmâh*) and 'return' (*shûvâh*) suggests that the MT should stand. God is depicted as arising to execute judgment and then returning to his throne on high (cf. also Ps. 68:1, 18).

Judge me, O LORD, according to my righteousness, according to my integrity, O Most High. O righteous God, who searches minds and hearts, bring to an end the violence of the wicked and make the righteous secure (*vv. 8b-9*). The psalmist now comes back to his own need, and the prayer here is the central one for the whole psalm. As over against his enemies he stands in integrity before the LORD, who alone can search the inner recesses of the heart (cf. Ps. 17:3; Jer. 11:20; 17:10; 20:12; Rev. 2:23). The NIV's title for God in verse 9, 'O Most High', is a translation of what traditionally has been taken to be an Hebrew preposition with suffix (*'alây*) that means 'on' or 'over me'. Some confusion may have existed between the preposition *'al* and an abbreviated divine name, *'al* or *'alî*, 'Most High', and here NIV may be correct in accepting that this is an epithet for God.[6] Repetition of the idea of righteousness marks the confidence of the psalmist before God's judgment. He knows that the righteous God, who establishes the righteous, will confirm his righteousness in the face of his opponents.

3. God — A Certain Saviour (*vv. 10-16*)
My shield is God Most High, who saves the upright in heart. God is a righteous judge, a God who expresses his wrath every day. If he does not relent, he will sharpen his sword, he will bend and string his bow. He has prepared his deadly weapons; he makes ready his flaming arrows (*vv. 10-13*). The military language is carried on first of all by referring to

---

[6] For discussion on this question, see *TWOT*, 2, pp. 669-70. P. C. Craigie, *Psalms 1-50*, p. 98, accepts that the word *'alây* is the divine name in verse 8, but not in verse 10. For M. Dahood's innovative discussion on this matter, see 'The Divine Name "eli" in the Psalms', *TS* 14 (1953), pp. 454-57.

God as his shield,[7] the protector of the upright in heart. As in verse 8, the NIV takes the Hebrew word ʿ*al* to be an epithet for God in combination with *ʾelohîm*, 'God Most High'. This is the best explanation of a difficult expression. He is the divine warrior who protects his people (for the word 'shield', see the comment on 3:5). Then the military metaphor is continued by reference to God getting his weapons (sword, bow, and flaming arrows) ready to attack. God is 'sifting out the hearts of men before His judgment seat', and he has 'loosed the fatal lightning of His terrible swift sword' (Julia Ward Howe, 'Mine eyes have seen the glory').

He who is pregnant with evil and conceives trouble gives birth to disillusionment. He who digs a hole and scoops it out falls into the pit he has made. The trouble he causes recoils on him; his violence comes down on his own head (*vv. 14-16*). The main idea expressed in these verses appears in other contexts in the Old Testament wisdom literature (see, for example, Ps. 34:21 and Job 4:8). It also appears in the New Testament in Galatians 6:7-8. The metaphor of a pregnant woman is taken over and applied to the sinner plotting against the righteous. He conceives the plan, only to find that it does not eventuate. Like a hunter who digs a trap for an animal, he falls into it himself. Whatever action he takes, he discovers that it comes back on himself. This last thought is often alluded to in the Old Testament (cf. e.g. Ps. 37:14-15; Prov. 26:27).

4. God — Worthy of Praise (*v. 17*)
I will give thanks to the LORD because of his righteousness and will sing praise to the name of the LORD Most High. No mention is made of the ultimate outcome of the distress. While the psalmist wanted immediate action to free him from his troubles (see vv. 6-9), yet he may have been disappointed that the answer did not come speedily. But what was most important (and we need to learn the lesson as well) is that he was given a new perspective on the problem by taking it to

---

[7] M. Dahood has argued that the word 'shield' (*mâgên*) means 'sovereign', but the evidence is not persuasive. For criticism of this idea, see P. C. Craigie, *Psalms 1-50*, p. 71.

God in prayer. He could rest in the confidence that God would deal justly and would vindicate him. No wonder that he can sing a doxology to the LORD! That praise was in honour of God's righteousness. Here, the additional name for God is the 'Most High' (*'elyôn*). This title for God occurs thirty-one times in the Old Testament, of which eighteen are in the Psalter. It emphasises the majesty of God, and it mainly appears in contexts in which universal claims are made in connection with Israel's God.[8] It was clearly an early title for God (see its use in Gen. 14:18, 19, 20, 22). In confidence David sings praise to the name of his God.[9] That does not mean simple repetition of God's name, but praise for the revelation that God has made of his nature. He is indeed a saviour and a righteous judge.

---

[8] See the extended note, 'Yahweh is El Elyon', in W. VanGemeren, 'Psalms', pp. 123-24.

[9] The form of the verb 'I will sing' (*'azammᵉrâh*) is cohortative ('let me sing'), not the regular imperfect. Thus the implication may be that the psalmist is among other singers in a public setting for worship. See Samuel Terrien, *The Psalms: Strophic Structure and Theological Commentary* (Grand Rapids: Eerdmans, 2003), p. 122.

Psalm 8

For the director of music. According to the gittith.
A psalm of David.

Creation is the focus of this hymn of praise. It is the latter part of Genesis 1 turned into a song. Biblical Hebrew has no word for 'thank you', but it manages to express thanks in a way rather like many of our English expressions are used when a gift is received ('It's the very thing I wanted!'; 'How beautiful it is!'). As psalmists and prophets understand more of God's character and works, they extol them. The expressions of delight in God's works, as here in verse 1, are themselves a mode of thanking him for them. Here a joyful song praises God's creative activity. The term *gittith* in the title may indicate a musical instrument (a Gittite lyre) or a bright melody to which it was sung. All three psalms that have this word in the title (Pss. 8, 81, and 84) are joyful songs of thanksgiving. *Gittith* is probably from the name of the town Gath in the south-west of Israel.

1. God's Majesty (*vv. 1-2*)

The psalm opens with a declaration of the majesty of God's name. **O LORD, our Lord, how majestic is your name in all the earth! You have set your glory above the heavens. From the lips of children and infants you have ordained praise because of your enemies, to silence the foe and the avenger** (*vv. 1-2*). God is addressed by the use of the covenantal name, LORD, to which is added 'our Lord', using the common word for 'Lord' (*'âdôn*).[1]

---

[1] Here the word for 'lord' is plural in form, as is usual when it applies to the God of Israel, though it takes singular agreement ('*your* name'). This is an honorific usage, probably modelled on the word for 'God' (*'ᵉlohîm*). The singular form is used of God only in the phrase 'the God of all the earth'. For discussion on this grammatical point, see *IBHS*, pp. 122-23; *DIHG~S*, p. 19.

The pronoun 'our' most probably relates to Israel, rather than to mankind. The NIV rendering of the second part of verse 1 is possible, but it omits the particle *ᵃsher* that commences the clause and takes the verb *tᵉnâh* as a past tense ('you have set'). The clause is difficult as both the syntax and the verb are anomalous. Possibly the particle links the two clauses together by carrying forward the idea of God's majesty, even though 'splendour' (*'addîr*) in the first clause is replaced by 'majesty' (*hôd*) in the second. The verb is either an imperative with an emphatic ending ('set'), or a perfect ('you have set').[2] God's character is seen in the created world, and to believing eyes the whole world manifests God's glory.

> Heaven above is softer blue,
> Earth around is sweeter green;
> Something lives in every hue,
> Christless eyes have never seen.
> (George Wade Robinson, 'Loved with everlasting love')

There is a fuller explanation of God's glory in creation in verse 3. Even the young children can be used by God to establish his 'strength',[3] and such praise is able to quieten that of his enemies. God is able to use the weak things of this world to confound the mighty (1 Cor. 1:27). Jesus quoted verse 2 in Matthew 21:16 when rebuking the authorities who wanted him to quieten the children shouting his praise when he entered Jerusalem. The quotation is from the LXX version and confirms the place of even little children in offering acceptable praise.

2. Man's Insignificance (*vv. 3-5*)

When I consider your heavens, the work of your fingers, the moon and the stars, which you have set in place, what is man that you are mindful of him, the son of man that you

---

[2] Many other suggestions have been made over the years. Mitchell Dahood, *The Psalms I, 1-50*, (Anchor Bible: Garden City, NY: Doubleday & Co., 1965). p. 49, proposed that the particle and the verb be taken together as a single word, giving the verbal form 'I will worship' (*'ashâretannâh*). Though this suggestion was taken up by P. C. Craigie, *Psalms 1-50*, p. 105, yet it gives a form not otherwise attested in the Old Testament.

[3] The word '*oz* primarily refers to 'strength' or 'might'. However, it occurs in several passages in which ascribing strength to God implies praise of him for his overwhelming majesty.

care for him? (*vv. 3-4*). In comparison with the majesty of all creation, which is an expression of the majesty of God (cf. 'your heavens, the work of your fingers'), man's position seems so very insignificant. The words chosen for 'man' in this verse (Hebrew *ᵉnôsh* and *ben 'ādām*) seem to be deliberately chosen to highlight his frailty. The expected answer to the question the psalmist asks has to be, 'Nothing!'

You have made him a little lower than the heavenly beings and crowned him with glory and honour (*v. 5*). It is better to follow the NIV margin and insert 'than god' instead of 'than the heavenly beings'. The Massoretic Hebrew text has 'God' (*ᵉlohîm*). Though the translation 'heavenly beings' does occur in some of the early translations, yet that is probably due to a theological reason. Versions such as the LXX, the Syriac, and the Targums were probably trying to avoid the idea that man was invested with such great dignity. However, man occupies a special position in creation, in that he alone of all the creatures was made in the image and likeness of God (Gen. 1:26-27; 5:1). Because of his creation he has to reflect God's glory in a special way as he rules as his vice-regent, and God's attitude to mankind continues to be, in spite of man's sinfulness, one of favour and blessing. The reference to God's action is not just to the past, but his abiding bestowal of 'glory and honour'.

3. Man's Role in Creation (*vv. 6-8*)

You made him ruler over the works of your hands; you put everything under his feet: all flocks and herds, and the beasts of the field, the birds of the air, and the fish of the sea, all that swim the paths of the seas (*vv. 6-8*). Man was given dominion over the rest of creation (Gen. 1:28-30; 9:1-3), and these verses show how comprehensive this rule was. At the apex of creation (note the distinctiveness of the account of man's creation in Gen. 1:26-30 as compared with the preceding narrative) man's rule extended over all the rest of creation, a fact reaffirmed after the flood (Gen. 9:2-3). The words 'you put everything under his feet' find their fullest meaning in Jesus' dominion through his resurrection and exaltation (1 Cor. 15:27; Eph. 1:22; Heb. 2:6-8). What is pictured here of man in respect to creation is yet to have its fullest significance in the great re-creation that will follow the return of Christ.

4. God's Praise Renewed (*v. 9*)
O LORD, our Lord, how majestic is your name in all the earth! Just as the psalm begins, so it ends. It started on the note of praise. Then the reasons for praise were unfolded, and finally the psalm ends with more praise. This is a pattern often followed with psalms of thanksgiving. Either the opening is repeated, or given at the end with some slight variation (cf. Ps. 117:1, 2).

Psalm 9

For the director of music. To the tune of 'The Death of the Son'. A psalm of David

Psalms 9 and 10 form a unit, as they together comprise an acrostic (see Introduction), and in early versions such as the LXX and the Vulgate they are a single entity. The acrostic pattern is not complete, as several letters of the Hebrew alphabet are missing and some letters are not in the usual order. Psalm 9 employs the Hebrew letters Alef–Kaf, though Dalet is missing in verses 5-6. Lamed–Taw are found in Psalm 10, though Mem and Nun are reversed in verses 3-6, while Ayin and Pe are similarly reversed in verses 7-9.[1] The use of an acrostic clearly appealed to some poets, and it must also have brought responsive appreciation from hearers or readers. Acrostics may well have served a teaching purpose in that they were a device to assist in memorising a poem. The emphasis on Psalm 9 is on praise of God who governs the whole world, while in Psalm 10 the main focus is an appeal to God in distress caused by personal enemies. Thoughts and words also bind the two psalms together:

Psalm 9	Psalm 10
The LORD is … a stronghold *in times of trouble* (v. 9)	Why do you hide yourself *in times of trouble* (v. 1)
He does not *forget* the cry of the afflicted (v. 12)	He says to himself, 'God has *forgotten*' (v. 11)

---

[1] For recent discussion on the acrostic psalms, see D. N. Freedman and J. C. Geoghegan, 'Alphabetic Acrostic Psalms' in D. N. Freedman, *Psalm 119: The Exaltation of the Torah* (Winona Lake, Ind.: Eisenbrauns 1999), pp. 13-19.

Psalm 9	Psalm 10
O Lord, see how my enemies *pursue* me (v. 13)	In his pride the wicked does not *pursue* him (v. 4)
	Why does he say in his heart, 'He won't *pursue* [me]' (v. 13)
Their feet are caught in the *net* they have hidden (v. 15)	He catches the helpless and drags them off in his *net* (v. 9)
Let the *nations* be judged in your presence; … let the *nations* know they are but men (vv. 19-20)	The Lord is king for ever and ever; the *nations* will perish from his land (v. 16)

On balance it seems best to assume that the two psalms, while having certain similarities, were written independently, and brought together at this point in the Psalter because of common ideas and words.

The inscription, 'For the director of music. To [the tune of] "The Death of the Son", A psalm of David', contains commonly used words, but the phrase 'To the death of the son' does not occur elsewhere in the Psalter. This involves dividing one word in the MT (*'almût*) into two (*'al mût*). Various suggestions have been made,[2] but no consensus has emerged. Perhaps an old explanation going back as far as Grotius (1583-1645) should be again considered. He proposed that a transposition of letters had taken place with the words 'of the son' (*labên*) and that the true reading should be *nâvâl*, Nabal. Hengstenberg refined this suggestion further, by taking *nâvâl*, not as a proper name, but as the noun 'a fool'.[3] This gives a translation 'on the dying of a fool' which suits the context (see especially

---

[2] See a summary in W. VanGemeren, 'Psalms', pp. 116-17.
[3] E. W. Hengstenberg, *Commentary on the Psalms*, pp. 141-42.

verses 3, 5, 6, 12, 17) and also can be supported by David's words regarding Abner, 'Died Abner as the fool dies?' (*hakk^{e}môt nâvâl yâmût 'avnêr*, 2 Sam. 3:33).

1. A Song of Thanksgiving (*vv. 1-2*)
I will praise you, O LORD, with all my heart; I will tell of all your wonders; I will be glad and rejoice in you; I will sing praise to your name, O Most High (*vv. 1-2*). These verses contain several terms that concentrate on praise, and probably public praise in the sanctuary: *praise, tell, be glad, praise, sing praise*. To the opening one is added, *with all my heart*, to indicate the depth of his 'praise'. The 'wonders' were the deeds that the LORD alone could and did perform, such as the great redemptive acts connected with the Exodus (see the first use of the word in Exod. 3:20). It is a word used especially in the Psalms (twenty-four occurrences out of forty-one), and often with the same verb as here (*sappêr*, 'count, recount'). The 'name' is a reference not to a title for LORD but the revelation he had made of himself. The psalmist sings praise to his covenant God (*LORD*) and to his exalted sovereign (*Most High*). Similar language is used at the opening of Psalm 75.

2. Acknowledgment of Personal Help (*vv. 3-6*)
My enemies turn back; they stumble and perish before you. For you have upheld my right and my cause; you have sat on your throne, judging righteously. You have rebuked the nations and destroyed the wicked; you have blotted out their name forever and ever. Endless ruin has overtaken the enemy, you have uprooted their cities; even the memory of them has perished (*vv. 3-6*). These verses refer back to historical incidents that are the foundation of praise. God had intervened, and the psalmist's enemies had turned back from their evil plans. They perished before the righteous God. The verb 'to stumble' often occurs in the poetical books in this metaphorical sense of being brought to ruin.

Along with verse 8, these verses contain very significant declarations joining together the concepts of God as judge and his acting in righteousness (*tsédek*). An accumulation of related terms occurs, relating to both personal and national levels of judgment: 'right' (*mishpât*), 'cause' (*dîn*), 'to judge' (*shâfat*), and 'justice' (*mêshârîm*). Judgment had been executed on the psalmist's behalf by God, who from his kingly throne executed his just decrees. Even the Gentile nations had felt God's 'rebuke', using a word elsewhere applied to dramatic actions of God such as the flood (cf. Ps. 106:9; Isa. 54:9). Nations had been blotted out before him so that no recollection of them remained. The use of the verb 'blot out' (*mâchâh*) is important, as it almost always has theological significance.[4] It is first used of the blotting out by the flood (Gen. 7:22-23), and also both in threats to Israel (Deut. 9:14; 29:20) and to describe the reality of God's judgment against Jerusalem (2 Kings 21:13). Here the application is to enemy nations that have been blotted out and brought to ruin. The duration of this is stressed by the use of 'for ever and ever' and 'endless'. Not being remembered at the time of death is the fate of evildoers and Israel's enemies (Exod. 17:14; Deut. 25:19; Ps. 34:16), while the righteous are remembered for ever (Ps. 112:6; Prov. 10:7).

3. The Rule of the King/Shepherd (*vv. 7-10*)

The thought of God as judge leads on to statements concerning his general rule and his protective care. **The LORD reigns forever; he has established his throne for judgment** (*v. 7*). In contrast to the enemies whose names are blotted eternally, the LORD sits enthroned for ever. Here the picture seems to move to the scene at the end of time, when all shall appear before the LORD's throne of judgment.

An action of judgment occurred in the past (v. 5), but future judgment is still in store. **He will judge the world in righteousness; he will govern the peoples with justice** (*v. 8*). Unlike human judges, God judges righteously. His administration will not be marred by the flawed justice of human systems. The whole of the inhabited world (Heb., *têvêl*) will be subject to his rule. This verse is used again in the later Royal Psalms to describe the end-time judgment of the divine king (Pss. 96:13; 98:9).

---

[4] See W. C. Kaiser's note in *TWOT*, 1, pp. 498-99.

The LORD is a refuge for the oppressed, a stronghold in times of trouble. Those who know your name will trust in you, for you, LORD, have never forsaken those who seek you *(vv. 9-10)*.

For any afflicted persons, there is the assurance that God is a 'refuge' or 'stronghold' (in the NIV translation these words render the same Hebrew word [*misgâv*] that occurs twice in verse 9). The main idea of the Hebrew word is a place with high fortifications (cf. Isa. 25:12), but it never occurs as a synonym for a Canaanite high place (Hebrew *bâmâh*). 'In times of trouble' the oppressed find refuge with the LORD (cf. the use of the identical expression in 10:1 and a similar one in 37:39). 'Oppressed' is a synonym for 'afflicted' in verse 12. The character of those who take refuge is described as 'those who know your name'. Unlike the names of the wicked that are blotted out (v. 5), God's name is the revelation of his person. Those who love him have come to a personal knowledge of him, and therefore they put their confidence in him. The verb 'to trust' *(bâtach)* is one of the most frequent ways employed in the Old Testament and especially in the Psalms to denote the confidence that comes through reliance on God.[5]

None of those who seek God ever find themselves left in the lurch. The verb 'to seek' appears often in the Psalms, especially in the general sense of asking help or assistance from the LORD (cf. Ps. 14:2). Verse 10 is also significant, for after speaking of God in the third person in verses 1-9, the change is made to the second person: 'those who know *your name*,' 'for *you*, O LORD', 'those who seek *you*'. This has the effect of drawing attention to the personal relationship that David enjoyed with his God. Such expressions regarding God's character towards his believing community were rooted in the psalmist's own experience of God's grace and power.

4. A Doxology *(vv. 11-12)*
Sing praises to the LORD, enthroned in Zion; proclaim among the nations what he has done. For he who avenges blood remembers; he does not ignore the cry of the afflicted

---

[5] For discussion of the wider use of this verb and other related ones, see G. J. Wenham, *Faith in the Old Testament* (TSF, n.d.); O. Adutwum, '*BATACH* in the Book of Psalms', *IBS* 15 (1993), pp. 28-38.

(*vv. 11-12*). The psalmist returns now to the theme of praise found at the beginning of the psalm (vv. 1-2). The call is most probably to the assembled people at the sanctuary, as the psalmist wants all who hear to join with him in praising God for his goodness and righteous acts. The LORD who is enthroned on Zion (the presence of the ark in Jerusalem is intended) is to be praised, and his deeds declared to the Gentile nations. Just as God sat on a heavenly throne (v. 7), so he dwelt in an earthly way in the tabernacle which was in Zion by his own appointment (see Ps. 132:13-14). Proclamation of God's deeds is to take place among the Gentile nations. 'The deeds' are clearly the same as 'the wonders' in verse 1, even though different Hebrew words are used. What his deeds consist of is made clear in verse 12. God was the one who would avenge those who took (or attempted to take) the life of others (cf. Gen. 4:10; 9:5). His sovereign deliverance of his people would be proclaimed as his 'wonders'. God's faithfulness is asserted in the phrase 'he does not ignore (lit. 'forget') the cry of the afflicted'. Not till later in the Psalms is there fuller expression of this wish that all the nations might know the LORD's deeds (cf. Pss. 18:49; 57:9, and also the Introduction).

5. An Appeal for Help (*vv. 13-14*)

The tone of the psalm changes at this point to become more like a lament, with appeals to God for his mercy and deliverance. These appeals are going to be repeated in a different form at the end of the psalm (vv. 19-20). **O LORD, see how my enemies persecute me! Have mercy and lift me up from the gates of death, that I may declare your praises in the gates of the Daughter of Zion and there rejoice in your salvation** (*vv. 13-14*). Stemming out of the assurance that God is the avenger, given in the preceding verse, the psalmist appeals in respect to his own case. Statements of God's character often form the basis for individual prayer. The NIV does not follow the word order of the MT, which puts the appeal for mercy at the beginning. It is better to follow the RSV and the NASB, which render: 'Be gracious to me. Behold ...,' and this highlights the appeal for mercy. David's persecution by his enemies had reached the point where he felt he had reached the gates of death itself. Death is looked at as if it was a territory, or a city with doors (cf. Rev. 1:18, 'the keys of death and Hades'). The psalmist wants mercy to be shown to him so that he, in turn, can declare God's praises. The highest desire he had is not just his own deliverance but the opportunity to praise his deliverer. Those delivered by God desire to declare the praises of him who called them out of darkness into his marvellous light (1 Pet. 2:9). 'The Daughter of Zion' is a personification of Jerusalem as a young girl, perhaps better rendered as 'Daughter Zion'. 'Daughter' is used of other cities and countries (cf. 'daughter of Tyre' [Ps. 45:12], 'daughter of Babylon' [Ps. 137:8], 'daughter of Edom' [Lam. 4:21]). Here it is a personification of Zion, and the phrase also serves to emphasise the father/daughter relationship between God and the city he had chosen (see Pss. 2:6 and 132:13-14). There, surrounded by the inhabitants of Jerusalem, he longs to sing and rejoice in God's salvation.

6. The Wicked Ensnared (*vv. 15-18*)

The nations have fallen into the pit they have dug; their feet are caught up in the net they have hidden. The LORD is known by his justice; the wicked are ensnared by the work of their hands. *Higgaion Selah* (*vv. 15-16*). Attention now comes back to the nations (see verse 5). The outcome for the wicked is described in terms of them falling into their own pit, being caught in the net they have set, or being trapped in their own snares. What they wanted to do to Israel has become their own portion. They were to know the consequences of their own plotting, not on others, but on themselves (cf. Pss. 5:10; 7:14-16). The work of their own hands turns on them. The reference to the LORD's justice picks up the theme of verse 4. The opening of verse 16 makes it plain that God's hand was also in this. 'The wicked' (synonymous with 'nations' in verses 5, 15, 17 and 19) are subjects of God's justice, which turns their plots against themselves.

The meaning of 'higgaion' is uncertain, but it may come from a Hebrew root that means 'to murmur', 'sigh', 'meditate'.[6] It also occurs in Psalm 92:4 of lyre music, but the same derivation would fit that context as well. Hence, here it probably denotes that the last part of the psalm is to be rendered softly in keeping with the solemnity of the subject. For 'Selah', see the comments on Psalm 3:2.

7. The Destiny of the Wicked (*vv. 17-18*)

The wicked return to the grave, all the nations that forget God. But the needy will not always be forgotten, nor the hope of the afflicted ever perish (*vv. 17-18*). Those who forget God return to Sheol (see comment on Ps. 6:5). Earlier in this psalm there is mention of 'forgetting' (v. 12, NIV 'ignore'). Here it means people who do not think about the true God and serve him, but rather strive against his people. The verdict expressed against them may not mean immediate judgment and death, but that which is treasured up for them in the future (see verse 20). The verb 'to forget' appears again in verse 18, but with what a great contrast! God will never forget his poor and afflicted ones. He will never allow their hope to perish. Their expectation is based on God's sure word to his children.

8. A Final Appeal (*vv. 19-20*)

Arise, O LORD, let not man triumph; let the nations be judged in your presence. Strike them with terror, O LORD; let the nations know they are but men (*vv. 19-20*). It is clear that the opposition to the righteous (and especially to the psalmist himself) was still present, and therefore he asks for God's speedy help (for 'arise' cf. Ps. 7:6). The language used here goes back to Moses' words in Numbers 10:35 when the ark was being moved: 'Rise up, O LORD! May your enemies be scattered; may your foes flee before you' (cf. also Ps. 68:1-2). The psalmist does not want frail man to be able to rejoice in triumph. The Hebrew word used for man carries with it implications of human frailty and weakness, especially in

---

[6] See P. C. Craigie, *Psalms 1-50*, p. 116.

contrast, as here, to God's power (Hebrew *ʾenôsh* as compared with the more common *ʾâdâm*). What was needed was a fresh demonstration of God's power such as had been shown at the Exodus. The word 'terror' implies this, for it is used in Deuteronomy 4:34 of God's awesome deeds when he brought Israel out of Egypt. By a repetition of such divine action the nations would truly know their own frailty and insignificance before the LORD. An appearance of God would fill his enemies with apprehension as they realised that they could not stand before him.

Psalm 10

Almost all the psalms in the first book (Psalms 1-41) have a title. The only exceptions are 1, 2, 10, and 33. The fact that a title is missing for this psalm is another indication that it is to be considered in conjunction with Psalm 9, whose title also covers this psalm. The note of appeal to God is much more prominent here, though at the end of the psalm there is an affirmation that God the king is also a prayer-hearing God. Though the word 'nations' appears in verse 16, yet the thrust of the complaint is against an individual oppressor *within* Israel. The fact that the word used for the 'wicked' (Heb., *râshaʿ*) almost always appears in the singular supports this position. The one exception is in verse 2b, where the NIV translation has to be emended to read 'caught in the schemes *they* have devised'. The use of the plural is understandable in this verse, as it is describing the more general setting before concentrating on the individual problem of persecution.

The style of this complaint is marked out, not only by the use of standard expressions, but also by the repetition of them. These include:

the wicked [man]	verses 2, 3, 4, 13, 15 (2×)
says to himself	verses 6, 11, 13
schemes, evil thoughts	verses 2, 4
lie in wait, ambush	verses 8-9 (twice the verb *'ârav* and once the derived noun *ma'ᵃrâv*)
weak, afflicted	verses 2, 9 (2×), 12, 17

in secret, hide	verses 8, 9 (the noun *mistâr*), 11 (the verb *sâtar*)
to seize	verse 9 (2×)

The effect of this repetition is to heighten the appreciation of the reader for the heart-rending situation in which David found himself. He states and restates the agony of one who was persecuted without cause and without cessation.

1. A Heartfelt Cry (*vv. 1-2*)

Why, O Lord, do you stand far off? Why do you hide yourself in times of trouble? (*v. 1*) The psalmist is in deep trouble and turns to the one who is a stronghold at such times (see 9:9). The introductory word is 'Why?' This speaks of the hurt and disappointment he feels, but it also includes the idea of expectation of God's help. There is also the note of puzzlement at the treatment believers receive from persecutors. Later Psalms 37 and 73 help to provide the answer to that puzzle. No indication is given that it was because of the psalmist's sin that God had placed himself afar off (contrast Jer. 23:23). The idea that God conceals himself from troubled believers occurs elsewhere (see Ps. 55:1 and Lam. 3:56), though such concealment is a figment of their imagination.

In his arrogance the wicked man hunts down the weak, who are caught in the schemes he devises (*v. 2*). This short statement of the situation is explained more fully later in the psalm (see especially vv. 7-10). The imagery of hunting is frequently employed in Hebrew poetry as by analogy the readers or hearers could transfer the concepts easily into their own situation. In the second clause of this verse the subject of the verb 'caught' is 'they'. While this could refer to the wicked being caught in their own snares, more probably the NIV is correct to take it as meaning the poor are entrapped. However, the verb 'devise' is plural as well, so that the translation has to be 'caught in the schemes *they* devise'. This provides the general statement, before individual specification of the attitude and actions of the wicked person follow.

2. The Pride of the Wicked (vv. 3-6)

He boasts of the cravings of his heart; he blesses the greedy and reviles the LORD. In his pride the wicked does not seek him; in all his thoughts there is no room for God (vv. 3-4). It is part of the routine of sinners to glorify themselves. Right from the time of the first sin they have wanted to elevate themselves to be as God (Gen. 3:5). They can extol the very longings that ultimately come to expression in outward transgression. Sin also causes wrong understanding of the deeds of other sinners, as well as of God's character. Hence the sinner praises greedy and ruthless men, while God is blasphemed. He makes no attempt to seek after God and shuts him out of all his thoughts. Part of the nature of sinful man is to suppress the knowledge he has of the truth and to fail to glorify God and give thanks to him (Rom. 1:18-21).

His ways are always prosperous; he is haughty and your laws are far from him; he sneers at all his enemies. He says to himself, 'Nothing will shake me; I'll always be happy and never have trouble' (vv. 5-6). The wicked enjoy prosperity, but it makes them even more arrogant. They live in seeming freedom from divine judgment (it is better to take the Hebrew word *mishpât* as 'judgment' rather than the NIV 'law'). Towards their enemies they show contempt and make the boastful claim that they will always stand firm. Such arrogance will continue into the future, as though the wicked person could control it as well as the present circumstances. The second part of verse 6 is difficult to translate and interpret, and an awkward verse division complicates it further. A literal rendering is: 'which (*'asher*) not in evil'. The NKJV ('I shall never be in adversity') or ESV ('I shall not meet adversity') are closest to the MT. The NIV translation accepts an emendation of the text, with *'asher* being revocalised as *'osher*, 'happiness'.[1] It is part of the wicked man's arrogance to claim exemption from trouble and from judgment. He considers himself unassailable.

---

[1] This is followed in *DCH*, I, p. 436: 'in happiness, not in misfortune'. The only time the word *'osher* appears with certainty in the MT is Gen. 30:13 where Leah says, 'How happy I am!'

3. The Character of the Wicked (*vv. 7-11*)

A description of sinful man now follows, with emphasis on his role as an oppressor. Some commentators take 'curse' with the preceding verse, in order to allow the letter *pe* to begin verse 7,[2] and so supply another letter of the alphabet to try and complete the acrostic pattern. However, the pattern is still incomplete even if that is done, and hence this suggestion does not carry much weight.[3] **His mouth is full of curses and lies and threats; trouble and evil are under his tongue. He lies in wait near the villages; from ambush he murders the innocent, watching in secret for his victims** (*vv. 7-8*). The description at the start of verse 7 of sinful man (with a tongue that is always speaking lies) is taken over by Paul from the LXX and used in his description of the utter sinfulness of man without Christ (Rom. 3:14).[4] Continually the wicked pour out their evil words against others, with the mouth being ready with its arsenal of deadly weapons. In addition to words, they act with violence against others. There is no reason to suggest anything other than a literal understanding of the description here. They act like lions in attacking their prey. Similar imagery occurs quite frequently in the Psalter (cf. Pss. 17:12; 37:32; 56:6; 59:3; 64:4).

He lies in wait like a lion in cover; he lies in wait to catch the helpless; he catches the helpless and drags them off in his net. His victims are crushed, they collapse; they fall under his strength. He says to himself, 'God has forgotten; he covers his face and never sees' (*vv. 9-11*). The spiritual conditions behind these verses are unknown to us. However, we have enough evidence from the prophets to confirm the accuracy of the description given here. There were clearly

---

[2] See, for example, P. C. Craigie, *Psalms 1-50*, p. 122. His translation, 'I won't slip throughout all generations. Happiness without misfortune – so has he sworn', in addition takes *'âlâh* not as 'curse' but as the verb 'he has sworn'.

[3] See the excellent note by Craigie, 'Excursus III: Acrostic Psalms', ibid., pp. 128-31.

[4] Paul does not quote the LXX precisely, and even it differs from the MT, mainly in that in place of 'deceits' the LXX has 'bitterness'. This appears to be caused by the LXX translators taking the Hebrew word *mirmôt* as coming from the verb *mârar*, 'to be bitter', rather than from *râmâh*, 'to deceive'.

many occasions when force was used against the poor and needy in Israel (see Hos. 4:2; 6:8-9; Isa. 1:15-17, 21-23; Jer. 7:9; Ezek. 22:2-5). Sheer brute force had been used and the helpless were felled. In addition, the wicked have been deceitful and cunning as they set traps for the righteous. In verse 11 the thought of verse 6 is taken up and developed further. The inner thoughts of the wicked are exposed, for what has taken place outwardly is only the expression of inward godlessness. The wicked are depicted as claiming that, as God does not see them, they can act sinfully with great boldness. Jesus, in his teaching, developed the whole concept of inner sin coming to expression in outward actions (see Matt. 5:21-30; Mark 7:20-23).

4. A Call to God (*vv. 12-13*)
Arise, Lord! Lift up your hand, O God. Do not forget the helpless. Why does the wicked man revile God? Why does he say to himself, 'He won't call me to account'? (*vv. 12-13*). The appeal to God is urgent. This is emphasised by the call to him to 'arise'. This is the fourth time in the first ten psalms that the words 'Arise, Lord' are used (see the comment on 3:7; note the other occurrences in 7:6 and 9:19).[5] The urgency is also stressed by the use of three different names for God in these verses. He is first of all addressed as covenant Lord (Heb., *yhwh*), then as God (Heb., *'ēl*), and finally by another word for God (Heb., *'elōhîm*). To lift up the hand clearly means to punish (cf. v. 15; see also 2 Sam. 18:28), or to put it positively, to rescue his afflicted ones (as in Ps. 138:7). Those who reviled God thought that he would not seek them out. They had already declared themselves as atheists (vv. 4,11), and now they proudly boast that they will be left alone to carry out their evil deeds.[6] Sinners ever need to be reminded that ultimately

---
[5] The expression also appears in 17:13 and 132:8, while 'Arise, O God' is used in 74:22 and 82:8.

[6] The NIV rendering 'He won't call me to account' follows the LXX and the Syriac in reading the verb as the 3 pers. sing., but the MT has 2 pers. sing., lit. '*you* will not seek me'. Probably the rendering should be indirect speech in English: 'Why does he say to himself that you won't call me to account?' The Hebrew verb here (*dârash*) is rightly translated 'call to account' as one of its uses conveys this sense of demanding or requiring something. It is then a quasi-legal term.

they will be called to account before the judgment seat of God (2 Cor. 5:10).

5. A Song of Confidence (vv. 14-18)
How different were things in reality! **But you, O God, do see trouble and grief; you consider it to take in hand. The victim commits himself to you; you are the helper of the fatherless. Break the arm of the wicked and evil man; call him to account for his wickedness that would not be found out** (vv. 14-15). The opening words in the NIV ('But you, O God') are good, in that they bring out the emphasis of the MT on the fact that God had indeed seen what was happening. The same effect can be gained by rendering: 'You have seen the trouble and vexation, yes you have!'[7] God saw everything that happened, in contrast to the claim that he neither saw (v. 11) nor punished (v. 13). The orphan is singled out as representative of that group for whom the LORD ever showed great care (Exod. 22:22-24; Mal. 3:5). Here the orphan represents helplessness and desertion. Those in need have the reassurance that God sees their trouble and that he acts as their helper. In verse 15 the psalmist asks God to break the powerful arm of the wicked so that he cannot continue in his evil way. God is said to seek out the wicked for punishment (Heb., lit. 'you seek [to punish] his wickedness. Surely you can find it!').

The LORD is King for ever and ever; the nations will perish from his land. You hear, O LORD, the desire of the afflicted; you encourage them, and you listen to their cry, defending the fatherless and the oppressed, in order that man, who is of the earth, may terrify no more (vv. 16-18). The psalmist ends with a song of complete confidence in the LORD, and he was so certain of being heard by him that he describes the result of his prayers as a present reality. He recognises that the LORD exercises his kingship over the whole land, and will even destroy the enemies from it. That thought is remarkable, because in the psalm the enemies are opponents *within* Israel. However, the concept of judgment on the enemies reminds

---

[7] This is the translation in Craigie, *Psalms 1-50*, p. 121.

him that God will also deal with the external enemies of Israel. Verse 17 contains the assurance that the prayers he has already expressed for the afflicted are indeed heard by God (notice the variety of terms the psalmist uses for the needy: *weak*, verse 2; *innocent*, verse 8; *helpless*, verse 12; *fatherless*, verses 14 and 18; *afflicted*, verse 17; *oppressed*, verse 18). What God does is to make the heart firm (NIV 'encourage'; for the negative use of this expression, see Ps. 78:8). Man, who boasts of his might, is but frail man (Heb., *ᵉnôsh*, cf. Ps. 9:19) who will no longer be able to terrify others. He is 'of the earth', a mere earthling who cannot stand before the judge of all. This psalm reminds us that under persecution and oppression we must turn to God for relief. Our pattern is Jesus who, 'when they hurled their insults at him, he did not retaliate; when he suffered, he made no threats. Instead, he entrusted himself to him who judges justly' (1 Pet. 2: 23-24). The same epistle counsels us that if we suffer we are to commit ourselves to our faithful creator and continue to do good (1 Pet. 4:19).

Psalm 11
For the director of music. Of David.

This is a song of confidence, probably composed when David fled from Absalom, though David had previously fled several times (see 1 Sam. 19:1-3, 12; 20:1; 21:1, 10; 22:1, 3; 23:13; 24:1-2; 26:1; 27:1). He knew very well what it was to be a fugitive. If the psalm does come from the time of Absalom's revolt, then verse 1 may contain the advice his friends were giving him. They were telling him to flee for safety as he had done when Saul was persecuting him to 'the Crags of the Wild Goats' (1 Sam. 24:2). But he knew that his protection was only with the LORD. While the opening verse speaks of David's trust, the remainder of the psalm is in the third person and has application to the broader situation in life in which the character of the righteous and the wicked is displayed. It is a continuation of the theme of Psalm 1, marking the sharp distinction in God's sight of these two groups in society (see the sharp contrasts in verses 5-7).

1. The Needy Situation Described (*vv. 1-3*)
In the LORD I take refuge. How then can you say to me: 'Flee like a bird to your mountain (*v. 1*). The Psalm opens and closes on a confident note: 'In the LORD I take refuge … the LORD is righteous.' The opening words give the basic theme of the psalm – confident trust in the LORD, using a verb (*châsah*) and its cognates that form an important part of the devotional vocabulary of Israel. In his critical situation friends were giving David advice. They were suggesting he should fly or escape like a bird to a mountain hideout. The verb is plural, so perhaps his friends and associates were

153

intended to flee as well. The designation, 'your mountain', has been taken by some to indicate the well-known retreat that David had previously used.[1] But the imagery is simply that of birds seeking shelter in the nooks and crannies of hills, a well-known and apposite illustration.

For look, the wicked bend their bows; they set their arrows against the strings to shoot from the shadows at the upright in heart (*v.* 2). Elsewhere the wicked are also described as bending the bow (Ps. 37:14). The thought of the bird fleeing is carried over from verse 1, and now the imagery is of a hunter going out after the birds with his bow. The language of fleeing to the mountains to escape may well be a reflection of the advice to Lot (Gen. 19:17; and see v. 6 later in this psalm). The godless are ready to shoot their arrows at the upright without being seen, taking their aim from some concealed hiding place (cf. Ps. 10:8-9).

When the foundations are being destroyed what can the righteous do?' (*v.* 3). There was so much upheaval that even the foundational principles of society were being shaken. There was no truth or justice any more. The final sentence could refer to the past: 'What has the righteous done?' i.e., to deserve this. Yet it is better to follow the NIV and take it as a question of despair: 'What can the righteous do?' In times when justice and righteousness no longer reign supreme in society, what can the upright do? The answer follows in the second section of the psalm.

2. The Source of Confidence (*vv.* 4-7)

The question of despair asked by the psalmist's friends now finds its answer. **The LORD is in his holy temple; the LORD is on his heavenly throne. He observes the sons of men; his eyes**

---

[1] Several awkward things confront the reader in this verse: (1) the switch from 1st pers. in 'I take refuge' to the 2nd plural masc., 'you say' (2) the consonantal text gives the verb 'flee' as 2nd pers. masc. plural imperative, while the Qᵉre reading has it as 2nd pers. fem. sing. (3) the last two words (*harᵉkem tsippôr*, lit. 'your (masc. plur.) mountain [like] a bird') are often emended to *har kᵉmo tsippôr*, ' [to] a hill like a bird'. While the interchange between singular and plural may be difficult, it is best to stay with the MT rather than attempting to emend the text.

examine them. The LORD examines the righteous, but the wicked and those who love violence his soul hates (*vv. 4-5*). Normally there is a spoken prayer after an expression of great need, but one is lacking here. Rather the psalmist points to the LORD on high, seated on his judgment throne. There was the visible presence of God in the tabernacle, but he was also the exalted heavenly ruler. From heaven he saw all that happened, and with penetrating gaze, he was able to test the works of all mankind. The verb translated 'examine' (*bâchan*) is often used of testing metals by fire and is a favourite word in Jeremiah (Jer. 11:20; 17:10; 20:12). While it is similar in meaning to 'put to the test' (*nâsâh*) and 'refine' (*tsâraf*), yet it seems to point to knowledge gained intuitively, and is therefore the most apt of the three in relation to spiritual realities.[2] Even the actions in darkness (v. 2) were open to his sight. The LORD examines the righteous, but his soul hates the wicked and those who love violence. Both righteous and unrighteous come under God's judging eye (cf. Paul's words, 'we must all appear before the judgment seat of Christ', 2 Cor. 5:10), though God's attitude is quite different with each of the two. His innermost being ('his soul') hates the violent man, presumably an indication that the psalmist's enemies were of this kind.

On the wicked he will rain fiery coals and burning sulphur; a scorching wind will be their lot (*v. 6*). The thought of fire used for testing metals changes in verse 6 to become a picture of the fiery judgment. For believers the fire will test the quality of their work (1 Cor. 3:13), while for unbelievers the fire will come as the exterminator of evil. 'Fiery coals and burning sulphur' remind us of what happened to Sodom (Gen. 19:24), and also point forward from the psalmist's time to another sulphur rain that will be poured out on Gog (Ezek. 38:22). A similar fate will be the lot of the wicked in general. The reference to the scorching wind is a description of the east wind that blows over Israel, bringing with it the desert heat.

For the LORD is righteous, he loves justice; upright men will see his face (*v. 7*). How differently God will act towards

---

[2] See the comments by B. K. Waltke, *TWOT*, 1, p. 100.

the righteous! He himself is righteous and he loves justice, i.e. the righteous deeds done by his people. The phrase 'loves justice' could mean that God loves to do righteous deeds, but this is less likely in the context. The final outcome is that the upright in heart will see God's presence manifested in his saving deliverance of them. It is possible that the vision of God here is the ultimate vision of him that every believer will have after death (see the two important passages for this concept, Psalm 17:15; Job 19:26-27). The psalmist returns at the end of the psalm to the same confession he made at the beginning.

Psalm 12

For the director of music. According to sheminith.
A psalm of David.

Psalms like this one show us the contrasts in spiritual life within Israel. So many had turned away from obedience to the LORD that it seemed that the godly had disappeared altogether. Psalm 120 is similar in that it depicts the godly living within Israel as though they were among barbarians. The other contrast in the psalm is between the lying words of the ungodly and the sure words of the LORD. The word *sheminith* has already occurred in the title of Psalm 6 (see comment).

1. The Vain Speech of the Ungodly (*vv. 1-4*)
Help, LORD, for the godly are no more; the faithful have vanished from among men (*v. 1*). The opening word is a cry of desperation. The Hebrew word used (*hôshî'âh*) is normally followed by an object: 'help *me*.' Here, and also in the Hebrew text of Psalm 118:25, the shout is never finished. It is like a drowning person calling out, 'Help.' The Hebrew verb is the one from which the names Joshua and Jesus come. The urgency of the request concerns the apparent disappearance of the faithful from the land. They are described by use of the words for covenantal loyalty (Heb., *châsîd*) and faithful (Heb., *'emûnîm*; cf. the fanatical Israeli group *Gush Emunim, assembly of the faithful*). The spiritual division of society into two contrasting groups was recognised later by Elijah (1 Kings 19:9-18), and manifested particularly in Jesus' rejection by his own (John 1:10-11).

Everyone lies to his neighbour; their flattering lips speak with deception (*v. 2*). Life was marked by deceit, so that everyone spoke against his neighbour. No society or church fellowship can continue if this is the case (cf. Eph. 4:25). With double hearts (Heb., *a heart and [still another] heart*) they spoke, so that their words did not agree with reality.

May the LORD cut off all flattering lips and every boastful tongue that says, 'We will triumph with our tongues; we own our lips – who is our master?' (*vv. 3-4*). The psalmist adds to his cry for help (v. 1) an appeal for the LORD to intervene by cutting off all deceivers and those who boast in their arrogance. The verb 'cut off' goes back to the threat in Genesis 17:14 that any unfaithful covenantal person will be 'cut off'. Rather than cutting a covenant with the LORD, they will be cut off, i.e. executed. The fact that synonyms include 'die' and 'be destroyed' confirms that this is the meaning of the term. These people are described further as proud boasters.[1] Their lips are at their service and they challenge anyone to prevail against them. Later, the prophets had to rebuke the people for the sins of the tongue (Hos. 4:1-2; Jer. 12:6), while the New Testament reaffirms how the tongue is a fire, corrupting the whole person (James 3:6).

2. The Sure Speech of the LORD (*vv. 5-8*)

'Because of the oppression of the weak and the groaning of the needy, I will now arise,' says the LORD. 'I will protect them from those who malign them' (*v. 5*). Prayer was made and speedily answered. No indication is given of how the LORD's words came to the psalmist. It could have been by the ministry of a priest, just as Eli ministered God's word to Hannah (1 Sam. 1:17). The answer is more direct than English translations are able to convey. The cry of help in verse 1 (*hôshî ʿâh*) is followed now by an assurance that the LORD is going to bring salvation (*yêshaʿ*, from the same root, *yâshaʿ*) for him. God hears the cry of the weak and needy and arises

---

[1] The NIV alternative reading, 'our lips are our ploughshares', is based on a suggestion by Dahood that instead of reading *'ittânû* ('with us'), *'ittênû* ('our ploughshares') should be the emended vocalisation. For Dahood's viewpoint, see his *Psalms I: 1-50*, pp. 73-74. However, the MT text, 'our lips are with us', makes good sense and it should be retained.

to help (cf. Pss. 7:6; 9:19; Isa. 33:10). He is the deliverer of the oppressed (Pss. 72:12; 103:6).

The second part of verse 5 is uncertain. The Hebrew text says, 'I will bring (lit. set, put) salvation to him who puffs for it.' Various attempts have been made to emend the text but without any certainty. Most probably, the meaning is that God will provide deliverance to those who pant with intense desire for it. The NASB rendering is good: 'I will set him in the safety for which he longs', or the NLT, 'Now I will rise up to rescue them as they have longed for me to do'.[2]

And the words of the LORD are flawless, like silver refined in a furnace of clay, purified seven times (*v. 6*). The contrast with the words of the deceivers is so clear. The LORD's words are pure, i.e. they have been purified like silver in the furnace, and so they stand forever (cf. the use of the same expression for the law of the LORD in 19:9). The reference to 'seven times' simply denotes the completeness of the process. The LORD's words contain no dross, and so can be relied upon. The implication is that the words of the deceivers are all dross!

O LORD, you will keep us safe and protect us from such people forever (*v. 7*). The message from the LORD has brought reassurance to the psalmist. In the MT text the two verbs in this verse have different suffixes. 'Keep us safe' has a third person masculine plural suffix ('keep *them* safe'), while 'protect' has a first person plural suffix ('protect *us*'). The early versions and a number of Hebrew manuscripts make both first person plural, and this is the way in which most English versions render the verse. Protection will be provided from 'such people' (the Hebrew has 'from this generation'; cf. Jesus' words in Matt. 17:17, 'O unbelieving and perverse generation'). 'Generation' is used in the broad sense of a type of people who share the same mindset, a group bound together by common interests.

---

[2] P. C. Craigie, *Psalms 1-50*, p. 136, chooses to follow the lead of the LXX and Syriac and renders: 'I shall appear in radiance to him', though he admits that 'the emendation is by no means certain'. For suggestions that appeal to Ugaritic, see D. Pardee, '*Yph*, "Witness in Hebrew and Ugaritic'*, VT* 28 (1978), pp. 204-13, and P. D. Miller Jr., '*Yâpîah* in Psalm XII 6', *VT* 29 (1979), pp. 495-501.

The wicked freely strut about when what is vile is honoured among men (*v. 8*). The psalm returns in its conclusion to its opening ideas. The ungodly are still parading around and 'among men' (*bᵉnê 'âdâm*, repeated from verse 1) and what is vile is still highly regarded. The end of the psalm is a reminder that believers have to persevere in prayer, even as wickedness continues or even abounds. Our pattern has to be that of Jesus who suffered at the hands of liars (John 8:44-47) and who 'offered up prayers and petitions with loud cries and tears to the one who could save him from death, and he was heard because of his reverent submission' (Heb. 5:7).

Psalm 13

For *the director of music. A Psalm of David.*

This short psalm has all the characteristics and structure of a lament or appeal for help. It moves from the desolation of the opening verses, with the sense of God's abandonment, to the strong confidence in his abiding mercy in the closing ones. Like other similar psalms no clue is offered as to the reason for the abrupt change in mind and heart (cf. comments on Psalm 6:8-10). The content of the psalm reminds the reader that as many as the LORD loves he rebukes and chastens (Rev. 3:19), and a sense of desolation does not necessarily mean that God has removed from them his favour and steadfast love.

1. A Cry of Distress (*vv. 1-2*)
How long, O LORD? Will you forget me forever? How long will you hide your face from me? How long must I wrestle with my thoughts and every day have sorrow in my heart? How long will my enemy triumph over me? (vv. 1-2). The fourfold cry, 'How long?' dominates the opening stanzas. The psalmist feels himself forgotten by God, and even suggests that God does not remember him as his covenantal servant. While the NIV translation of the Hebrew word *nétsach* as 'forever' is possible, yet it appears here without a preposition such as *lᵉ* or *'ad*. In some instances it can be used as a superlative, 'utterly', and this makes excellent sense here: 'Will you utterly forget me?'[1] The thought of 'forever' is alien to the context, as the concluding section of the psalm shows. 'How long?' is a phrase of urgency, even of desperation. God can reach

---
[1] For this meaning, see *DCH*, V, pp. 739-40.

the end of divine endurance as he did with Israel: 'How long will these people treat me with contempt? How long will they refuse to believe in me, in spite of all the miraculous signs I have performed among them? I will strike them down with a plague and destroy them ...' When Moses pleaded God's covenantal mercy he relented and forgave the people (Num. 14:10-25). Here we have the same link made between 'How long?' and God's covenantal mercy (v. 5). The personal feelings that predominate in a situation like this are inward thoughts. These thoughts may be of sorrow, yet the word used here (*'êtsâh*) is not the normal word for 'thoughts' but rather for 'plans' or 'advice'. The idea may be that the psalmist, in his hour of need, is thinking up possible ways to escape from his difficulties and evade his tormentors. Sorrowful thoughts occur all the time as the psalmist faces his foes, that seemingly include illness and death (see verse 3). He is faced with a continuous battle as his enemies rise up against him.

2. A Plea to the LORD (*vv. 3-4*)
Look on me and answer, O LORD my God. Give light to my eyes, or I will sleep in death; my enemy will say, 'I have overcome him,' and my foes will rejoice when I fall (*vv. 3-4*). In his opening lament the psalmist has spoken of God hiding his face (v. 1). Now his plea is for the LORD to 'look' (i.e. to consider, scrutinise) and to answer his questions. Illness is understood as a darkening of the eyes. Hence the psalmist prays for light to dawn on him so that he will not experience death. There is a tender note in the way he makes his plea. He says, 'O LORD *my* God.' The pronoun 'my' injects an affectionate aspect into the prayer and also a note of believing confidence. Those who approach God in prayer 'must believe that he exists and that he rewards those who earnestly seek him' (Heb. 11:6). The metaphor of death as sleep developed in many languages because of the similarities between a dead person and one who is sleeping. Here the psalmist prays that God will let his eyes see ('give light to my eyes') lest he sleep in death. If his God does not answer him he will die, and all his foes will then take joy in gloating over what has happened

to him (cf. Ps. 38:16). They will claim that they have prevailed and rejoice in his downfall.

3. A Certain Confidence (vv. 5-6)

A marked difference exists between the psalmist's foes and himself, and the opening of verse 5 sets them over against each other. But I, he says, **trust in your unfailing love; my heart rejoices in your salvation. I will sing to the LORD, for he has been good to me** (vv. 5-6). His confidence is in the covenantal love of the LORD that expresses itself in his deliverance. This is one of the passages in the Old Testament in which 'unfailing love' (*chésed*) is parallel with 'salvation' (*y^eshû'âh*). If a distinction is to be made between them, then 'unfailing love' is displayed in God's acts of 'salvation'.[2] Hence the psalmist can overflow with loving praise and he asks God to let his heart rejoice when that salvation appears. This understanding of verse 5 (that his deliverance is yet in the future) is confirmed by the Hebrew idiom in the final verse, which means that he will sing praise 'as soon as he has dealt bountifully with me'. Deliverance, though yet to come, is acknowledged and praised in believing trust. Believers can always look forward in anticipation of God's deliverances, and they can be filled with 'an inexpressible and glorious joy' as they await on the return of Christ the ultimate salvation of their souls (1 Pet. 1:8-9).

---

[2] See Gordon R. Clark, *The Word Hesed in the Hebrew Bible* (Sheffield: JSOT Press, 1993), pp. 156-58. He makes the further point that while God's people experienced and were aware of both 'unfailing love' and 'salvation', the Gentile nations only saw the demonstration of 'salvation'.

Psalm 14

For the director of music. Of David.

Psalms 14 and 53, while not exactly identical, are so close that one is basically a replica of the other. The main differences lie in the use of divine names (Ps. 14 uses LORD [*yhwh*] four times; Ps. 53 consistently uses God, [*'elohîm*]), the addition of a title to Psalm 53, slight verbal differences in the opening verses, and more major differences in the closing verses (Ps. 14:5-6 = Ps. 53:5). The verbal changes in general involve the change of a common word for a more unusual one, though no indication exists in the text as to the reason behind the changes.[1] Most probably Psalm 14 is the earlier version, but the importance of its teaching must have been recognised and an alternative version used as well in worship. Finally, both forms were incorporated into the present Psalter.

The content of Psalm 14 is very similar to Psalm 12, for while speaking of universal sinfulness, both also contrast the way of the wicked with the way of the righteous. Further amplification is given of the condition of 'the sons of men' (see references in psalms that immediately precede: 11:4, 12:1, 8), and the repetition of the phrase 'there is no-one who does good' (v. 1) in verse 4, with the additional phrase, 'not even one', highlights human depravity.

The style of the psalm is closest to Psalms 1 and 2, or to the wisdom literature, especially illustrated by the Book of

---

[1] There is a good note in E. W. Hengstenberg, *Commentary on the Psalms*, I, pp. 205-07, on the differences between Psalms 14 and 53. He argues that 'these alterations (with the exception of the "all" in ver. 4) have all the same character, – everywhere, in Ps. liii., is the rare, the uncommon, the strong, and the elevated, substituted for the common and the simple' (p. 205).

Proverbs. Psalm 14 is not concerned with intellectual atheism. Its focus is rather on the person who is a practical atheist because he has renounced the covenant and therefore the covenantal God. The New Testament points more fully than the Old Testament to the ultimate wisdom of God which is found in Jesus Christ (1 Cor. 1:23-25).

1. A Description of the Fool (*vv. 1-3*)

The fool says in his heart, 'There is no God'. They are corrupt, their deeds are vile; there is no one who does good (*v. 1*). The Hebrew word for fool or folly (*nâvâl*) marked out those who had renounced their allegiance to the covenantal God and consequently to one another. It was used, for example, of the nation in Isaiah 9:15-17, and English expressions like 'outcast' or 'sacrilegious person' may convey better the meaning.[2] The fool lacks the wisdom with which the fear of the LORD begins. He not only says but lives as if 'there is no God'.

The second part of verse 1 clearly shows the normal character of such fools. Their actions are corrupt and an abomination to the LORD. They do not do what is good. This may imply more than general goodness, and specifically, failure to follow covenantal commitments.

The LORD looks down from heaven on the sons of men to see if there are any who understand, any who seek God. All have turned aside, they have together become corrupt; there is no one who does good, not even one (*vv. 2-3*). An anthropomorphic description (one in terms of human characteristics) is given of God's actions to emphasise how he sees all people. He looks out for those who 'understand' (*maskîl*). The Hebrew word stands in contrast to 'fool' in verse 1, and is a synonym for 'wise', 'spiritually understanding'. Another expression for the godly is used at the end of verse 2. They 'seek God,' i.e. they approach the face of God in prayer.

The divine verdict is given in verse 3. The godless, far from seeking God, have turned aside and they have become corrupt. The words, 'there is no one who does good,' are repeated from verse 1, with the addition of the emphatic,

---

[2] See *DCH*, V, pp. 593-94.

'not even one'. Almost certainly there is an allusion here to Genesis 6:5-12, where the account is given of how God looked on the earth and saw how great was the corruption, 'for all the people on earth had corrupted their ways' (Gen. 6:12). While different verbs meaning 'to see' are used, the same verb for 'to be corrupted' (*shâchat*, Hi.) occurs in both passages, and also the extent of the corruption (Gen. 6:12, *kol-bâsâr*; Ps. 14:3, *hakkol*) is stated in similar terms. Paul takes over words from verses 2 and 3 to give further confirmation to his assertion that none are righteous before God (Rom. 3:10-12). In the course of time the passage in Romans 3:10-18 was included in the text of the LXX in Psalm 14, and even appears in some Hebrew manuscripts, having been translated into Hebrew.

2. The Oppression of the Righteous (*vv. 4-6*)

Will evildoers never learn—those who devour my people as men eat bread and who do not call on the LORD? (*v. 4*). It becomes clear that not everyone has turned aside from the LORD, for there are those whom the psalmist can call 'my people'. They are the objects of oppression on the part of 'fools', or, as they are called here, 'evildoers'. Their problem is that they do not have spiritual knowledge, or more specifically, they do not understand their responsibility to their covenantal lord.[3] As a consequence they have spurned him and this shows in that they 'do not call on the LORD'. This last phrase can be used in the Old Testament in the sense of proclaiming the LORD (cf. what God himself did for Moses, Exod. 33:19), but it also means, as here, to use God's name in prayer (Gen. 4:26). The character of the righteous is such that they depend upon God and his grace, and demonstrate it by their prayerful attitude.

There they are, overwhelmed with dread, for God is present in the company of the righteous. You evildoers frustrate the plans of the poor, but the LORD is their refuge (*vv. 5-6*). These are difficult verses to interpret. In both of them

---

[3] For the argument that the verb 'know' (Heb., *yâdaʿ*) has covenantal connotations, see H. B. Huffmon, 'The Treaty Background on Hebrew YADA', *BASOR* 181, pp. 31-37.

there is a contrast between the evildoers in the first part of the verse, and the righteous in the second. There does not seem to be any direct connection between the two clauses other than direct contrast. The evildoers live in fear as a result of their folly (lit. 'they feared a fear'),[4] and they oppress the poor. On the other hand, the righteous have God in their midst, in their assembly.[5] They also have the assurance that while they are being oppressed, the LORD is their refuge.

3. A Prayer for Deliverance (v. 7)

Oh, that salvation for Israel would come out of Zion! When the LORD restores the fortunes of his people, let Jacob rejoice and Israel be glad! (v. 7). The psalmist longs for the coming salvation of the LORD. Clearly the psalm dates from a time when Zion was the religious centre (i.e. after David's bringing of the ark there). The words 'restoring the fortunes' need not be a reference to the pending return from exile. Rather, the Hebrew phrase (lit. *restores the captivity*) can be taken in a general way as speaking of a real change in the people's circumstances. Salvation would come from the LORD. Every saving action of God in the Old Testament was a precursor of the far fuller salvation that Jesus would bring. It is not surprising that the psalm ends on a note of joy, for salvation brings forth a song from the people of God. When the ultimate redemption is completed, a great multitude will sing: 'Salvation belongs to our God who sits on the throne, and to the Lamb' (Rev. 7:10).

---

[4] For this usage, called a cognate accusative, see *GKC* §117p. The effect of this is to strengthen the idea of the verb.

[5] Hebrew has two words that are identical in orthography and pronunciation (*dôr*), one meaning 'generation' and the other 'assembly'. The NIV rendering is preferable here, especially since the word is preceded by the preposition 'in' (*bᵉdôr*). Cf. ESV, 'with the generation of the righteous'. See *DCH*, II, p. 430.

Psalm 15

A psalm of David.

Psalm 15 and Psalm 24 have much in common. They both ask about coming into the presence of the LORD at his holy hill, and they both answer in a similar way. The character of the godly worshipper is set out clearly. Both psalms probably originated with the removal of the ark of the covenant to Jerusalem by David (2 Sam. 6). It is possible that the opening questions were asked by the worshippers as they approached the sanctuary, and then the priests answered with the appropriate responses that specify the character of true worshippers.

The concerns in the opening part of this psalm are reflected elsewhere in the Old Testament. Passages such as Jeremiah 7:1-7 and Ezekiel 18:5-9 show that the prophets expressed the same requirements on worshippers as the psalmists (see especially the reference in Jeremiah 7:2 to entering into the gates of the LORD's house). The closest parallel, however, to Psalm 15:1 is Isaiah 33:14-16, where the questions bear a close resemblance: 'Who of us can dwell with the consuming fire? Who of us can dwell with everlasting burning?' Both verbs for 'dwell' used in the opening questions in the psalm (*gûr* and *shâkan*) occur in Isaiah 33:14, 16, while the answer given mentions six characteristics: righteous walk, upright speech, no extortion, no bribes, no participation in plotting murder, and rejection of planned evil deeds. The general principle being stated in all these passages is that personal character will determine one's destiny. It is not the person who says 'Lord, Lord' who will enter the kingdom of heaven, but the one who does God's will (Matt. 7:21-23).

1. The Question Asked (*v. 1*)

Lord, who may dwell in your sanctuary? Who may live on your holy hill? The two clauses are clearly used in parallel with one another. Two different verbs are used ('dwell', 'live') and two different descriptions of God's dwelling place are given ('sanctuary', 'holy hill'). The Hebrew word for 'sanctuary' is *'ōhel*, 'tent', which, while strictly the outer covering of the 'tabernacle' (*mishkân*), is often used as synonymous with it. The mountain of the Lord has been spoken of in the Song of Moses (Exod. 15:17). When David captured Mount Zion (2 Sam. 5:7) he took up residence there and made it the dwelling place for the ark of the Lord. From that point onwards there was never any question as to where the central place of worship should be. The worshipper now asks who can sojourn as the Lord's guest. The verb 'sojourn' (*gûr*) does not only imply temporary dwelling as Psalm 61:4 shows: 'I long to dwell in your tent *for ever*'. To 'live' or 'dwell' (*shâkan*) is a verb used of living in a tent and from it one of the names for the tabernacle was derived (*mishkân*). The principle underlying the tabernacle in the Old Testament came to its fullest expression in Jesus taking upon himself human flesh: 'The Word became flesh and dwelt (lit. 'tabernacled') among us' (John 1:14).

2. The Answers Provided (*vv. 2-5a*)

The answer comes in a pattern of two sets of positive conditions, with two corresponding sets of negative conditions.

Positive	Negative
Verse 2a	Verse 3a
Verse 2b	Verse 3b
Verse 2c	Verse 3c

Positive	Negative
Verse 4a	Verse 5a
Verse 4b	Verse 5b
Verse 4c	

He whose walk is blameless and who does what is righteous, who speaks the truth from his heart (*v. 2*). The first group of positive conditions does not include sacrificial requirements, nor do any of the others. The concentration is on moral characteristics. The first one, walking blamelessly (*tâmîm*), is virtually a synonym for being godly, and speaks of the wholeness of the person. It is a term that is used of a person's close relationship with the LORD, and is very close in meaning to 'upright' (*yâshâr*) and 'righteous' (*tsâdîq*). The second one starts to be more specific, demanding righteous actions, while the third one asks for truthful speech.

The relationship with the LORD has to be demonstrated in deeds and words ... **and has no slander on his tongue, who does his neighbour no wrong and casts no slur on his fellow man** (*v. 3*). The negative conditions now follow. The first one implies no wrong use of his tongue. Literally it is, 'he has not spied with [or possibly, tripped over] his tongue.' The idea of spying is clearly carried over here in regard to stealthy behaviour in the area of speech. Nor has he done any harm to his neighbour, or made fun of the faults or situations of his friends (or possibly relations). The Hebrew word *qârôv* can refer to nearness (both geographical and temporal), but also for nearness in human relationships (cf. its use in 2 Sam. 19:42 [Heb. 43]).[1]

... **who despises a vile man but honours those who fear the LORD, who keeps his oath even when it hurts,** (*v. 4*). The second set of positive conditions included honouring those who fear God and despising those who are rejected by God. The NIV 'vile man' is too weak a translation of the Hebrew word *nim'âs* (Ni. part. of *mâ'as*). Something closer to 'rejected' or 'reprobate' is needed. 'The fear of the Lord' is a standard Old Testament expression, occurring twenty-one times, mostly in wisdom literature. It is a multifaceted concept, but in passages such as this it designates those who walk uprightly. This group in Israel comprised those who served the LORD with devotion and formed part of the worshipping community (cf. its use in parallel with *qâhâl râv*,

---

[1] The use of this word in Isa. 33:13 provides another link between that context and Ps. 15.

'great congregation', in Psalm 22:25).[2] Thus spiritual attitudes are important in the worshipper. The third condition in this verse is difficult to translate and interpret. The NIV rendering is one possibility. It could also mean 'he has sworn to do no wrong and does not alter', i.e. he keeps his pledged word without any change.

... who lends his money without usury and does not accept a bribe against the innocent (*v. 5a*). The final two conditions are negative and both relate to money. They are activities that strike at the very heart of societal life. It was forbidden for an Israelite to lend with interest to a fellow Israelite (Lev. 25:36-37; Deut. 23:19). It was, however, permissible to lend with interest to a foreigner (Deut. 23:20). To take interest from a fellow Israelite who was in financial difficulties would only compound the situation. Just as God had shown mercy and compassion to his people, so they in turn had to act compassionately to those in need (see Lev. 25:35-37). Also, no bribe could be taken to ensure the conviction of the innocent (cf. Exod. 23:8; Deut. 16:19). Perverted justice was no justice at all. The exemplar for true justice was God himself, 'the righteous judge' (Pss. 7:11; 67:4). Passages in the prophetical books such as Isaiah 33:14-16 and Micah 6:6-8 may well be building upon these conditions given in verses 2-5a.

3. The Promise (v. 5b)

He who does these things will never be shaken. The final word in the psalm is one of reassurance. The person who fulfils its conditions will not be moved, i.e. be removed from the house of the LORD and from the LORD's presence. The answer to the opening question in verse 1 in effect is: 'Whoever does these things shall dwell in his sanctuary for ever'.

---

[2] 'The fear of the LORD' has two dimensions to it. On the one hand, there is a vertical dimension involving both general and special revelation. On the other hand, there is a horizontal dimension involving emotional responses as diverse as awe and love. See the discussion by Bruce Waltke, 'The Fear of the Lord: The Foundation for a Relationship with God', in J. I. Packer and L. Wilkinson, *Alive to God: Studies in Spirituality presented to James Houston* (Downers Grove: Inter-Varsity Press, 1992), pp. 17-33. Other full discussions are provided by John Murray, *Principles of Conduct: Aspects of Biblical Ethics* (London: Tyndale Press, 1957), pp. 229-42, and Henri Blocher, 'The Fear of the Lord as the "Principle" of Wisdom', *TB* 28 (1977), pp. 3-28.

Psalm 16

A miktam of David.

The title attributes the psalm to David, and both Peter and Paul in the New Testament confirm this (Acts 2:25-32; 13:36). The word *miktâm* occurs here and in the titles of five other psalms (56, 57, 58, 59, 60). Only here and in Psalm 58 is there omission of details linking this particular psalm with incidents in David's life. The explanations of *miktâm* vary. Some have thought that it is a musical term whose meaning is now lost. In rabbinical sources the most common explanation was that it was formed by a prefix *mi-* together with the word *kétem*, 'gold', and meant a golden piece or one artistic in form or character. The oldest interpretation is that of the LXX, which translated it as *stêlographia*, an inscription on a pillar or monument. This is assuming that it comes from a verb meaning 'to inscribe', and therefore a *miktâm* is a song that is to be inscribed on a tablet or some similar surface.[1]

This is a song of confidence. While the psalm commences with a cry for help, it is quickly silenced by the sense of God's favour and the hope to which he looks forward. The psalm was probably written while David was an outlaw, when he was alienated from his property and exposed to false gods.

---

[1] *DCH*, V, p. 276, identifies this tentatively as designating a particular type or kind of psalm, especially in relation to writing on a tablet. Some want to read *miktâm* in the heading of Hezekiah's song in Isaiah 38:9, but the manuscript evidence overwhelmingly supports the reading *miktâv*, 'writing'. This heading is unique in the Old Testament in that it is the only case in which a poem within a *narrative* section has such a heading. See my discussion in *Isaiah: A Covenant to be Kept for the Sake of the Church* (Fearn: Christian Focus Publications, 2005), pp. 256-57.

He repudiates the thought of yielding allegiance to such gods, for his trust is firmly placed in Israel's Saviour.

The most difficult part of the psalm is verses 2-4a. Several perplexing points of translation have to be faced, and also the place of this section within the psalm as a whole.

1. An Opening Prayer (*v. 1*)

Keep me safe, O God, for in you I take refuge. As no details are given of any particular crisis in David's life it is best to take this appeal at the beginning of the psalm to be for God's continuing protection. Those who have already experienced this protection know how to pray, for, like David, they have taken refuge in him. This request is a favourite with him (see Pss. 7:1 and 11:1). The New Testament expands this concept. The Lord Jesus prayed that the believing community given to him should be 'kept' (John 17:11), while the assurance is given that the believer is 'preserved in Christ Jesus' (Jude 1).

2. The Words of an Idol Worshipper (*vv. 2-4a*)

I said to the LORD, 'You are my Lord; apart from you I have no good thing'. As for the saints who are in the land, they are the glorious ones in whom is all my delight. The sorrows of those will increase who run after other gods. There are problems in giving a good English translation of these verses and fitting them satisfactorily into the psalm as a whole.[2] The verb at the beginning of verse 2 is not first person singular (as given in the NIV, '*I* said'), but second person singular ('*you* (fem.) said').[3] The following comments assume that the words are those of an idol worshipper who claimed allegiance to the LORD but who followed other gods. He tried to maintain a

---

[2] The note in A. F. Kirkpatrick, *The Book of Psalms*, pp. 74-75 remains an excellent summary of different approaches to these verses, supplemented by the footnotes in BHS, p. 1097. See also R. Bratcher and W. Reyburn, *A Translator's Handbook to the Book of Psalms* (New York: UBS, 1991), p. 140-41.

[3] Though many manuscripts do have *'āmartî*, 'I said', the harder reading is *'āmart*, 'you (fem. sing.) said'. The object addressed has then to be 'my soul' (as expressly supplied in Pss. 42:6 and 43:5). This would result in a translation very near to the NIV rendering. If the MT consonantal text is retained but the vocalisation changed to *'āmartā*, then the verb is 2nd pers. masc., 'you (m.) have said'.

spoken commitment to the LORD ('my Lord') and a claim that all his goodness was to be found in him ('apart from you I have no good thing'). However, the reality was that he followed foreign gods, calling them in verse 3 'holy ones' and 'mighty ones'. Because of the parallelism between 'to the LORD' and 'to the holy ones', it is best to assume that the verb 'to say' is understood at the commencement of verse 3: '[You have said] to the holy ones'.[4] His real pleasure was solely in these heathen deities. The psalmist gives his verdict on all those who follow this example (v. 4a). The word rendered 'run' in the NIV is better taken as meaning 'acquire' or 'exchange' (cf. Ps. 106:20; Jer. 2:11).[5] Those who exchange the true God for idols will always increase their sorrows. This may be an allusion to the fertility rites practised in the heathen religions (cf. Isa. 57:7-8).

3. A Song of Confidence (*vv. 4b-6*)

I will not pour out their libations of blood or take up their names on my lips (*v. 4b*). Heathen worship holds no attraction for a true believer. David says emphatically that he will not share in their false sacrifices, nor even take their names on his lips. He will shun any association that might link him with such false beliefs.

LORD, you have assigned me my portion and my cup; you have made my lot secure. The boundary lines have fallen for me in pleasant places; surely I have a delightful inheritance (*vv. 5-6*). Here is the reaffirmation of the blessings that the LORD had given him, and which stand in such contrast to the sorrows that the idol worshipper experiences (v. 4a). 'Portion and cup' refers to the overflowing bounty that God had given him. The imagery is related to that concerning God's provision for the Levites (Num. 18:20; Deut. 10:9; 18:1-2). His allocated territory was certain, and the places where the lines had been marked for him were pleasant. He is not speaking

---

[4] This is the viewpoint of P. C. Craigie, *Psalms 1-50*, p. 155.
[5] See *DCH*, V, p. 167. While there is evidence pointing to a verb *mâhâr*, 'to acquire', there is none confirming the suggestion in *DCH*, that this may be a verb 'to serve'.

of an earthly inheritance, such as the tribes received, but of God's gift of himself.

3. The Reward of Confidence (*vv. 7-11*)
The psalmist breaks into a song of thanksgiving for the wisdom that has come to him from the LORD. **I will praise the LORD, who counsels me; even at night my heart instructs me. I have set the LORD always before me. Because he is at my right hand, I will not be shaken** (*vv. 7-8*). The NIV rendering 'praise' is an unnecessary alteration as the Hebrew verb is 'to bless' (*ᵃvârêk*, 'I will bless'), though in this type of context 'bless', with God as the object, is not significantly different from the verb 'to praise' (*hâlal* Pi.). 'At night time' (or possibly the plural form in Hebrew, *lêlôt*, denotes dark nights) he considers and meditates on this instruction. True meditation is never with a blank mind, but is based on God's revealed word. 'Heart' is literally the kidneys, which the Hebrew people considered as the seat of the emotions.

Verse 8 gives further expression to the thought of refuge in verse 1. The LORD is always before his eyes, and he is ever at his right hand. There is no 'he' in the MT, but the context demands that 'the LORD' continues as the subject. The right hand is the position that is mentioned as the place of the helper (Pss. 109:31; 121:5). Because the LORD is with him, he knows assuredly that he will not be moved.

Safety with the LORD produces a further song of praise from David. **Therefore my heart is glad and my tongue rejoices; my body also will rest secure, because you will not abandon me to the grave, nor will you let your Holy One see decay** (*vv. 9-10*). Various synonyms, for 'I' (in addition to 'kidneys' in the previous verse) appear in these verses: 'my heart', 'my glory' (the NIV follows the LXX text and reads 'my tongue'),[6] 'my flesh', and 'my soul' (NIV 'me'). David is not separating soul from body, but simply indicating that the whole person

---

[6] Though the LXX has *hê glôssa mou* ('my tongue'), no Hebrew text has this reading. A different suggestion, that *kewôdî*, 'my glory', be revocalised as *kewêdî*, 'my liver', has greater merit, as this would add 'liver' to the accumulation of references to bodily parts. See R. L. Harris in *TWOT*, 1, p. 427.

is living securely. The verbs in this verse are awkward (the first, a perfect; the second, a *vav* consecutive; the third, an imperfect), but in the context the NIV rendering is perfectly legitimate.[7] Verse 10 occupies a special place in biblical thought because it is quoted in reference to Jesus' resurrection. David is asserting that the LORD will not abandon his life to Sheol, nor let his faithful one (i.e. David) see corruption. He knows that his prayer of verse 1 ('help me') is answered and that he will not die, or alternatively, that he will be preserved from a premature death. But David also speaks prophetically by the Holy Spirit and looks to the resurrection of the Messiah. His eye is on one of his descendants (see Acts. 2:27) and his words have a far deeper meaning than the surface reading of them would suggest. They pointed to the fact that the Christ would not be abandoned in the grave nor his body see corruption (Acts 2:31).

You have made known to me the path of life; you will fill me with joy in your presence, with eternal pleasures at your right hand (*v. 11*). This final verse uses words and ideas already employed earlier in the psalm ('make known', 'life', 'joy', 'your presence', 'pleasure', 'evermore'). He wants to experience God's leading in the path through life (cf. 'the path of the righteous', Prov. 4:18; and 'the path of peace', Luke 1:79). Fullness of joy is to be found where the LORD reveals his presence (cf. Pss. 4:7; 21:6), and the pleasant places and things (see v. 6) from the LORD's hand will last right through life. Hence 'lasting pleasures' would be a preferable translation to the NIV's 'eternal pleasures'.

---

[7] Two Hebrew manuscripts read the impf. *yismach* instead of *sâmach* in the opening clause, but this seems to be an attempt to conform the text to what was perceived as the more normal verbal aspect.

Psalm 17

A prayer of David.

A psalm such as this shows how strongly the covenantal hope supported troubled and persecuted believers in the Old Testament period. The psalmist calls on God and asks for a further display of covenantal mercy, such as God showed in acts of deliverance at the time of the Exodus. There is dependence upon words from the Song of the Sea (Exod. 15:1-18) and also from the Song of Moses (Deut. 32). There are also many points of connection between Psalms 16 and 17. Some of these are: the prayer, 'keep me' (16:1; 17:8); communion with God at night (16:7; 17:3); the use of the Hebrew word *'ēl* for God in prayer (16:1; 17:6); the reference to the right hand of God (16:8; 17:7, 14); and the pleasures of God's presence (16:11; 17:15). The two psalms may well form a pair composed near the end of David's life.

1. A Prayer from an Innocent Person (*vv. 1-5*)
Hear, O LORD, my righteous plea; listen to my cry. Give ear to my prayer – it does not rise from deceitful lips. May my vindication come from you; may your eyes see what is right (*vv. 1-2*). The request that David makes is given in three forms: 'hear', 'listen', and 'give ear'. Likewise his description of his plea is threefold: '[my] righteous [plea]'; 'my cry'; and 'my prayer'. The varied language draws attention immediately to the intensity of his requests and the deep need in which he found himself. He disclaims any deceitfulness on his part. This type of protestation of innocence is common to the Psalter (cf. 18:20-24; 26:1). These should not be understood as self-righteous claims

to sinless perfection. They are affirmations that the writers were essentially devoted to God, that they were innocent of the slanderous accusations of their enemies, and hence they were worthy of God's protection. The psalmist knows that right judgment will come from the LORD[1] and he is quite prepared to leave his life open before his all-seeing eye. He is willing to have sentence passed by his judge.

Though you probe my heart and examine me at night, though you test me, you will find nothing; I have resolved that my mouth will not sin (*v. 3*). David claims that all of God's testing, however probing it may be (two of the terms, 'probe' [*bâchan*] and 'test' [*tsâraf*], are from metallurgy), will find no dross in his life. He knew the dangers of the sins of the tongue, as he was the victim of accusations. Yet he set himself to refrain from transgressing with his mouth. The final clause in the verse has received various explanations, though the overall meaning is clear enough.[2]

As for the deeds of men – by the word of your lips I have kept myself from the ways of the violent. My steps have held to your paths; my feet have not slipped (*vv. 4-5*). The psalmist isolates himself from the wicked for, in contrast to them, he has kept to God's word and his steps have followed his paths. Attention to the divine revelation has kept him in a right way. His enemies were clearly violent in action as well as in word. By following God's directions he had shunned their way of life and had not deviated from God's paths. The idea of following certain paths is often tied in with the concept of the feet slipping (for examples, see Pss. 38:16; 94:18). When the verb 'to slip' is preceded by a negative, it conveys the idea of absolute certainly and dependability.

---

[1] The Hebrew word *mishpât* has many nuances, but most common is the use here to denote a judgment issued by a court, or by God as the great judge over all. While the translation 'judgment' would have been acceptable, yet the NIV 'vindication' respects the context where the idea of a favourable judgment is present.

[2] The MT has the word *zammotî*, which seems to be an irregular inf. of the verb *zâmam*, plus suff. 1 sing. This gives a translation: 'my thoughts do not extend beyond my mouth'. The NIV follows the LXX which presupposes a verbal form *zimmâtî*, 'I have determined'.

2. A Fresh Appeal in the Face of Danger (*vv. 6-12*)

From pressing dangers the psalmist turns again to God. **I call on you, O God, for you will answer me; give ear to me and hear my prayer** (*v. 6*). The 'I' with which this verse begins is emphatic. He has just described himself in the previous verses and he now calls urgently to his God, whom he knows will answer. Many times the psalmists refer to calling upon God, and then receiving answers. God also invites his people to call on him, and promises an answer (Ps. 91:15). Certainty about this encourages expectancy. The second half of the verse is virtually an abbreviated form of verse 1. 'Give ear to me' corresponds to 'give ear to my prayer', while 'hear my prayer' is parallel to 'hear ... my righteous plea'.

Show the wonder of your great love, you who save by your right hand those who take refuge in you from their foes. Keep me as the apple of your eye; hide me in the shadow of your wings from the wicked who assail me, from my mortal enemies who surround me (*vv. 7-9*). The basis of his appeal is the covenantal bond (*chªsâdekâ*, 'your gracious acts of commitment'),[3] which he wants to be revealed as wonderful.[4] He longs for a fresh manifestation of God's power and redeeming mercy as was shown during the Exodus. The language here echoes that in the Song of the Sea (Exod. 15:6-7, 11-13). Historical recollection often forms the basis for present prayer in the Psalms. David knew that God saved those who take their refuge in him. The expression 'the LORD's right hand', used three times in the Song of the Sea (vv. 6 [2×] and 12), denotes his omnipotence and power to rescue his people from their enemies. It forms the theme of praise in many psalms (cf. 18:35; 44:3; 48:10; 98:1).

---

[3] The singular, 'your mercy', is more common, but the plural form as in this verse, 'your mercies', does occur (see for example, Pss. 89:2; 107:7; Isa. 63:7). I have tried in the translation above to bring out the force of the plural by using the expression 'gracious acts of commitment', because the appeal is to the great acts of God in redeeming his people.

[4] It is hard to be sure whether the verb that commences this verse is the Hi. of *pâlâh* or *pâlâʾ*. NIV deviates from the MT (*hiflêh*, 'treat with distinction'), but is following the well-attested variant verbal form (*haflêʾ*, 'do wonders'). See P. C. Craigie, *Psalms 1-50*, p. 160.

Allusion to the Exodus continues in verse 8. God found Israel in the wilderness and guarded her as the apple of his eye (Deut. 32:10). The idiom for 'apple of the eye' used there of the people as a whole is taken over here, when an individual Israelite prays for himself. The thought of being protected under the LORD's wings is probably taken from Deuteronomy 32:11, whence the imagery of the eagle is introduced. God provides protection from all the dangers (cf., for use of the idea of God's wings, Pss. 36:7; 57:1; 61:4; 63:7; 91:4). The danger is from enemies (also called 'the wicked') who attack his life. They come against him with murderous intent.

They close up their callous hearts, and their mouths speak with arrogance. They have tracked me down, they now surround me, with eyes alert, to throw me to the ground. They are like a lion hungry for prey, like a great lion crouching in cover (*vv. 10-12*). A fuller description is given of these enemies. They shut up their hearts. The Hebrew text says 'they shut up their fat'. Probably this is another reference to Deuteronomy 32 and specifically to God's Jeshurun (Israel), who grew fat and kicked (Deut. 32:15).[5] The idea of rebelliousness carries over here, for the enemies will not bow before God's majesty and they attack his servant David. He felt surrounded on every side (v. 11) for they were waiting for their chance to overthrow him. The most threatening enemy is singled out in verse 12 (cf. with the use of the plural in verses 10-11), or perhaps the leader of the band. He is likened to a crouching lion which is ready to leap out at his prey from his secret hiding place. The words 'lion' and 'young lion' (not 'great lion' as in NIV) are often used in parallel (see Amos 3:4; Isa. 31:4). It is not surprising that the New Testament depicts the devil as a roaring lion (1 Pet. 5:8).

3. Another Urgent Prayer (*vv. 13-15*)
Rise up, O LORD, confront them, bring them down; rescue me from the wicked by your sword (*v. 13*). The military language,

---

[5] The word 'Jeshurun' only occurs in Deut. 32:15; 33:5, 26, and in Isa. 44:2. It could be a diminutive, 'my little upright one', but no example exists in biblical Hebrew of a diminutive ending in – *un*. As a derivative of the root *yâshar* it probably means to be upright, so marking Israel off from the surrounding nations as the nation to which God's law was given. Cf. Deut. 4:5-8.

already noted in Psalms 3:7; 7:6; 10:12, is again used by David. He appeals with urgency to his divine protector to come as a warrior ('your sword') and subdue his enemy, delivering him from his enemy, rescuing him from his clutches.

O LORD, by your hand save me from such men, from men of this world whose reward is in this life. You still the hunger of those you cherish; their sons have plenty, and they store up wealth for their children (*v. 14*). The enemies are described as being 'men of this world' who will only know rewards in this life. They will know nothing of having the LORD as their portion, which is the condition of the righteous (Ps. 16:5). The New Testament speaks of the same type of people who belong to the world (John 15:19), who are people of this world (Luke 16:8), and whose mind is on earthly things (Phil. 3:19). From such men David seeks rescue by God's hand (cf. the use of 'right hand' in verse 7).

The final part of this verse speaks of God's blessings on his cherished ones. They have plenty to eat, they have many children (taking 'sons' as the object of the verb), and are able even to pass on their superabundance to their children. However, such people may have an abundance of earthly riches, but they are not rich towards God (Luke 12:21).

And I – in righteousness I will see your face; when I awake, I will be satisfied with seeing your likeness (*v. 15*). The contrast with the worldly men of verse 14 is most obvious. Any satisfaction they get has to be in this life. For David, there was the prospect of satisfaction beyond the grave, because he gives us in this verse a glimpse of eternity. The language is similar to that used by Moses when speaking of his relationship with the LORD (Num. 12:8). David grasps something, however tenuous, of a doctrine of resurrection, which is spoken of elsewhere as an awaking from sleep (see Isa. 26:19; Dan. 12:2). The Greek LXX translation clearly read the verse in this way in pre-Christian time for it added the words 'in the vision of your glory'. God's actual presence would then be his joy and satisfaction. It is the pure in heart who will see God (Matt. 5:8).

Psalm 18

For the director of music. Of David the servant of the LORD. *He sang to the* LORD *the words of this song when the* LORD *delivered him from the hand of all his enemies and from the hand of Saul. He said:*

This psalm is tied into historical circumstances both by its title and by the fact that it occurs in a duplicate form in 2 Samuel 22:1-51. Because of its length, as the longest hymn in the Psalter, and also because of questions relating to its parallel in 2 Samuel, several comments need to be made before proceeding to its exegesis.

1. The essential text is the same in the two songs, though there are numerous minor differences. These should not be exaggerated, however, for the general spirit of the two songs remains identical. Numerous discussions already exist noting the differences, with extensive notes on Hebrew vocabulary, grammar and textual questions.[1]

2. In spite of all that has been written on this subject, it is impossible to assert with confidence which is the earlier song, or whether both come from the same author. The two texts confront the reader without sufficient clues to come to definitive answers on questions relating to the origin and transmission of these songs.

3. The heading of both Psalm 18 and 2 Samuel 22 place the songs in a historical context – 'when the LORD delivered him [David] from the hand of all his enemies and from the hand of Saul'. In the texts explicit reference to David only occurs at the end (Ps. 18:50; 2 Sam. 22:51). In 2 Samuel, the song follows an account of Saul's death and then a summary of various

---

[1] For detailed listing of the variations in the Hebrew text, see F. Delitzsch, *Psalms*, I, pp. 269-78; F. M. Cross and D. N. Freedman, 'A Royal Song of Thanksgiving: 2 Samuel 22 = Psalm 18', *JBL* 72, 1 (1953), pp. 15-34; P. C. Craigie, *Psalms 1-50*, pp. 168-71.

campaigns against the Philistines (2 Sam. 21:15-22). It is quite possible that this song was utilised in celebratory worship after a series of incidents in which David was delivered by the LORD. The real enemy, in any case, was death and the grave (Ps. 18:5-6).

4. In form it is similar to victory songs like Exodus 15:1-18 and Judges 5, though the details of any specific victory are not given. David achieved many victories, and this song seems to be a royal thanksgiving psalm when he looks back on all that the LORD did for him. The pictorial language makes it a graphic description of God's help, and how God preserved David for, and established him in, his kingship.

5. A strong connection exists between this song and that of Hannah (1 Sam. 2:1-10). The central theme of Hannah's song is expanded in this one. Each finishes with reference to the LORD's support of his anointed king. The difference in Psalm 18 is that it post-dates the covenant with David (2 Sam. 7) and hence the reference to David's successors ('to David and his descendants for ever', verse 50).

6. The pattern of the psalm is straightforward. It starts and finishes with reference to God as the rock of Israel (vv. 1-2 and 46-50), having therefore a prologue and an epilogue. The centre of the psalm is composed of two main passages, verses 3-30 and 31-45.

1. An Introductory Song of Praise (*vv. 1-2*)

I love you, O LORD, my strength (*v. 1*). The psalm begins with an unusual verb for 'love' (Hebrew *râcham*, Qal 1 sing.), which in the form used here occurs nowhere else in the Old Testament. While not the most common usage, the verb is applied to a mother's love for her baby (Isa. 49:15), or of a father's love for his children (Ps. 103:13). Much more frequent is another form of the verb (Hebrew Pi.) that occurs over thirty times with God as the subject. David expresses his heartfelt love to the LORD (cf. Ps. 116:1 where the more common verb *'âhav* occurs) and confesses that he is his 'strength', i.e. his strong helper. This is the first of eight titles for God that are clustered together, all with the personal suffix 'my'. This fact points to the faith from which David speaks and of the bond between himself and the LORD.

The LORD is my rock, my fortress and my deliverer; my God is my rock, in whom I take refuge. He is my shield and the horn of my salvation, my stronghold (*v. 2*). The first two titles point to the majesty of God as David's hiding place. He has his refuge in the cliff (Hebrew uses a different word for 'rock' later in the verse) and it is a fortress for him. Linked with those first two titles, the third one could be expected to be 'a place of refuge', but the vowels in the Hebrew text make it the participle 'my deliverer' (Hebrew *m^efalêt* instead of *miflât*). 'Rock' is an old title for God (Deut. 32:4, 15, 18, 31, 37), stressing God's permanence and the security he affords those who trust in him. To call him 'my shield' immediately brings to mind God's words to Abraham (Gen. 15:1), a passage in which Abraham is reassured of God's protection.[2] 'Horn' is descriptive of power in battle (and only here is it a title for God), and finally 'stronghold' completes the list by giving added emphasis to God's protective care for his servant.

2. The Account of God's Salvation (vv. 3-19)
The two major sections of the psalm are introduced with a note of praise that is in essence a summary of their main theme (vv. 3 and 30).

a) *Praise for Redeeming Grace* (*v. 3*) **I call to the LORD, who is worthy of praise, and I am saved from my enemies**. God is worthy of praise (the Hebrew word, *m^ehullâl*, comes from the same root as 'Hallelujah'), and David expresses his settled conviction that he can call on God and he will answer. He knows, and what follows in this psalm is a testimony to the fact, that God can save him from his enemies.

---

[2] It is possible that the Hebrew consonants in this word 'shield' (*m-g-n*) may denote a 'donor' or 'giver'. If this meaning applies here, it would suggest that the LORD was to reward Abraham greatly. See M. Kessler, 'The "Shield" of Abraham?' *VT* 14 (1964), pp. 494-97; G. Rendsburg, 'Notes on Genesis XV', *VT* 42 (1992), pp. 266-72. The biblical passages listed in *DCH*, V, p. 134, should also be noted.

b) *A Divine Appearance (vv. 4-19)* The dangers that David has faced are described, before a description is given of God's saving work. **The cords of death entangled me; the torrents of destruction overwhelmed me. The cords of the grave coiled around me; the snares of death confronted me** (*vv. 4-5*). Death came very near to David. He felt tied by its cords and terrified by its torrents. The Hebrew text says 'torrents of Belial'. 'Belial' occurs in Deuteronomy 13:13 and 15:9. Various derivations of 'Belial' have been suggested. Jerome held that it meant 'without a yoke', and hence signified 'lawless'. Another common interpretation is that it means 'without profit', 'worthless'. In more recent times it has been proposed that it is an abstract noun meaning 'destructiveness'. This last definition certainly fits the context here, where 'torrents of destruction' is paralleled by 'the cords of Sheol' and 'the snares of the grave'.[3] The cords of Sheol (NIV 'grave') were pulling David there and he felt entrapped by death. David must have felt his life to be in danger for many years, and in this poetic description he expresses his feelings in the face of constant deadly situations.

In my distress I called to the LORD; I cried to my God for help. From his temple he heard my voice; my cry came before him, into his ears (*v. 6*). The prayer of faith comes from his lips. He says, 'my God' (cf. v. 2). In his need he knew to turn to the God with whom he had a living relationship, and to him he makes his heartfelt cry. God heard from his 'temple', a word that describes both the place where God is honoured and worshipped, and where he sits enthroned in majesty (cf. Isa. 6:1-7). The psalmist was assured that when he 'cried for help' his 'cry' had come to the LORD's ears (the verb and the noun come from the same Hebrew root, *sh-v-ʿ*). The description of his rescue that follows is given in poetic terms as a theophany, i.e. a visible manifestation of God. God came to him in a way similar to his coming to Sinai of old (Exod. 19:16-19), or to

---

[3] For literature on the subject, see the references in *DCH*, II, pp. 608-9, especially J. A. Emerton, 'Sheol and the Sons of Belial', *VT* 37 (1987), pp. 214-18.

Elijah on his visit there (1 Kings 19:11-12).[4] Similar descriptions of a theophany are given in Psalms 68:7-8 and 77:14-20. God's great acts of salvation are pictured in similar terms by psalmist and prophet alike (Ps. 97; Hab. 3).[5] The psalmist makes the connection between his experience and that of the children of Israel in days long past. He is the second Moses who has seen God's great redemptive work as at the Red Sea (see v. 16).

The earth trembled and quaked, and the foundations of the mountains shook; they trembled because he was angry. Smoke rose from his nostrils; consuming fire came from his mouth, burning coals blazed out of it (*vv. 7-8*). First, there is an earthquake, and in Hebrew poetical style the first two verbs are similar in sound (*vattigʿash vattirʿash hâʾârets*), the assonance adding to the overall effect. The first of these verbs is repeated at the end of the verse (*vayitgâʿªshû*). The expression, 'the foundation of the mountains,' is borrowed from Deuteronomy 32:22. God had heard his servant's cry and was ready to do battle with those who were attacking him. His anger was aroused and he was preparing to come as he had done at Mount Sinai. The description points to a powerful sense of God's presence. The divine warrior comes to display his wrath against his, and the psalmist's, enemies.

He parted the heavens and came down; dark clouds were under his feet. He mounted the cherubim and flew; he soared on the wings of the wind. He made darkness his covering, his canopy around him—the dark rain clouds of the sky (*vv. 9-11*). The theophany moves on from the earthquake to the picture of dark clouds enveloping the earth (cf. Deut. 5:22). The heavens are described as though they were a curtain that could be split to allow God to come down. He brought storm clouds down, while he himself flew on cherubim. Because

---

[4] The English versions fail to mark the connection between Moses' and Elijah's experience at Mt Sinai by translating the opening of 1 Kings 19:9 as 'and there he came to *a* cave'. The MT has '*the* cave', which seems to point to the cleft of the rock in which Moses was placed as the glory of the LORD passed by.

[5] For some apposite comment on how this psalm and other similar poetic passages far surpass narrative description, see Elmer Martens, *God's Design: A Focus on Old Testament Theology* (Grand Rapids: Baker Books, 1994), p. 164.

of the parallelism in verses 9-10 'cherubim' may here be a poetic term for clouds. In the midst of the storm the LORD was there, controlling all the forces at his disposal. He comes with majesty to bring deliverance.

Out of the brightness of his presence clouds advanced, with hailstones and bolts of lightning. The LORD thundered from heaven; the voice of the Most High resounded. He shot his arrows and scattered the enemies, great bolts of lightning and routed them. The valleys of the sea were exposed and the foundations of the earth laid bare at your rebuke, O LORD, at the blast of breath from your nostrils (*vv. 12-15*). The storm now breaks. Thunder and lightning come from the LORD's presence. The light that streams from the LORD becomes a consuming fire for his enemies. The bolts of lightning are likened to a warrior's arrows with which he attacks and routs the enemies. The representation of the LORD's voice as being thunder is common in the Old Testament (cf. Ps. 29:3-4; Job 37:2-5; Joel 3:16). The use of the divine title 'Most High' in verse 13 serves to designate how exalted he is over all, including the enemies. The NIV translation deviates from the MT at the end of verse 13 in that it omits the repeated words 'with hailstones and bolts of lightning'. Though some Hebrew manuscripts and the LXX do not repeat these words, yet the repetition reinforces the idea of God's dramatic intervention in human affairs as if it had the suddenness and power of a mighty storm.[6] Earth experiences turmoil as God's breath pours forth as a storm. Even the very foundations of the earth are uncovered as the storm blows upon it. The language in verse 15 is reminiscent of that in the Song of the Sea in Exodus 15:8.

He reached down from on high and took hold of me; he drew me out of deep waters. He rescued me from my powerful enemy, from my foes, who were too strong for me. They confronted me in the day of my disaster, but the LORD was my support. He brought me out into a spacious place;

---

[6] The repetition is retained in other modern versions such as RSV, NASB, NKJV, and ESV. The fact that the repetition does not occur in 2 Samuel is not decisive, as the two passages are not identical at many points.

he rescued me because he delighted in me (*vv. 16-19*). The hand of the LORD was then stretched out to save David. The figurative language describes a divine arm that reaches down to rescue David from the overwhelming flood. At the end of verse 16 the theophany ceases and the description then reverts to an ordinary one. The LORD delivered him from his powerful enemy. This is probably a reference to Saul, while the plural 'my foes' may very well include Saul's henchmen. When he was confronted by them he found that the LORD was his 'support'. In the context the Hebrew word used (*mishʿân*) suggests not only support or stay but also provider. He found that the LORD brought him out of his narrow and confined situation into a place where there was so much liberty. To be in 'a spacious place' denotes freedom from the restraints and oppression that he had experienced earlier. Hence this song may come from a later time in David's life when he could look back on the troubles he endured in years past. God's delight in his servant was because he was indeed his anointed kingly servant. He was the man after God's own heart (1 Sam. 13:14), the man of his choice. This was no arrogant boast for he was the man with whom God had made a covenant promising him an enduring dynasty (2 Sam. 7, and cf. also the wording of verse 50 of this psalm). The following verses that deal with David's integrity before the LORD point to his life and obedience as being also part of the reason for God's delight in him.

c) *The Goodness of God (vv. 20-30)* **The LORD has dealt with me according to my righteousness; according to the cleanness of my hands he has rewarded me** (*v. 20*). David is not claiming sinless perfection (see the comments on Psalm 17:1) but is asserting his own integrity before the LORD (cf. Paul's words in Acts 24:16, 'a conscience void of offence toward God and men'). He was walking in righteousness and his hands were clean. According to his character God had rewarded him. Even the king was not exempt from showing obedience to the LORD's commands. That is why it was stipulated that the king had to have a copy of the law for himself (Deut. 17:18).

For I have kept the ways of the LORD; I have not done evil by turning from my God. All his laws are before me; I have not turned away from his decrees (*vv. 21-22*). He had not turned aside from the ways of the LORD, but had guarded his steps carefully. Never had he acted rebelliously and departed from his God. This is an unusual use of the verb 'to commit wrongdoing' (*râshaʿ*), but in the context it clearly does mean turning away from God to commit evil deeds. The judgments and ordinances of the LORD were constantly before him, as if placarded before his eyes. At no time had he turned away from God's commands and consciously set his requirements aside (cf. Ps. 101:2).

I have been blameless before him and have kept myself from sin. The LORD has rewarded me according to my righteousness, according to the cleanness of my hands in his sight (*vv. 23-24*). The word 'blameless' should not be read as if it meant 'sinless'. It speaks rather of the legal obedience of a covenantal servant, and it reappears later in this psalm in verses 25, 30, and 32. It denotes the wholehearted dedication of a person to a sanctified life. The repeated reference to guarding is a reminder of the watch that the Bible teaches believers to have over their lives ('Keep yourself pure', 1 Tim. 5:22; 'keep oneself from being polluted by the world,' James 1:27). Verse 24 repeats the thought of verse 20. Such repetition of the opening thought of a section at its close was a typical poetic device that calls attention to a major idea or theme.

To the faithful you show yourself faithful, to the blameless you show yourself blameless, to the pure you show yourself pure, but to the crooked you show yourself shrewd. You save the humble but bring low those whose eyes are haughty (*vv. 25-27*). These verses confirm what has been already said of God's character and his way of dealing with his servants. To the faithful covenant servant (*châsîd*) God shows himself merciful (*châsad*, Hitp.).[7] To the man of integrity, he acts with integrity towards him. To the pure, God responds with a demonstration of his own purity. Other Old

---

[7] It is only here and in 2 Samuel 22:26 that the verb occurs, as over against the 246 times that the noun *chésed* appears in the Old Testament.

Testament passages give the full doctrine. God dealt with Israel in terms of his covenant and thus not according to their sins (Ps. 103:10; cf. also Ps. 143:2).

After these assertions about the godly, one assertion is dedicated to the ungodly with an introduction that sets it over against what has preceded ('*but*, to the crooked ...'). It may not seem good to call God 'shrewd' (*pâtal*, Hitp.). The Hebrew word can have a more neutral meaning closer to 'inscrutable'. David is saying that God will deal with the person who mocks him over his covenantal dealings, just as he has already described God's dealings with his own personal enemies. This section of the psalm points to the way in which God deals with a person according to his/her character. It is only divine grace that makes the difference in God's attitude to the godly and the ungodly, and that, therefore, determines the abiding destiny of both at the final judgment (Rev. 22:11).

You save the humble but bring low those whose eyes are haughty. You, O LORD, keep my lamp burning; my God turns my darkness into light (*vv. 27-28*). A summary statement is given in verse 27 that ties the themes together about which David has been speaking. God shows his gracious character in delivering the afflicted, whereas the proud and arrogant are humbled by him. 'He mocks proud mockers but gives grace to the humble' (Prov. 3:34), words that are quoted by Peter with the added instruction: 'Humble yourselves, therefore, under God's mighty hand, that he may lift you up in due time' (1 Pet. 5:6). David goes on to describe his deliverance in terms of God providing a lamp for him, and giving him light in his darkness. A special application of the idea of David's lamp is made in 1 Kings 11:36 when God promised, through Ahijah the prophet, that David would always have a lamp. The same promise is repeated in 1 Kings 15:4 and 2 Kings 8:19.[8]

With your help I can advance against a troop; with my God I can scale a wall. As for God, his way is perfect; the

---

[8] Cf. also the words of David's men when David was rescued when in danger from a Philistine: 'Never again will you go out with us to battle, so that the lamp of Israel will not be extinguished' (2 Sam. 21:17). For further information on the varied Old Testament use of the word 'lamp' (Hebrew *nêr*), see *TDOT*, X, pp. 14-24.

word of the LORD is flawless. He is a shield for all who take refuge in him (*vv. 29-30*). Now David returns to the theme of the opening of the psalm and specifically to God's help for him in his battles. With confidence he could attack an enemy troop (or possibly, following NIV margin, 'can run through a barricade'), or leap over a wall. The thoughts that have preceded lead David to praise his God. He extols the LORD's ways, i.e. his actions, his dealings with David, and proclaims them as complete. Along with his actions his word is mentioned. It has been tested (the word comes from metalworking), and almost the same language is used of God's spoken word in Psalm 119:140. The final statement in this section is virtually a brief summary of verse 2. For all who, like David, put their confidence in the LORD and trust him as their refuge, he proves to be a shield.

3. The Character of God (*vv. 31-45*)
David as king had good reason to praise the LORD for the help he provided him. He does so in words extolling him as the only God, and the one who so blessed him during his military campaigns.

a) *Praise for Redeeming Grace (vv. 31-32).* **For who is God besides the LORD? And who is the Rock except our God? It is God who arms me with strength and makes my way perfect** (*vv. 31-32*). As with the section beginning at verse 3, this section also commences on a note of praise that virtually summarises the section. It is a statement of the creed of Israel with its implicit monotheism.[9] The rhetorical questions are an important way of emphasising that there was no other God except the LORD (cf. the way Isaiah, in particular, uses similar language and style in chaps. 40-48). The style here is typical of hymnic sections of the Old Testament, especially when descriptions of God's character and work are given. As in Isaiah 40:21-22, three clauses follow the questions, each beginning with a participle:

---

[9] This is a counterpart to the Islamic claim, 'There is no God but Allah', and preceding it by many centuries. Even the New Testament contains assertions that pre-date the Islamic one. See particularly, 1 Corinthians 8:4, 'there is no God but one.'

31 For who is God besides the LORD?
   And who is the Rock except our God?
32 It is God
   the one who arms me (*ham*ᵉ*'azz*ᵉ*rênî*) with strength
   who makes (*m*ᵉ*shavveh*) my feet like the feet of a deer;
   who trains (*m*ᵉ*lammêd*) my hands for battle.

The use of this pattern helps to draw attention to the concepts, as David explains why God is incomparable.[10] The language concerning God as a 'rock' has already been used by David in verse 2, in dependence on Deuteronomy 32. This is one of many references to Deuteronomy throughout this song. The word for God (Hebrew *'ᵉlôah*) is a relatively uncommon word, but it seems to be employed to give variation in the use of the divine names.[11] God had indeed strengthened David for his battles and made his way perfect. This last expression must here mean that God had so assisted David that his life turned out well and especially that his kingship was a fulfilment of God's purposes.

He makes my feet like the feet of a deer; he enables me to stand on the heights. He trains my hands for battle; my arms can bend a bow of bronze (*vv. 33-34*). Like a swift and sure-footed deer he was able to escape his enemies and stand upon the heights, i.e. upon mountain strongholds he had captured. Almost the same expression comes at the conclusion of the Book of Habakkuk (Hab. 3:19). God gave to David the physical strength he needed to engage in battle. This line from verse 34 is used again in Psalm 144:1. So strong was David that he could even use a bow that required considerably more than normal strength.

You give me your shield of victory, and your right hand sustains me; you stoop down to make me great. You broaden the path beneath me, so that my ankles do not turn

---

[10] A further grammatical point reinforces the use of the participles. Following the first two, the Hebrew text uses *imperfect* forms: *vayyittên … yaʿᵃmîdênî*, that have the sense of present time, 'and makes my way' and 'he enables me to stand'. For this grammatical point, see DIHG-S, § 113(e).

[11] The word *'ᵉlôah* occurs 57× in the Old Testament, mainly in the Book of Job (41×). It appears in early poetry (Deut. 32:15, 17), but then seems to have dropped out of use until the time of the exile and after. For further information, see *TWOT*, 1, pp. 43-44.

(*vv. 35-36*). David recognises that it was not his own strength that won him victories. God had provided for him a 'shield' (see comment on verse 2 and the footnote) and constantly supported his servant (cf. the use of 'right hand' in Ps. 16:8). The last part of verse 35 is a remarkable anthropomorphic expression, for David says that God's condescension has made him great. God had stooped to David and taken a humble shepherd boy and made him king. All of God's acts of mercy to his children and expressions of his condescension came to fullest expression in Jesus' coming in human flesh. David's path was made plain and broad before him so that he was able to go along it without impediment and also he did not suffer any injury.

b) *Complete Victory (vv. 37-42).* **I pursued my enemies and overtook them; I did not turn back till they were destroyed. I crushed them so that they could not rise; they fell beneath my feet** (*vv. 37-38*). In a psalm of thanksgiving for his victories, David now details some of the events surrounding them. He had pursued his enemies and did not turn back till his mission was completed. His armies had so smitten the enemies that they were unable to arise, and hence they were in subjection under his feet.

You armed me with strength for battle; you made my adversaries bow at my feet. You made my enemies turn their backs in flight, and I destroyed my foes (*vv. 39-40*). Once again David acknowledges that his victories did not come from his own strength or from that of his army. It was the LORD who had girded him for war (see verse 32 for the earlier use of the same idiom and using the same verb, *'âzar*, Pi.), and his opponents have been made to prostrate themselves before him. The word used for his 'adversaries' can mean opponents in general, though it could also designate rebellious subjects (see its use in Deut. 28:7 for enemies of Israel). Verse 40 contains a Hebrew idiom that is not brought out in the NIV translation. The meaning is that God gave the enemies into his hands so that he could put his foot on their necks. This was the sign of victory in the Near East. The AV rendering is correct: 'Thou hast also given me the necks of my enemies.'

An illustration of the practice is provided by Joshua's action regarding the kings of Jerusalem, Hebron, Jarmuth, Lachish, and Eglon (Josh. 10:22-24; cf. also the prophecy concerning Judah that his hand would be on the neck of his enemies, Gen. 49:8). **They cried for help, but there was no one to save them — to the LORD, but he did not answer. I beat them as fine as dust borne on the wind; I poured them out like mud in the streets** (*vv. 41-42*). In their distress David's enemies prayed – presumably to their own gods – but no saviour appeared on the scene. In their extremity they prayed to the LORD.[12] While it is possible that the enemies were Saul and his supporters, the fact that they prayed to Israel's God does not necessarily mean that the enemies were people within Israel. At times of crisis heathen people used the name of the LORD in prayer (see Jonah 1:14). There was no answer from the LORD and David continued his attack until they were destroyed. The metaphors concerning 'dust' and 'mud' depict the definitive nature of David's victories.

c) *Kingdom Extension (vv. 43-45).* **You have delivered me from the attacks of the people; you have made me the head of nations; people I did not know are subject to me. As soon as they hear me, they obey me; foreigners cringe before me. They all lose heart; they come trembling from their strongholds** (*vv. 43-45*). David's victories had not only been internal to Israel but external as well. He subdued surrounding nations and so became their head. This meant that he was sovereign over them, hence the saying they were subject to him, i.e. they became his servants. It is not clear if the foreigners in verses 44-45 are those subdued through further foreign victories or those already conquered. Probably the former is correct. Kings like Tou of Hamath heard of David's victories and quickly made peace with him (2 Sam. 8:9-10). The accounts of David's battles were enough to cause them to come trembling from their strongholds. When David was succeeded by his

---

[12] The Hebrew text has ʿ*al yhwh*, whereas 2 Samuel 22:42 has ʾ*el yhwh*. No emendation is needed as the prepositions ʾ*el* and ʿ*al* were often used interchangeably.

son Solomon the territorial boundaries of Israel extended to the promised limits for the land (1 Kings 4:20-21, 25).

4. David's Doxology to the LORD (vv. 46-50)

Having reviewed his past victories, David now sings a triumphal song: **The LORD lives! Praise be to my Rock! Exalted be God my Saviour!** (v. 46). That truth was so evident from his past experience, for not only does the LORD live but he reveals that to his own believing people. This parallels the familiar words in the Psalter, 'the LORD reigns' (cf. Pss. 97:1; 99:1). It may also be a deliberate counter-assertion to the Canaanite cry regarding Baal, who, when he supposedly returned from the dead, was greeted with the words, 'For Baal the Mighty is alive, for the Prince, the Lord of the earth exists'.[13] Seeing that this is a statement it is probably best to take the following words as a statement too: 'My rock is worthy to be praised!' Likewise the third phrase: 'God my Saviour is exalted!' All three statements stem from David's own experience of the LORD.

He is the God who avenges me, who subdues nations under me, who saves me from my enemies. You exalted me above my foes; from violent men you rescued me (vv. 47-48). Vengeance is something that belongs to the LORD (Deut. 32:35), and room must be left for God's wrath (Rom. 12:19). The MT has the plural 'vengeances' denoting the judicial acts by which the LORD had vindicated David. Here he acknowledges that God had indeed avenged him, and that he had brought foreign nations under his sovereignty.[14] God was his Saviour who had also exalted him over all his enemies, and had not allowed those who attacked him with malicious intent to prevail.

Therefore I will praise you among the nations, O LORD; I will sing praises to your name (v. 49). Assuming that such foreign nations were brought under his authority, David

---

[13] *DOTT*, p. 131.
[14] For 'subdue', the MT has *vayadbêr*, whereas 2 Samuel 22:49 has *ûmôrîd*. Emendation is not necessary as this is probably *d-v-r* II, 'to destroy', 'to subdue'. See *DCH*, II, p. 396; Craigie's comments, *Psalms*, p. 171; and Dahood, *Psalms 1-50*, I, p. 118.

says that he will praise the LORD among the Gentiles. No attempt is made at self-aggrandisement. Rather, he wants to make public proclamation of what the LORD has done for him. Quotations from Deuteronomy 32:43, Psalm 117:1, and Isaiah 11:10 are used along with this verse in Romans 15:9-12 to show that participation of the Gentiles in gospel blessings was anticipated in the Old Testament.

He gives his king great victories; he shows unfailing kindness to his anointed, to David and his descendants forever (v. 50). The final verse of the psalm changes from first person ('I') to third person ('his anointed, 'David'). This could be a later addition by another inspired poet, or else David referred to himself in this way. Two things are said about the LORD. First, he had given and was still giving great victories to David. This may be another pointer to the fact that the psalm was composed much earlier than its position in 2 Samuel would suggest. Secondly, the LORD shows covenantal mercy to his anointed.[15] It cannot be doubted that 'his anointed' is defined by the word 'David' which follows. David was the anointed king to whom great promises were given concerning his seed (see 2 Sam. 7: 8-16). The mention of 'seed' points even to Christ in whom the promises to David's house find their ultimate fulfilment (Luke 1:30-33; Rom. 1:2-4). David, in his varied experiences set out in this song of thanksgiving, is a pointer to Jesus who bears the name 'Christ', 'anointed one'.

---

[15] The idiom here is 'to show covenantal mercy to' someone (ʿoseh chésed lᵉ). The phrase itself, and the use of the participle ʿoseh in particular, points to the enduring nature of the LORD's commitment to David and his descendants.

Psalm 19

For the director of music. A psalm of David.

God has manifested himself clearly. His great power is seen in the created world around us. But the revelation that comes from that display of his power is not in words. For revelation in words, we have to turn to the Scriptures, which are indeed the Word of God. Both forms of revelation are celebrated in this nineteenth psalm, though the focus is more on the wonder and beauty of God's Word. It begins with reference to the demonstration of God's power in the natural world before changing to the perfection of his law. That change is marked by the use of the covenantal name for God – 'Lord' (*yhwh*), used seven times in the second major section, while in the first it is absent. Instead, the general name 'God' (*'ēl*) is used in verse 1, followed by the appropriate personal pronouns in the following verses. The point is clearly that while natural revelation points to God, yet true knowledge only comes through the divinely given law. Sin causes distortion, and it is only through the aid of God's Spirit that we can see clearly God's revelation of himself in nature (cf. Paul's teaching in Romans 1:18-23).

1. God's Glory in Nature (*vv. 1-6*)

The beautifully balanced opening sentence sets the theme for the first section. **The heavens declare the glory of God; the skies proclaim the work of his hands** (*v. 1*). The first part of the verse has the subject ('the heavens'), the verb ('declare'), and the object ('the glory'). Then in typical Hebrew poetic style it has parallel expressions in the second half with the word order reversed (object, verb, subject). The created world declares in an ongoing way the glory of God. Its testimony is never finished. The second verse continues the same idea and does so with similar poetic artistry. **Day after day they pour forth speech; night after night they display knowledge** (*v. 2*). Day by day the message of creation bubbles forth.[1] Night by night the majesty of the stars is a witness to the creator. Creation cannot contain itself, but constantly proclaims the glory of God. The heavenly bodies are not divine (Deut. 4:19; 17:3), nor do they have control over human destiny.[2] **There is no speech or language where their voice is not heard. Their voice goes out into all the earth, their words to the ends of the world** (*vv. 3-4a*). Nowhere in the world is isolated from this message, for it penetrates everywhere. The voice of creation is a universal messenger. The NIV deviates from the MT to follow the lead of the LXX and the Latin Vulgate in reading *qôlām*, 'their voice', instead of *qavvām*, 'their measuring line'. The MT text makes good sense, though, as it asserts that the measuring line of the heavens is over the whole earth, a truth confirmed by the following words.[3] The voice (or call) of the heavens and earth has gone to the uttermost part. This is a proclamation or a summons from God to mankind. Nonetheless this is a muted message for it cannot say anything about God's grace or the way of approach that he has provided to his throne.

In the heavens he has pitched a tent for the sun, which is like a bridegroom coming forth from his pavilion, like a

---

[1] The verb 'bubble forth' (*nâvaʿ*, Hi.) is an uncommon verb, only used once of water bubbling forth (Prov. 18:4). However, it is also used as here in the figurative sense of God's praise coming forth in a stream in Psalms 78:2, 119:171, and 145:7.

[2] Cf. the comments of Derek Kidner on Genesis 1:16-18: 'Sun, moon and stars are God's good gifts.... As *signs* (14) they will speak for God, not fate (Jer. 10:2; cf. Mt. 2:9; Lk. 21:25, 28), for they *rule* (16, 18) only as lightbearers, not as powers. In these few simple sentences the lie is given to a superstition as old as Babylon and as modern as a newspaper-horoscope': *Genesis: An Introduction and Commentary* (London: Tyndale Press, 1967), p. 49.

[3] The Hebrew text simply says '*their* line', just as it says 'in *them*' in verse 4b. In both cases the pronouns refer back to 'the heavens' and 'the firmament' in verse 1.

champion rejoicing to run his course. It rises at one end of the heavens and makes its circuit to the other; nothing is hidden from its heat (*vv. 4b-6*). The picture is enlarged with a description of the sky as the tent that God has provided for the sun. Despite all its glory, the sun is still a created thing, set in its place by God. Just as the bridegroom comes out from under his canopy, or the virile athlete runs his race, so the sun comes forth to run its daily course. It covers a daily circuit, and from the standpoint of human observation it goes from one edge of the heavens to the other. Its heat penetrates everywhere. The description of the sun is clearly based on Middle Eastern experience. How many receive the message of creation? Paul says in effect: 'Very few.' For although men 'knew God, they neither glorified him as God nor gave thanks to him, but their thinking became futile and their foolish hearts were darkened' (Rom. 1:21). It is only a believer who can truly see in creation the hand of God, and give him praise for the wonder of his works.

2. God's Glory in His Word (*vv. 7-10*)
The last clause in verse 6 serves as a bridge between the first and second parts of the psalm. Just as the sunshine reveals everything, so does God's Word search our hearts. It is 'sharper than any double-edged sword, it penetrates even to dividing soul and spirit, joints and marrow; it judges the thoughts and attitudes of the heart' (Heb 4:12).

The law of the Lord is perfect, reviving the soul. The statutes of the Lord are trustworthy, making wise the simple. The precepts of the Lord are right, giving joy to the heart. The commands of the Lord are radiant, giving light to the eyes. The fear of the Lord is pure, enduring forever. The ordinances of the Lord are sure and altogether righteous (*vv. 7-9*).

There are several noteworthy things about these verses. First, instead of the word 'God' (Hebrew *'ēl*) used when speaking of creation, the psalmist now uses the covenantal name Lord (Hebrew *yhwh*) when speaking of the Scripture. Secondly, he uses six parallel expressions to describe the

Scriptures ('law', 'statutes', 'precepts', 'commands', 'fear', and 'ordinances'). While each name adds something more to the description, yet together they form a multifaceted picture of God's Word. Thirdly, we have a balancing list of six attributes ('perfect', 'trustworthy', 'right', 'radiant', 'pure', and 'sure'). Fourthly, accompanying each title is a descriptive phrase telling what the Scripture does ('reviving the soul', 'making wise the simple', 'giving joy to the heart', 'giving light to the eyes', 'enduring forever', 'altogether righteous').

The description starts in verse 7 with the revelation of the LORD being referred to as his perfect law. That is, it was divine instruction that brought refreshment in weakness or despair. The Hebrew word used here, *tôrâh*, comes from a verb 'to teach' or 'instruct' (*yârâh*). To call it 'perfect' is to say that it is an expression of the pure will of God. Likewise the LORD's statutes are trustworthy, and they bring wisdom to those who lack it, the 'simple'. The psalmist is not indicating a special class of people, for he would certainly include all in the description of 'simple' (cf. our Lord's words in Matthew 11:25). The Hebrew word translated 'simple' (*petî*) has a good sense in the Psalms where it indicates those who lack wisdom but who can gain it by receiving knowledge. In contrast, when used in Proverbs it marks out the 'gullible', who, unless they repent, will be reckoned alongside the fools and mockers.[4]

In verse 8 the psalmist moves on to speak of the righteous precepts that are a source of joy and satisfaction. The verb 'to rejoice' (*sâmach*) is frequently used in the Psalter, with the source of joy being found in God's presence, or else in things emanating from him like his precepts, as here. From another angle they are sincere commands that bring light to the eyes. Spiritual illumination comes through God's own revelation of himself. When David speaks of the fear of the LORD in verse 9 he is not concerned with the inward experience of a believer. As it is in parallel with other terms relating to Scripture it must mean the 'law', which had as one of its purposes to

---

[4] For the contrast in usage between Psalms and Proverbs, see *TWOT*, II, p. 743; Bruce K. Waltke, *The Book of Proverbs: Chapters 1-15*, NICOT (Grand Rapids: Eerdmans, 2004), pp. 111-12.

bring men to fear the LORD (cf. Deut. 4:10; 17:19). The word 'fear' is used elsewhere in this objective sense (Ps. 34:11; Prov. 1:29). Moreover, this 'fear' stands in perpetuity as the abiding manifestation of God. The final concluding statement in verse 9 sums up the character of the law – it is true becomes it comes from God who is true. It is altogether righteous since it comes from the righteous God himself.

They are more precious than gold, than much pure gold; they are sweeter than honey, than honey from the comb (*v. 10*). This section concludes with the assurance of how precious and sweet is God's Word. It is far more valuable than purified gold; it is far sweeter than honey. For those in the ancient world who did not have an abundance of sugar, there was nothing sweeter than honey. Similar expressions about God's law are found in Psalm 119 (gold, 119:72, 127; honey, 119:103).

3. The Response to God's Word (*vv. 11-14*)

By them is your servant warned; in keeping them there is great reward. Who can discern his errors? Forgive my hidden faults (*vv. 11-12*). Now comes the reflection on what has been said about God's precious Word. They brought meaning (or perhaps better, 'enlightenment') to David, as they continue to do to us, and there is great blessing in walking in the pathway of God's commands. David knew that there was no complete and perfect obedience to be given to God's law and therefore he asks concerning his 'errors'. The Hebrew word he uses here (*shᵉgî'âh*) is related to the word used for the sins for which atonement could be sought (*shᵉgâgâh*, Lev. 4:2, 22, 27). His plea is for forgiveness to blot out even inadvertent sins. There has to be sensitivity of heart before the LORD so that we can pray this prayer with David. A true response to this truth is to seek cleansing even from faults not obvious to our eyes.

Keep your servant also from wilful sins; may they not rule over me. Then will I be blameless, innocent of great transgression (*v. 13*). The danger of sin was present with David. Hence he asks for preservation from presumptuous and wilful sins, which have a tendency to rule over people.

The Hebrew word for 'wilful' is *zêd*, only used here in reference to sins. Usually it is applied to people who are arrogant or impudent. Such sins are like a wild animal waiting to catch its prey, as Cain found out to his cost (Gen. 4:7). They take hold of people and make them their slaves (John 8:34). If kept from such sins David would be heart-whole with the LORD and not guilty of the 'great transgression'. Elsewhere in the Old Testament this phrase commonly refers to adultery (see Gen. 39:9), but here it probably means sin in general.

May the words of my mouth and the meditation of my heart be pleasing in your sight, O LORD, my Rock and my Redeemer (*v. 14*). The psalm opened with the thought of the heavens speaking. It closes with the psalmist asking that *his* words would be pleasing to the LORD. He is referring to the words of this song in particular, and acknowledges that it is his speech and meditation that he desires to be acceptable to his Rock and his Redeemer (for the idea of meditation, see the comment on 1:2). The use of 'rock' ties in closely with the way it has appeared in the previous psalm (see Ps. 18:2, 31, 46). The psalm that began on the note of the glory of all God's creation, closes on the note of a personal relationship with the Saviour.

Psalm 20

For the director of music. A psalm of David.

Before battles it was customary in Israel and Judah to pray to the LORD and to seek an answer from him. Thus Jehoshaphat prayed before his battle with Moab and Ammon, a Levite responded, and then all the people worshipped (2 Chron. 20:5-19). Psalm 20 seems to come from a similar situation and be intended as a song to be sung before a battle. Like Jehoshaphat's prayer, this one seems to be influenced in its thought and language by Solomon's prayer at the dedication of the temple (see especially 2 Chron. 6:18-21). The early part may have been sung by all the people after the king had offered sacrifices. They look forward to rejoicing in his victory (v. 5), and then an individual (probably a Levite) makes a declaration, and finally all the congregation respond in praise. The poetry of this psalm is marked out by repetition of key words that form an important stylistic feature (cf. 'answer(s)', vv. 1, 6, 9; 'name', vv. 1, 5; 'remember', vv. 3, 7; 'fulfil', vv. 4, 5; 'save(s)', vv. 5, 6, 9).[1]

1. A Prayer Before Battle (*vv. 1-5*)

May the LORD answer you when you are in distress; may the name of the God of Jacob protect you (*v. 1*). The psalm begins and ends with similar words (closer in Hebrew than the English translation suggests). 'Answer in the day of ...' is clearly a key term. The appeal is to the LORD, or as he is also described, 'the God of Jacob'.This term occurs again in an

---

[1] The NIV obscures the repetition by translating some of the Hebrew words with different English words: 'remember' (v. 3), 'trust' (v. 7), 'fulfil' (v. 4), and 'grant' (v. 5).

abbreviated form in Psalm 24:6, and it is common elsewhere in the Psalter (Pss. 46:7,11; 75:9; 76:6; 81:1; 84:8; cf. also Isaiah's term, 'The mighty one of Jacob,' Isa. 49:26; 60:16). 'The name' of the LORD is clearly God himself (cf. Isa. 30:27) through whom enemies were overcome (Ps. 44:5). It is the self-revelation of his character.

May he send you help from the sanctuary and grant you support from Zion (*v.* 2). The date of writing was clearly after the ark was brought to Jerusalem, and the establishment of the sanctuary on Mount Zion. The following verse, with reference to sacrifices, shows that it is the earthly and not the heavenly sanctuary that is meant. The combination of the idea of God's name being associated with the sanctuary and prayer to God at the temple are drawn from Solomon's prayer (1 Kings 8:27-30; 2 Chron. 6:18-21).[2] The people's plea is that when they leave for battle they go with the LORD's help and sustaining power.

May he remember all your sacrifices and accept your burnt offerings Selah (*v.* 3). The sacrifices could be all those of the past, but probably what is meant are those offered on the particular occasion of going into battle (cf. 1 Sam. 7:9; 13:9). The first word for sacrifice (*minchâh*) is a general term that covers many types, while the second is the burnt offering (*'ôlâh*), in which everything was consumed as a symbol of dedication to God. The use of 'Selah' marks a break after these opening petitions, though the exact significance of its presence is hard to determine (for discussion on this term, see the comments on Ps. 3:2).

May he give you the desire of your heart and make all your plans succeed (*v.* 4). What is intended is that the plans of the king for the battle would come to fruition. His heart's desire and his counsel were that he would overcome the enemy, and for that the people pray: 'May God give it!' The verb translated 'succeed' (*mâlê'*, Pi.) is used again at the end of verse 5 (NIV 'May the LORD *grant*').

---

[2] For a detailed discussion on the temple and its significance, see W. A. VanGemeren, 'Appendix: The Ark of the Covenant and the Temple, Symbols of Yahweh's Presence and Rule', 'Psalms', pp. 809-15.

We will shout for joy when you are victorious and will lift up our banners in the name of our God. May the LORD grant all your requests (v. 5). The scene moves now to the future when those at present praying will be among those rejoicing in victory. Songs of rejoicing will be heard as the people celebrate God's salvation or victory. Jubilant shouting will mark the outcome of battle. They will also erect or wave banners, possibly the tribal banners under which they camped (Num. 1:52).[3] The final clause in the verse repeats the idea of verse 4 in describing full realisation of the king's requests.

2. God's Declaration of Victory (v. 6)

Now I know that the LORD saves his anointed; he answers him from his holy heaven with the saving power of his right hand (v. 6). The introductory 'now' (*'attâh*) is important, as it is an adverb that often marks a change in narrative and especially in the prophetical books introduces imminent activities of the LORD, either in blessing or cursing (see, for a good example, Isa. 43:1). Here it precedes the declaration that the LORD saves his anointed. The deliverance is still in the future but the assurance is given that the LORD hears and answers the cry of the king. While some have taken 'anointed' to be the future eschatological king, the context points to its use as designating a contemporary king.[4] The LORD answers from his holy throne on high. His 'right hand' describes in anthropomorphic terms God's power and ability to deliver.

3. A Song of Thanksgiving (vv. 7-9)

Some trust in chariots and some in horses, but we trust in the name of the LORD our God (v. 7). Without trusting in the LORD the use of horses and chariots was useless. There was a constant temptation for God's people to trust in human might or agencies to give deliverance. Even Moses had to learn the lesson in this respect (see Exod. 2:11-14, and Stephen's

---

[3] The parallel expression is 'shout for joy', and hence the idea is that in victory parades banners would be waved as part of the celebration.

[4] See the discussion by G. Vos, 'The Eschatology of the Psalter', in *The Eschatology of the Old Testament*, ed. James T. Dennison Jr. (Nutley, NJ; P. & R. Publishing, 2001), pp. 131-40.

comment in Acts 7:23-29). There could be no trusting in horses, chariots, bows, or swords (Ps. 44:5-7), but only in the LORD himself (see the use of 'name' already in verses 1 and 5) who was their God. Also, since the ideal condition of God's kingdom was to be peace, consequently this was meant to be the condition of Israel as a theocracy at all times. Some in Israel clearly followed the untheocratic principle of trust in human might, against which prophets and psalmists warned.[5]

They are brought to their knees and fall, but we rise up and stand firm (*v. 8*). The outcome of battle, if the LORD was on their side, was that their enemies would be humbled and fall. The word 'fall' often occurs in military contexts as here and denotes falling to death (see the account of Sisera's death in Judg. 5:27: 'At her feet he sank, he fell; there he lay. At her feet he sank, he fell; where he sank, there he fell – dead'). In contrast the Israelites will arise and stand their ground.[6]

O LORD, save the king! Answer us when we call! (*v. 9*) Again the whole congregation joins in singing, as the worshippers repeat the opening intercession. They want God to show his power in delivering the king in battle. This cry of the people lies behind the British expression of loyalty to the sovereign, 'God save the King/Queen!'[7] The New Testament use of 'Hosanna' particularises this cry and does so by way of its use in Psalm 118:25. The psalm that began with the cry of 'answer', finishes on the note of entreaty with the repetition of the word 'answer'.

---

[5] Cf. passages such as Hosea 14:3: 'Assyria cannot save us; we will not mount war-horses,' and Isaiah 31:1: 'Woe to those who go down to Egypt for help, who rely on horses, who trust in the multitude of their chariots and in the great strength of their horsemen, but do not look to the Holy One of Israel, or seek help from the LORD.'

[6] See my discussion of this usage of the verb 'fall' in *NIDOTTE*, 3, p.130.

[7] The LXX rendering is *kurie, sôson basilea sou* ('Lord, save your king') and the Vulgate's *Domine salvum fac regem* is the origin of our familiar 'God save the king!'

Psalm 21

For the director of music. A psalm of David.

This psalm is closely connected in theme with the preceding one. It is a song that recounts past victories which the LORD gave, and which expresses trust that he will do the same yet again for his people. It is also a psalm with strong covenantal overtones. This is best seen in verse 7. On the LORD's part he shows covenantal commitment (*chésed*) to his people; on the people's part (represented by the king) they respond in trust (*bâtach*). The former never altered, but time and again the people had to be challenged in regard to their commitment to the LORD. At the heart of this psalm is this fresh affirmation of the covenantal faith, and this is confirmed by the blessings in verses 2-7, and promised divine protection in verses 8-13. As with the previous psalm, the conclusion returns to the opening theme forming an *inclusio*. Just as the king can rejoice in the LORD's strength (v. 1), so will the people sing of the LORD's strength and might (v. 13).

1. Rejoicing in the LORD's Victories (*vv. 1-7*)
O LORD, the king rejoices in your strength. How great is his joy in the victories you give! (*v. 1*). The people join in a song of praise to the LORD because of the assistance he has provided for the king. The LORD's strength (*'oz*) has been manifested in the battles of the past. At the end of the psalm reference is made again to this aspect (v. 13), and though a different noun is used (*gevûrâh*), it is synonymous in meaning. So much of the history of Israel and Judah was dominated by battles, as the people extended or endeavoured to maintain

their boundaries. All these victories were the LORD's, and the king and people together rejoiced in them.

You have granted him the desire of his heart and have not withheld the request of his lips. *Selah (v. 2).* Prayer before battle was customary in Israel (see vv. 1-4 in the previous psalm). Now the people acknowledge that when the king prayed, God answered him. In time of need, the LORD had not refused to listen to the requests that the king made. Though the word for 'victory' (*yᵉshûʿâh*) is singular, the context implies repeated demonstrations of God's saving power.

You welcomed him with rich blessings and placed a crown of pure gold on his head. He asked you for life, and you gave it to him — length of days, for ever and ever *(vv. 3-4).* The blessings of the kingship are described, using the crown as a symbol of all the good things that the LORD bestowed upon the king. It is only a poetical figure to sum up the many gifts that God gave to the Davidic kings. The word used for 'crown' (*ʿᵃtârâh*) is a general word and one most frequently used in metaphorical expressions like this one.[1] In regard to verse 4 the question can be posed: 'When was the request made, and when was the answer given?' Most probably before going into battle the king asked that his life would be spared. When he came back after the battle he knew that God had prolonged his life in accordance with his prayer. The expression 'length of days, for ever and ever' does not mean eternal life. The expression is used even of heathen kings (Neh. 2:3; Dan. 2:4), and here it means prolonged life extending into the foreseeable future,[2] or possibly continuation of the Davidic line.

Through the victories you gave, his glory is great; you have bestowed on him splendour and majesty. Surely you have granted him eternal blessings and made him glad with the joy of your presence *(vv. 5-6).* After the God-given victories the king received not only life but 'splendour and majesty'

---

[1] In contrast, the word *nêzer* is used both for the royal crown (2 Sam. 1:10; 2 Kings 11:12, Ps. 89:39) and the holy headband of the High Priest (Exod. 29:6; 39:30; Lev. 8:9). The connecting link between these two usages is the idea of consecration to God's service.

[2] Cf. also the use of 'length of days' (*ʾórek yâmîm*) in Psalm 23:6, and see the commentary on that verse.

(*hôd vᵉhâdâr*). These are attributes of God himself (Pss. 96:6; 104:1; 111:3), but the king reflected these characteristics as he occupied the divinely appointed office. As in verse 4 the thought is not of blessings of eternal life, but of long-lasting blessings. Other possible interpretations would be blessings of enduring value, or blessings whose flow to recipients was continuous. While it is not expressly stated, the idea behind the expression is that the king was a mediator of God's blessings to others. The first main part of the psalm comes to climactic expression in the following words:

For the king trusts in the LORD; through the unfailing love of the Most High he will not be shaken (*v. 7*). This is the key verse of the psalm, and the one connecting verses 1-6 with verses 8-13. It is in the third person, not in the second person as is the rest of the psalm. Covenantal love shown by the Most High is the foundation of the whole relationship.[3] If that trust continues, then the king will not be moved or shaken, an expression denoting fixity of purpose and life (cf. its use in Pss. 15:5; 16:8; 46:5; 112:6). The response of the people has to be one of trust in the LORD, just as the king placed his ground of hope in him.

2. Confidence in the LORD's Future Victories (*vv. 8-12*)

Now the focus switches to the future, and to deliverances that the LORD will provide. It is the king who is being addressed. **Your hand will lay hold on all your enemies; your right hand will seize your foes. At the time of your appearing you will make them like a fiery furnace. In his wrath the LORD will swallow them up, and his fire will consume them** (*vv. 8-9*). Just as verses 2-7 described the *blessings* of God on the king, so now verses 8-12 set out the *curses* that the king visits on his enemies. When the king appears (using language which is often used of God himself) he will destroy his enemies with the aid of the LORD. Double parallelism occurs in verse 8: 'your hand'/'your right hand', and 'your enemies'/'your haters' (i.e 'those who hate you'). The same verb (*mâtsâ'*, 'to find') is used twice, probably with the meaning 'to find out, to search for'.

---

[3] For comment on the 'Most High', see Psalm 7:17.

Just as the contents of a burning oven are destroyed, so shall the enemies perish. This is described as a divine action, even though the king and his forces would accomplish it. **You will destroy their descendants from the earth, their posterity from mankind. Though they plot evil against you and devise wicked schemes, they cannot succeed; for you will make them turn their backs when you aim at them with drawn bow** (*vv. 10-12*). The destruction of the enemies would be so complete that they would leave no descendants behind them. This was a curse often expressed in the ancient Near East (cf. Jeremiah 22:30 in reference to King Jehoiachin). The idea is that the lack of descendants would mean that these particular enemies through lack of followers would never be in a position to attack again. However much they devise plans, and scheme against the king, they will not succeed, for the LORD has them on the run, so that their backs are exposed to the pursuing troops.

3. The Prayer of the Congregation (*v. 13*)

Be exalted, O LORD, in your strength; we will sing and praise your might. The psalm ends with a prayer asking for God to reveal his strength and majesty. There are military overtones here in keeping with the subject matter of the psalm (cf. Num. 10:35). The request for God to be exalted is echoed later in the Psalter (see Ps. 57:5, 11). The might of the LORD is to be the subject of praise by the people as a whole ('we'), just as verses 2-7 were such praise regarding the past victories.

Psalm 22

To the director of music.
To the tune of 'The Doe of the Morning'. A psalm of David.

This is a priceless psalm, and in many ways the supreme example in the Psalter of an appeal for help. According to the title, it is a cry from David to the LORD, and there are features in the psalm that point to it being connected with incidents in David's life (see v. 2, which shows that the appeal was made over a considerable period of time). He calls on God in whom 'our fathers put their trust' (v. 4), which seems to be a reference to earlier fathers of the nation, or possibly even to the patriarchs, Abraham, Isaac, and Jacob. It may be, as Calvin claims, that David sums up here various incidents of suffering and persecution in his life.[1]

There are strong connections between this psalm and Jeremiah's writings (cf. Ps. 22:6b with Jer. 49:15; Ps. 22:7a with Jer. 20:7b; Ps. 22:7b with Lam. 2:15 and Jer. 18:16; Ps. 22:9-10 with Jer. 1:5; 15:10; 20:14, 17-18).[2] Yet the fact that it is quoted thirteen times in the New Testament, and nine times alone in the account of Jesus' suffering and death, points to a fuller meaning realised only in our Lord's messianic affliction. Because of this Psalm 22 has even been referred to as 'the Fifth Gospel'.[3] Though the primary reference in the psalm must be to David and his experiences, there is an

---

[1] John Calvin, *A Commentary on the Psalms of David* (London: Thomas Tegg, 1840), I, p. 232.

[2] For the reference to Jeremiah, see W. L. Holladay, 'The Background of Jeremiah's Self-Understanding, Moses, Samuel, and Psalm 22', *JBL* 83 (1964), pp. 153-64.

[3] See, S. B. Frost, 'Psalm 22: An Exposition', *CJT* 8 (1962), pp. 102-15.

indirect messianic application (see my broader discussion on the messianic element in the Introduction). This explains why in the North African churches in Augustine's time (AD c. 354–430) this psalm was sung at the Easter celebration of the Lord's Supper. Similarly, it has been traditionally associated with communion services of the Scottish churches since the Reformation.

1. Invocation and Call for Help (v. 1-2)

The psalm opens with a despairing cry. **My God, my God, why have you forsaken me?** (*v. 1a*). The ultimate expression of desolation is Jesus' use of these words on the cross (Matt. 27:46; the words quoted, *Eloi, Eloi, lama sabachtani*, are the Aramaic equivalent of the Hebrew words here in v. 1). The idea of being forsaken by God occurs several times in the Old Testament, especially in passages in which God accuses his people of sinning against him (Judg. 10:13; 1 Sam. 8:8; 1 Kings 11:33; 2 Kings 22:17). Neither here nor in Psalm 44, which is a communal lament on being forsaken by God, is there any suggestion of sin on the part of the speakers.

Why are you so far from saving me, so far from the words of my groaning? O my God, I cry out by day, but you do not answer, by night, and am not silent (*vv. 1b-2*). Even though the speaker has called God 'my God', yet he feels that salvation is so far away from him. The words of his groaning are addressed to God day and night, and yet no answer seems to come. A sense of abandonment comes over the psalmist, and God's silence troubles him. The word 'far' (*râchôq*) is repeated in verses 11 and 19, which helps to maintain the sense of isolation throughout the psalm.

2. The Basis of Faith (vv. 3-5)

Yet you are enthroned as the Holy One; you are the praise of Israel. In you our fathers put their trust; they trusted and you delivered them. They cried to you and were saved; in you they trusted and were not disappointed (*vv. 3-5*). Verse 3 can be translated as the NIV does, or we can adapt slightly the NIV margin and render: 'You the Holy One are enthroned on the praises of Israel.' Whichever option is taken, the idea is present that God is the object of Israel's praise, and he is indeed the Holy One. The Hebrew word for holiness used here (*qâdôsh*) comes from a Semitic root that means 'cut off' or 'separate'. It denotes God's transcendence and his ethical purity. It is used in a threefold refrain in Psalm 99 and also in the threefold call of the seraphim in Isaiah 6:3. The psalmist appeals to Israel's history to show why he is calling upon God with expectancy. The explanation for this is that their forefathers had put their trust in him. Three times the verb 'to trust' is used (Hebrew *bâtach*), and this is one of the great 'faith' words of the Old Testament and the most frequent of them.[4] Those who had called on Israel's God in times of great need had experienced his saving mercy. Their faith was not misplaced. All who trust or take refuge in the LORD will never be put to shame, for he will save them (cf. Ps. 71:1).

3. Lament (*vv. 6-8*)

The psalmist now bemoans his condition, in that he is barely left as a man. **But I am a worm and not a man, scorned by men and despised by the people** (*v. 6*). There are many similarities here to the language of Isaiah, who calls Israel a 'worm' (Isa. 41:14), and who says of the Servant of the LORD that he is so disfigured that people can hardly recognise him as a man (Isa. 52:14; 53:2-3). The use of 'worm' highlights the psalmist's perception of himself, for he is weak and insignificant, while the parallel expressions in the second part of the verse indicate the result of others' perception of him.

All who see me mock me; they hurl insults, shaking their heads: (*v. 7*). All who see his suffering take delight in it. They shake their heads, not in compassion, but out of joy that he has been brought to this condition, and they cast

---

[4] For a helpful discussion on this and other words relating to faith, see G. J. Wenham, *Faith in the Old Testament*.

reproaches in his face. They react to his condition and need with derision.

What they say to him is: **'He trusts in** (Hebrew *gol*, which is an imperative: lit. *roll on*) **the LORD; let the LORD rescue him. Let him deliver him, since he delights in him'** (*v. 8*). Of course, this is said in jest, with no expectation that God would intervene and save his servant. But later in the psalm we see that the prayer of the psalmist was indeed answered, for God did not turn his face away and refuse to listen (v. 24). 'Rescue' and 'deliver' are used as synonyms, while the verb 'delights in' (*châfêts*) is used of God's pleasure in his servants such as David (2 Sam. 22:20) or in their observance of his law (Isa. 56:4).

4. A Confident Appeal (*vv. 9-11*)

All the songs of appeal have as a characteristic an expression of trust in the LORD and commitment to him. It comes here in the words: **Yet you brought me out of the womb; you made me trust in you even at my mother's breast. From birth I was cast upon you; from my mother's womb you have been my God. Do not be far from me, for trouble is near and there is no one to help** (*vv. 9-11*). The words of the mockers are now turned against them, as the psalmist says that from infancy he has been trusting in the LORD. The same verb for 'trust' is used as has already appeared in verses 4-5. The God in whom he trusts is said to be 'my God', echoing the appeal to God in verse 1. Verses 9 and 10 are paired, in that the expressions in verse 9 are paralleled in verse 10, though in reverse order:

> You/brought me/from the womb/you made me
> trust in you/upon my mother's breasts:
> Upon you/I was cast/from the womb/from the
> womb of my mother/my God are you.[5]

---

[5] The two Hebrew words for 'womb' (*béten* and *rêchem*) are synonymous, and are used in parallelism also in Job 3:11; 10:18-19; 31:15; Ps. 58:3; Isa. 46:3, and Jer. 1:5. See Y. Avishur, *Stylistic Studies of Word-Pairs in Biblical and Ancient Semitic Languages* (Neukirchen-Vluyn: Neukirchener 1984), p. 70.

The request, 'Do not be far from me', also echoes verse 1, as he pleads with God to reverse the present seeming separation between them.

5. Another Lament (*vv. 12-18*)
The imagery in these verses is dramatic, for various metaphors are used to describe graphically the ordeals he has been through. **Many bulls surround me; strong bulls of Bashan encircle me. Roaring lions tearing their prey open their mouths wide against me. I am poured out like water, and all my bones are out of joint. My heart has turned to wax; it has melted away within me. My strength is dried up like a potsherd, and my tongue sticks to the roof of my mouth; you lay me in the dust of death. Dogs have surrounded me; a band of evil men has encircled me** (*vv. 12-16a*). Such metaphors are part of biblical poetry, for they serve to engage the mind and to stir emotions. We can feel for the psalmist as he describes his enemies as bulls, lions, and dogs, while he himself has a heart of wax, strength as dry as a potsherd, a tongue stuck to his palate, and he feels as if he is already in the grave. On every side the psalmist is hemmed in by those who seek to kill him. The reference to Bashan is to an area east of the Jordan that was well known for its cattle (cf. Amos 4:1).

They have pierced my hands and my feet (*v. 16b*). This part of verse 16 has for long provided difficulty for commentators as the Hebrew text does not seem to make good sense.[6] It reads literally, 'like a lion, my hands and my feet.' All the early translators into Greek, Latin, Syriac, and Arabic found this verse a problem, and instead of 'like a lion', they all insert a verb: 'they pierced', or 'they bound', or 'they put to shame'. Unless we propose some textual change and read something like, 'My hands and feet are exhausted', we are left with the problems. If so, then the

---

[6] Of the older commentators full notes can be found in E. W. Hengstenberg, *The Psalms*, I, pp. 383-87, F. Delitzsch, *The Psalms*, I, pp. 317-20, and J. J. S. Perowne, *The Book of Psalms:* I, pp. 255-56. For modern bibliography on this psalm as a whole and also the textual problem in verse 16, see Samuel Terrien, *The Psalms*, pp. 226-28.

word normally translated 'lion' may well be a verb 'to bind'. Hence, the translation would be: 'they bound my hands and feet'.[7] The only other alternative would be to understand a verb, e.g. 'like a lion [they maul] my hands and feet', or else assume that the force of the verb in 16a is carried over into 16b: 'they surround me, like a lion, [even] my hands and my feet.' The point of mentioning hands and feet is that 'hands' form the means of defence against the enemy, the feet the means of escape. While the New Testament quotes Psalm 22 so often, yet never once is this verse referred to the crucifixion.[8]

I can count all my bones; people stare and gloat over me. They divide my garments among them and cast lots for my clothing (*vv. 17-18*). The final act of indignity is that the sufferer, who can count all his bones that are out of joint (see v. 14a), is the laughing stock of his persecutors, who strip him of his clothing. The enemies gaze with pleasure on one destined for death; they take pleasure in his humiliation. The dividing-up of the garments is not for gain, but to indicate that all is now finished for the afflicted sufferer. The words of the psalmist come to highest fulfillment in the death of the sufferer *par excellence*, Jesus.

6. A Further Appeal (*vv. 19-21*)
Once more the psalmist cries to his God, commencing with the same language as at the end of his previous appeal in verse 11.

---

[7] Several factors must be considered in assessing proposed alterations to the text. (1) The Hebrew manuscript evidence is almost without exception supportive of the reading 'like a lion'. (2) The word for 'a lion' (*ʾărî*) fits the context as lions have already been mentioned in verse 13 and will again be part of the scene in verse 21, even though a slightly variant form of the word is used in these verses (*ʾaryēh* instead of *ʾărî*). (3) The evidence of the versions, though supporting a verbal form (either *kāʾrû*, 'they pierced', or *kārû*, 'they bound'), is not uniform. (4) Modern emendations, such as given by P. C. Craigie, *Psalms 1-50*, p. 196, involve even greater alteration to the MT.

[8] Another objection to the interpretation that assumes that this verse points to the crucifixion of Jesus is that crucifixion does not appear to have been practised in Israel at the time at which the psalm was composed. Deuteronomy 21:22-23 deals with impalement on a tree after execution. See my comments on these verses in *Deuteronomy: The Commands of a Covenant God* (Fearn: Christian Focus Publications, 2001), p. 201.

But you, O LORD, be not far off; O my Strength, come quickly to help me (*v. 19*). There has been a progression in the psalm in regard to this idea of God being far off. First, there was the recognition of this fact (v. 1); then, the appeal for him to come near, noting there was none to help (v. 11); and, finally, with an added emphasis ('But you' is emphatic), an urgent appeal for God to come quickly. The form of address to God uses the word *ᵉyâlûtî* which is a *hapax legomenon*. The NIV translation 'my strength' is also adopted by many commentators, and it is probably preferable to 'my help' found in the RSV, NRSV, NEB, and REB.[9] While the petitioner is so near to death and in utter despair, yet, like the poet in Psalm 88, he can still direct an appeal to God for deliverance.

Deliver my life from the sword, my precious life from the power of the dogs. Save me from the mouth of the lions; you have heard me from the horns of the wild oxen (*vv. 20-21*). The enemies are again depicted as wild animals ('dogs', 'lions', 'wild oxen'), crowding in on him waiting for his death. But now he knows with assurance that God has heard him (following the NIV margin).[10] This interpretation then regards verses 20 and 21a as forming a triple appeal for deliverance, including deliverance from 'the horns of the wild oxen' ('Save me from the mouth of the lions and from the horns of the wild oxen'). This section of the psalm is then concluded with the words 'you have answered me', which both show the change that has come about since the psalmist said 'you do not answer' (v. 2) and also provide a fitting introduction to the final songs of thanksgiving that conclude the psalm.[11] 'You have answered me' is the transition point leading into the expression of praise for God's deliverance.

---

[9] For fuller information see P. C. Craigie, *Psalms 1-50*, p. 197, and *NIDOTTE*, 1, p. 377.

[10] The MT has *ᶜᵃnîtânî*, that appears to be from the verb *ᶜânâh* I, 'to answer'. The LXX has *tên tapeinôsin mou*, 'my humiliation', which, while fitting in with the general context, yet is based on a reading that deviates from the MT. The same objection can be made against Samuel Terrien's suggestion (*The Psalms*, p. 233) that the word means 'my wounded flesh', taking the root of the word to be *ᶜânâh* III, 'to afflict'.

[11] In interpreting verses 20-21 in this way I am following E. W. Hengstenberg, *The Psalms*, I, pp. 389-90. More recently P. C. Craigie, *The Psalms*, pp. 197, 200 has adopted a similar position.

7. Two Songs of Thanksgiving (*vv. 22-26, 27-31*)

What a contrast between the beginning and end of the psalm! Now that God has heard, the psalmist wants to proclaim God's character ('name' often has this connotation in Hebrew) to his fellow Israelites. The shift from penitent supplication to praise, though sudden, is not without parallel (cf. Ps. 6:8-10). **I will declare your name to my brothers; in the congregation I will praise you. You who fear the LORD, praise him! All you descendants of Jacob, honour him! Revere him, all you descendants of Israel! For he has not despised or disdained the suffering of the afflicted one; he has not hidden his face from him but has listened to his cry for help** (*vv. 22-24*). The reason for this praise is that God has remembered his afflicted one, and answered his call for help. The synonymous expressions for the people of God are important: 'my brothers', 'the congregation', 'you who fear the LORD', 'all you descendants of Jacob/Israel'. The word used for 'congregation' (Hebrew *qâhâl* = Greek *ekklēsia*) refers to the assembled people of God, and denotes an enduring feature of Israel's existence. When called 'the great congregation', this assembly is simply being described as the major gathering of God's people in Old Testament times (see Pss. 22:25; 35:18; 40:9, 10). David even adopts a missionary spirit, as he encourages others to honour and revere the LORD. The words of verse 22 are used in Hebrews 2:12 in reference to Jesus not being ashamed to call believers his brothers. He revealed his Father's will to them, and in turn this resulted in their becoming his brothers.[12] Deliverance by the LORD is the greatest, and most basic, motivation for missionary service. David refers to himself in the third person here, calling himself 'the afflicted one', in order to bring into sharper focus God's mercy to him. Other humans would turn their faces away from the afflicted, but God, who is not a man, has listened and heard his cry. Furthermore, the psalmist unites with other sufferers as they together praise the Lord.

From you comes my praise in the great assembly; before those who fear you, will I fulfil my vows. The poor will eat and

---

[12] See in particular the discussion of verse 23 in relation to Hebrews 2:12 in S. Kistemaker, *The Psalm Citations in the Epistle to the Hebrews* (Amsterdam: Wed. G. VanSoest N. V., 1961), pp. 83-85.

be satisfied; they who seek the LORD will praise him – may your hearts live forever! (*vv. 25-26*). He acknowledges that from the LORD alone comes the reason for his praise; it is all of his doing. As in verses 22-23, after his deliverance by the LORD, he sings his praise at the sanctuary in the presence of other God-fearers. He also brings a thank-offering that he had vowed during his trouble (Lev. 7:16), and in accordance with the custom in reference to the tithes (Deut. 14:28-29; 26:12) and at the harvest (Deut. 16:11), the widows, orphans, and poor in the community share in the meal. The final phrase in verse 26 may well have been a customary expression used at meals, asking for divine provision always to be the portion of those present at that time. Other similar statements without any introductory comment or explanation, that are in effect exclamations, occur in Psalms 31:14a; 45:6a; and 87:6b.[13]

David widens his vision at the end of this psalm and prophesies that all the nations and even children yet to be born will join in praise to the LORD. **All the ends of the earth will remember and turn to the LORD, and all the families of the nations will bow down before him, for dominion belongs to the LORD and he rules over the nations. All the rich of the earth will feast and worship; all who go down to the dust will kneel before him – those who cannot keep themselves alive** (*vv. 27-29*). In the context the primary meaning is that even far off nations will hear about David's deliverance and turn to the LORD in repentance. Gentile nations will come and bow in subjection to him who has all dominion and authority (cf. Pss. 72:8-11; 96:10-13). Just as direct address to the assembled people occurs in verse 26, so in verse 27 there is direct address to God: 'all the families of the nations will bow down *before you.*' This is the reading of the MT, but NIV and other versions adopt the translation 'before him'. In doing so they are following the LXX and the Syriac versions, which are also supported by Jerome. These verses are part of the missionary vision of the Old Testament, as prophets and psalmists sing of God's kingdom being extended to incorporate Gentile believers. The thought

---

[13] Here the use of the jussive form (*yᵉchî*, 'may [your hearts] live') may be an intentional use in order to vary the verb sequences, addressing directly the persons who have just been spoken of in the preceding context. For the grammar, see *IBHS*, p. 570.

of verse 29 is that rich and poor alike will join in worship of the LORD, sharing together in a communal meal, though this will be an eschatological feast rather than the votive meal mentioned in verse 26.[14] There will be no separation of rich and poor in that day, for the wealthy and those so poor that they are on the brink of the grave will both bow in submission to their Saviour.

Posterity will serve him; future generations will be told about the Lord. They will proclaim his righteousness to a people yet unborn – for he has done it (*vv. 30-31*). Within Israel coming generations will serve the LORD, for generation after generation shall be told about the wonderful deeds of the LORD. Those yet to be born will in their day hear of the LORD's righteousness (cf. Psalm 78:1-7). In this context 'righteousness' has the idea of 'salvation', 'deliverance'. The final words of the psalm stress that salvation is indeed of the LORD alone: 'for he has done [it].' Neither the subject nor the object are expressed in the Hebrew text, but the preceding references to the way in which the Lord heard the cry of the psalmist makes it plain that it is the deliverance by the LORD that is in view. The psalm that began on such a sorrowful note ends with the theme of universal joy in God's redemption.

David's experiences as set out in this psalm are not his alone, but in particular they are a pointer to the coming sufferings of the Lord Jesus. On the Cross our Lord used both its opening words ('My God, My God, why have you forsaken me?') and also its closing words ('It is finished', cf. 'for he has done it'). He is the one who has identified with us in our sufferings, which the writer to the Hebrews stresses in his exposition of the work of Jesus (Heb. 2:10-18; 4:15-16; 5:7-10). Having been made perfect through suffering, he is able to be a merciful and faithful high priest for his people, and even to unite with them in singing praise for God's salvation.

---

[14] Many commentators and translators think that the opening word of verse 29 should be emended from *'ākᵉlû* ('they shall eat') to *'ak lô* ('indeed to him', cf. *BHS*, RSV). If this suggestion is followed, then a further emendation is required to change the following verb from being a *vav* consecutive to a simple future by deleting the initial *vav*. As eating has already been mentioned in verse 26, it seems best to retain the MT, avoiding both word division, revocalisation, and deletion.

Psalm 23

A psalm of David.

Probably no psalm is better known nor more universally loved than this one. Because of its lack of details it is impossible to date this psalm, or to link it with any specific event. Its general nature, however, helps us to identify with it as it proclaims the depth of personal relationship between the LORD and a believer. It is steeped in a covenantal setting, and it has many affinities with descriptions of the Exodus experience. It uses the metaphor of the shepherd to speak of God's loving concern for his sheep and the richness of provision he makes for them.

1. The Divine Shepherd (*vv. 1-4*)
The LORD is my shepherd, I shall lack nothing (*v. 1*). The covenantal nature of this psalm is emphasised by the fact that the opening word is the distinctive covenantal name for God. The psalmist makes the declaration that this LORD is his own shepherd. He is appropriating language for himself that applied to the nation as a whole (see Pss. 79:13; 95:7; 100:3; Isa. 40:11; Ezek. 34). In the same way Christian believers can speak in personal terms of Christ's work (cf. Gal. 2:20b: he 'loved *me* and gave himself for *me*'). Just as God saw to it that the children of Israel lacked no good thing after the Exodus, so also the individual believer will lack nothing (cf. Deut. 2:7).

He makes me lie down in green pastures, he leads me beside quiet waters, he restores my soul. He guides me in paths of righteousness for his name's sake (*vv. 2-3*). The function of the shepherd with respect to the flock as a whole is now particularised to his care for the individual sheep. He leads to pasture and to water, and thus brings what seems like new life to the soul. The first part of verse 3 defines further what has already been said in verse 2. All the paths of the LORD are paths of righteousness, and he leads his people in them 'for his name's sake'. The verb 'leads' (*nâhal*) re-echoes the use of the same verb at the Exodus (Exod. 15:13), while 'for his name's sake' (*l*ᵉ*ma'an sh*ᵉ*mô*) is also used of the Exodus experience (Ps. 106:8).

Even though I walk through the valley of the shadow of death, I will fear no evil, for you are with me; your rod and your staff, they comfort me (*v. 4*). The many ravines in Palestine suggest the metaphor of this verse. In all the facets of life, including the most feared ('the valley of shadow of death', or alternatively, 'the valley of deepest darkness'),[1] the shepherd's rod and staff give comfort and assurance. David knew from his pastoral experience how helpful the rod and staff were, and so transfers the idea to God as the great and good shepherd. If God is with believers, then why should they fear? (cf. Rom. 8:31-39).

2. The Gracious Provision (*vv. 5-6*)

You prepare a table before me in the presence of my enemies. You anoint my head with oil; my cup overflows. Surely goodness and love will follow me all the days of my life, and I will dwell in the house of the LORD forever (*vv. 5-6*). The scene changes from food and water for sheep to banquet fare for humans. While it is possible that the psalmist is thinking of the special meals at times of sacrifice, yet it is more probable that he is thinking of the other meal times or special feasts. 'Table' is not to be understood as like Western wooden ones, but a skin or hide spread on the ground, though the verb 'to prepare' (*'ârak*) implies

---

[1] The Hebrew word in question, *tsalmâvet*, occurs eighteen times, all in poetry. The debate is whether the traditional derivation and the translation, 'valley of the shadow of death,' should be retained, or a derivation sought from the root *ts-l-m*, 'to become dark', and giving a rendering like 'deep darkness'. The traditional rendering has strong support, and the reference to death certainly brings in the emotional element present in situations of fear or danger. For this view, and a summary of other positions, see *NIDOTTE*, 3, pp. 807-10.

thoughtful preparation.[2] The shepherd lavishes his care on his children. He anoints the head, and gives so liberally that it is like an overflowing cup. Oil was used on festive occasions and, along with perfumes, symbolised joy (cf. Ps. 133:2). All this is because of the covenantal relationship.

The psalmist is sure that the blessings of the covenant and God's steadfast love will pursue him to the end of his life. The two Hebrew words used here (*tôv* and *chésed*) have strong covenantal connotations,[3] and together they form a fixed pair.[4] He commits himself to come back constantly to God's house. The Hebrew text has 'I will return', while the commonly accepted English translation (as in NIV) follows the LXX.[5] God's house (the tabernacle or later the temple) will be the constant abode of his people. The final phrase in the Hebrew text is simply 'length of days', that parallels 'all the days of my life' in the first part of the verse. The phrase denotes a long life (cf. Job 12:12), not an eternal life.[6] A lifelong experience of God's tender care brings a commitment to be always found in the LORD's house. This reference to God's house provides a key word that links this and the four following psalms (Pss. 23-27), and it forms a central and unifying theme

---

[2] Victor Hamilton draws attention to the fact that the basic meaning of this verb 'is "to arrange in order" for the sake of accomplishing a useful purpose. It is never used to describe arranging something arbitrarily or haphazardly' (*NIDOTTE*, 3, p. 536). Samuel Terrien points out that the corresponding Arabic word for 'table' continues to mean an animal skin or woven rug thrown on the ground (*The Psalms*, p. 241).

[3] See in particular A. R. Millard, 'For He is Good', *TB*, 1966, pp. 115-17, and the literature he cites. For fuller discussion of the covenantal significance of *tôv* and *tôvâh*, see P. Kalluveettil, *Declaration and Covenant: A Comprehensive Review of Covenant Formulae from the Old Testament and the Ancient Near East* (Rome: Biblical Institute Press, 1982), pp. 42-47.

[4] For further discussion on this point, see M. L. Barré, 'The Formulaic Pair *ṭwb (w) ḥsd* in the Psalter', *ZAW* 98 (1986), pp. 100-05.

[5] I have discussed the interpretation of this verse, including the question of whether the verb is 'to return' or 'to dwell', in 'The Conclusion of Psalm 23', *The Tyndale Paper* (Australia), XXXIV, 1 (March, 1989), pp. 1-8.

[6] It is strange that later Protestant commentators took the Hebrew to mean 'eternal life' when Renaissance and Reformation scholars had correctly understood it to have a temporal connotation. For some examples of the exegesis of Psalm 23 in those periods, see William Yarchin: *History of Biblical Interpretation: A Reader* (Peabody: Hendrikson, 2004), pp. 175-83.

within them. In Psalm 24 the poet asks about the character of the person who comes into the LORD's presence (vv. 3-4), while Psalm 25 has explicit references to covenant (vv. 6, 7, 10, 14). Psalm 26 contains the declaration that the author loves the house where the LORD lives (v. 8), followed in the next psalm by expressions of longing to dwell in the LORD's house (Ps. 27:4) and confidence in the protection the temple affords (Ps. 27:5).

Psalm 24
Of David. A psalm.

From Jewish tradition we know that this psalm was sung every Sabbath morning in the temple when the wine offering was made. The LXX evidence agrees with this as it adds to the title the words, 'for the seventh day of the week'. The psalm opens with an affirmation of the LORD's sovereignty over everything. It moves on to describe the character of the true worshipper, and then ends on the kingship of God as the ark is brought into Jerusalem.

1. The LORD of Creation (*vv. 1-2*)
The earth is the LORD's, and everything in it, the world, and all who live in it; for he founded it upon the seas and established it upon the waters (*vv. 1-2*). The opening words of this psalm are quoted by Paul (1 Cor. 10:26) to show that all foods can be eaten, because they all come from the LORD. The words were very familiar in Jewish circles because they were part of prayers said at mealtimes.[1] Paul was clearly thinking of mealtimes when he uses this quotation as his later comment on partaking of a meal and giving thanks to God make evident (1 Cor. 10:30). He does not draw a conclusion from his use of the quotation, but the reader is expected to understand that even though meat may be offered to idols, because it comes from God, it may be eaten. Central to the psalm's message is that the LORD is not only the God of Israel; he is the God of the whole world. To him it belongs, as well as all who live in it. It is his, because he is the creator of it. The founding of the earth is

---
[1] Cf. *Berakot* 35a-b.

described in terms reminiscent of other ancient Near Eastern creation accounts. Other passages in the Old Testament use similar language (Pss. 104:5-6; 136:6; Job 38:4-11).

2. The Character of True Worshippers (*vv. 3-6*)

Who may ascend the hill of the LORD? Who may stand in his holy place? (*v. 3*). These questions are very like those in Psalm 15:1. They may well have been asked as the ark was being brought into Jerusalem, but they also clearly have a wider connotation. The psalmist is asking regarding the character of the worshipper who approaches God's dwelling and stands his ground there.[2]

The answer to the questions specifies four characteristics. **He who has clean hands and a pure heart, who does not lift up his soul to an idol or swear by what is false** (*v. 4*). Purity of action and purity of desire are both demanded, which Jesus later spoke of when he said: 'Blessed are the pure in heart, for they will see God' (Matt. 5:8). Likewise there could be no compromise with idolatry. The Hebrew word translated 'idol' (*shâv'*) is simply 'vanity', but this word is applied to false gods in the Old Testament (see Pss. 24:4; 31:6; Jer. 18:15). The phrase clearly refers to an Israelite who is not living a life of obedience to the LORD. The final characteristic describes a life of falsehood by singling out one special form that it takes – false swearing.

He will receive blessing from the LORD and vindication from God his Saviour. Such is the generation of those who seek him, who seek your face, O God of Jacob. Selah (*vv. 5-6*). What is impossible for sinful man to do is ultimately received as a gift of God. The content of the blessing becomes much clearer in the New Testament, where it is seen as spiritual and eternal gifts (see Matt. 25:34; Gal. 3:14; Eph. 1:3). God the Saviour is also the vindicator of his people, as he lives up to his part of the covenant and faithfully blesses them. 'Seekers' is a common Old Testament expression for true worshippers

---

[2] This comment is based on the fact that the Hebrew verb for 'stand' (*qûm*) can be used in the sense of 'endure', 'survive'. Cf. Nahum 1:6a: 'Who can *endure* his fierce anger?' with the parallel verb being ʿ*âmad*.

who seek the LORD in prayer and who turn to him in their need. The conclusion of verse 6 is awkward in the Hebrew text, as after the words 'who seek your face', it simply says 'Jacob'. The NIV follows the common view that this is probably a case of ellipsis, so that the words 'God of' have to be added to complete the meaning. While this understanding is old (the LXX contains it), yet it would be very unusual if mention of God was omitted. In the context, with the reference being to those who seek God, it makes better sense to take it to be an identification of the true worshippers with their forefather Jacob. He was the one who pled with God: 'I will not let you go unless you bless me' (Gen. 32:26). It makes good sense to understand the comment at the end of the verse to be: '[They are] Jacob.'

3. The Triumph of the King of Glory (*vv. 7-10*)

Lift up your heads, O you gates; be lifted up, you ancient doors, that the King of glory may come in. Who is this King of glory? The LORD strong and mighty, the LORD mighty in battle (*vv. 7-8*). This psalm either dates from the bringing of the ark to Jerusalem (see 2 Sam. 6), or the return of the ark after a victorious battle. In the midst of the people is the ark, 'which is called by the Name, the name of the LORD Almighty, who is enthroned between the cherubim that are on the ark' (2 Sam. 6:2; cf. also Num. 10:35). It represents God himself, and therefore the call goes out for the gates of Zion to receive the LORD. The removal of the ark to Jerusalem marked the end of the battles to obtain possession of the land. The LORD comes as a mighty warrior to his rightful dwelling place.

Lift up your heads, O you gates; lift them up, you ancient doors, that the King of glory may come in. Who is he, this King of glory? The LORD Almighty – he is the King of glory. *Selah* (*vv. 9-10*). The words of verse 7 are repeated almost exactly (the only change is from 'be lifted up' to 'lift up'). The final question draws attention to the character of this triumphant king. The king of glory is the LORD Almighty (*yhwh ts^{e}vâ'ôt*). This name for God, 'LORD of hosts' or 'LORD Almighty', occurs here for the first of its fifteen appearances in the Psalter. It often carries military overtones, and so designates the LORD of the armies. This would be most fitting here, as the LORD leads his armies into Jerusalem.[3] The procession into the temple is also an occasion to acknowledge afresh the LORD as the glorious king. He is LORD of creation (vv. 1-2) and also the exalted king of salvation (vv. 7-10).

---

[3] The term 'LORD' or 'God of hosts' (for both forms were used) can have a variety of meanings. 'Hosts' can refer to the angels, the heavenly bodies, the armies of Israel, or even the universe. An excellent summary of the Old Testament usage is provided by J. E. Hartley in *TWOT*, 2, pp. 750-51, and further discussion on its use in the Psalms can be found in J. P. Ross, 'Yahweh Seba'ot in Sam and Ps', *VT* 17 (1967), pp. 76-92.

Psalm 25

Of David.

This beautiful psalm reads well in English, but our translations disguise another aspect of it. In Hebrew it is an acrostic like Psalms 9-10, with each successive verse beginning with the next letter of the Hebrew alphabet.[1] Four of the exceptions are that the letter *vav* is missing, the letter *qôf* is missing, the letter *rêsh* occurs twice in consecutive verses, and after the final letter of the alphabet is used in verse 21, another verse follows introduced by the letter *pê*.[2] This too may be deliberate, because the first letter (*alef*), the middle letter (*lamed*), and the final letter (*pe*) form a Hebrew word that means 'to learn' or 'to teach' (*lâmad*). The theme of teaching is so central to the psalm, with its repeated mention of being taught God's ways. The background of this instruction is God's covenant love, which the psalmist wants to make known.

It has been suggested that the psalm revolves around a chiastic structure that follows this pattern:[3]

---

[1] For discussion on the acrostic psalms, see the Introduction.

[2] Psalm 34 exhibits some of the same variations of the acrostic pattern, in that the letter *vav* is omitted, and that after the alphabet is completed, the final verse commences with the letter *pê*. Another detail about the pattern in Psalm 25 is that all the verses consist of two clauses, except the opening and closing verses which only have one clause each. Clearly the pattern of the psalm has been carefully conceived.

[3] Nineteenth century scholars suggested this pattern, and it has been revived lately by Samuel Terrien, *The Psalms*, p. 253. Craigie, *The Psalms*, pp. 217-18 discusses it, but considers there is insufficient evidence to sustain it. An alternative pattern is given by David A. Dorsey, *The Literary Structure of the Old Testament: A Commentary on Genesis–Malachi* (Grand Rapids: Baker, 2004), p. 184.

A		vv. 1-3	A plea for help
	B	vv. 4-7	Claiming God's mercy
	C	vv. 8-10	Covenant love
	D	v. 11	Core verse: a plea for pardon
	C¹	vv. 12-14	Meditation on the covenant
	B¹	vv. 15-18	Prayer for deliverance
A¹		vv. 19-21	Prayer for protection

Verse 11 does seem to be the fulcrum around which the rest of the psalm revolves, but some of the other proposed parallels are not so certain. It is better to simply take it that the psalm can be broken into three sections. In the first one (vv. 1-7) he addresses God in the second person, while changing to the third person in the second section (vv. 8-15). The final section (vv. 16-22) reverts to direct address to God in the second person.

1. Prayer to the LORD (*vv. 1-7*)
To you, O LORD, I lift up my soul; in you I trust, O my God. Do not let me be put to shame, nor let my enemies triumph over me (*vv. 1-2*). A word of prayer is addressed directly to God. The close relationship between the psalmist and his God is indicated by the way in which he addresses him and by the confident appeal he makes. He claims the LORD as '*my* God', that is the language of faith. He couples this with a declaration of trust in him.[4] The themes of trust and confident waiting on God are a feature of this song (see the ideas of waiting for God in vv. 2, 5, and 21, and of taking refuge in God in v. 20). Because of that relationship he can go on to make his appeal to God. What he wants is help against his enemies. Later in the psalm he is going to describe more closely his affliction (vv. 16-18). If there is no help from God, an audience of gloating enemies will rejoice over his downfall. For Christians there is the assurance that by faith in Christ we come to possess a hope that will never disappoint us (Rom. 5:1-5).

---

[4] For the Hebrew usage of 'trust in' (*bâtach bᵉ*), see the comment on Psalm 9:10. No great difference exists in meaning between this verb and *châsâh bᵉ* that is used in verse 20, though D. J. Wiseman has suggested that *châsâh* may denote 'more precipitate action' (*TWOT*, I, p. 307).

No one whose hope is in you will ever be put to shame, but they will be put to shame who are treacherous without excuse (*v. 3*). In this verse a different word is used to express confidence in the LORD. No one who truly 'waits on' the LORD will find their prayer disregarded, for they are displaying confidence in him. The Hebrew verb used (*qâvah*) is one of several that our English versions translate by the word 'wait', but it is distinctive in that it does not denote passive waiting on God. Rather, it points to prayer that involves action, striving with God in prayer. The root idea is associated with tension, which explains why the noun from it can mean both a cord (Josh. 2:18, 21) and the ground of hope (Job 4:6; Ps. 71:5).[5] On the other hand, those who deal treacherously with God (the verbs 'wait' and 'deal treacherously' stand in contrast with God as the object) will find that there is no deliverance for them. 'Put to shame' tends to suggest in English that the inner state of mind is primarily in view, whereas the Hebrew usage points rather to public disgrace.

Show me your ways, O LORD, teach me your paths; guide me in your truth and teach me, for you are God my Saviour, and my hope is in you all day long (*vv. 4-5*). Two things especially are needed by the psalmist and they are interconnected. He needs enlightenment regarding God's ways, and then he needs God's help to rescue him from his present troubles. In the context God's 'ways' are not the general moral principles to be observed, but rather the ways of deliverance to be provided by him. This is made plain in verse 5 by the clause '*for* (Hebrew *kî*) you are God my Saviour', and also by verse 9, where the 'ways' are those in which God guides as deliverer. He looks for further instruction from the LORD, with the Hebrew root *d-r-k* appearing twice in verses 4-5 (*derâkîm* 'ways' and *dârak* Hi. 'lead [me]'). To be 'led in the truth' (Hebrew *'emet*) means the truth that belongs to

---

[5] No exact equivalent occurs in the New Testament, though the idea is present in the reference to our Lord being in agony (*agônia*) so that 'he prayed more earnestly' (Luke 22:44). Similarly, Epaphras is described by Paul as 'wrestling in prayer' (*agônizomenos*) for the Colossians (Col. 4:12). For a discussion on the various Hebrew verbs used regarding 'waiting on the Lord', see J. G. S. S. Thomson, 'Wait on the Lord', *ET* 66 (1954), pp. 196-98.

God (cf. the expression in verse 10, 'all the ways of the LORD are loving and *faithful* [Hebrew *ᵉmet*]). Appeal to his God involves acknowledgment that he is the God of his salvation or deliverance ('God my Saviour'). The use of this description of God is in reference to his distress. Constantly he looks in trust to his God. The last sentence in verse 7 is usually taken to mean that David was constantly looking to his God, but an alternative interpretation is possible. It is possible to translate 'I wait for your sign [of deliverance] all day long', and this makes very good sense in the context.⁶

Remember, O LORD, your great mercy and love, for they are from of old. Remember not the sins of my youth and my rebellious ways; according to your love remember me, for you are good, O LORD (*vv. 6-7*). There is a threefold use of 'remember' in these verses. He asks for forgiveness of past sins, for God not to remember his sins, and finally for God to remember him as an individual. His past sins troubled him, even the rash sins of youth, and he did not want them held against him. He can pray confidently because he is basing his prayer on the character of God. He is the covenant God who displays covenant love to his people, and acts towards them with generous compassion.

2. The Goodness of the LORD (*vv. 8-15*)

The final statement of verse 7 is amplified at the start of verse 8. **Good and upright is the LORD; therefore he instructs sinners in his ways. He guides the humble in what is right and teaches them his way** (*vv. 8-9*). God is good, and one way in which he shows that goodness is in teaching sinners his ways. He desires that they know his ways and so be guided in true paths. He wants all men to come to a knowledge of the truth (1 Tim. 2:4) and repent of their sinful ways. God's scholars should always be humble, for 'he mocks proud mockers but gives grace to the humble' (Prov. 3:34; also quoted in 1 Pet. 5:5).

---

⁶ The Hebrew word translated by the NIV 'is in you' is *'ôtʿkâ*, which can be the object marker (*'et* with pronominal suffix 2 m.s.) or the noun *'ôt* (with pronominal suffix 2 m.s.) meaning a 'sign'. I have commented on this word in *Isaiah: A Covenant to be Kept for the Sake of the Church*, pp. 83-84.

All the ways of the LORD are loving and faithful for those who keep the demands of his covenant. For the sake of your name, O LORD, forgive my iniquity, though it is great (*vv. 10-11*). A cluster of terms point to the covenant relationship, and the general demands of God on Israel as a whole are individualised in passages such as this when personal responsibility is the issue. Being in covenant with the LORD always brought with it demands. The same is true of Christians who have to show their love to Jesus by obedience to his commands (Matt. 28:20; John 14:15). Here the psalmist says that God's ways reflect his character in that they are also loving and faithful.[7] The NIV rendering is a little free at the end of verse 10 because the Hebrew text uses two synonyms to describe the formal relationship with the Lord – 'his covenant and his testimonies'. The NLT is better: 'The LORD leads with unfailing love and faithfulness all those who keep his covenant and obey his decrees'. This is a reminder that the relationship binding the believers to the LORD was of a formal nature with a solemn ceremony in which they swore allegiance to him. Because God is both 'good and upright' the psalmist asks for forgiveness. God cannot overlook sin, but in his mercy can forgive. No matter how great the sin, it can be forgiven. He remains today just and the justifier of the person who believes in Jesus (Rom. 3:26).

Who, then, is the man that fears the LORD? He will instruct him in the way chosen for him. He will spend his days in prosperity, and his descendants will inherit the land (*vv. 12-13*). Already the psalmist has described what fearing the LORD involves – including praying, and receiving his instruction. Now he says that that instruction will be in the way of God's will. While the NIV translation 'the way chosen

---

[7] The pair 'unfailing love' (*chésed*) and 'faithfulness' (*ʾemet*) come together fifty-one times in the Old Testament. The usage suggests that they express a single idea, but this is hard to bring out in English translation. 'Unfailing love' comes near to it, as the meaning of *chésed* seems more dominant than that of 'truth' or 'faithfulness'. On this expression, see Gordon R. Clark, *The Word Hesed in the Hebrew Bible*, pp. 235-55. The New Testament use of 'grace and truth' (John 1:17) echoes this phrase, and both the older Hebrew translation of the New Testament and the modern one retain the two Hebrew words *chésed* and *ʾemet*.

for him' is possible, it is better to understand it as an active choice the individual makes—'the way he must go', or 'the way he should go'. Such a man will enjoy rest and safety, while his descendants will continue to occupy the land of Canaan. Elsewhere the psalms teach that the wicked will be uprooted from the land and perish (Pss. 1:5; 37:10-11), a repetition of the covenant curse first stated in Leviticus 26:27-35 and then also in Deuteronomy 4:26-27.[8]

The LORD confides in those who fear him; he makes his covenant known to them. My eyes are ever on the LORD, for only he will release my feet from the snare (*vv. 14-15*). The covenant also meant a close bond of friendship with the LORD. There existed a reciprocal relationship in which believers feared the LORD (with a child's, not a slave's, fear) and the LORD disclosed to them more of himself and his covenant.[9] It also meant that in times of trouble, such as the psalmist presently faced, the believer fixed his eyes on the LORD. Only he could deliver from all the traps that the enemies had laid.

3. A Tender Appeal (*vv. 16-22*)
Turn to me and be gracious to me, for I am lonely and afflicted. The troubles of my heart have multiplied; free me from my anguish. Look upon my affliction and my distress and take away all my sins (*vv. 16-18*). Again the psalm returns to direct address to God. The psalmist was facing troubles from within (his own sins) and troubles from without (hatred from his enemies). From both he pleads for release. He senses his loneliness, i.e. he was without a helper, and consequently he makes his appeal for God's graciousness to be shown to him. He feels hemmed in by his troubles and he wants to be taken out of his distress. Knowing that God would forgive for his own name's sake (see verse 11), he asks again for the removal of his sins along with help

---

[8] This teaching is an important aspect of the way in which the concept of 'the land' is dealt with in Deuteronomy. See 6:18; 8:1; 11:8, 21; 16:20; 28:11; 28:58-63; 30:17-20.

[9] The opening word in Hebrew of verse 14 is *sôd*, which can have the meaning of 'secret' (cf. the older English translations, 'the *secret* of the LORD'). However, in this context, as in Psalm 55:14, it means 'trustworthy speech' or 'close fellowship'.

in his troubles. Whereas in verse 16 'affliction' is paralleled with 'loneliness', in verse 18 it is linked with 'distress'. This indicates something of the breadth of meaning that 'affliction' can have, ranging from personal illness to social ostracism. **See how my enemies have increased and how fiercely they hate me! Guard my life and rescue me; let me not be put to shame, for I take refuge in you. May integrity and uprightness protect me, because my hope is in you** (*vv. 19-21*). The call for God to 'see' is really a call to help.[10] The trouble surrounding him was not just verbal abuse. He was facing physical danger from the enemies. That is why he asks for God to rescue him, lest his enemies should be able to gloat over him. As his song draws to a close he returns to the theme of trusting in the LORD and also the idea of facing shame or reproach (see vv. 2-3). He had no other helper, for his trust was in the LORD alone. God's character ('integrity and uprightness') was the basis for his plea, and his desire is to reflect in his life God's own character (cf. v. 8). There is no reference to God's answer in the psalm itself, but clearly the praise portion which has preceded (vv. 8-14) suggests an expectancy on the part of the psalmist.

4. A Prayer for the Nation (*v. 22*)

Redeem Israel, O God, from all their troubles! (*v. 22*). This final verse begins with the letter *pe* (like *p* coming after *A–Z* in English). This has led many to think that this verse was added when the psalm began to be used in formal worship situations. The fact that it uses the name 'God' and not 'LORD' also supports this. On the other hand, the references to the covenant in the psalm may well have led into this final verse with reference to all Israel. What was true of the psalmist, was also true of the whole nation, or to put it in another way, the whole psalm was applicable to Israel. If an individual could appeal for help in his personal troubles, why should Israel not appeal for deliverance as well? The call for redemption is equivalent to a call for deliverance (cf. Ps. 3:8, 'Deliverance belongs to the LORD').

---

[10] The MT begins with a verb whose initial consonant is *rêsh*, whereas the letter expected in the acrostic pattern is *qôf*. Craigie, *Psalms 1-50*, pp. 216-17, emends provisionally by inserting a verb starting with *qôf* and meaning 'meet', but no textual support for this is available.

Psalm 26
Of David.

This psalm does not appear to be an individual complaint to God, for there is no mention of illness or of persecution. Rather, the context from which it comes seems to be worship at the tabernacle. The psalmist renounces connection with ungodly men (vv. 4-5, 9-10), and longs to be in the assembly of the righteous proclaiming the wonderful deeds of the LORD (vv. 6-8, 12). His love is for God's altar (v. 6), God's house (v. 8), and God's people (v. 12). Possibly this song was later used as worshippers came individually to the temple precincts to worship at the LORD's altar.

1. A Confession of Trust (*v. 1*)
Vindicate me, O LORD, for I have led a blameless life; I have trusted in the LORD without wavering. The psalmist expresses his confident trust in the LORD, for he has maintained his confidence without slipping from his ways.[1] His appeal to God is for vindication as he comes to the temple again to worship. He knows that all authority is of God, who is going to preside at the last great judgment (Ps. 96:13). To him he cries again for vindication, since the central issue of his life is his relationship with his God. The combination of the noun 'perfection' (*tôm*) and the verb 'to walk' (*hâlak*) is frequently

---

[1] The NIV rendering 'without wavering' represents the Hebrew *lô' 'em'âd*, 'I shall not slip.' Those whose trust is in the LORD will not depart from his ways (cf. also Ps. 37:31), whereas those who lack integrity before him are sure to slip (Job 12:5; Ps. 69:23; Prov. 25:19).

used to indicate blameless conduct. The same combination occurs again in verse 11.[2]

2. A Prayer and an Affirmation (*vv.* 2-5)

Stemming from his confession of trust in verse 1, the psalmist moves on to make his request from the LORD. **Test me, O LORD, and try me, examine my heart and my mind; for your love is ever before me, and I walk continually in your truth** (*vv.* 2-3). Here three synonyms are used to describe putting to the test. The first of these ('test') is commonly used of God, and often has a very spiritual connotation. The second ('try') is the general word for testing or refining, while the third ('examine') is the more specific, being a term from metallurgy meaning 'smelt' or 'refine'. The psalmist is so confident of his standing that he is willing to submit to the all-seeing eye of the LORD. His attention was continually fixed on God's covenantal love and his whole conduct (his 'walk') was based on God's truth. The fact that the appeal is based on God's 'love' (Hebrew, *chésed*) is characteristic of hope in times of trouble (see also Psalms 13:5; 17:7; 33:18, 22; 36:7; 143:8; and 147:11).

I do not sit with deceitful men, nor do I consort with hypocrites; I abhor the assembly of evildoers and refuse to sit with the wicked (*vv.* 4-5). Anyone like the psalmist, committed to the LORD and his truth, shuns the association with those who show no love to the LORD. There is no desire to be in constant contact with them as individuals, for they are utterly deceitful.[3]

---

[2] Many, including C. S. Lewis, *Reflections on the Psalms* (London: Geoffrey Bles, 1958), pp. 66-67, misunderstand protests of innocence on the part of the psalmists. Instead of looking at them as holding a position that leads 'straight to "Pharisaism"' in the sense which Our Lord's own teaching has given that word', they must be viewed as expressing knowledge that there is 'no condemnation' for them in God's presence. Such a view of their innocence lies behind their confident appeal to their deliverer.

[3] The expression 'deceitful men' (*mᵉtê shâv'*) employs an unusual word for 'men', which can be used both for those of good or bad character. While *shâv'* can mean 'an idol' (cf. 24:5), here it probably is best to retain a translation like 'deceitful'. This is necessary in the context because of the following word that the NIV translates as 'hypocrites' (*naʿᵃlâmîm*). Most probably this is a Ni. part. of the verb *ʿâlam*, indicating those who hide themselves and their actions. It parallels, therefore, the other terms used here for deceitful men, evildoers, and the wicked.

Nor will they identify with such people when they gather together, finding them abhorrent because of their wickedness.

3. Approaching the Place of Worship (vv. 6-8)

Coming to the temple the psalmist now speaks of the nature of true worship. **I wash my hands in innocence, and go about your altar, O LORD, proclaiming aloud your praise and telling of all your wonderful deeds** (*vv. 6-7*). The idea of washing one's hands probably comes from Exodus 30:17-21, where Aaron and his sons were commanded to wash their hands and feet before they did service at the altar. Here the idea is figurative. Nowhere is such a ceremony of going round the altar commanded in the law, but apparently such an occasion involved singing songs of thanksgiving to the LORD. It may be that the king had a special function at this ceremony. It was an opportunity for praise and proclamation. 'Proclaiming aloud your praise' is more literally to 'proclaim with the voice of thanksgiving' (NASB). While the Hebrew noun for 'thanksgiving' (*tôdâh*) is used in a technical sense in reference to the peace offering called a thank-offering (Lev. 7:12), here it is used in its other more general meaning of a song of praise. To tell of the LORD's wonderful deeds means to recount the great acts of God, especially those associated with his work as saviour and deliverer.[4]

I love the house where you live, O LORD, the place where your glory dwells (*v. 8*). Past association with the place of worship, which is intended especially as the place of God's presence, meant that David could speak of his love for it. It was where God's glory took up an abiding presence, and it is noticeable that God's glory is specially mentioned in connection with the ark of the covenant (see Psalm 24:7; 1 Samuel 4:21; and 1 Kings 8:10-11).

4. Another Prayer (vv. 9-10)

Do not take away my soul along with sinners, my life with bloodthirsty men, in whose hands are wicked schemes,

---

[4] The Hebrew verb used here (*sâfar*) in the Qal form means 'to count', while the Piel form means 'to re-count, to tell'. The English verb 'tell' once had two distinct meanings, though the second one (to count) has almost dropped out of use except for the name of a specific bank employee, a teller.

whose right hands are full of bribes (*vv. 9-10*). The thought of entering into God's house immediately suggests the contrast – being with ungodly sinners. Any evildoer who attempted to draw near to God would be destroyed (Ps. 5:4-6). David does not want to be killed by God's judgment along with other ungodly people, and so he prays that God will not take away his life. The sins he mentions were probably intended as a general description of sinful actions, though they could also have been things of which he was unjustly accused.

5. Continuing Trust (*vv. 11-12*)
But I lead a blameless life; redeem me and be merciful to me. My feet stand on level ground; in the great assembly I will praise the Lord (*vv. 11-12*). At the close of the psalm, reference is made back to verse 1, picking up again the theme of integrity before the Lord. Entry into God's presence was not to be determined by merit, but only by grace. Hence the psalmist prays for redemptive mercy to be shown to him. The reference to 'level ground' could be to the floor of the tabernacle, or else the phrase could be a metaphor for uprightness of life. When, by grace, he entered the assembly of God's people, the psalmist would there bless the Lord. The psalm, which began on a note of trust (v. 1), ends here on the note of praise.

Psalm 27
Of David.[1]

This personal appeal to the LORD is made in the face of pressing attacks, though nothing in the psalm enables precise identification of them to take place. There are expressions of a military nature in the psalm that suggest that David is speaking as king. Especially in verse 3 the picture is of a battle situation in which he and his country are facing serious attacks. Yet his trust is in the LORD and he can encourage himself and others to take heart and to wait for him. He knows that the enmity that he is experiencing is not so much against him as against the LORD.

1. Confidence in the LORD (*vv. 1-6*)
The LORD is my light and my salvation – whom shall I fear? The LORD is the stronghold of my life – of whom shall I be afraid? (*v. 1*). David sums up what the LORD was to him in three words – 'light', 'salvation', and 'stronghold'. 'Light' may well have carried overtones of a military nature, for it is used in Psalm 18:28-29 of military victory. 'Salvation', in a context like this, can be virtually equivalent to deliverance and victory. 'Stronghold' notes the safety that the LORD affords, and the protection he was to David and his people. Is it surprising then that, by his two questions, he can assert his complete trust in his deliverer?

---

[1] The LXX adds *pro tou christhênai*, 'before he was anointed'. This could in effect be a claim that the psalm was composed before David was anointed at Hebron, though it is so indefinite that it could be a reference to some other anointing, for example, of a high priest.

When evil men advance against me to devour my flesh, when my enemies and my foes attack me, they will stumble and fall (v. 2). It is not clear if 'devouring the flesh' is to be taken as a metaphor for destruction, thus comparing his enemies with wild animals. It could also refer to personal attacks of a verbal kind, such as false witnesses could make (see verse 12). This latter viewpoint is probably correct, as in Aramaic the phrase 'to eat the flesh' means 'to slander', an interpretation followed by the RSV, 'uttering slanders against me'. Whatever the oppression he was certain of God's intervention and that no attack would succeed. God would ensure that the enemies stumbled and fell.

Though an army besiege me, my heart will not fear; though war break out against me, even then will I be confident (v. 3). This verse is an expansion of the idea of verse 1, 'Whom shall I fear?' Even if faced with a siege against Jerusalem, or a bold attack on him, yet the psalmist will trust in what God is to him. He had promised himself as a deliverer, and on that David stakes his confidence. The repetition of words and sounds in the opening of each of the statements in this verse makes them stand out.

> 'im-tach^{a}neh 'âlay mach^{a}neh ... Though an host encamp against me ...
> 'im-tâqûm 'âlay milchâmâh ... Though war arises against me ...

One thing I ask of the Lord, this is what I seek: that I may dwell in the house of the Lord all the days of my life, to gaze upon the beauty of the Lord and to seek him in his temple (v. 4). The opening of verse 4 has no parallel anywhere in the Old Testament. It is a statement of exclusive trust in the Lord. His faith is such that he wants to live continually in God's presence. In particular he wants to see the glory of the Lord symbolised by the ark of the covenant and the associated ceremonies of worship, and to be able to see the Lord at the sanctuary. Such 'seeking' may well have been in connection with the military dangers he faced, when advice from the priest concerning the will of the Lord would be sought. The clause 'that I may dwell in the house of the Lord all the days of my life' is very similar to words in Psalm 23:6, 'that I may return to the house of the LORD for length of days'.[2] 'House' (*báyit*) can designate the temple (see 2 Sam. 7:13; Ps. 122:1), and this is made clear in the context by the use of 'temple' (*hêkâl*) later in the verse. Expressions such as these may well have been part of the standard religious language in Israel. The desire to 'see' God may refer to visionary experience, such as Isaiah experienced (Isa. 6:1), but the verb used can have wider connotations of perception and appreciation. Hence it is probably synonymous with the verb to 'seek'.

For in the day of trouble he will keep me safe in his dwelling; he will hide me in the shelter of his tabernacle and set me high upon a rock (*v. 5*). Confident trust enables the psalmist to express how safe he felt. Probably the references to 'dwelling' and 'tabernacle' are general in character, and are not directed specifically to the dwelling place of the ark.[3] The final words of the verse support this interpretation, because lifting high on a rock suggests safety and protection in general (cf. Ps. 3:3). The expression 'hide me in the shelter' is very striking in Hebrew because both verb and noun come from the same root (*yastirênî bᵉsêter*), rather like saying in English, 'hide me in the hide.'

Then my head will be exalted above the enemies who surround me; at his tabernacle will I sacrifice with shouts of joy; I will sing and make music to the LORD (*v. 6*). The outcome of the LORD's protection is that the psalmist experiences deliverance from his enemies, and with thankful heart he wants to sacrifice and praise the LORD. Sacrifices of thanksgiving would be offered after military victories, and with joyful song the LORD would be praised (for an example, see 1 Sam. 4:6). The idea of a sacrifice of praise goes back to

---

[2] Here the verb is vocalised as *shivtî* ('dwell') as compared with *shavtî* ('return') in Psalm 23:6. No need exists to suggest as BHS does, that this expression has been taken over by a copyist and inserted at this point in Psalm 27. There is no grammatical reason to support this, and it is hard to explain why, if this happened, the whole clause was not repeated, i.e. including 'length of days' instead of 'all the days of my life'.

[3] The phrase 'in his dwelling' is the Qᵉre reading (*bᵉsukkô*), whereas the Kᵉtiv reading is 'booth' (*sukkâh*). The Massoretic vocalisation seems to be correct (cf. Psalm 76:2), and gives a good parallel to the following 'tent' (*'ôhel*).

Leviticus 7:12, and this is reflected in the New Testament phrase, 'a sacrifice of praise' (Heb. 13:15). If this psalm was used in later worship situations in the Old Testament church, it may have been that a sacrifice would be offered at this point in its recitation.

2. Prayer for Divine Assistance (*vv. 7-13*)

Hear my voice when I call, O LORD; be merciful to me and answer me (*v. 7*). The flow of thought from the first part of the psalm continues on into the second part, with several key words being repeated. Now the psalmist cries to God to hear his request and to show compassion to him in his need. Praise has turned into prayer. Here he prays in general terms, while later (see v. 11) he becomes more specific. The appeal to God to 'hear the voice' is one of the standard expressions of petition (see other examples in Pss. 64:1; 119:149; 130:2), while the plea for mercy is a repetition of the prayer already uttered in the previous psalm (Ps. 26:11). 'Answer me' is a frequent cry that both acknowledges the supplicant's need and invokes God's favour.

My heart says of you, 'Seek his face!' Your face, LORD, I will seek (*v. 8*). The translation of this verse is difficult, as all the ancient translations show. The main problem is that in Hebrew the imperative 'seek' is second person plural, while the context requires second person singular. The NIV margin provides an alternative that may be the best solution at the moment: 'To you, O my heart, he has said, "Seek my face".'[4] The expressions 'seek God' and 'seek his face' may go back to Deuteronomy 4:29. If so, the psalmist is acting in the spirit of that verse as he indicates that he is indeed seeking admission to God's presence in order to ask a favour.

Do not hide your face from me, do not turn your servant away in anger; you have been my helper. Do not reject me or forsake me, O God my Saviour (*v. 9*). He wants God's presence to be manifest to him, not hidden as when God is

---

[4] This suggestion still does not solve all the problems, for it presupposes a singular imperative ('seek') whereas the MT has the plural. For discussion of other suggestions, and also possible emendation, see P. C. Craigie, *Psalms 1-50*, p. 230.

angry with his children. He acknowledges that God has been his helper, using a Hebrew expression that suggests God's abiding nature as his helper.[5] What he was in the past, he continues to be to David. The psalmist pleads that his Saviour will not thrust him away in his need.

Though my father and mother forsake me, the LORD will receive me (*v. 10*). This expression is not to be taken literally, as though David's parents are abandoning him. Rather, it expresses the new relationship that David as king has with the LORD. God now fills the role that David's parents previously occupied. The king is adopted as God's son (Ps. 2:7) and therefore is sheltered by him.

Teach me your way, O LORD; lead me in a straight path because of my oppressors. Do not turn me over to the desire of my foes, for false witnesses rise up against me, breathing out violence (*vv. 11-12*). The specific request he makes is for guidance in God's way and for direction in a straight path (cf. the same type of request in Psalm 25:4-5). He wants to be kept in God's paths, though his oppressors are attacking him.[6] He fears their designs on him, for they are speaking lies against him and their purpose is to destroy him.[7] The opponents could well be foreign nations who do not want Israel's king to be walking in the ways of her covenant LORD.

I am still confident of this: I will see the goodness of the LORD in the land of the living (*v. 13*). The commencement of this verse in Hebrew presents a problem, one that was apparent to the Massoretic scholars for they marked it with unusual notation, placing dots both above and below each of the three consonants of the opening word. They also added a note drawing attention to the fact that this is the only

---

[5] The construction consists of the verb *hâyâh* and a substantive with suffix, '*ezrâtî*, 'my help'. This is used instead of the perfect of the verb '*âzar*, 'to help'.

[6] See the footnote on 5:9 for discussion on the word 'oppressors'. This is one of the contexts where the translation 'slanderers' would be appropriate, especially since 'false witnesses' are mentioned in the following verse.

[7] 'The desire of my foes' is an idiomatic Hebrew expression (lit. 'the life of my foes') that occurs again in Psalm 41:2.

occurrence in the Hebrew Bible of this phenomenon.[8] The best explanation of the difficulty is to suggest that verse 13 contains an opening clause that is never finished by the addition of an apodosis. The translation then can be: 'If I did not believe that I would see the goodness of the LORD in the land of the living ...!' The unspoken result is that he would perish. While the NIV and similar translations do not follow exactly the grammatical structure of the Hebrew text, yet they convey faithfully the meaning. The verse is a confident assertion of trust in the LORD and the conviction that David would see his saving power. He knew that he would not be cut off in the midst of his days (Psalm 102:24, lit. 'in the half of my days'). The land of the living is simply the opposite of the land of the dead (see Pss. 52:5 and 116:9, and Isa. 38:11).

3. A Call to Wait (v. 14)

Wait for the LORD; be strong and take heart and wait for the LORD (v. 14). This final verse appears to be a call to others to follow the psalmist's example, though it is possible that it is addressed to himself as a word of self-encouragement. The repetition of the word 'wait' gives particular force to the idea, emphasising waiting with tenseness or eagerness.[9] From a strong faith in the LORD flows mighty deeds in his name. The 'heart' stands for the centre of the psalmist's whole life. With all of his being he is willing, like Joshua (Deut. 31:7 and Josh. 1:6-7), to serve the LORD.

---

[8] The Massoretic note reads: 'One of 4 occurrences written with a final א and the only occurrence in the Bible of a word with special diacritical points both above and below all consonants, except the consonant *vav*, and this is one of 15 words in the Bible with special diacritical points.' See *The Masorah of Biblia Hebraica Stuttgartensia: Introduction and Annotated Glossary*, Page H. Kelley, Daniel S. Mynatt, and Timothy G. Crawford (Grand Rapids: Eerdmans, 1998), p. 140. The note on this verse by P. C. Craigie, *Psalms 1-50*, p. 230, gives a good summary of the difficulty.

[9] *CHAL*, p. 315. See also the footnote on Psalm 25:3.

Psalm 28
Of David.

While the setting of this psalm seems to be very similar to that of Psalm 26, it also has affinities with both Psalms 23 and 25. The reference to the LORD as the shepherd in the last verse connects it with Psalm 23. Like Psalm 25, it ends with prayer for the Israel of God. The interconnection of Psalms 23-28 suggests that it formed a group of songs linked together by common themes. The period of Absalom's rebellion against David may form the historical background of both this psalm and Psalm 26. The peril of the psalmist, his enemy's hypocrisy, and the mention of the sanctuary, all point in this direction. It is an appeal on behalf of the people and their anointed king (God's anointed one, 'his messiah', v. 8) against enemies from within their own nation. Many of the expressions in the psalm are paralleled elsewhere, forming part of the language of individual and corporate prayer.

1. A General Plea (*vv. 1-2*)
To you I call, O LORD my Rock; do not turn a deaf ear to me. For if you remain silent, I will be like those who have gone down to the pit. Hear my cry for mercy as I call to you for help, as I lift up my hands toward your Most Holy Place (*vv. 1-2*). There is but one 'rock' for the psalmist and that is the LORD (cf. Ps. 18:2). To him he makes his appeal and asks that he will not refuse to listen to him. He doesn't want God to remain deaf to his plea. This would really mean being 'inactive', 'not helping'. If God doesn't intervene, then death stares him in the face. 'To go down to the pit' is an Old Testament expression for

death (cf. Psalms 30:3; 88:4; and 143:7).[1] The poet recognises he needs mercy, for his situation is desperate. He has his hands lifted up, as it were, out of the pit, waiting for God to rescue him. Alternatively, here and elsewhere the expression 'to lift up the hands' could be to a posture symbolising being ready to receive from God an answer to prayer. The 'Most Holy Place' ($d^ev\hat{\imath}r$) appears to designate the inner sanctuary of the tabernacle/temple, the place that symbolised God's earthly presence.[2]

2. Deliverance from his Enemies (vv. 3-5)

Do not drag me away with the wicked, with those who do evil, who speak cordially with their neighbours but harbour malice in their hearts (v. 3). The psalmist did not want to be associated with wicked people. He characterises them in three ways. They practise evil, on the surface they speak peacefully to their neighbours, and in their hearts they treasure up evil. 'To practise evil' is a phrase that occurs about twenty times, in Job, the Psalms and Proverbs. It may designate men who were skilled in magic or idolatrous ritual, for the Hebrew word for evil in this phrase (*'âven*) sometimes denotes idolatry (cf. *Beth-aven*, Hos. 5:8; 10:5, 8).

Repay them for their deeds and for their evil work; repay them for what their hands have done and bring back upon them what they deserve. Since they show no regard for the works of the LORD and what his hands have done, he will tear them down

---

[1] 'Pit' (*bôr*) and *she'ôl* are often synonymous terms, though in Ezekiel 32:18-32 a distinction is made between them. *Bôr* can also mean a cistern, and then by transference of ideas, a prison. The best discussion on the Hebrew terms for death is W. VanGemeren, 'Appendix: Sheol-Grave-Death in the Psalms', 'Psalms', pp. 569-73.

[2] The Hebrew phrase 'toward your Most Holy Place' (*'el d^{e}vîr qodsh^{e}kâ*) only occurs here. The word *d^{e}vîr* is never used of the holy of holies in the wilderness tabernacle. It occurs sixteen times, mainly in the descriptions regarding the building of the temple. However, some ambiguity exists regarding its meaning, for while it does denote the holy place, it also seems to be distinguished from it, designating a back or side room of the temple (see 1 Kings 8:6). For further discussion, see Earl S. Kalland in *TWOT* 1, p. 181 (and the literature cited), and G. H. Jones, *1 and 2 Kings* (New Century Bible: London: 1984), 1, pp. 169, 195.

and never build them up again (*vv. 4-5*). Words such as these, calling for vengeance on enemies, seem to some as contradictory to Christian belief in love and forgiveness. However, a much broader view has to be taken of them (see the fuller discussion in the Introduction, p. 72-76). David is asking for the curses of the covenant to be visited on those who are in breach of its requirements.[3] To repay what people deserve is a technical legal expression. The LORD is a God of retribution (Ps. 94:2; Jer. 51:56) who gives to the wicked their due. They have yet to learn that there is a marked contrast between the works of their hands (v. 4) and the works of the LORD's hands (v. 5). The form of the cursing here echoes Deuteronomy 28 and it has many similarities to passages in Jeremiah (cf. verse 5b with Jer. 24:6; 42:10; 45:4). While the psalmists call for retribution now, the prophets in their declarations regarding retribution focus more on the future.

3. Praise for the Deliverer (*vv. 6-9*)
Praise be to the LORD, for he has heard my cry for mercy. The LORD is my strength and my shield; my heart trusts in him, and I am helped. My heart leaps for joy and I will give thanks to him in song (*vv. 6-7*). There is a direct link between the words of thanksgiving and the earlier part of the psalm. He had asked, 'Hear my cry for mercy' (v. 2a). Here he says that the LORD has heard his cry for mercy. He has received the assurance of the LORD's intervention on his behalf (v. 5), and now he praises him for deliverance. This, in concise form, is a song of thanksgiving. It starts with an introduction (v. 6a) and ends with a conclusion (v. 7c, d). It has a confession in verse 7a, and a recounting of the deliverance in verses 6b and 7b. He acknowledges his refuge, and he can sing a jubilant song about the LORD,[4] now and always. Even in his great need he did

---

[3] The general theme of God's retribution as taught in the Old Testament is dealt with by J. Robert Vannoy, 'Retribution, Theology of' in *NIDOTTE*, 4, pp. 1140-49.
[4] The MT, 'and from a song' (*ûmishshîr*), is awkward in the context. Consonantal emendation is unnecessary as here and in Psalm 137:3 the word is *mâshîr*, 'a song'. This means that, as in Ugaritic, biblical Hebrew had two words for 'song', *shîr* and *mâshîr*. Cf. *DCH*, V, p. 522, and the bibliography on p. 883.

not cease to trust in the LORD, and in deliverance the psalmist confesses where his help lies. The combination of 'shield' and another word like 'strength', 'help', or 'sun' is frequent in the Psalms to convey the ideas of God as protector and defender of his people. The use of the military term 'shield' also ties in with the concepts of the divine warrior and the holy war.[5]

The LORD is the strength of his people,[6] a fortress of salvation for his anointed one (*v. 8*). The psalmist's confession continues with the acknowledgment that the LORD is not only his strength, but that of his people in general. What he is to the king in person ('his anointed one'), he is also to the believing community as a whole. A play on words occurs, for the LORD is both the strength (*ʿoz*) of his people and their fortress (*mâʿoz*).

Save your people and bless your inheritance; be their shepherd and carry them forever (*v. 9*). This verse confirms the impression that the setting of the psalm is a time of national danger. David prays for salvation of the people of Israel, and blessing for God's inheritance. The concept of Israel as God's special, chosen heritage (Exod. 34:9; Deut. 4:20) is carried over in New Testament thought (see Eph. 1:3-6). The idea of the loving shepherd is reminiscent of Psalms 23:1; 80:1; 100:3; and Isaiah 40:11.

---

[5] Cf. the comments on Psalm 3:5. For a summary discussion of the concept of the divine warrior, see Tremper Longman III, 'Divine Warrior', *NIDOTTE*, V, p. 545-49.

[6] The NIV 'of his people' involves an alteration of the text from 'for them' (*lâmô*) to 'for his people' (*lᵉʿammô*). But the variant form of the preposition *lᵉ* with suffix can indicate 'for *them*' as well as 'for *him*'. The form of suffix in this case is one of a considerable number of occurrences in Hebrew poetry that are certainly archaic and that remain unexplained. On this point, see *IBHS*, p. 189.

Psalm 29

A psalm of David.

This is a mighty song of victory, and an exaltation of the power of the Lord. The sevenfold repetition of 'the voice of the Lord' (*qôl yhwh*) led Delitzsch to call it 'the psalm of the seven thunders'.[1] It has often been pointed out that this psalm has certain similarities to poetry known from Canaanite sources. This does not necessarily imply borrowing poetry and simply changing the name from Baal to the Lord (*yhwh*). It could be a polemical psalm directed against the heathen notions of the Canaanites, and in particular a denial of the place of Baal in the world of nature.[2] The fact that all the geographical references in the psalm are to places outside the area controlled by Israel (Lebanon, Sirion/Hermon, the desert of Kadesh) simply reinforces this point. The Lord is the mighty creator who has all the forces of nature at his control, both within and without Israelite territory. The emphasis on 'the Lord' comes out also in the fact that the name appears eighteen times in this short psalm. It also has similarities to other victory songs such as Exodus 15:1-18 and Judges 5:2-31, which also use storm imagery to describe victory in battle. A Jewish tradition, as early as around 250 BC, associated this psalm with the Feast of Tabernacles. The LXX reflects this in that it adds to the title '[on

---

[1] F. Delitzsch, *Psalms*, I, p. 367. The phrase 'the seven thunders' comes from Rev. 10:3.

[2] Cf. the conclusion of P. C. Craigie, *Psalms 1-50*, p. 245 on this question of possible borrowing from Canaanite sources: 'it is clear that there are sufficient parallels and similarities to require a Canaanite background to be taken into account in developing the interpretation of this psalm, but it is not clear that those parallels and similarities require one to posit a Canaanite/Phoenician original of Ps. 29.'

the occasion] of the solemn assembly', though in later rabbinic tradition this psalm was linked to the Feast of Weeks.[3]

1. A Call to Praise (*vv. 1-2*)

Ascribe to the LORD, O mighty ones, ascribe to the LORD glory and strength. Ascribe to the LORD the glory due his name; worship the LORD in the splendour of his holiness (*vv. 1-2*). The opening call is for the LORD's glory and strength to be acknowledged, and this is done using two significant features of Hebrew poetry, repetition and development. The pattern of these verses can be set out in diagrammatic form:

a – b – c	ascribe	to the LORD	O mighty ones
↓ ↓	↓	↓	
a – b – d	ascribe	to the LORD	glory and strength
↓ ↓ ↓	↓	↓	↘
a – b – d + e	ascribe	to the LORD	the glory of his name. Worship the LORD in the splendour of his holiness.[4]

'Glory', when an attribute of God, normally refers to visible beauty of God when he reveals himself, while the word 'strength' is often associated with victory in battles, as is the reference to God's name (see Exod. 15:3, for example). Those addressed are called 'sons of God' (*bᵉnê 'ēlîm*), which here and in Psalm 89:7 most probably denotes the angels.[5] The speaker requests the heavenly host to join in praise of the LORD. What is fittingly his, should be rendered to him in praise and adoration. Even angelic beings have to bow in submission to him.[6] The final phrase of verse 2 could refer to the manner in which the LORD was worshipped (as in NIV translation), or

---

[3] *Soferim* 18:3.

[4] For this basic structure, see Carroll Stuhlmueller, *Psalms I:1-72* (Collegeville, Minnesota: Michael Glazier, 1983), p. 171.

[5] Extensive bibliography exists in relation to this phrase. See P. C. Craigie, *Psalms 1-50*, p. 241-47; S. Terrien, *The Psalms*, pp. 274-75; *NIDOTTE*, 1, pp. 375-77.

[6] The verb 'to worship' is probably from a root *ch-v-h*, and carries the idea of prostration. It is normally used of communal worship, but it does occur less frequently of individuals. For details on the derivation and meaning, see *TDOT*, IV, pp. 248-56; *TWOT*, I, pp. 269-71.

it could refer to the garments that the servants wore. Some commentators have suggested that it refers to the dress that the priests wore on special occasions (see 2 Chron. 20:21). If that is correct, then a translation like 'the adornment of the king' is quite close in meaning to the NIV translation.[7]

2. The Mighty Voice of the LORD (vv. 3-9)

The voice of the LORD is over the waters; the God of glory thunders, the LORD thunders over the mighty waters *(v. 3)*. Mention is made seven times of the LORD's voice in this central section of the psalm. Thus it is clearly the focal point, as the psalmist uses the language of the storm to refer to God's power and glory. The picture of the LORD's coming is in terms of the thunderstorms that originate over the Mediterranean (v. 3), then cross the hill country (vv. 5-7) and finally peter out over the eastern desert (v. 8). Over all the mighty waters he reigns supreme, and he speaks as with a clap of thunder. The phrase 'the God of glory' is reminiscent of Psalm 24:7-10 with fourfold mention of 'the king of glory'.[8]

The voice of the LORD is powerful; the voice of the LORD is majestic *(v. 4)*. No verbs occur in this verse. Either the verb 'to be' has to be inserted in English (as in the NIV translation), or the verb 'to thunder' carries over from the previous verse. 'Powerful' (*koach*) is virtually the equivalent of 'strength' (*'oz*) in verse 1, while 'majestic' (*hâdâr*) is from the same root as 'splendour' (*hᵃdârâh*) in verse 2.

The voice of the LORD breaks the cedars; the LORD breaks in pieces the cedars of Lebanon *(vv. 5)*. The reference to Lebanon is interesting, because it marked the border with the Canaanite territory to the north. The cedars of Lebanon were

---

[7] The meaning of this rare word has been a problem even as far back as the time when the LXX was being translated. The LXX has 'court' (*aulê*), but no support for this comes from Hebrew manuscripts. Also, the LXX translation requires an emendation in the next word to make it read 'in *his* holy court'. An association with a Ugaritic word *hdrt*, 'revelation' or 'vision', is unlikely.

[8] Other links with Psalm 24 are the waters (v. 2), the sanctuary (v. 4), and celebration of the LORD's kingship (vv. 7-10).

well known, and they represented the strength of Lebanon itself. But they could be shattered by the majestic voice of the LORD. When he commanded, they split in pieces.

He makes Lebanon skip like a calf, Sirion like a young wild ox. The voice of the LORD strikes with flashes of lightning (*vv. 6-7*). Now Lebanon itself and nearby Sirion come directly into the picture. 'Sirion' is Mount Hermon (see Deut. 3:9), and here it is used as basically synonymous with Lebanon. God's voice makes these great mountains skip like young animals, for the creator has power over his creation.[9] Perhaps an earthquake is in view. The likening of the LORD's voice to lightning is in keeping with Near Eastern ideas, for lightning was often used in visual depictions to denote weaponry used in battle.

The voice of the LORD shakes the desert; the LORD shakes the Desert of Kadesh (*v. 8*). It is hard to know whether a specific desert is in view here, or whether it is just a general reference to the semi-desert steppe country. While the locality could be the Kadesh, situated about 50 miles (80 km) southwest of Beersheba (Kadesh Barnea), more probably it refers to Kadesh on the Orontes, a Hittite capital about 80 miles (128 km) north of Damascus. This places it in geographical proximity to Lebanon and Hermon. Whatever the exact location, the point is that the LORD exercises control over vast territories.

The voice of the LORD twists the oaks and strips the forests bare. And in his temple all cry, 'Glory!' (*v. 9*). This verse presents a contrast between what is happening outside (thunder, lightning, earthquake), and which disturbs the whole natural world, with what is happening in God's sanctuary. It is not clear if this sanctuary is the heavenly one, or the one

---

[9] The NIV translation assumes that the final *mem* on the verb (*vayyardîqêm*) is not the third person plural suffix but an enclitic *mem* (see Glossary for explanation). J. C. L. Gibson, *Canaanite Myths and Legends* (Edinburgh: T. & T. Clark, 1977), p. 150, regards this as one of the two 'reasonably certain survivals in Hebr. poetry' of this phenomenon: *vayyarqîd + m*, 'he made Lebanon skip'. Cf. also his later reference to enclitic *mem* in *DIHG—S*, pp. 24-5. The fullest bibliography on this matter can be found in *DCH*, V, pp. 823-25.

situated in Jerusalem. Perhaps the two were combined in the thought of the people, the earthly sanctuary being made after the fashion of the heavenly one. In the sanctuary there is peace, and a cry of 'Glory' arises. This provides a beautiful ending to this part of the psalm, for there is no parallel expression accompanying it and it calls attention to the way in which the psalm opened with a twofold command to praise (v. 1, 'ascribe to the LORD ... ascribe to the LORD glory and strength').

3. A Concluding Song of Praise (*vv. 10-11*)

The LORD sits enthroned over the flood; the LORD is enthroned as King forever. The LORD gives strength to his people; the LORD blesses his people with peace (*vv. 10-11*). The final verses of the psalm rejoice in the fact that the LORD is the eternal king. There seems to be a reference back to the creation account in Genesis 1 and to the story of the flood, recalling the manner in which God is sovereign over his creation, including the waters. What God is in himself (v. 1), he gives to his people, and having won victory for them he bestows his peace. The psalm that starts with 'glory to God in the highest' ends with 'peace upon earth'.

Psalm 30

A psalm. A song. For the dedication of the temple. Of David.

This song of thanksgiving is a joyful response to what God has done. Wailing has turned to dancing (v. 11), and there is praise to the LORD for the fact that he spared his servant, delivering him from death. The anguish on the part of the psalmist is reflected in the poetry, especially that the rhythmic patterns of the Hebrew text are very irregular. The staccato effect accentuates the distress of heart. The title is ambiguous. The Hebrew word translated 'dedication' (*ch^anukâh*) could mean 'initiation, commencement of use',[1] while the word 'temple' (*báyit*) is the Hebrew word for 'house' or 'palace'. This may be a Davidic psalm intended for use in his palace, or alternatively for the temple when it was built. It is possible that these words relating to the dedication of the temple were added to the superscription much later after the restoration of the temple following the exile. It is a song that concentrates on the LORD, using that title nine times, and twice he is called 'my God'. It is also much more concrete in its description of the danger from which the psalmist has been delivered than those in many other psalms.

1. A Grateful Song (*vv. 1-5*)
I will exalt you, O LORD, for you lifted me out of the depths and did not let my enemies gloat over me (*v. 1*). The verb

---

[1] The Jewish Feast of Dedication (Hanukkah) is post-biblical in origin. It commemorates the rededication of the temple in 165 BC by Judas Maccabeus, and later Jewish practice included the singing of Psalm 30 at the feast. The 'Feast of Dedication' is noted in John 10:22. For further details concerning it, see *TDOT*, 5:19-21.

261

'exalt' in a setting like this has the meaning of praising (cf. Ps. 99:5). The 'depths' from which the psalmist is lifted is clearly sickness, as becomes explicit in the following verses. Had he succumbed to that illness and died as a result of it, then his enemies would have taken great delight. The verb 'to lift' really means 'to draw [water]' and is paralleled by 'you brought me up' in verse 3.[2]

O Lord my God, I called to you for help and you healed me. O Lord, you brought me up from the grave; you spared me from going down into the pit (*vv.* 2-3). The psalmist directed his cry for help to God, and he found that he was restored. The verb 'to cry for help' (*shâva'*) is found more often in the psalms than in any other Old Testament book, and it is usually used in autobiographical settings such as this one. On most occasions it is used, as here, in a psalm of lament. In verse 3 'Sheol' (or the grave) and 'the pit' (*bôr*) are used in parallel to describe death.[3] What was involved in calling on the Lord is spelt out in more detail in verses 8-10.

Sing to the Lord, you saints of his; praise his holy name (*v.* 4). The psalmist wants the whole congregation to share with him in praising the Lord for his deliverance. He calls the members of the congregation 'saints' or 'holy ones'. The word used (*châsîd*) is clearly related to the Hebrew word *chésed*, 'mercy', and 'the holy ones' were probably called this because, having received God's mercy, they also were characterised by it in their lives. 'His holy name' is literally 'his holy memorial', which is an echo of Exodus 3:15, 'This is my name for ever, the name by which I am to be remembered from generation to generation.'

For his anger lasts only a moment, but his favour lasts a lifetime; weeping may remain for a night, but rejoicing comes in the morning (*v.* 5). The first part of this verse has long been recognised as proving difficult to translate. The LXX renders: 'For anger is in his wrath, but life in his favour.' This does not make much sense unless 'anger' is equivalent to

---

[2] This is the only time that the Pi. form of this verb occurs in the Old Testament. The Hebrew word for 'bucket' (*dᵉlî*) comes from this root (*d-l-h*). Cf. Isaiah 40:15, 'like a drop in a bucket'.

[3] See f.n. 1 on Psalm 28 for discussion on *she'ol* and *bôr*.

'death'. Certainly, the context here shows a contrast between death and life, and the idea that the Hebrew word *régaʿ* (NIV 'moment') means 'death' has had advocates both among older commentators and those in recent time.[4] This idea receives support, moreover, by the fact that the Hebrew word for 'life' (*cháyyîm*) is never used to refer to a 'lifetime'. Rather, it appears in contrast to death. In the second part of the verse, sorrow is depicted as if it was a guest that intruded into our lives. It takes up temporary lodging,[5] but it is eventually replaced by joy. The light of God's love chases away the night of sorrow and gloom.

2. A Detailed Description of His Deliverance (*vv. 6-12*)

When I felt secure, I said, 'I will never be shaken' (*v. 6*). The detailed description of the trouble from which the LORD had delivered him starts here. Looking back on his life before the onset of sickness, the psalmist realises that in his health he had been complacent and self-sufficient. This was something that a member of the covenant community should not have been (see Deut. 8:17-18). Prosperity and safety both came from the LORD.

O LORD, when you favoured me, you made my mountain stand firm; but when you hid your face, I was dismayed (*v. 7*). David has already spoken of 'favour' in verse 5. It is the response of God to repentance and faith on the part of his people. The contrast he presents is between being firmly established by God (as though set firm on a mountain) and trembling when God removes his favour. David was perplexed when God took away the signs of his gracious presence.

The psalmist now recalls his prayer to the LORD at the time of his trouble. **To you, O LORD, I called; to the Lord I cried for mercy: 'What gain is there in my destruction, in my going down into the pit? Will the dust praise you? Will it proclaim your faithfulness?** (*vv. 8-9*). These words show how, when realising his true condition, he turned to the LORD, seeking

---

[4] See in particular, M. Dahood, *Psalms I: 1-50*, pp. 182-83; P. C. Craigie, *Psalms 1-50*, pp. 250-51; E. W. Hengstenberg, *Commentary on the Psalms*, I, pp. 288-89.

[5] The verb is *lîn*, 'to lodge the night'.

mercy from him. His argument was that his death would not be any profit to God. All it would do would be to rob God of an offering of praise and confession.

Hear, O LORD, and be merciful to me; O LORD, be my help (*v. 10*). This is the outcome of the reasoning of the psalmist in the preceding verse. He now knew that his former feelings of self-sufficiency were gone. Instead he recognises that he needs the LORD's mercy if he is to recover from his sickness and join in praising him again. The only helper he has is the LORD. The repetition of the same verb in verses 8 and 10 serves to emphasise the urgency of his appeal (v. 8, 'I cried for mercy'; v. 10, 'be merciful to me').

You turned my wailing into dancing; you removed my sackcloth and clothed me with joy, that my heart may sing to you and not be silent. O LORD my God, I will give you thanks forever (*vv. 11-12*). In an expansion of verse 5b, the psalmist describes the complete reversal in his circumstances. Here the allusions are to the outward signs of sorrow (wailing and wearing of sackcloth) being removed. Instead, he has God-given joy and his whole being (his heart, his soul) is able to sing and praise the LORD.[6] Death would have brought silence. Recovery brings praise. The final verse is a reaffirmation of the praise with which the psalm began. It can be compared with the final verse of Hezekiah's song after he received mercy from the LORD and was spared: 'The LORD will save me, and we will sing with stringed instruments all the days of our lives in the temple of the LORD' (Isa. 38:20).

---

[6] For 'my heart' the Hebrew text has 'glory'. For this as a term of self-reference, see the note on Psalm 7:5. The LXX inserted the personal pronoun 'my', but this is not confirmed from Hebrew manuscripts.

Psalm 31

For the director of music. A psalm of David.

The indications, within the psalm itself, of its setting are not precise enough to allow certainty. Clearly the psalmist faced scheming enemies, who were slandering him. It may even have been a warlike situation, as there are various expressions that suggest the need for defence in the heat of battle. It is typical of songs of complaint in that, while the urgent needs come to the fore, yet there is thankful recognition for the wonderful love of the LORD shown to him. This individual lament falls into two parts (vv. 1-8, 9-24) that are more or less parallel, though the second part is more expansive. In both parts the steadfast love of the LORD sustains the psalmist (see vv. 7 and 16).

1. A Prayer for Deliverance (*vv. 1-8*)

In you, O LORD, I have taken refuge; let me never be put to shame; deliver me in your righteousness (*v. 1*). This opening is very like that of Psalm 71:1-3. The NIV translation captures well the emphasis at the commencement of the psalm. The psalmist points away from himself to the LORD, in whom he had taken refuge.[1] This is accentuated by the fact that there is

---

[1] The verb used here for 'to trust' (*châsâh*) is normally construed with the preposition *b^e*. It occurs most commonly in the Psalms, and in particular in songs of lament. In them it draws attention to the confident hope of the psalmist, even when circumstances seem so discouraging. The phrase used here, 'in you I trust' (*b^e kâ châsîtî*), seems to have become a stylised expression, and is often associated with other almost synonymous verbs such as 'trust' (*bâtach*), 'wait for' (*qâvâh*), and 'wait' (*yâchal*). For comment on the expression as a stylised form, see R. C. Culley, *Oral Formulaic Language in the Biblical Psalms* (Toronto: University of Toronto Press, 1967), p. 53; and for general discussion on this verb, *TWOT*, V, pp. 64-75.

no parallel expression to match it, and therefore it stands as an introduction to the whole psalm. In a context such as this 'put to shame' has the idea of being confused and disappointed. 'Righteousness' is not a reference to God's justice, but rather to his power to save. It often has this meaning in prophetical passages such as in Isaiah chapter 40 onwards.

Turn your ear to me, come quickly to my rescue; be my rock of refuge, a strong fortress to save me (*v.* 2). The opening prayer is expanded now, as the psalmist appeals for speedy help. In a pressing situation he asks that God would listen to him, and then hastily answer. 'To turn the ear' is a common expression in the Psalms (cf. Pss. 17:6; 71:2; 86:1; 88:2) and is an appeal to God to pay heed to the supplications of his worshippers. The terms the psalmist uses in the second part of the verse point to a military situation, for he is asking for protection and safety from a fierce enemy.

Since you are my rock and my fortress, for the sake of your name lead and guide me (*v.* 3). After asking for God to be his fortress, he now declares that is exactly what God is to him! That conviction is a fruit of his praying. He calls him 'my rock' and 'my fortress', and requests that for the honour of his name he will take him to a safe place. These metaphors denoting security and protection commonly occur in close proximity to verbs of 'trust'. The reference to 'name's sake' seems to go back to the experiences of the Exodus, when God, for his name's sake redeemed his people from their bondage and showed his mighty power (see Ps. 106:7-8).

Free me from the trap that is set for me, for you are my refuge. Into your hands I commit my spirit; redeem me, O LORD, the God of truth (*vv.* 4-5). For the first time in the psalm specific mention is made of the enemies, and he asks for deliverance from their snares. This is not just a metaphor, but an allusion to real life in the ancient Near East. Drawings exist that show Mesopotamian kings enclosing captured enemies in a net.[2] Again the overtones of the Exodus deliverance are here, with the expression 'free me' being one of the common

---

[2] J. B. Pritchard, ed., *Ancient Near East: An Anthology of Texts and Pictures* (Princeton: Princeton University Press, 1973), 1, p. 288.

expressions to describe God's bringing his people out of Egypt (see Exod. 13:3, 9, 14, 16; 20:2). He has just declared that God is his rock and fortress, and now he says that God is his refuge.

Verse 5 is well known because of the use of the first part of it by the Lord Jesus upon the Cross: 'Father, into your hands I commit my spirit' (Luke 23:46). Jesus used these words in a similar spirit of trust as the psalmist when he spoke them. Knowing that he had finished the work he had come to do (his 'exodus', Luke 9:31),[3] he committed his life into the Father's hands. This action of Jesus also became a model for his disciples (cf. the case of Stephen, Acts 7:59). The words should not be taken to mean that the psalmist was simply resigning himself to his fate. Rather, they indicate the strong faith of one who has complete confidence in God's ability to save and to keep. 'Redeem' is a further reference to the exodus, and just as God had acted in this way for his people (see Deut. 7:8), so now the psalmist asks for similar redemption for himself from the faithful God ('God of truth').

I hate those who cling to worthless idols; I trust in the LORD (v. 6). The phrase 'who cling to worthless idols' only occurs here and in an almost identical form in Jonah 2:8. It refers to false gods that disappoint their worshippers, who in time of crisis find them impotent to help. Calling them vanities goes back to Deuteronomy 32:21. Later it was to become a favourite expression of Jeremiah to describe the idols (see Jer. 2:5; 8:19; 10:15; 14:22; 16:19). The contrast between those people and the psalmist is made plain in the final clause. The true source of help was the LORD, and the psalmist expresses his trust in him. This was the response that covenant commitment required, and it is just putting in another way the confession the psalmist had made in his opening words (v. 1).

I will be glad and rejoice in your love, for you saw my affliction and knew the anguish of my soul. You have not handed me over to the enemy but have set my feet in

---

[3] In the Greek text of Luke 9:31 the word for 'departure' is *exodos*. This is a significant link in thought between the Old Testament exodus from Egypt and the ministry and the work of Jesus. It is also interesting to consider the way in which Jesus quotes on the cross from a psalm that is replete with exodus terminology.

a spacious place (*vv. 7-8*). God's covenant love (*chésed*) had been the psalmist's stay, and it provoked a spirit of rejoicing, for God had taken note of his servant's pitiable condition, his heartfelt anguish. He records how God had heard his cry and delivered him, putting him into a broad place. This last phrase is a favourite one of David (see Pss. 4:1; 18:19, 36), and it describes the release from oppression into a condition of freedom. He had not been abandoned to the enemy, because the LORD had intervened, and song and joy were but the rightful response to his dealings with David.

2. A Description of Sorrows (*vv. 9-18*)
The central part of the psalm is a description of the psalmist's sorrows and afflictions. **Be merciful to me, O LORD, for I am in distress; my eyes grow weak with sorrow, my soul and my body with grief** (*v. 9*). The appeal he makes for mercy is set over against the oppressive situation in which he lives. Whereas he had pled on the basis of God's righteousness earlier (v. 1), he now pleads on the basis of God's mercy. He sets out in detail before the LORD his misery and anguish, using language that has already appeared in Psalm 6:7.[4] No word for 'grief' occurs in the Hebrew, hence it is better to simply conclude the verse with 'my soul and body [too]'. His whole being is consumed with anguish, so that he feels that all strength is gone.

My life is consumed by anguish and my years by groaning; my strength fails because of my affliction, and my bones grow weak (*v. 10*). It is better to accept the NIV marginal reading of 'guilt' in place of 'affliction', for the Hebrew word ʿāwôn can carry ideas both of a misdeed and its punishment. This is the only place in the psalm in which mention is made of the psalmist's own sin. It is a blessing when suffering turns the heart inward to see one's true condition before the LORD. He pictures himself as an old man, stumbling along in his weakened condition, whereas he previously had been so

---

[4] The phrases are almost identical in Psalms 6:7 and 31:9, the only difference being that the former has *mikaʿas*, 'from sorrow', while the latter has *bʿkaʿas*, 'in sorrow'. No real difference in meaning is observable.

strong. The expression 'to have one's bones weakened' is a frequent idiom in the Old Testament to describe the reaction to acute pain or emotional distress (cf. Job 33:19, 21; Psalms 6:2; 38:3; Lam. 1:13). Neat parallelism occurs in verses 9 and 10, as the rare verb 'to grow weak' (*'âshash*; it only appears elsewhere in Ps. 6:7) is used near the beginning of verse 9 and at the end of verse 10.

Because of all my enemies, I am the utter contempt of my neighbours; I am a dread to my friends – those who see me on the street flee from me (*v. 11*). He faces problems on every side – enemies assail him, neighbours shun him, even friends turn away from him in public places as if he had a dreadful, infectious disease. The NIV rendering '*utter* contempt' is an attempt to bring out the force of the Hebrew word *me'ōd* that often translates as 'very' or 'greatly', but here the syntax of the sentence is unusual: 'I am a reproach, and to my neighbours greatly.' Since readers would probably expect a noun parallel to 'reproach' to appear, many attempts have been made to propose emendation. However, the fact that the LXX translates it as *sphodra* ('very [much], exceedingly') certainly points to the MT being correct.[5] This is all because he is facing such opposition from his enemies, and no one wants to associate with him any longer.

I am forgotten by them as though I were dead; I have become like broken pottery (*v. 12*). The hurt of his situation is described in these words. He is so shunned by his acquaintances that it is as if he were dead. The NIV translation fails to bring out clearly the presence of the Hebrew word *millêv* ('from the heart') after the words 'I am forgotten', and the insertion of 'by them', while implied by the context, does not correspond to any words in the MT. Here the NKJV translation is better: 'I am forgotten like a dead man, out of mind.' In the final clause the psalmist thinks of himself as just being a cast-off piece of pottery, broken and of no more use!

---

[5] The note in *BHS* lists four suggestions that have been proposed: *mânôd* ('shaking [of the head]'), *mâgôr* ('terror'), *morâ'* ('fear'), and *mâdôn* ('quarrel'). While all are plausible, yet the uniformity of the MT reading suggests that alteration of the text is not an option.

For I hear the slander of many; there is terror on every side; they conspire against me and plot to take my life (*v. 13*). The first part of this verse is like Jeremiah 20:10, though there the expression 'terror on every side' is what the people were saying. The phrase 'terror on every side' (Hebrew *mâgôr missavîb*) is a frequent one in Jeremiah's writing (see Jer. 6:25; 20:3; 46:5; 49:29; Lam. 2:22). Here the picture is simply of back-biting enemies who attack from all sides and who plot together to take his life. The same phrase is used in Psalm 2:2 of the rebellious rulers plotting against the LORD. Not just slander, but death threats come against him.

But I trust in you, O LORD; I say, 'You are my God' (*v. 14*). In the midst of all his afflictions the psalmist can turn to the LORD and make confession of his faith in him. The sudden transition between this and the preceding verse is remarkable. What matters most in his situation is the relationship between himself and the LORD. The pronouns 'I' and 'you' stand next to each other in the Hebrew text before the verb, and emphasise the bond between the psalmist and the LORD: 'But I, upon you I trust ...'. In addition to this profession of absolute trust, the psalmist confesses that the LORD is indeed his only God.

My times are in your hands; deliver me from my enemies and from those who pursue me (*v. 15*). By 'times' the psalmist means all the circumstances of life. The same word is used in 1 Chronicles 29:30 of the circumstances of David's lifetime. Because all of his life is in God's control, he can appeal to him to come and rescue him from his present distress. Having made his confession of trust, he is on even surer ground as he renews his cry for deliverance. A sharp contrast exists between committing himself *into* the LORD's hand in the first part of the verse, and praying for deliverance *from* the enemy's hand in the second part.

Let your face shine on your servant; save me in your unfailing love (*v. 16*). The first phrase is an allusion to the priestly blessing in Numbers 6:24-25: 'The LORD bless you and keep you; the LORD make his face shine upon you and be gracious to you.' The psalmist appeals for saving mercy to be shown him in his distress. His request is doubly based on the covenant: he is the LORD's servant (*'avdekâ*), and he pleads on the basis of the LORD's unfailing covenant love (*chasdekâ*).

Let me not be put to shame, O LORD, for I have cried out to you; but let the wicked be put to shame and lie silent in the grave (*v. 17*). The appeal is for a completely different result to come for the psalmist than for his enemies. In regard to them he wants them to be put to shame. In English the idea of shame stresses the inner feelings, whereas in Hebrew thought it is more outward disgrace. 'To lie silent in the grave' is equivalent to saying 'dead'. Those in Sheol are both inactive and silent.[6]

Let their lying lips be silenced, for with pride and contempt they speak arrogantly against the righteous (*v. 18*). The reference to lying lips goes back to the thought of verse 13. In their arrogance the ungodly speak against the righteous, such as the psalmist. He now asks for an end to their slander, so that no longer will the deceitful words of his enemies be a trouble to him.

3. Praise and Thanksgiving (*vv. 19-24*)

The psalm draws to a close with a beautiful acknowledgment of the LORD's mercies and with a call to all God's saints to love him. **How great is your goodness, which you have stored up for those who fear you, which you bestow in the sight of men on those who take refuge in you** (*v. 19*). The psalmist extols the wonderful goodness of God, a goodness (*tûv*) that is promised because of God's covenant with his people.[7] His servants are described by the parallel expressions 'who fear you' and 'who take refuge in you'. The LORD has stored up his love, described in terms of precious things that are set aside (cf. Ps. 119:11 for use of the verb *tsâfan* of treasuring up God's word in the heart). The demonstration of that love to his servants, however, is done publicly. Those who continue to set their trust on the LORD receive blessings from him that are apparent to others.

---

[6] For further information on the Hebrew word *sh⁰'ôl*, see comment on Psalm 6:5.

[7] See f.n. 3 on Ps. 23 in reference to *tûv*.

In the shelter of your presence you hide them from the intrigues of men; in your dwelling you keep them safe from accusing tongues (*v. 20*). God himself is a place of refuge and protection for his people. Just as God stores up love for his people (v. 19), so he stores them up (using the same Hebrew verb) in a secure place, and so protects them against the slander of men. The NIV 'your dwelling' is clearly intended to form the parallel to 'your presence' in the first clause, but the MT simply has 'a shelter' (*sukkâh*). Since the almost identical phrase occurs in Psalm 27:5, it is preferable to translate simply 'You will hide them in a shelter.' This is one particular way in which God's love is shown to them.

Praise be to the LORD, for he showed his wonderful love to me when I was in a besieged city. In my alarm I said, 'I am cut off from your sight!' Yet you heard my cry for mercy when I called to you for help (*vv. 21-22*). The expression 'praise' or 'blessed' often comes at the beginning or at the end of a psalm of thanksgiving (cf. 28:6; 66:20; 144:1). The reason for such ascription of praise to the LORD is because of an unique and sovereign display of his covenant love. 'Showed his wonderful love' attempts to convey in English the idea that God has acted to manifest his love in a way that belongs to him alone. The expression is unique in that it combines a verb that is used of divine action (*pâlâ'*, Hi.) with the common noun (*chésed*) denoting God's affection expressed primarily in the covenant. It is hard to know whether the reference to a besieged city is a true historical allusion (to a city such as Ziklag) or a metaphorical description of the acute distress in which he was. Verse 22 tells the story of his deliverance. The cry for mercy (v. 9) has been heard. When in a state of disquiet ('alarm') he had claimed that he was cut off from God's sight. This is the only occurrence of this particular word for being 'cut off' (*gâraz*, Ni.), but the context makes clear that it is a metaphorical description of being rejected by God. Using other verbs, the Old Testament describes being cut off from God's hand (Ps. 88:5), from God's house (2 Chron. 26:21), and from the land of the living (Isa. 53:8). The reality was, though, that God heard the psalmist's cry for help and responded.

Love the LORD, all his saints! The LORD preserves the faithful, but the proud he pays back in full. Be strong and take heart, all you who hope in the LORD (*vv. 23-24*). An experience of God's mercy leads to a desire to see others sharing in it. He calls on all of God's saints, that is, all who have been objects of his mercy, to respond in love to him. This word for saints (Hebrew *châsîd*) occurs most often in the Psalms, and later it became the word for the orthodox party in Judaism in pre-Christian times (*the Chasidim*). All who firmly rely on the LORD will be guarded by him. On the other hand, those who vaunt themselves in their pride will find that the LORD renders to them just punishment. The final call is to strengthen themselves as they hope in the LORD. 'To hope' is practically synonymous with other expressions such as 'to trust' or 'to wait for'. The ultimate expression of believing trust is set out for the Christian in Romans 8:28-29.

Psalm 32

Of David. A maskil.

This is the first time in the Psalter that the technical term *maskîl* is used in the title.[1] It also occurs in Psalms 42, 44, 45, 52-55, 74, 78, 88, 89, 142, and in 47:7. A difficulty that faces the reader and interpreter of the Psalms is that it is uncertain whether it refers to the content of the psalm in question, or the musical accompaniment. The description of a group of Levites, the Maskilim, who 'showed good understanding of the service of the LORD' (2 Chron. 30:22), may be the best clue as to the meaning of the term. In that context a *maskîl* seems to be a song or a collection of songs for use in worship by a special group of Levites who are called *maskilîm*.[2]

The central theme of this psalm is the free grace of God in forgiving sin. Paul speaks of it as illustrating 'the blessedness of the man to whom God credits righteousness apart from works' (Rom. 4:6). No precise mention is made here of the nature of the sin itself. He clearly had been through a deep experience of knowing God's disfavour and of suffering illness at his hand. But with a fresh experience of God's unfailing mercy, he can sing this song of thanksgiving. This psalm forms another of the penitential psalms of the early church.

1. The Blessing of Pardon (*vv. 1-2*)
The psalm opens on a note of rejoicing because of the free grace of God. **Blessed is he whose transgressions are**

---

[1] *Maskîl* is a participial formation from the Hi. of the verb s-k-l. The root essentially means to have insight and hence success.

[2] See the note by Marvin Tate, *Psalms 51-100* (Word Biblical Commentary: Dallas: Word Books, 1990), p. 33.

forgiven, whose sins are covered. Blessed is the man whose sin the LORD does not count against him and in whose spirit is no deceit (*vv. 1-2*). Three terms for sin are used. 'Transgressions' (*pesha'*) refers to acts of rebellion against God, while 'sins' (*chᵃtâ'âh*) is the broadest term for sin in the Old Testament. It denotes in general a missing of the mark, and hence an offence against God. The third term ('*âwôn*), also translated as 'sin' in the NIV, has the idea of distortion or twisting from the right way. The wonderful thing that the psalmist can sing about is that all three kinds of sin can be forgiven by God. He can remove sin as far as the east is from the west (Ps. 103:12).

The three expressions for sin are paralleled by three expressions for forgiveness: 'taken away' (*nâshâh*, pass. part.), 'covered' (*kâsâh*, pass. part.), and 'not reckoned' (*châshav*). The psalmist, though, is not speaking of forgiveness in general. Rather, he is relating his own experience of the grace of God. For us today the New Testament makes it plain that forgiveness comes through the same free grace of God displayed in the death and resurrection of Jesus. 'He was delivered over to death for our sins and was raised to life for our justification' (Rom. 4:25).

2. A Personal Confession (*vv. 3-5*)

We now have a glimpse back to the period before the psalmist came to repentance and made his confession to the LORD. **When I kept silent, my bones wasted away through my groaning all day long. For day and night your hand was heavy upon me; my strength was sapped as in the heat of summer. Selah** (*vv. 3-4*). The time of silence was the time prior to his confession of guilt. The psalmists repeatedly speak of God being silent, but God also has cause to complain of the silence of his children. The physical effects brought on by his spiritual condition included a wasting of bones and a sapping of strength. The verb used of his bones (*bâlâh*, 'wasted away') is one normally used of clothes wearing out (cf. Josh. 9:13). Other psalms, such as 6:2-7, 102:3-5, and 119:83, also describe the physical effects of spiritual conflict. Constantly[3] he was aware of God's hand upon him, but resisted the promptings of his conscience to turn to the LORD in repentance. **Then I acknowledged my sin to you and did not cover up my iniquity. I said, 'I will confess my transgressions to the LORD' – and you forgave the guilt of my sin. Selah** (*v. 5*). The three words for sin already used in verse 1 also appear here, while the phrase 'the guilt of my sin' (lit. 'the iniquity of my sin') is a combination of two of these terms. The silence is broken and the psalmist recounts abruptly his change of heart. When God's Spirit brings true repentance there is no attempt to cover one's sin and guilt. The psalmist had openly confessed his sin, and he knew the reality of God's forgiving mercy. The confession and the forgiveness are simultaneous (cf. 1 John 1:9).

3. Instruction for the Godly (*vv. 6-10*)

Therefore let everyone who is godly pray to you while you may be found; surely when the mighty waters rise, they will not reach him. You are my hiding place; you will protect me from trouble and surround me with songs of deliverance. Selah (*vv. 6-7*). Having experienced forgiveness for himself, the psalmist now wants others to seek the LORD as well. The godly[4] can find God (Isa. 55:6), whereas proud sinners discover that God has withdrawn himself from them (Prov. 1:28; Hos. 5:6).[5] The person, who in faith prays to the

---

[3] The Hebrew expression used here (*yômâm vâlay'lâh*; lit. 'daily and night') is a standard one to express continuity. At times the words occur in reverse order without any difference in meaning.

[4] The NIV also uses 'saint' as a translation of the Hebrew word *chasîd*. See comment on Psalm 31:23.

[5] The translation 'while you may be found' represents the MT 'at the time of finding only' (*l^eêt m^etso' raq*). Three main approaches to a problem text have been taken. (1) As NIV to compare the expression with Isaiah 55:6 and translate accordingly. (2) To emend 'finding' (*m^etso'*) to 'distress' (*mâtsôq*), which is followed by NRSV, RSV, NEB, JB. (3) To assume that this is a case of ellipsis, with the omitted object being 'his heart'. Cf. the full phrase 'when he comes to search his heart' in 2 Samuel 7:27. All these proposals still have to deal with the unusual use of *raq* ('only'). Probably it should be taken with the following clause and rendered 'assuredly'.

LORD, will find him, and knows that he keeps his children safe, even when the mighty waters look like overwhelming them. There may be an allusion here back to the flood in Noah's day. A believer will be safe because he has found a sure hiding place with the LORD (cf. 27:5; 31:20). When God protects his people he also gives them a joyful spirit and enables them to sing songs of deliverance (lit. 'songs of escape').

I will instruct you and teach you in the way you should go; I will counsel you and watch over you (*v. 8*). Some have taken these words to be what God said to David. But in the context they appear to be part of David's response to the LORD. Elsewhere he pledged himself to teach sinners the ways of the Lord (Ps. 51:13). Here he assures another godly person that he will both give instruction and also keep a watchful eye upon him. If another believer was caught in a similar set of circumstances to those which had overtaken him, he would be able to instruct him in the ways of the Lord.

Do not be like the horse or the mule, which have no understanding but must be controlled by bit and bridle or they will not come to you (*v. 9*). This could be advice against stubbornness in general, but in the context it may well be suggesting that there should be none of the hesitancy that David had in confessing his sin (see vv. 3-4). A sinner should not be constrained like a rebellious animal to come to the LORD. Out of a sense of need he should make his confession and seek pardon.

Many are the woes of the wicked, but the LORD's unfailing love surrounds the man who trusts in him (*v. 10*). The contrast is drawn between the sinner and the person constantly trusting in the LORD. The one knows many distresses (possibly 'sicknesses', cf. the use of the same Hebrew word in Isa. 53: 3, 'man of sorrows'), whereas the other has the knowledge of God's covenant love. Trust is the abiding characteristic of a believer.

4. A Call to Praise (*v. 11*)
Rejoice in the LORD and be glad, you righteous; sing, all you who are upright in heart! (*v. 11*). The call to praise concludes

the psalm. It is very similar to other calls such as Psalm 97:12. It fits in well with the thought of the psalm because of the place 'the righteous' has in it (see especially v. 6). The verb 'sing' (*rânan*) is first used in the Old Testament in connection with a divinely appointed sacrifice (Lev. 9:24). In its later usage it normally denotes joy in connection with God's great saving acts. 'Righteous' and 'upright in heart' are parallel terms describing the condition of those who have received God's mercy.

Psalm 33

This is a hymn of praise to the LORD, and it is his creative work that is especially in focus. It is a short commentary on Genesis 1 (see particularly vv. 6-9), and then the implications of the LORD's mighty power for Israel are applied. The creator of the world is the creator of Israel and he is able to keep and deliver a people whom he chose for his own. Some of the language is drawn from Genesis 1, while other parts are dependent upon the Exodus account, and in particular the poetry of Exodus 15.

The psalm falls into the normal pattern for hymns (see section on hymns in the Introduction), having an introductory call to praise the LORD, followed by the reasons for this, and a conclusion that expresses confident trust in the covenantal love of the LORD. The double use of *chésed* towards the end of the Psalm (vv. 18 and 22) picks up and amplifies the earlier use of the same word in verse 5. This is the last of the psalms in Book 1 that has no title.

The position of this psalm following Psalm 32 may well be deliberate. The theme of praise at the end of Psalm 32 is taken up in a renewed way at the beginning of Psalm 33. Also, the commands in 32:11 and 33:1 are both addressed to 'the righteous' (*tsaddîqîm*), and the repetition of the verb 'sing [joyfully]' (*rânan*) is another link. While Psalm 33 has twenty-two verses (the exact number of letters in the Hebrew alphabet), no acrostic pattern is evident.[1]

---

[1] Eight Hebrew manuscripts actually join Psalms 32 and 33 together. However, this may have happened since Psalm 33 had no title, though the LXX and Qumran both include one.

1. A Call to Praise (*vv. 1-3*)

Praise is something appropriate for the righteous, and so this psalm commences with a call to jubilant song. **Sing joyfully to the LORD, you righteous; it is fitting for the upright to praise him** (*v. 1*). The verb rendered here 'to sing' (Hebrew *rânan* Pi.) is first used in Leviticus 9:24, where a shout of jubilation accompanied a burnt offering. It occurs most frequently in the Psalms and Isaiah, often in parallel with other terms for 'joy', 'rejoicing', and 'praise'. It also occurs in parallel with 'song' (*shîr*, Ps. 59:16) and the verb denoting 'playing an instrument' or 'singing' (*zâmar*, Ps. 98:4). Certainly 'jubilation' seems to be the main connotation, whether by 'music' (cf. 2 Chron. 20:22) or by 'singing' (Ps. 71:23). The word rendered 'fitting' by the NIV occurs again in Psalm 147:1: 'How good it is to sing praises to our God, how pleasant and *fitting* to praise him!' In that context, because of the parallelism, the word seems to suggest that praise is lovely. Such an idea fits in well here too. Praise is to be expected from the righteous, but when rendered it is also lovely. 'Righteous' (*tsaddîqîm*) and 'upright' (*yᵉshârîm*) occur as parallel terms to describe the believing community.

Praise the LORD with the harp; make music to him on the ten-stringed lyre. Sing to him a new song; play skilfully, and shout for joy (*vv. 2-3*). The choice of only two instruments is meant to be representative of the whole range of instruments used in ancient Israel (see Ps. 150 for a fuller list). The thought of a 'new song' can be interpreted in two ways. The use of the word 'new' has suggested to some commentators that it designates an eschatological or end-time song, just as 'new heavens and new earth' designate the great physical change that is coming. This would be in agreement with the use of the expression in Psalms 96:1 and 98:1, and it would also suit the use of the same phrase in Revelation 5:9. However, the phrase appears to be sometimes more general in its use (here and in Ps. 149:1), so that it marks out the freshness of praise that is rendered to the LORD.

2. The Reasons for Praise (*vv. 4-19*)

For the word of the LORD is right and true; he is faithful in all he does. The LORD loves righteousness and justice; the earth is full of his unfailing love (*vv. 4-5*). The first reason given for praise concerns the word of the LORD. The use of the word 'for' (Hebrew *kî*) is one of the distinctive characteristics of psalms such as this, as it marks out the things for which praise is to be given to the LORD (see also v. 9). The things that mark out God's Word are those that first of all distinguish him (uprightness, truth, righteousness, justice, and covenant love). Then in the work of creation, as he speaks the word and the world comes into being, his love is seen displayed there. He always acts in a manner consistent with his own character, for God cannot deny himself.

By the word of the LORD were the heavens made, their starry host by the breath of his mouth. He gathers the waters of the sea into jars; he puts the deep into storehouses (*vv. 6-7*). This is the start of a description of the creative work of God, for it was the LORD's word that caused the heavens to come into existence. The word 'host' has a variety of meanings in the Old Testament. It can be used for an army, for the angelic beings, or, as here, for the stars. The NIV correctly identifies its meaning here by adding the word 'starry'. The gathering of the waters (see Gen. 1:9-10) is described in poetical language as if God gathered up all the seas into a heap,[2] or as if he put the deeps (cf. Gen. 1:2) into stores.

Let all the earth fear the LORD; let all the people of the world revere him. For he spoke, and it came to be; he commanded, and it stood firm (*vv. 8-9*). By God's powerful word the world came into being. Since then, as Paul teaches in Romans 1:20, 'God's invisible qualities – his eternal power and divine nature — have been clearly seen, being understood from what has been made, so that men are without any excuse.' God's voice was heard, and creation resulted. It is not expressly called 'creation out of nothing', but that certainly is the implication of what is taught here and elsewhere in the

---

[2] Though early versions such as the LXX imply by their translations that the gathering of the waters of the sea was 'into jars' (NIV and other modern translations), the MT should be retained as it makes good sense and the parallel expression in Exodus 15:8 confirms this.

Old Testament about creation. As this revelation is universal, then everyone in the world should bow in adoration and reverence before him. In a context such as this, 'fear' does not mean 'to be afraid', but rather to 'adore' or 'revere'.

The LORD foils the plans of the nations; he thwarts the purposes of the peoples. But the plans of the LORD stand firm forever, the purposes of his heart through all generations. Blessed is the nation whose God is the LORD, the people he chose for his inheritance (*vv. 10-12*). The second reason for praise comes in verses 10-12. God is not only great in his creative work, but also in the outworking of his providence in history. The Bible ties together very closely the ideas of creation and providence. Nations may plot, but God intervenes to work out his own purposes. Israel was to see various kingdoms rise and fall. Through Isaiah, the LORD told the surrounding nations that their strategies would fail, and their purposes would not stand (Isa. 7:7; 8:10). God's purposes are sure, and his plans continue generation after generation. The contrast is so marked. Human schemes are temporary and fail; the LORD's plans are enduring and successful. After speaking of creation and providence, the psalmist now reaches the point where he speaks of the unique position of Israel. It was part of God's purpose that he chose Israel to be his people, and his inheritance. The truth stated here is reiterated in Psalm 135:4: 'For the LORD has chosen Jacob to be his own, Israel to be his treasured possession.' The verb 'choose' (*bâchar*) in the Old Testament always involves the idea of careful, well thought-out choice, and mostly (as here) it is used to designate the choice that expresses God's eternal purpose. God chose Israel to be his 'inheritance' (see Exodus 34:9 and Deut. 4:20), and how happy should Israel be in knowing that is so! The choice was based, not on any superiority or greatness of Israel, but solely on God's sovereign love (Deut. 7:7-10).

From heaven the LORD looks down and sees all mankind; from his dwelling place he watches all who live on earth – he who forms the hearts of all, who considers everything they do (*vv. 13-15*). The third reason for praise is that God's eye is over all his creation. The fact that it is 'from heaven' that he looks down, emphasises the rule that he has over everything. The LORD can see much more than just the outworking of sinful purposes by men (cf. vv. 10-11). He can even see into the hearts that he has made. He is the creator of those hearts, and this action is described using a word ('form', Hebrew *yâtsar*) that is used in Genesis 2:7, 8, 19 of the original creative work (see also its use in Pss. 74:17 and 94:9; Isa. 45:18; and Jer. 10:16). It is a word that describes the divine potter forming man from the dust of the ground.

No king is saved by the size of his army; no warrior escapes by his great strength. A horse is a vain hope for deliverance; despite all its great strength it cannot save (*vv. 16-17*). The fourth reason for praise is that God's might delivers his people. There is reference to displays of human strength that fail. It is not simply the size of a king's army that guarantees success in battle. Nor does an individual warrior manage to escape by his own ability. The horse was noted for its strength in battle, but Israel was warned not to trust in it for military victories (Isa. 30:15-16; 31:1). The Egyptians had learned at the Exodus that the horse and its rider could be overthrown by the LORD, for the LORD fought for his people (Exod. 15:1-4). The cluster of expressions denoting salvation or deliverance in these verses serves to highlight how vain it is to trust in human or earthly powers.

But the eyes of the LORD are on those who fear him, on those whose hope is in his unfailing love, to deliver them from death and keep them alive in famine (*vv. 18-19*). The contrast is marked by the introductory word at the beginning of verse 18. The 'but' (Hebrew *hinnêh, behold*) marks out the transition to the opposite idea. The LORD does not only look down on all mankind (v. 13), but he has a special interest in the God-fearing community. The parallel description of them (they who fear the LORD and who hope for his covenant love) also occurs in passages such as Psalm 119:74. The verb 'to hope for' (*yâchal*, Pi.) has the idea of expectant looking for something, coupled with the idea of patient waiting. In this case, it is that the God-fearers look to the LORD's covenanted mercy to deliver them in time of trouble. He is able to save from death (from enemies) or to preserve alive in times of famine. This seems to mean more than just to be kept alive. Rather it is preservation to enjoy God's presence and blessing, and to henceforth live in relationship with him.

3. A Declaration of Trust in the LORD (*vv. 20-22*)

A change takes place at this point, as the third person forms in the earlier part of the psalm give way to the first person plural ('we', 'our', 'us'). The conclusion is an affirmation of communal confidence in the LORD. The creator of both the world and Israel is well able to provide protection. **We wait in hope for the LORD; he is our help and our shield** (*v. 20*). Now the song of confidence sounds again from the psalmist. The NIV rendering 'wait in hope' aptly captures the sense of the Hebrew verb used here (*chākāh*), for it denotes eager expectation and confident trust. The assertion that follows about the LORD is taken up as a refrain in Psalm 115, 'He is their help and shield' (vv. 9, 10, 11). Both descriptions of God are fitting in a psalm that has spoken about battle. God supports and strengthens his people, and because he is their protector it is not surprising that he is called their shield.

In him our hearts rejoice, for we trust in his holy name (*v. 21*). After the acknowledgment which has just been made of the LORD's help, the psalmist now shows that the communal response was one of joy. Where there is believing trust in God's character, then there can be songs of joy that extol what he is to his people. The aspect of God's holiness is most important, for he is distinguished from his creatures in his character and his works. His character is the guarantee of blessing for those who trust in him.

May your unfailing love rest upon us, O LORD, even as we put our hope in you (*v. 22*). The psalm concludes with a prayer for covenant mercy to rest upon the believing community. This is putting verse 18b into the form of a prayer. The repetition of the two key words 'unfailing love' and the verb 'to hope' serves to point to the nature of the relationship between the community of Israel and the LORD. The song of joyful trust, evident at the outset of the psalm, continues right through to its close.

Psalm 34

Of David. When he pretended to be insane before Abimelech, who drove him away, and he left.

This is an acrostic psalm, with each verse of it beginning with a letter of the Hebrew alphabet. The only irregularities are that one letter is omitted (*vav*) and that an extra *pe* is added to commence the last verse (see the introductory comment on Psalm 25, as it similarly omits *vav* and has a supernumerary *pe*). Using an acrostic pattern placed certain restrictions on an author, but the thought flows well throughout this psalm. As an acrostic appeals more to the eye than the ear, its use in the Old Testament attests to a cultured and literate community in Israel. Attempts have been made to identify further alphabetical features about this psalm but they are unconvincing.[1]

It is a song of thanksgiving, though it is hard to be certain what the precise situation was in which the psalmist was placed. There is no reason to doubt the accuracy of the title, and to relate the psalm to this specific period of David's life. The word 'Abimelech' (which means, 'my father is king') may well have been a title for the Philistine kings, just as 'Pharaoh' was for the Egyptians. If this was so, then the king referred to would be Achish (1 Sam. 21:10).

A link exists with the previous psalm, in that the words 'But the eyes of the LORD are on those who fear him' (33:18a) are paralleled in this psalm by the words 'The eyes of the LORD are on the righteous' (34:15a). Also, in both psalms the repeated occurrence of the word 'LORD' is striking, with

---

[1] See especially A. R. Ceresko, 'The ABCs of Wisdom in Psalm XXXIV', *VT* 35 (1985), pp. 99-104.

it being used thirteen times in Psalm 33 and fifteen times in Psalm 34. More commonly psalmists intersperse use of the divine name (*yhwh*) with metaphorical expressions. Repetition of other words throughout the psalm also gives a feeling of literary unity to it.[2]

Another feature of this psalm is the presence of expressions that are very typical of wisdom literature in general. These include the invitation to 'taste and see', followed by the declaration, 'Blessed is the man ...' (v. 8). The invitation to the children to come and receive instruction (v. 11) is also redolent of a wisdom setting.

1. An Introductory Hymn (*vv. 1-3*)

I will extol the LORD at all times; his praise will always be on my lips (*v. 1*). As part of his thanksgiving the psalmist pledges himself to bless the LORD always, and to have his praise constantly on his lips. This is a vow that he is making, and he does so to the covenant LORD of Israel. The constant repetition of the name of the LORD is a striking feature throughout the psalm (see vv. 1-4, 6-11, 15-19, 22). So great has been the LORD's mercy to him that he pledges himself to praise him repeatedly. The word 'always' (*tāmîd*) has the idea of constancy, and it is used in other similar expressions (cf. 'my praise shall be continually of you', Ps. 71:6 NKJV).

My soul will boast in the LORD; let the afflicted hear and rejoice (*v. 2*). The experience of joy that David had was one that he wanted others to know as well. He wanted his fellow afflicted ones to listen to this call and also to rejoice in the LORD. Some have thought that he is referring to those who have come to worship at the sanctuary, but this seems too restrictive. Elsewhere the psalmist says that all who swear by God's name will rejoice (Ps. 63:11).

Glorify the LORD with me; let us exalt his name together (*v. 3*). Human praise can never make God any greater than he is, but he desires praise that calls others to magnify his name in public acknowledgment of him. Most probably 'his name'

---

[2] Notice the threefold or more repetition of 'hear', 'deliver', 'fear', 'good', 'evil', and 'righteous'.

is to be understood as the object of the verb 'glorify', for the Hebrew has, 'glorify *for the* LORD with me'. It is common in Hebrew poetry not to repeat the same phrase in both parts of a verse.[3] What is sought is a united song of praise to the LORD.

2. A Testimony to Deliverance (*vv. 4-10*)

Now the psalmist relates his own experience of seeking the LORD and finding him. **I sought the LORD, and he answered me; he delivered me from all my fears. Those who look to him are radiant; their faces are never covered with shame** (*vv. 4-5*). The verb 'sought' often suggests a diligent seeking. His cry had been heard and had received a ready answer from the LORD, and he had found deliverance from the fears that had oppressed him. 'Fears' carries with it the idea of the terror that God's judgment brings (cf. the only other occurrences of the word in Isa. 66:4 and Prov. 10:24). To look to God is the same as seeking him, and those who do look will not do so in vain.[4] None who cry to him will know disappointment. Instead, there is a radiance about their faces as they receive from his hand, as God's face shines on them (cf. the Aaronic blessing in Num. 6:24-26).

This poor man called, and the LORD heard him; he saved him out of all his troubles. The angel of the LORD encamps around those who fear him, and he delivers them (*vv. 6-7*). These verses form a parallel with the preceding pair. Thinking back on his own condition David refers to himself as a poor man who cried to the LORD. That cry was heard and salvation or deliverance resulted. The outcome was that he knew deliverance or salvation was from the LORD. By means of his angel the LORD stations himself around his people as their

---

[3] This feature is a form of ellipsis, or gapping as it is sometimes called. It is much more common in Hebrew poetry than in prose, and in contradistinction to prose it may occur in poetry in the first clause, as here in Psalm 34:2. For further discussion, see *DIHG~S*, pp. 163-64.

[4] A little awkwardness exists in the translation 'Those who look to him', as the subject has not been introduced in the preceding verses. Some Hebrew manuscripts make the verb an imperative (pointing it *habbîtû* instead of the MT *hibbîtû*). The LXX has *proselthate* that presupposes reading something like *g*ᵉ*shû*, 'draw near'. Confirmation of the Massoretic vocalisation comes from the following suffix, '*their* faces'.

protector. The language involving 'camping' and 'deliverance' suggests a military situation, but, whatever the precise battles in which David had engaged, the expressions here are general in character. He is reflecting on the fact that those who fear the LORD will find in him a protector and deliverer.

Resulting from his own experience of the LORD the psalmist now calls to others to enter into a similar experience. **Taste and see that the LORD is good; blessed is the man who takes refuge in him** (*v. 8*). 'Taste' is used here, as in Proverbs 31:18, of discernment (lit. 'She [the wife] sees [Hebrew *tastes*] that her trading is profitable'). In the early church, because of the invitation to 'taste and see', this verse was appropriated for use at the Lord's Supper.[5] The reference to knowing that the LORD is good fits in well with the psalm as a whole, which, by its constant use of the divine name, emphasises the covenantal character of the relationship. It is significant that 'good' or 'goodness' are terms used in the Old Testament to describe the things promised by a covenant.[6] Peter adapts these words from the LXX version, omitting 'and see' as not essential to his argument (1 Pet. 2:3). The person, who takes refuge in the LORD, will know indeed the blessedness that he bestows on his children. The expression here, 'Blessed is the man ...' (*'ash*ᵉ*rê haggever*), seems just to be a poetic synonym for either *'ash*ᵉ*rê hâ'îsh* (Ps. 1:1) or *'ash*ᵉ*rê 'âdâm* (Ps. 32:2). The blessing closely resembles that which occurs at the end of Psalm 2.

Fear the LORD, you his saints, for those who fear him lack nothing. The lions may grow weak and hungry, but those who seek the LORD lack no good thing (*vv. 9-10*). The expression, 'the fear of the LORD', is one of the most comprehensive terms that the Old Testament has to describe a true believing attitude to the LORD. It is the devoted reverence of a trusting saint.[7] Those who do trust him will find that he fulfils his word to them and that they will not miss out on any of the good things he has promised in his covenant. Even

---

[5] *Apostolical Constitutions*, 8.13; Cyril, *Catech. Myst.* 5.17.
[6] See note on Psalm 23:6.
[7] For the concept of 'the fear of the LORD', see note on Psalm 15:4.

a powerful animal like the lion may go hungry, but none of God's children will lack food.

3. Instruction Offered (*vv. 11-20*)

Come, my children, listen to me; I will teach you the fear of the LORD. Whoever of you loves life and desires to see many good days, keep your tongue from evil and your lips from speaking lies (*vv. 11-13*). The style now becomes very like the wisdom style of the Book of Proverbs. The children addressed are students or pupils rather than literal sons, and the phrase is commonly used in the Book of Proverbs in this sense (cf. Prov. 1:8; 4:1). Hence the teacher is called a father (2 Kings 2:12; Matt. 23:9). In the Hebrew text verses 12-13 form a question that finds its answer in verses 14 and following (the NASB and NKJV both accurately reflect the MT). The question relates to the fundamental meaning of life. Verses 12-16 are quoted in 1 Peter 3:10-12, to enforce the lesson that we must not repay insult with insult.

Turn from evil and do good; seek peace and pursue it (*v. 14*). The life lived in the fear of the LORD is not just a state of heart and mind, but one that translates into action. It involves shunning evil and seeking good. Moreover, peace is to be sought as a harmonious relationship, and here it is largely relationship with other human beings rather than peace with God. He desires that his children will 'make every effort to do what leads to peace and to mutual edification' (Rom. 14:19). Jew and Gentile can both be brought into peace with one another through the blood of the cross (Eph. 2:14-16).

The eyes of the LORD are on the righteous and his ears are attentive to their cry; the face of the LORD is against those who do evil, to cut off the memory of them from the earth (*vv. 15-16*). The LORD keeps watchful guard over his children, and he is ever willing to heed their cry. The evildoers of verse 16 seem to be the righteous in name only, and against them God will display his anger if they set themselves to follow evil ways. The ultimate result is that they will perish from the earth, and no memory of them will remain. The language used here echoes the threat against covenant rebels of being 'cut off' (Gen. 17:14), and almost identical wording occurs again in Psalm 109:15.

The righteous cry out, and the LORD hears them; he delivers them from all their troubles. The LORD is close to the broken-hearted and saves those who are crushed in spirit (*vv. 17-18*). In the Hebrew text the subject of the verb 'cry out' is simply 'they'. The context at first suggests that the subject should be the evildoers, but as the main thrust of the passage concerns the righteous it is best to follow the NIV and understand the reference as being to them. Verse 17 is then to be understood as stating a general and abiding truth. The LORD ever hears the cry of his people and is ready to free them from their troubles. He is also ready to help. This and other similar expressions are used throughout the Psalms to convey the knowledge that God is able to save his people from whatever trouble they are in (cf. Pss. 25:22; 34:6; 54:7; 81:7). Two synonyms are used in verse 18 to describe the righteous – 'broken-hearted' and 'crushed in spirit'. Both are virtually equivalent to describing them as humble or contrite. The same combination of words occurs in Psalm 51:17. God's promise through the prophet Isaiah was that he would dwell 'with him who is contrite and lowly in spirit, to revive the spirit of the lowly and to revive the heart of the contrite' (Isa. 57:15). The adjective 'near' (*qârôv*) is used to designate closeness of relationship, so that God is near to all who call upon him in truth (Ps. 145:18). The Israelites claimed to be different from other nations in having God so near to them whenever they called on him (Deut. 4:7).

A righteous man may have many troubles, but the LORD delivers him from them all; he protects all his bones, not one of them will be broken (*vv. 19-20*). These verses are very similar in style to the Book of Proverbs, as they both state general truths, not promises to individuals. Trouble is the norm for the life of the righteous, but there is another norm applying as well, which is that God is the deliverer. The third use in this psalm of the same verb to 'deliver (*nâtsal*, Hi.) places emphasis on the truth that God indeed is the one who can rescue his people whatever their circumstances. Verse 20 puts the truth in a pictorial way. God will not allow his people to be brought into an extreme situation of danger, nor allow them to be made objects of derision and shame. When the soldiers came and found Jesus dead they did not break his bones, so that this scripture would be fulfilled (John 19:33-37). That was the highest expression of the idea of verse 20.

4. Concluding Summary (*vv. 21-22*)
Evil will slay the wicked; the foes of the righteous will be condemned. The LORD redeems his servants; no one will be condemned who takes refuge in him (*vv. 21-22*). The psalm ends with a short summary statement. Just as verses 15-16 contained a contrast, so there is another here. Those who give themselves to evil will find that in time they are destroyed by that evil. The enemies of the righteous will perish (taking the Hebrew verb *'âsham* here and in the following verse in this sense). That is to say, they will suffer the appropriate penalty as the consequence of their sin. On the other hand, the LORD redeems his servant. This final verse stands outside the acrostic pattern, just as the last verse of Psalm 25 does too. There is another similarity between these two psalms in that the letter *pe* is introduced to commence the final verse and in both cases it is the verb 'redeem' that is used. Also, the idea of finding refuge in the LORD occurs at the conclusion of both psalms (25:20; 34:22). Whereas the wicked perish, God saves his servants, and none perish who trust in him. All who seek refuge with him will find that they are preserved.

Psalm 35

Of David.

At first glance this appears to be an individual song of complaint. However, on closer examination it seems to be a psalm sung by the king. He appeals to God to intervene in a situation in which some treaty partners have proved false to their commitments. There are various phrases in the psalm that have either a legal or a military connotation. In general it is similar to the much shorter Psalm 20. A striking parallel expression to the opening of the psalm occurs in David's words to Saul: 'May the LORD be our judge and decide between us. May he consider my cause and uphold it; may he vindicate me by delivering me from your hand' (1 Sam. 24:15).

This psalm is composed of three main sections, each of which concludes with a promise of thanksgiving (vv. 10, 18, 28). The opening one (vv. 1-10) sets the tone for the others, and while it may appear different from them, yet definite links are apparent. For example, the thoughts of verses 4 and 17 are clearly connected, while the concept of 'ruin' occurs in both verses 8 and 17. The cluster of terms denoting 'shame' in verse 4 (the verbal roots *bôsh, kâlam, châpar*) recur in verse 26. The links between the second and third sections are closer. Fear of the reproaches of the enemy is mentioned in verses 11, 15, and 20, together with his enemies' glee over his distress in verses 15, 19, and 24-26. In both the second and third parts the enemies are depicted as voracious animals (vv. 15-17, 21, 25).

1. A Request for Help (*vv. 1-10*)
Contend, O LORD, with those who contend with me; fight against those who fight against me (*v. 1*). This verse is very

terse in Hebrew. It can be rendered, 'Contend, O LORD, with my contenders, and fight with my fighters'. The Hebrew verb translated 'contend' (*rîv*) often occurs in a legal or covenant setting (cf. Jeremiah 2:9: 'I bring charges', *'ārîv*; Micah 6:1: 'Plead your case before the mountains', *rîv*).[1] The cognate noun ('strife', 'defence') appears in verse 23. The psalmist wants God to fight his legal battles and also to defend him against his attackers. If the attack was caused by a treaty partner who had gone back on a formal agreement, then both battles were in fact identical.

Take up shield and buckler; arise and come to my aid. Brandish spear and javelin against those who pursue me. Say to my soul, 'I am your salvation' (*vv.* 2-3). 'Shield' (*māgēn*) and 'buckler' (*tsinnāh*) were two different types of shields used in battle. The shield was the smaller round one carried by infantry, while the buckler was a larger rectangular shield that protected the whole body. The appeal is for God to enter into battle for the psalmist, lifting up weapons both to defend and to attack. Though 'spear' (*ḥᵃnît*) is a common word, 'javelin' is more problematical. As it is vocalised in the MT (*sᵉgor*), it appears to be an infinitive from the verb 'to close' (cf. AV, 'and stop *the way*'). Different vocalisation (*seger* or *sāgār*) yields a translation 'battle axe' or 'javelin'. The psalmist also longs for reassurance from God by means of a declaration that he is his deliverer. The phrase 'I am your salvation' may well be an abbreviated form of a phrase like 'I, the LORD, am your saviour' (Isa. 49:26; 60:16).[2]

May those who seek my life be disgraced and put to shame; may those who plot my ruin be turned back in dismay (*v.* 4). At this point there is a change from direct address to God (vv. 1-3) to indirect appeal in the form of curses on his enemies.

---

[1] This word is not common in the Psalter (for other instances see 43:1; 74:22, 103:9; 119:154). Literature on this topic includes H. B. Huffmon, 'The Covenant Lawsuit and the Prophets', *JBL* 78 (1959), pp. 286-95; J. Limburg, 'The Root RIB and the Prophetic Lawsuit Speeches', *JBL* 88 (1969), pp. 291-301; M. De Roche, 'Yahweh's *rîb* Against Israel: A Re-Assessment of the So-Called "Prophetic Lawsuit" in Pre-exilic Prophets', *JBL* 102 (1983), pp. 563-74.

[2] This suggestion is made by W. VanGemeren, 'The Psalms', p. 287.

Curses such as these are not to be regarded as expressions of personal vindictiveness. They are best taken as expressions of a covenant servant desiring God to deal with his enemies (see section on imprecatory psalms in the Introduction). Here David prays that his enemies will be disgraced (*yêvoshû*) and shamed (*v^eyikkâl^emû*). These two verbs (*bôsh, kâlam*) often occur together in the Old Testament. In English 'shamed' has the idea of inner feelings, whereas the Hebrew verb conveys the idea of public disgrace. His enemies were seeking his life, and he wants them to be put to open shame.

May they be like chaff before the wind, with the angel of the LORD driving them away; may their path be dark and slippery, with the angel of the LORD pursuing them (*vv. 5-6*). The reference to 'chaff before the wind' suggests complete worthlessness (cf. Ps. 1:6). The idea of the angel of the LORD pursuing the enemies probably comes from the role that the angel played in the defeat of the Egyptians (Exod. 14:19-25). In the previous psalm the angel of the LORD was the guardian of his people (Ps. 34:7). Here he is the one who brings destruction on the enemies.

Since they hid their net for me without cause and without cause dug a pit for me, may ruin overtake them by surprise – may the net they hid entangle them, may they fall into the pit, to their ruin (*vv. 7-8*). As often in psalms like this, the psalmist proclaims his innocence. His enemies have acted against him without just cause, with emphasis on this because of the repeated use of 'without cause' (*chinnâm*, 'gratuitously'). Their actions are unprovoked on his part (cf. similar assertions in Pss. 109:3 and 119:161). He feels trapped by their plots, but prays that these plots will turn upon themselves and they will be caught by their own craftiness.

Then my soul will rejoice in the LORD and delight in his salvation. My whole being will exclaim, 'Who is like you, O LORD? You rescue the poor from those too strong for them, the poor and needy from those who rob them' (*vv. 9-10*). The psalmist anticipates that his prayer will be heard and answered. Thus he is able to express his delight in the LORD as his saviour and deliverer (cf. the declaration in verse 3). He is confident that his present situation will be overturned, and that the judgment he has invoked on his enemies will come to pass. The question, 'Who is like you, O LORD?' is typical of victory songs, and it is probably an echo of the one sung after the Exodus: 'Who among the gods is like you, O LORD? Who is like you – majestic in holiness, awesome in glory, working wonders?' (Exod. 15:11). The psalmist is so conscious of his own weakness ('poor and needy'), yet he knows that his salvation rests with the LORD alone.

2. A Description of the Enemies (*vv. 11-18*)

This new section of the psalm sets out the psalmist's innocence in the light of the persecution he is facing. He urges this as a reason why God should intervene and help him. **Ruthless witnesses come forward; they question me on things I know nothing about. They repay me evil for good and leave my soul forlorn** (*vv. 11-12*). The phrase 'ruthless witnesses' is literally 'witnesses of violence' (*'êdê châmâs*; cf. Exod. 23:1; Deut. 19:16). The scene is that of an irregular court. He is questioned by these violent men about crimes about which he knows nothing. The expression 'they questioned me' reflects legal terminology, as the verb 'to ask' (*shâ'al*) can be used of questioning a witness in a court of law.[3] The translation 'on things I know nothing about' is a possible interpretation of the MT. The alternative is to take the words (lit. 'who/which I do not know') as denoting the accusers of whom he has no knowledge. Either, they could have been friends whose appearance was so changed that he did not recognise them, or else they used messengers with whom he was unfamiliar. The parallelism with 'ruthless attackers' and the repetition of the same phrase 'those I do not know' in verse 15 suggest that this is the better interpretation.[4] The result of these illegalities is that he is punished for things he has never done, and so is left desolate. He is like a child who has lost his mother.

---

[3] T. H. Gaster, 'Questioning a Witness in a Court of Law', *VT* (1954), p. 25.

[4] This reflects the argumentation of W. VanGemeren, 'Psalms', p. 289.

Yet when they were ill, I put on sackcloth and humbled myself with fasting. When my prayers returned to me unanswered, I went about mourning as though for my friend or brother. I bowed my head in grief as though weeping for my mother (*vv. 13-14*). These verses contain several of the Old Testament terms for mourning. Sackcloth was an outward sign of mourning, and worn against the skin it was very uncomfortable. Fasting was practised in dangerous and sorrowful situations. 'To go about in mourning' is a phrase to describe mourners who show their deep grief by going about without washing, and by wearing soiled clothes. To pray with bowed head (lit. 'my prayer returns to my bosom') like the tax collector did (Luke 18:13) meant that physical posture and inward agony were seen to be united. How different was the psalmist's attitude to his enemies than theirs to him! Even if his enemies had been the closest of family, he could not have shown more grief for them.

But when I stumbled, they gathered in glee; attackers gathered against me when I was unaware. They slandered me without ceasing. Like the ungodly they maliciously mocked; they gnashed their teeth at me (*vv. 15-16*). A very unusual word is used here for attackers (*nêkîm*). It seems to come from a Hebrew verb meaning to strike (*nâkâh*), but in form it should probably be passive ('stricken', 'crippled'). It is used in Isaiah 66:2 of those who are crushed in spirit.[5] If this meaning is taken here, it implies that even those who were in a similar state as the psalmist did not try to console him. Rather, they gloated over his condition, and wounded him further with their bitter words. The NIV translation 'when I was unaware' should be emended to 'whom I did not know', as it is a repetition of the same phrase in verse 11.

While the general meaning is clear, the opening of verse 16 is extremely difficult to interpret. Literally it translates: 'as profane men, mockers for a cake.' While this may mean mockers who do so in pursuit of food, yet various changes

---

[5] Another alternative is to accept Dahood's suggestion that this is an occurrence of the Qal form of this verb that is otherwise unattested. This involves revocalising the word as *nokîm*. See M. Dahood, *Psalms I*, p. 213.

have been proposed.[6] The simplest solution is to take the word rendered 'cake' as meaning 'a circle', so that the meaning is that the psalmist faced mockers who stood in a circle around him. The verb 'to gnash the teeth' only occurs five times in the Old Testament and in each of the passages in the Psalms in which it occurs the context indicates that the machinations of the wicked against the righteous come to naught (see, in addition to v. 16, Pss. 37:12 and 112:10).

Now there is direct appeal to the LORD to step into the situation and deliver him. **O Lord, how long will you look on? Rescue my life from their ravages, my precious life from these lions. I will give you thanks in the great assembly; among throngs of people I will praise you** (*vv. 17-18*). 'How long?' occurs when there is a feeling of utter abandonment (Pss. 13:1; 79:5; 89:46). He wants his life delivered from the present bitter attacks by these evil men. The reference to 'my precious life' may suggest that he is very self-centred, but the word almost invariably is used of those loved by God. Such love by God brought protection (cf. Benjamin, Deut. 33:12). Our attitude to our own lives must be taken in Christian terms, and like Paul we must only view them in relation to God's purpose for us (Acts 20:24). The promise is made that not only will praise be given to God in an individual way, but also in the presence of others as the people of God assemble for worship. The phrase 'the great congregation' seems to be referring to the same assembly as the simple 'the congregation' (for other occurrences of 'the great congregation', see 1 Kings 8:65; 2 Chron. 20:14; 30:13; and Ps. 22:25). This note of thanksgiving is very fitting following on the cries of lament in the preceding verses.

3. A Call for God's Help (*vv. 19-27*)

Direct appeal to the LORD is now made, replacing the curses earlier in the psalm. **Let not those gloat over me who are my enemies without cause; let not those who hate me without reason maliciously wink the eye** (*v. 19*). Once more the innocence of the

---

[6] For discussion of various proposals, see W. VanGemeren, 'Psalms', p. 290; M. Dahood, *Psalms I*, pp. 212-13; *DCH*, 5, p. 383; A. A. Anderson, *The Book of Psalms I* (London: Marshall, Morgan & Scott, 1972), p. 282.

psalmist is maintained for he is being persecuted 'without cause' and 'without reason'. He does not want such people to be able to gloat (lit. 'rejoice') over his trouble. The Hebrew verb translated 'wink' has the idea of pinching something together. 'Wink' is probably too much associated with merriment in English. It would be better to use an expression like 'narrow the eyes' which may better depict the hostility.

They do not speak peaceably, but devise false accusations against those who live quietly in the land (*v. 20*). Further indication comes here of the treaty or covenant background to the psalm. The term 'peace' was used in international treaties of the ancient Near East to designate the relationship between the parties. Thus Joshua made peace with the Gibeonites, establishing a treaty relationship between Israel and themselves (Josh. 9:15). Clearly the psalmist's enemies were breaching the terms of the treaty, and making false claims against those living in quietness in the land. The phrase 'those who live quietly in the land' only occurs here, apparently designating the congregation of faithful worshippers.[7]

They gape at me and say, 'Aha! Aha! With our own eyes we have seen it.' O LORD, you have seen this; be not silent. Do not be far from me, O Lord (*vv. 21-22*). The enemies make the claim that they have seen something that broke the requirements of the covenant they had made. The cry 'Aha!' is an exclamation of joy over the fact that they have discovered something with which they can accuse the psalmist. But someone else had seen the situation. God had been witness to the treaty, and the psalmist appeals to him to intervene. 'Do not be silent' and 'do not be far from me' are simply ways of asking for God's immediate help to rectify the situation.

Awake, and rise to my defence! Contend for me, my God and Lord. Vindicate me in your righteousness, O LORD my God; do

---

[7] The difficulty in understanding the phrase is not just because it is a *hapax legomenon*. The word in question (*râgêa'*) comes from a root *r-g-'* that has two divergent meanings, 'to stir' or 'act in a moment', and 'to be at rest'. Context has to be the determining factor, and in this psalm the phrase seems to designate those who experience the tranquility 'that results from having ceased one's own efforts and from having found security through trust in God' (John N. Oswalt, *NIDOTTE*, 3, p. 1054).

not let them gloat over me (*vv. 23-24*). Legal terminology is used to show the action that is needed by the LORD. The request for God to contend for him, with which the psalm opened, is now repeated. He is asked to 'awake', i.e. to stir himself and to act on behalf of the psalmist, for he seems so distant. God is not hostile but seems so indifferent. The psalmist longs for deliverance, and the phrase 'vindicate me in your righteousness' may refer to victory in battle as much as to legal vindication. The final clause of verse 24 is the same as the first in verse 19.

Do not let them think, 'Aha, just what we wanted!' or say, 'We have swallowed him up' (*v. 25*). If God does not intervene, then this would be the consequence. These enemies would be able to think and say, 'We got our wish!' Again the exclamation 'Aha!' denotes joy. With rejoicing they would be able to claim that the psalmist had been destroyed (cf. Ps. 124:3 for the idiom concerning being swallowed).

May all who gloat over my distress be put to shame and confusion; may all who exalt themselves over me be clothed with shame and disgrace. May those who delight in my vindication shout for joy and gladness; may they always say, 'The LORD be exalted, who delights in the well-being of his servant' (*vv. 26-27*). This section of the psalm moves to a close with a contrast between two groups of people. For those who desire his ruin, the psalmist asks again (see v. 4) that they will be covered with shame and disgrace, as though they were wearing it like clothes. On the other hand he longs for his supporters to be able to rejoice in what the LORD has done for him. The covenant theme is continued here with reference to the well-being (lit. 'the peace') of the LORD's servant. Human treaties might promise peace, but it is only the LORD who can give it. True peace is a gift of the Saviour (John 14:27). The response from the psalmist is praise for God's salvation.

My tongue will speak of your righteousness and of your praises all day long (*v. 28*). He will ever speak (the same word as used in Ps. 1:2 for murmuring or meditating) of his deliverance, and make mention of God's praise. It is noticeable that God's praise is closely tied in here and elsewhere with God's acts of deliverance (see Exod. 15:11; and Pss. 78:4 and 106:47).

Psalm 36

For the director of music. Of David the servant of the LORD.

There are features in this psalm that resemble appeals to God, but there are also other features which are more like wisdom psalms such as Psalms 37 or 73. Perhaps it is best to compare it to the first psalm, though it deals with the subject matter in reverse order. In fact, there are four sections in the psalm. It starts with the wicked, progresses to God's covenant love (*chésed*), prays for the continuation of that love, and then reverts to the fate of the wicked. This chiastic pattern is clearer in the Hebrew text, but it can be set out in this fashion:

1. **The character of the godless** (vv. *1-4*)
   Subject: the wicked [*râshâ'*] (v. *1*)
2. **The covenant love of the** LORD (vv. *5-9*)
   Subject: covenant love [*chésed*] (v. *5*)
3. **Continuation of the** LORD**'s love** (v. *10*)
   Subject: covenant love [*chésed*] (v. *10*)
4. **The fate of the wicked** (vv. *11-12*)
   Subject: the wicked [*râshâ'*] (v. *11*)

This psalm, along with others such as Psalm 32, shows how wisdom teaching found a congenial place in the worship of Israel. The characteristics of the godly and the ungodly are described graphically, setting out both their way of life and also the attitude of God to them. On the one his favour rests; from the other, his grace is withheld.

1. The Character of the Godless (*vv. 1-4*)

The opening verse is called by the notable nineteenth-century commentator, J. A. Alexander, one of the most difficult verses in the whole book.[1] **An oracle is within my heart concerning the sinfulness of the wicked: There is no fear of God before his eyes** (*v. 1*). The word translated 'oracle' is a technical term (*n^e'um*), occurring again in Psalm 110:1. It is used repeatedly in the prophets to introduce a divine proclamation. Here it is either used of the psalmist, as the NIV takes it, or else it refers to the decision the wicked man has made: 'I have resolved in my heart to do evil'.[2] While not without problems, these interpretations at least are trying to interpret and translate the MT without changing it.

The second part of the verse is the psalmist's comment on the character of the wicked man. He has none of the terror inspired by God, and hence God is excluded from the whole horizon of his life. The phrase is not the normal one for the fear of God (*yir'at yhwh*) but one that speaks more of terror (*pachad 'elôhîm*). Paul quotes these words in Romans 3:18 as giving the cause of all the manifestations of sin he has just listed.

For in his own eyes he flatters himself too much to detect or hate his sin. The words of his mouth are wicked and deceitful; he has ceased to be wise and to do good (*vv. 2-3*). The nature of sin is that it is self-deceptive. Without a true relationship with the LORD the transgressor does not view himself aright, and therefore is unable to acknowledge or come

---

[1] J. A. Alexander, *The Psalms Translated and Explained* (Edinburgh: Andrew Elliot and James Thin, 1864; republished by Zondervan, n. d.), pp. 155-56.

[2] The phrase *n^e'um pesha'* is a *hapax legomenon*. The use of *n^e'um* is almost invariably with *yhwh*, designating a word from the LORD given to a prophet and then transmitted to his hearers. But it is not only the opening phrase that is difficult, but also the word 'in my heart' (*libbî*). The fact that a few Hebrew manuscripts have *libbô*, 'his heart', only shows that scribes recognised a problem and sought to overcome it. Older commentators discussed the problem (cf. in addition to Alexander, F. Delitzsch, *Psalms*, II, pp. 1-4; Hengstenberg, *Psalms*, II, pp. 12-14). Good modern discussions can be found in Craigie, *Psalms 1-50*, p. 290, and VanGemeren, 'Psalms', p. 293. Craigie proposes that *n^e'um*, 'oracle', should be added to the title, and this is accepted by C. C. Broyles, *Psalms* [NIV International Biblical Commentary] (Peabody, MA; Hendrickson, 1999), pp. 174, 177. However, both Craigie and Broyles proceed to accept the emendation 'his heart'.

to hate his sin. Pride rules his motives and his self-sufficiency creates the inability to feel any sense of sin. His words reveal his true character, and being under the dominion of sin he has ceased acting wisely and doing good.

Even on his bed he plots evil; he commits himself to a sinful course and does not reject what is wrong (*v. 4*). As part of his way of life, the evil man thinks that in the solitude of his own bedroom he can plot evil without God knowing. Instead of thinking about God's goodness while in bed (Ps. 63:6) he is deliberately setting himself to plot further evil for the next day. He sets himself upon a path that is not good, the MT making not-good a single word (*lô'-tôv*).

2. The Covenant Love of the LORD (*vv. 5-9*)

In stark contrast to these descriptions of the wicked is the covenant love (*chésed*) of the LORD. **Your love, O LORD, reaches to the heavens, your faithfulness to the skies** (*v. 5*). The idea of this verse is very similar to the opening of Psalm 89, which is proclaiming the wonder of God's grace shown in his covenant with David (Ps. 89:1-4). Both 'love' and 'faithfulness' describe the unchanging commitment of God, his total dependability in keeping his pledged word. It is beyond human ability to grasp the full extent of this love (cf. Ps. 103:11 and Paul's words in Eph. 3:18-19).

Your righteousness is like the mighty mountains, your justice like the great deep. O LORD, you preserve both man and beast (*v. 6*). Another pair of attributes are ascribed to God, indicating how his character affects both men and animals. Both 'righteousness' and 'justice' are terms that carry on the idea of God's covenant commitment. They are compared to the great, unchanging parts of God's creation in order to demonstrate how unchangeable they are.[3] He will continue to preserve both men and animals. The allusion here is probably to the covenant with Noah, in which God pledged himself

---

[3] In the MT 'like the mighty mountains' is 'like the mountains of God' (*kʰharê 'êl*). This construction in effect has the force of a superlative in linking a word with a divine name. Most probably the usage arose from the idea that God created the thing in question. See, for further comment, illustration, and literature, *DIHG~S*, p. 46; *IBHS*, pp. 154 n. 33, 268.

never again to cut off all life by means of a flood (Gen. 8:21-22; 9:9-17).

How priceless is your unfailing love! Both high and low among men find refuge in the shadow of your wings (*v. 7*). An exclamation or a doxology is a fitting response to what has just been said. The NIV takes the Hebrew word *ʾelohîm* to stand for men of high station. It is better to take it in its normal meaning of 'God', and so render: 'How precious is your unfailing love, O God! Men find refuge. ...' This also forms a neat parallel with 'O LORD, you preserve ...' in the previous verse. An expression of God's covenant love is seen in the truth that men can find shelter with him, just as Israel did of old (cf. Deut. 32:10-11 and Ps. 17:7-8).

They feast on the abundance of your house; you give them drink from your river of delights. For with you is the fountain of life; in your light we see light (*vv. 8-9*). God's grace is depicted as feasting or drinking. As people came to the sanctuary they found that God provided richly for them. The idea of feasting may come from the practice of participating in the fellowship meals. Linked with this is the picture of drinking from a cool fountain of water. It may be that 'house' here is God's creation as a whole, from which men and animal alike receive the bounty. All of life is traced back to God as its source. The word 'delights' (pl. *ʿadānîm*) only occurs three times in the Old Testament, and there may be an illusion to the Garden of Eden, the garden of delight (*ʿêden*). The imagery is furthered in the Book of Revelation with reference to drinking from the fountain of life (Rev. 21:6). Then the psalmist changes the imagery to light. This statement in verse 9 is similar to the opening verse of Psalm 27 where God is said to be light and salvation. This idea anticipates the gospel message of the New Testament that Jesus is indeed the true light (John 1:4-9; 1 John 1:5-7).

3. The Continuation of the LORD's Love (*v. 10*)
Continue your love to those who know you, your righteousness to the upright in heart (*v. 10*). The verb used at the outset of this verse (*mâshak*) conveys the idea of drawing

out or prolonging something. It forms a prayer here that the covenant love of the LORD will be maintained for those in a vital relationship with him. 'To know the LORD' is an expression denoting close fellowship with him, because strangers to him do not have this knowledge (cf. 1 Sam. 2:12; 3:7). The parallel phrase repeats the same idea in variant language, continuing the close connection between covenant love and righteousness (see v. 5). As in Psalm 33:1, 'the upright in heart' is a term that describes the believing community.

4. The Fate of the Wicked (*vv. 11-12*)
May the foot of the proud not come against me, nor the hand of the wicked drive me away (*v. 11*). The thought of the wicked plotting evil ways against the righteous is taken up again from the beginning of the psalm. The psalmist prays for protection against the foot and hand of the wicked that would trample him down or drive him far away from the place of blessing and salvation.

See how the evildoers lie fallen – thrown down, not able to rise! (*v. 12*). Whereas the earlier picture of the wicked in this psalm was one of busyness in their own sinful ways, now their end is depicted with startling brevity. 'There they lie!' exclaims the psalmist. The place or time is not mentioned, making the statement an even greater threat. The person who does not live in the fear of the LORD will ultimately perish.

Psalm 37
Of David.

None of the previous acrostic psalms (9-10, 25, and 34) is as elaborate as this one. Every letter of the Hebrew alphabet is included, and two verses are allocated to each letter. In its general theme the psalm is most closely related to Psalm 73, though it has numerous verses that have parallels in the Book of Proverbs. Many of the statements are in the form of proverbs, which are general assertions of a truth rather than promises to individuals. Twice (in verses 25 and 35) the psalmist refers to his own experience in which he had seen something of the character of both the righteous and the wicked. Its teaching centres on the source of true blessing, and it encourages its readers to follow the ways of the LORD. It concludes on the note of salvation for those who find refuge in him (v. 40). While the alphabetic pattern places constraints on the author, yet there does seem to be some divisions in the psalm.

This psalm was utilised by the Qumran community in pre-Christian times. Considerable parts of a commentary on it have survived (4QPs37), in which the community itself becomes 'those who wait for the LORD' (v. 9), while the wicked are interpreted as their opponents.[1]

1. A Call to Trust in the LORD (*vv. 1-9*)
The opening and close of the psalm are marked by imperatives and prohibitions. **Do not fret because of evil men or be**

---

[1] For further discussion on this document, see J. M. Allegro, 'A Newly Discovered Fragment of Ps 37 from Qumran', *PEQ* LXXXVI (1954), pp. 69-75, and D. Pardee, 'A Restudy of the Commentary on Psalm 37 from Qumran Cave 4', *Revue de Qumran* VIII (1973), pp. 163-94.

envious of those who do wrong; for like the grass they will soon wither, like green plants they will soon die away (*vv. 1-2*). The Hebrew word for 'fret' (*chârâh*) comes from a stem meaning to burn, and it is used here in a reflexive form; 'Do not let yourself burn [with envy]'. It is only in this psalm (vv. 1, 7, 8) and Proverbs 24:19 that this form occurs.[2] The parallel expression points to envy of the ill-doing of the wicked and their short-lived prosperity. The problem faced in this psalm, as in Psalm 73, is the seeming prosperity of the wicked. The psalmist says to his readers, 'Don't be jealous of the wicked, for they are just like grass, which seems to be flourishing and then is gone'. The comparison with the grass is used elsewhere in the Psalms to teach the frailty of all human life (Ps. 103:15).

Trust in the LORD and do good; dwell in the land and enjoy safe pasture. Delight yourself in the LORD and he will give you the desires of your heart (*vv. 3-4*). What was needed was not envy, but trust in the LORD! This command has as its background the possession by Israel of the land of promise. What was needed was continuing commitment to the LORD and the appropriate obedience to his word which would result in them 'doing good'. The references to the land are reminiscent of passages such as Deuteronomy 11, in which 'the land' was a summary of all the blessings promised under the covenant. 'Enjoy safe pasture' is the NIV's attempt to translate a difficult clause in the MT (*r$^{e^c}$êh $^{\,e}$mûnâh*, lit. 'shepherd faithfulness'). It is preferable to take the word 'faithfulness' as an adverb, 'faithfully', and the resulting translation, 'shepherd faithfully', gives a good parallel to 'dwell in the land'.[3] There was to be enjoyment in the LORD (the verb is a very rare one in the Old Testament), and the assurance is given that he would respond to the prayers of his people.

The theme of verses 3-4 is repeated in alternative language in verses 5-6. **Commit your way to the LORD; trust in him and he will do this: He will make your righteousness shine**

---

[2] It is a mistake to think that the Hitpael of this verb refers to passionate anger as over against simple anger in the Qal form. The Qal already has intensive force. See the comment by B. K. Waltke, *The Book of Proverbs Chapters 15-31*,(NICOT: Grand Rapids: Eerdmans, 2005), p. 286 n. 59.
[3] For fuller discussion, see W. VanGemeren, 'Psalms', p. 299.

like the dawn, the justice of your cause like the noonday sun *(vv. 5-6)*. The call is to commit (lit. 'roll', *gôl*) their way on the LORD (cf. Ps. 22:9). When this expression is compared with Proverbs 16:3 – 'Commit to the LORD whatever you do, and your plans will succeed' – it seems to suggest that heavy demands, like a great burden, are to be rolled onto the LORD. He is able to do whatever is demanded. The New Testament equivalent is to cast all our anxiety upon him because he cares for us (1 Pet. 5:7). The outcome of this trust will be that the cause entrusted to him will flourish just like the appearance of the sun in its glory. NIV takes the Hebrew word *'ôr (light)* as 'dawn', but the parallelism suggests 'sun' is the better rendering.

Be still before the LORD and wait patiently for him; do not fret when men succeed in their ways, when they carry out their wicked schemes *(v. 7)*. The situation confronting the readers of this psalm was that the prosperity of wicked men was causing them problems. When they thought about it they were becoming angry and resentful. What they should have done was to be silent before the LORD (cf. the use of the same verb already in Pss. 4:4 and 30:12, and also in Ps. 62:1) and to wait patiently for him to deal with the situation. The command 'Do not fret' is taken up from the opening verse and is repeated in both this and the following verse. Present success of ungodly men is no true indication of God's favour or blessing.

Refrain from anger and turn from wrath; do not fret – it leads only to evil. For evil men will be cut off, but those who hope in the LORD will inherit the land *(vv. 8-9)*. Becoming angry about the situation is only to imitate the unrighteous ways of the wicked. Those ways are not to be followed, only forsaken. Inward turmoil over it results in more evil, and places one in danger of God's judgment. 'To be cut off' is used here as in Exodus 30:33, 38 and 31:14 of being put to death. To remain in the good land and enjoy its benefits required true faith and hope in the LORD. This latter expression complements the other expressions already used such as 'trust', and 'commit your way to the Lord'. To hope in the LORD indicates long, patient endurance in waiting on him. The New Testament parallels to it are our Lord's experience in Gethsemane (Luke 22:44: 'in anguish') and the description of Epaphras' prayers (Col. 4:12: 'always wrestling in prayer').

2. The Ruin of the Wicked (vv. 10-15)

A little while, and the wicked will be no more; though you look for them, they will not be found. But the meek will inherit the land and enjoy great peace (vv. 10-11). The seeming prosperity of the wicked is only an illusion, for they are going to be cut off. When one looks to see where they are (lit. 'you perceive his place'), they are gone. The contrast is that the meek shall abide in the land and enjoy (the same word as translated 'delight' in verse 4) abundant peace. The word 'meek' represents all those who are truly waiting on the LORD. It is often contrasted with the wicked as here in this verse, or with the scoffers (Prov. 16:19). They experience God as their deliverer (Ps. 10:17), receive grace from him (Prov. 3:34), and they know that he is finally going to save them (Pss. 147:6; 149:4). The concept of the land was so central for Old Testament believers that occupation of it could be used to summarise all the blessings that God had promised. Jesus, in the Sermon on the Mount (Matt. 5:5), broadened the concept of the meek inheriting the land. He spoke not just of 'land' but of the world. Then, too, he further developed the idea both by integrating it with his teaching on the kingdom and also by expanding the idea to embrace Jew and Gentile.

The wicked plot against the righteous and gnash their teeth at them; but the Lord laughs at the wicked, for he knows their day is coming (vv. 12-13). Those whose hearts are not right with God spend their time scheming against the righteous. In their bitterness they vent their rage by grinding their teeth as they display their anger.[4] In Psalm 2:4 the Lord mocks at the scheming of the hostile kings. Here he mocks at the wicked in general. The reason for this is that he knows that 'his day' is coming. This could refer to the Lord's 'day', but in the context it seems to be the wicked man's day. In effect

---

[4] For the expression 'gnash the teeth', see comment on 35:16.

it amounts to the same thing, for his day will be the final day of judgment.

The wicked draw the sword and bend the bow to bring down the poor and needy, to slay those whose ways are upright. But their swords will pierce their own hearts, and their bows will be broken (*vv. 14-15*). Hostility towards the righteous is the hallmark of the wicked. They plot to use weapons against them, and even to kill them. The verb 'to slay' (*tâvach*) is a very strong word, being used elsewhere normally of the slaughter of animals. However, what they will find is that their own schemes turn against themselves and they are destroyed by their own weapons. This theme, of evil turning back on its practitioners, is dealt with in Psalm 7:14-16 (see commentary; for the same idea, see Jer. 2:19 and 5:24-25).

3. The Blessing of the LORD (*vv. 16-26*)

Better the little that the righteous have than the wealth of many wicked; for the power of the wicked will be broken, but the LORD upholds the righteous (*vv. 16-17*). Money may be part of a happy life but it is not its real basis. The righteous may be poor, but that is better than thinking that wealth is what matters in life. Money in itself is not wrong. It is the love of it that the Bible condemns (1 Tim. 6:10). The wicked will find that their ability to acquire wealth will disappear. The word 'power' is literally 'arms', for often 'arm' ($z^e r\hat{o}^c a$) is used as a symbol for power (see Pss. 77:15 and 89:10). On the other hand, the sustenance of the righteous comes from the LORD. He is the constant provider for his people, and his role is emphasised in the Hebrew text (and all the ancient translations) by placing his name at the end of the verse.

The days of the blameless are known to the LORD, and their inheritance will endure forever. In times of disaster they will not wither; in days of famine they will enjoy plenty (*vv. 18-19*). The whole idea of Canaan as the land that God swore to give to Israel lies behind the words here. Canaan was the inheritance that the LORD provided (Exod. 15:17; Deut. 31:20), and his eyes were 'continually on it from the beginning of the year to the end' (Deut. 11:12). God knew each day of his people's lives, and he so met their needs that even in times of famine they enjoyed abundance. On occasions this was done by extraordinary means, as in the days of Elijah (1 Kings 17:1-6).

But the wicked will perish: The LORD's enemies will be like the beauty of the fields, they will vanish – vanish like smoke (v. 20). The stress here is on the passing nature of the wicked. This is emphasised by the use of two verbs, 'perish' and 'vanish', with the double use of the latter drawing attention to the accomplishment of God's wrath against the wicked. Two illustrations are involved. The first one is that of the beauty of the grass, which then fades. The second is of things being consumed by fire. Both of them draw attention to how fleeting is the existence of the wicked.

The wicked borrow and do not repay, but the righteous give generously; those the LORD blesses will inherit the land, but those he curses will be cut off (*vv. 21-22*). The contrast is between the wicked who borrow so extensively and are unable to pay when the crisis comes, and the righteous, who not only have sufficient for their own needs, but are also able to help others as well. In the Hebrew text of verse 21, two phrases are used both of the wicked and the righteous (borrow/not repay, show mercy/give). It is best to retain this parallelism with a translation such as the NKJV: 'The wicked borrows and does not repay, but the righteous shows mercy and gives.' The introduction of the reference to blessing and cursing in verse 22 recalls the sections in the covenant that list the appropriate blessings and cursings (Deut. 27:1-26; 28:1-6, 15-68). The description of death as a 'cutting off' goes back to the language of instituting a covenant (lit. 'cutting a covenant') and the threat of being cut off because of failure to keep the provisions of the covenant (Gen. 17:14).

The LORD delights in the way of the man whose steps he has made firm; though he stumble, he will not fall, for the LORD upholds him with his hand (*vv. 23-24*). The general principle being stated is that the righteous may experience falls during life, but yet the LORD will uphold them so that they are lifted up again (see the similar teaching in Prov. 24:16). The

LORD's pleasure is shown towards the righteous as they walk in his ways, and he establishes those ways. The righteous are not isolated from trouble, but when it comes, the LORD strengthens their hand (the same verb 'uphold' occurs here as in v. 17).[5]

I was young and now I am old, yet I have never seen the righteous forsaken or their children begging bread. They are always generous and lend freely; their children will be blessed (*vv. 25-26*). The elderly psalmist reflects on his knowledge of life, extending from being a lad (*naʿar*) until he has reached old age (*zâqantî*). While he has seen the righteous passing through difficult times (cf. vv. 7, 12, 14, 16, 19), yet he has never seen them completely forsaken by the LORD. Though they may have periods in life when it seems that the LORD has withdrawn his love, yet that is never final. The righteous are able to show compassion to others and share with them their resources. The lending is not in a commercial sense, for no interest was to be charged on such loans (Exod. 22:25). The final phrase of verse 26 points to the fact that not only will the righteous be provided by the LORD, but their children, in turn, will receive from him.

4. The Marks of the Righteous (*vv. 27-33*)

In the closing parts of the psalm there is a return to the style of the opening, with commands again evident. The theme of dwelling in the promised land continues. **Turn from evil and do good; then you will dwell in the land forever. For the LORD loves the just and will not forsake his faithful ones** (*vv. 27-28a*). Continuity of life in the promised land depended on obedience by the people (see Deut. 11:8-9: 'Observe therefore all the commands I am giving you today ... so that you may live long in the land that the LORD swore

---

[5] Ambiguity is present in both of these verses. The verb 'he delights' could have either 'the LORD' or 'the righteous man' as the subject. Then at the conclusion of verse 24, 'his hand' could be either the direct object of the verb ('he upholds his hand', i.e. the hand of the righteous man), or it could be as the NIV translates, 'the LORD upholds by his hand.' These ambiguities explain the difference in rendering by various English versions.

to your forefathers to give them and their descendants ...').[6] Following the LORD meant that they had to turn from evil and do good, which is a reference to living in a morally good way (1 Kings 8:36). The Hebrew text of verse 28a says that the LORD loves 'justice', but it seems best to take this as meaning 'the just' as in Proverbs 2:8. To those who are just and who are his loyal servants (*ch*ᵃ*sîdîm*, see on 4:3; 12:1; 18:25), there is the promise that God will never forsake them (Deut. 31:6, quoted in Heb. 13:5).

They will be protected forever, but the offspring of the wicked will be cut off; the righteous will inherit the land and dwell in it forever (*vv. 28b-29*). Verse 28b commences the section of the acrostic beginning with the letter *ayin*, though here and in verse 39 the conjunction *vav* must be disregarded.[7] The contrast is between the just and the wicked and their respective descendants. The seed (NIV 'children') of the righteous will be blessed (v. 26), whereas the seed (NIV 'offspring') of the wicked will be destroyed. This is a repetition in other words of what has already been stated in verses 9 and 22. The psalmist builds here on the concept of the land being an inheritance for Israel. God's covenant people had to maintain their inheritance by obedience to his demands. This is the fourth time that the psalmist has mentioned inheriting the land, and the variety of expressions used to designate the persons involved shows how close in meaning several of the phrases are ('those who hope in the LORD', v. 9; 'the meek', v. 11; 'those who the LORD blesses,' v. 22; 'the righteous', v. 29). The idea of this statement forms the background for Jesus' words in the Sermon on the Mount: 'Blessed are the meek, for they will inherit the earth' (Matt. 5:5).

---

[6] 'In the land' is not in the MT but it is clearly implied in the context (see vv. 22 and 29). Also, as this section of the psalm reverts to the themes of the early verses, it is certainly in parallel with verse 3, 'Trust in the LORD and do good; dwell in the land ...'

[7] The alternative to this is textual change. Craigie, *Psalms 1-50*, p. 296 says that the initial word needed for a strophe beginning with *ayin* 'was presumably dropped accidentally'. However, taking this approach requires further emendation to give a translation such as 'the wicked are destroyed for ever' that has some support from the LXX.

The mouth of the righteous man utters wisdom, and his tongue speaks what is just. The law of his God is in his heart; his feet do not slip (*vv. 30-31*). Again, there is a parallel with a saying in the Book of Proverbs (see Prov. 10:31). The righteous person ponders over God's wisdom and speaks about it. The word 'utters' is translated as meditate in Psalm 1:2, but it can also mean 'speak' (see on Ps. 35:28). Here meditation and speech are linked together, for the righteous man has God's law in his heart, and thus he speaks of what is wise and just. His steps do not slip because he has God's instruction as his guide.

The wicked lie in wait for the righteous, seeking their very lives; but the LORD will not leave them in their power or let them be condemned when brought to trial (*vv. 32-33*).[8] These two verses have the ring of the courthouse about them. Hence it may well be that 'seeking their very lives' (Hebrew lit. 'seeking to kill him') refers to action in a court to secure a verdict of guilty, one which amounted to 'legal' murder. The 'lying in wait' would then be giving false evidence against the righteous. But while men may condemn, God will acquit. The righteous judgment of God is here contrasted (as in 1 Cor. 4:3) with human judgment. Tertullian (AD c. 160-240), one of the great theologians of the early church, said: 'If we are condemned by the world, we will be acquitted by God.' The righteous will not be forsaken at this time of trial, but rather find vindication from the LORD.

5. Salvation from the LORD (*vv. 34-40*)

Wait for the LORD and keep his way. He will exalt you to inherit the land; when the wicked are cut off, you will see it (*v. 34*). The final verses of the psalm sum up its message, repeating ideas already seen in verses 7, 9, and 11. The psalmist issues a call for patient and expectant waiting for the LORD, which is coupled with following his paths.

---

[8] The NIV turns the singular forms of the MT into plurals in these verses. While the meaning is preserved, yet it is preferable to retain the singular: 'The mouth of the righteous speaks wisdom, and his tongue talks of justice. The law of his God is in his heart; none of his steps shall slide' (NKJV).

'The way of the LORD' is an expression that goes back to God's words concerning Abraham and his descendants (Gen. 18:19). David, at the end of his life, instructed his son Solomon to 'observe what the LORD your God requires: Walk in his ways, and keep his decrees and commands' (1 Kings 2:3). To 'exalt' in this context is practically equivalent to deliver (cf. Ps. 27:6). Once more the land of Canaan comes into focus here. When the wicked come to destruction, the righteous are going to be observers (for the same idea, see Pss. 52:6 and 91:8).

I have seen a wicked and ruthless man flourishing like a green tree in its native soil, but he soon passed away and was no more; though I looked for him, he could not be found (*vv. 35-36*). In the psalmist's own experience he had seen wicked and tyrannical men. They seemed to be like indigenous trees, well rooted and luxuriant. But when he next looked they were gone, and no searching could locate them. This is using the same illustration as in Psalm 1, but in the opposite way.

Consider the blameless, observe the upright; there is a future for the man of peace. But all sinners will be destroyed; the future of the wicked will be cut off (*vv. 37-38*). Another imperative follows. 'Consider' is the Hebrew verb 'to keep' or 'guard'. It is used here in the sense of 'regard', or 'pay attention to'. The object of this attention is the righteous man, called here 'the blameless' (see on Pss. 15:2 and 18:23) and 'the upright'. His final end (NIV 'future') is one of well-being and prosperity. His character and his destiny stand in marked contrast to the man of violence (v. 35). All transgressors will be destroyed, for at the end they will be cut off by the LORD.

The psalm ends with a summary of its entire message. **The salvation of the righteous comes from the LORD; he is their stronghold in time of trouble. The LORD helps them and delivers them; he delivers them from the wicked and saves them, because they take refuge in him** (*vv. 39-40*). The source of salvation is the LORD, who is a refuge in time of trouble. He sustains and delivers. The verb 'deliver' used (Hebrew *pâlat*) is almost exclusively a Psalter word. It is often used as here in a word of testimony regarding God's deliverances, and also it frequently has as its parallel the verb 'help'. The final words are important because they explain the reason for God's deliverances. The righteous have taken refuge with him, and hence he saves them.

Psalm 38

A psalm of David. A petition.

The title of this psalm does not provide much help in trying to put it into a historical setting. The description, 'a petition', is literally 'to bring to remembrance'. Some suggest a link with the memorial offering of Leviticus 2:2 and 24:7. The Aramaic Targum ties the psalm in with the daily memorial offering (Lev. 6:8-13), while the Greek Septuagint associates it with the Sabbath memorial offering (Lev. 24:5-9). It is better to think of the title as a later description of a psalm used by sufferers to bring their plight to God's remembrance. The situation the psalmist faced is twofold. On the one hand, he is suffering inwardly, but on the other hand he also has numerous enemies who are venting their hatred against him. These enemies are not mentioned in the early part, but from verse 12 onwards they dominate the text. Many affinities exist with Psalm 6, except that no recorded answer to the appeal for help occurs here.

The descriptions in the psalm are noteworthy because of the clusters of terms that are employed. God's attitude is described by words like 'anger', 'wrath', 'arrows', 'hand', and 'indignation'. The psalmist feels the pain in his 'flesh', 'bones', 'head', 'wounds', 'loins', 'heart', and 'eyes'. He describes his condition as being 'weighed down', 'bowed down', 'mourning', 'crushed' and 'sighing'.

Another feature of this psalm is that while it is not an acrostic, yet it is a poem of twenty-two lines, thus matching the number of letters in the Hebrew alphabet. The restriction of following the alphabetic sequence is gone, yet the use of twenty-two lines seems to be characteristic of laments.[1]

1. A Cry for Help (*v. 1*)

O LORD, do not rebuke me in your anger or discipline me in your wrath (*v. 1*). The opening of the psalm is almost identical to Psalm 6:1, though different words are used for 'anger', *kétsef* replacing *'af*. Comparison of the contexts in which these two words are used suggests that little difference in meaning exists between them. The psalmist knows that God will punish sin, but he asks God not to display his anger as he brings his case before him. He approaches the one who is 'the compassionate and gracious God, slow to anger, abounding in love and faithfulness' (Exod. 34:6). Confidence in the LORD's compassion underlies appeals in many of the Psalms (in addition to Psalms 6 and 38, see also Psalms 88 and 102).

2. A Description of Illness (*vv. 2-10*)

It is hard to assess the nature of the illness described here. There are features that suggest a dermatological condition (see vv. 5 and 7). It may have been a form of leprosy, which would also help to explain why the psalmist was so alienated from his friends and acquaintances (v. 11). **For your arrows have pierced me, and your hand has come down upon me** (*v. 2*). The arrows signify divine judgment, while the hand is often a symbol of power in the Old Testament. This verse is an acknowledgment of the sovereign way in which God had dealt with him, penetrating deeply into his heart and life (the same Hebrew verb is represented by 'pierced' and 'has come down'; cf. the use of this verb in Prov. 17:10: 'A rebuke impresses [penetrates deeply] a man of discernment more than a hundred lashes a fool').

Because of your wrath there is no health in my body; my bones have no soundness because of my sin. My guilt has overwhelmed me like a burden too heavy to bear (*vv. 3-4*). There is not always a connection between sin and sickness,

---

[1] Wilfred G. E. Watson, *Classical Hebrew Poetry: A Guide to the Techniques* (Sheffield: JSOT Press, 1984), p. 199.

but here the psalmist confesses his sin, as he does again later in the psalm (v. 18). Throughout his whole body he is experiencing the consequences of God's judgment upon him. His health is gone (lit. 'no *shalom* in my bones').[2] A comparison with Isaiah 1:6 is in order, as both the expressions 'no health in my body'//'no soundness in it' and the general tenor of the passages are so similar. He feels that he is being engulfed by his sin and its consequences. The word 'burden' is a fitting term to use of sin and guilt, and its use recalls Cain's words: 'My punishment is more than I can bear' (Gen. 4:13).

My wounds fester and are loathsome because of my sinful folly. I am bowed down and brought very low; all day long I go about mourning (*vv. 5-6*). The terms used here to describe the sickness denote the smell and the discharge of wounds, though they could be used as a figurative description of extreme suffering. 'Sinful folly' is a good translation of a Hebrew word that appears most commonly (twenty-two out of twenty-four appearances) in the Book of Proverbs (cf. especially Prov. 24:9). Verse 6 picks up the idea of sin being a burden (v. 4), as the psalmist suggests he is bent over because of his sin. He goes about in mourning constantly. In later Judaism it was customary for someone coming for trial to appear to be mourning. If this was also an earlier custom, it would suggest that the psalmist was recognising his own guilt and that he stood accused before the LORD.

My back is filled with searing pain; there is no health in my body. I am feeble and utterly crushed; I groan in anguish of heart (*vv. 7-8*). His back is ulcerated and fevered, and he repeats his mournful cry of verse 3: 'There is no health in my body.' This was the way in which Isaiah later spoke of the condition of the nation (Isa. 1:6: 'from the sole of your foot to top of your head *there is no soundness* …'). Physically and psychologically the psalmist is enfeebled

---

[2] For a good translation that brings out the use of the Hebrew word *shâlôm*, see Calvin Seerveld, *Voicing God's Psalms* (Grand Rapids: Eerdmans, 2005), p. 54: 'There's no shalom in my bones, because of my sins. Yes, my misdeeds have piled up over my head – they weigh down on me like a too heavy weight'.

to an intense degree. The two terms 'feeble' and 'utterly crushed' are practically synonymous, this point being underscored by the verbal construction.[3] He describes his anguished cries by using the verb (Hebrew *shâʿag*) that is normally used of the roaring of a lion. The same verb is used of the LORD roaring (Amos 1:2; Jer. 25:30; Joel 3:16). But here it is the tortured psalmist who cries out in his grief and pain.

All my longings lie open before you, O Lord; my sighing is not hidden from you. My heart pounds, my strength fails me; even the light has gone from my eyes (*vv. 9-10*). In his sickness and distress the psalmist knew that his whole life was open before the Lord. Nothing could be hidden from him, even all his 'sighings' (*kol-taʾᵃvâtî*). This is the real meaning of the word here, rather than 'longings'. When normal speech is impossible, sometimes only sighings can express emotional and physical anguish. God, who heard the groaning of his people in Egypt (Exod. 2:24), would understand his condition. His heart beats frantically,[4] and all his strength vanishes. The reference to the light going from the eyes is probably to the fact that his vitality had disappeared (cf. the note regarding Moses in Deut. 34:7: 'his eyes were not weak', for the opposite use of the idiom). The last clause in verse 10 has an awkwardness concealed by the NIV translation. Literally it is: 'And the light of my eyes *they* are not with me'. The plural pronoun 'they' should not be made to refer to the singular 'light'. Rather, it probably is intended as a reference to the 'eyes', emphasising their value for the body: 'and the light of my eyes – even them – I lack it'.

---

[3] The two verbs are connected by simple *vav*, not *vav* consecutive. When this occurs 'it repeats on the same time-scale or, it may be, slightly extends the reference of a previous verb, being thus more or less synonymous with it'. *DIHG~S*, p. 103. Cf. also the discussion in *IBHS*, pp. 497-98.

[4] The form of the verb here, *sᵉcharchar*, is a *hapax legomenon*. It appears to be a Peʿalʿal form derived from the root s-ch-r. The repetition of the last two consonants of the root is 'used of movements repeated in quick succession' and so yielding a translation like 'palpitate'. See *GKC* §55 d, and D. W. Thomas, '*libbî sᵉcharchar* in Ps. 38', *JTS* XL (1939), pp. 390-91.

3. Forsaken by Friends (*vv. 11-20*)

The following verses go on to describe the sense of desolation that David was experiencing. First of all, his friends left him, and then his enemies derided him. **My friends and companions avoid me because of my wounds; my neighbours stay far away. Those who seek my life set their traps, those who would harm me talk of my ruin; all day long they plot deception** (*vv. 11-12*). His friends (lit. 'those loving me') want to avoid contact with him. The affliction that he is undergoing was too much for them, and so they distance themselves from him. The word 'wounds' is literally 'affliction, smiting' (*nega'*), a word that is used for leprosy in the Old Testament (Lev. 13:2; Deut. 24:8), but also for other sicknesses. It is probably not just the repulsive nature of his illness that caused their alienation, but a realisation that it came from God. The contrast between those near to him, his neighbours, and the fact that they stand far away, is very poignant. From a distance they plot how they can ensnare him, and in conversation they speak about his ruin. The Hebrew poetry is enhanced by the fact that the first four words of the verse all contain the letter *shin*, so that the resulting assonance is striking to the ear.[5] All day long they are ready to plan things that will cause him even greater harm, and do so in deceitful ways.

I am like a deaf man, who cannot hear, like a mute, who cannot open his mouth; I have become like a man who does not hear, whose mouth can offer no reply (*vv. 13-14*). The psalmist rests his case with God, and he makes no attempt to justify himself to his accusers. He pretends he is both deaf and dumb, and he says it in emphatic fashion by repeating the main ideas in verse 14. Verbal forms of the verb 'to hear' (*shama'*) occur in both verses, as does the word 'his mouth'. He does not offer a response to the accusations of his friends and neighbours. The NIV translation 'reply' is a little too weak, as the

---

[5] Transliteration shows the assonance, with the use of the letter *qof* in the two opening words adding to the effect: *vay^enaq^eshû m^evaq^eshê nafshî v^edor^eshê râ' âtî dibb^erû havvôt*.

Hebrew word used (*tôkachat*) is often employed to designate an argument that is presented in court. The psalmist's trust is in God and he does not need to fill his mouth with arguments. In the midst of the lament the psalmist shows where his hope really lies. **I wait for you, O LORD; you will answer, O Lord my God** (*v. 15*). He directs his prayer to the LORD, confident that God will respond. By the end of the psalm there is still no recorded answer, but it is part of the nature of true faith to continue in expectant waiting.[6]

For I said, 'Do not let them gloat or exalt themselves over me when my foot slips' (*v. 16*). The Hebrew text of this verse has simply: 'For I said, "Lest they rejoice over me ..."' Something seems to be understood, such as, 'I will take heed of my ways ...' This was probably a prayer which had been prayed earlier, asking for healing lest his condition give his enemies occasion to rejoice. Even when he stumbled they took the opportunity to exalt themselves, priding themselves that they were not in the same position. After so many metaphorical expressions earlier, the psalmist now prays in very concrete terms. The triumph of the enemies would have meant his call for help had failed.

For I am about to fall, and my pain is ever with me. I confess my iniquity; I am troubled by my sin (*vv. 17-18*). It is hard to know to what 'falling' refers. It could be that in his heart he would come to a wrong conclusion about his present condition, and fail to see it in the light of God's word. He seems to even doubt the promise that God will not let the righteous fall (Pss. 15:5; 37:24; 112:6). Mental and physical distress was his constant companion. At the outset of the psalm he had acknowledged his sin (v. 3), and now he does so again. He was disturbed by it, and willingly makes known his condition before God.

Many are those who are my vigorous enemies; those who hate me without reason are numerous. Those who repay my good with evil slander me when I pursue what is good (*vv. 19-20*). The NIV is rather paraphrastic in its rendering of

---

[6] For a discussion on the various Hebrew verbs used regarding 'waiting on the Lord', see J. G. S. S. Thomson, 'Wait on the Lord', pp. 196-98.

the first part of verse 19. A literal translation of the MT is: 'And my enemies [are] alive: they are vast [or possibly, 'powerful']'.[7] While he seems near death, the psalmist's enemies are very much alive, and they have the numbers and power to enforce their will. Instead of 'my enemies [are] alive', one manuscript from Qumran reads 'my enemies without cause' (Hebrew *chinnâm* in place of *cháyyim*), which is an emendation frequently suggested (cf. Ps. 35:19). However, this manuscript may well have made a deliberate change, and it is preferable to stay with the MT. Without any justification the enemies repaid good with evil, and their hatred was inspired only by their own sinfulness.

4. An Appeal for Help (*vv. 21-22*)

The psalm ends with a prayer for speedy help. **O Lord, do not forsake me; be not far from me, O my God. Come quickly to help me, O Lord my Saviour** (*vv. 21-22*). At the centre of his life there is still true faith. No more mention is made of his sickness or of his enemies. He fears abandonment by God, and asks for urgent help to be granted. The final verse is the equivalent of saying, 'Come and save me quickly.' The ideas in both verses are very similar to those in Psalm 22:1, 11, 19. The two concluding words in Hebrew are 'Lord, my salvation', using the noun along with 'Lord' in phrases that are practically the equivalent of titles (cf. Ps. 51:14).

---

[7] The verb occurring here (*'âtsam*) seems to vary in meaning between the ideas of being numerous and being mighty. See the discussion in *NIDOTTE*, 3, pp. 487-99.

Psalm 39

For the director of music. For Jeduthun. A psalm of David.

There are aspects of this psalm that resemble some of those in the wisdom psalms (see the Introduction). This is especially so in relation to the teaching regarding the transitory nature of human life (vv. 4-6). It is not sickness that brings forth David's plea, but the knowledge that old age and death are approaching. This is a lament from an individual that does not seem to have been directly connected with any formal worship situation. The psalm moves through two parallel phases, which can be set out as follows:

1. Silence before the LORD (vv. *1-3*)
2. Prayer to the LORD (vv. *4-6*)
3. Appeal for Help (vv. *7-8*)
4. Silence before the LORD (v. *9*)
5. Prayer to the LORD (vv. *10-11*)
6. Appeal for Help (vv. *12-13*)

The name 'Jeduthun' in the title also occurs in the titles of Psalms 62 and 77. He was one of David's chief musicians (1 Chron. 9:16; 16:38, 41-42). It is unclear whether the use of the name is a reference to the musical director ('For the musical director, Jeduthun') or to a tune by this name.

1. Silence before the LORD (*vv. 1-3*)
The psalm opens with the psalmist telling his readers what his thoughts had been. **I said, 'I will watch my ways and keep my tongue from sin; I will put a muzzle on my mouth as long as the wicked are in my presence'** (*v. 1*).

He had wanted to speak, but because of the presence of the wicked he determined he would not. Perhaps he wanted to speak about the prosperity of the wicked or to ask questions about their relative ease in life. Instead, he muzzled himself and prevented himself speaking hasty or angry words that would have been sinful.[1] The NIV rendering 'I will put' follows a suggested emendation to avoid having the same Hebrew verbal form (*'eshmᵉrâh*) used in successive verses. While the suggested emendation (*'âsîmâh*) may be supported by the LXX (which renders the Hebrew word by *ethemên*), that does not justify the change.

But when I was silent and still, not even saying anything good, my anguish increased. My heart grew hot within me, and as I meditated, the fire burned; then I spoke with my tongue (*vv. 2-3*). His silence created other problems for him, for as he guarded his mouth his inner thoughts overwhelmed him. His anger is described by the terms 'grew hot' and 'burned'. From what follows in the next section it may be that the psalmist's concerns related to growing old and ultimately dying. He was like Jeremiah with a fire in his heart, which could not be contained (Jer. 20:9). Finally, he had to break his silence and speak, and the words 'then I spoke with my tongue' bring a dramatic end to the introductory verses.

2. Prayer to the LORD (*vv. 4-6*)

This section starts with a prayer, includes a description of the fleeting nature of life, and then has three assertions, which all start in Hebrew with the word 'surely' (Hebrew *'ak*). **Show me, O LORD, my life's end and the number of my days; let me know how fleeting is my life** (*v. 4*). The word 'end' is never used of geographical limits but always of either God's judgments,[2] or, as here, of the end of life. The psalmist wants divine instruction regarding the nature of human life. It is only temporary, and short-lived, and he prays that he may understand this. This section is very similar in idea to

---

[1] This is the only time that the word 'muzzle' (*machsôm*) appears in the OT, though the verb occurs in Deuteronomy 25:4 and Ezekiel 39:11.

[2] Cf. Amos 8:2 where there is word play between 'fruit basket' (*kâyits*) and 'the end' (*qêts*).

Psalm 90:1-12, where the counting of days is not just numerical but rather an understanding of human life and its frailty. **You have made my days a mere handbreadth; the span of my years is as nothing before you. Each man's life is but a breath. Selah** (*v. 5*). The MT places emphasis on this statement by the use of an introductory particle, 'Behold' (*hinnêh*). God's understanding of our lifetime is quite different from our own, for our lifespan is insignificant before him, a mere handbreadth.[3] The word for 'span' occurs in a similar passage in Psalm 89:47. The first of the three assertions introduced by the Hebrew 'surely' comes at the end of the verse: 'surely, each man's life ...'

Man is a mere phantom as he goes to and fro: He bustles about, but only in vain; he heaps up wealth, not knowing who will get it (*v. 6*). The second and third assertions starting with 'surely' come in this verse: 'Surely, like a shadow as man goes to and fro ... Surely, in vain he bustles about.' It is surprising that the word for 'mere phantom' is also the word for 'image' in Genesis 1:26, 27 (*tsélem*). But man is not God; he is only created in his image, and the image-bearer, because of sin, has a limited lifespan before death comes. All his activity is characterised as vanity, nothingness, and even his wealth will be enjoyed by others. The New Testament teaches that we should be content with God's provision, 'for we brought nothing into the world, and we can take nothing out of it' (1 Tim. 6:7).

3. Appeal for Help (*vv. 7-8*)

'But now, Lord, what do I look for? My hope is in you (*v. 7*). The expression 'But now' (*vᵉ attâh*) is far stronger in Hebrew than in English, for it marks off a new stage in the psalm.[4] It commences with a rhetorical question, to which the answer is given, 'I look expectantly to you'.[5] Both question and answer

---

[3] The word for 'handbreadth' (*téfach*) only occurs in this sort of context. It is clearly a building or architectural term as shown by its other occurrences in the Old Testament and in the documents from Qumran. Cf. *DCH*, III, p. 373.

[4] Cf. the comment in *NIDOTTE*, 4, p. 1031.

[5] For comment on the Hebrew words for 'waiting on the LORD' or 'looking to him', see f.n. 5 for Psalm 25.

suggest the very opposite of despondency and despair. The only hope for the psalmist was with God.
Save me from all my transgressions; do not make me the scorn of fools (*v. 8*). There is a confession implicit in these words. He prays for the forgiveness of his transgressions, no matter how many they are ('all of my transgressions'), including those already mentioned earlier in the psalm. His sinful thoughts and also wrong ideas concerning the meaning of life were part of his confession. Even a fool could note that he was so taken up with his enemies and the passing matters of human existence. He prays that he will be delivered from their reproaches.

4. Silence before the Lord (*v. 9*)
The second phase of the psalm begins here, with the idea of silence in verses 1-3 being taken up again. **I was silent; I would not open my mouth, for you are the one who has done this** (*v. 9*). He repeats from verse 2 the opening reference to his silence. However, there is a change here. Previously he had stopped himself from speaking, but now that he has seen what God has done, with his new insight he is content to stay silent. This is an acknowledgment that God's providence extends to all that happens in his life.

5. Prayer to the Lord (*vv. 10-11*)
Remove your scourge from me; I am overcome by the blow of your hand (*v. 10*). He is conscious of the Lord's rebuke, using the word 'scourge' to describe it (see the same word in Ps. 38:11, and accompanying comment). It is a military figure, and this is continued in the following phrase for the word 'blow' (*tigrâh*; only used here in the Old Testament) comes from a root that is associated with warfare. The distressing situation into which he has come is in fact the blow he has received.

You rebuke and discipline men for their sin; you consume their wealth like a moth — each man is but a breath. Selah (*v. 11*). The scourge from God is a form of rebuke to the psalmist. The biblical pattern is that 'the Lord disciplines those he loves, as a father the son he delights in' (Prov. 3:12, and cf. the use of these words in Hebrews 12:6). David now knows that human wealth can vanish quickly, just as a moth can eat some clothing. The final words of the verse are a repetition of the idea in verse 5, though what was a personal assertion only in that verse is now made applicable to everyone. It applies to all humanity (*kol-'ādām*), and the statement is made even more impressive by the introductory 'surely' (*'ak*) that the NIV omits: '*Surely* all mankind is a mere breath!' (ESV).

6. Appeal for Help (*vv. 12-13*)

'**Hear my prayer, O LORD, listen to my cry for help; be not deaf to my weeping. For I dwell with you as an alien, a stranger, as all my fathers were** (*v. 12*). As the psalm ends, there is another cry to God. David pleads with God to receive his prayer, saying, 'Hear ... listen ... be not deaf.' But he feels that he is a stranger in God's presence, even though he addresses God by using his covenant name, LORD. This is different from the idea that we are to live as strangers and pilgrims in this present world (1 Pet. 2:11). It takes its origin from the fact that the Israelites were themselves aliens in the promised land, for it belonged to the LORD (Lev. 25:23; 1 Chron. 29:15). Just as the strangers living among the Israelites depended upon their kindness, so the Israelites themselves depended upon God's mercy. As often, the two words 'alien' (*gêr*) and 'stranger' (*tôshāv*) are used synonymously.

Look away from me, that I may rejoice again before I depart and am no more' (*v. 13*). Normally psalmists ask for God to look upon them. Here the request is that God will *not* look upon him. In the context it must be a plea that God will avert his judgment from the psalmist. David longs to know the joy of the LORD before death comes.

Psalm 40

For the director of music. Of David. A psalm.

There are unusual features about this psalm. It is most uncommon to have a song of thanksgiving (vv. 1-10) followed by a lengthy complaint (vv. 11-17). The psalm moves from a song of joy concerning the past actions of the LORD to a heartfelt cry from the depths of despair. The *magnificat* becomes a most plaintive *de profundis* ('out of the depths').[1] It is also unusual because part of the psalm (vv. 13-17) is substantially repeated as Psalm 70. There are a few other examples of this in the Psalter (14 = 53; 57:7-11 = 108:1-5; 60:5-12 = 108:6-13).

The earlier experiences of the psalmist form the basis for his prayer for the present. He is pleading past mercies as the ground for this present trust in the LORD as his deliverer. Notwithstanding the use of a part in Psalm 70, which may suggest it was originally a separate composition, yet the repetition of words in the two sections of the psalm point to a unified composition.[2] Thus, the word 'thoughts' (*machsh^evotechâ*) in verse 6 is paralleled by the use of the verb from which it is derived (*châshav*) in verse 17, and 'I do not *seal* my lips' (v. 9) and 'Do not *withhold* your mercy' in verse 11 are both translations of the same Hebrew verb (*kâlâ'*). It may be that David added the second part when his circumstances changed for the worse. It should also be pointed out that

---

[1] This description of Psalm 40 has been attributed to Franz Delitzsch but it does not appear in his commentary on the Psalms.

[2] This is the view of A. Cohen, *The Psalms: Hebrew Text and English Translation with an Introduction and Commentary* (London: Soncino Press, 1969), p. 123.

strong links between this psalm and Psalm 35 are evident (cf. 35:4 with 40:14).

1. A Testimony to Grace (vv. 1-10)

I waited patiently for the LORD; he turned to me and heard my cry (v. 1). This is a testimony by the psalmist. He is relating what happened to him in the past when he cried to the LORD. The rendering 'waited patiently' is probably too passive a translation of the opening words. The verb means to wait expectantly or to hope in the LORD (see on Psalm 37:8-9), and the expression here is an emphatic one.[3] Perhaps a rendering such as, 'I indeed waited expectantly for the LORD' captures something of the meaning. The cry was heard and the LORD answered.[4]

He lifted me out of the slimy pit, out of the mud and mire; he set my feet on a rock and gave me a firm place to stand (v. 2). He describes his experience as if it was like being in a pit, or in a cistern such as the one Jeremiah was put into, which had no water, only mud (Jer. 38:6). From his place of distress, with its desolation and danger, God had delivered him. He was rescued and set on a firm foundation.

He put a new song in my mouth, a hymn of praise to our God. Many will see and fear and put their trust in the LORD (v. 3). With distress gone, there was a new song in his mouth. In later psalms such as Psalms 96 and 98, the phrase 'a new song' is linked with final, end-time events, as it is in Revelation 5:9 and 14:3. Here it denotes the salvation song that God gave him, as part of the sequence of actions by him ('he turned ... he heard ... he lifted ... he set ... he put'). His experiences will be a testimony to many others, who also will come and find refuge with this Saviour.[5] The use of '*our* God' draws attention to the fact that the psalmist was not alone in these experiences (cf. the references to 'the great congregation' in vv. 9-10).

---

[3] The verb preceded by the inf. absol.: *qavvoh qivvîtî*.

[4] For the words such as 'wait for', etc., see f.n. 5 on Psalm 25.

[5] Literature relating to the verb 'trust' (*bâtach*) and other similar verbs is cited in f.n. 5 on Psalm 9.

Blessed is the man who makes the LORD his trust, who does not look to the proud, to those who turn aside to false gods (*v. 4*). The contrast is now drawn between those who set (*sîm*) their trust on the LORD, and those who put their trust in idols. They are commended (for 'blessed', see on Psalm 1:1), for they have not followed the arrogant ones who deviate from the true God to trust in idols. This is the only occurrence of the word translated 'proud' (*rāhāv*), but the root appears to denote 'acting aggressively'. The final phrase in the MT adds to the difficulty of translation as it says 'those who turn aside to falsehood'. This may mean 'fraudulent images'[6] (cf. NIV 'false gods'), and this gives some support to the suggestion that the word 'proud' should be understood, not as a reference to people, but to 'pagan idols'.[7]

Many, O LORD my God, are the wonders you have done. The things you planned for us no one can recount to you; were I to speak and tell of them, they would be too many to declare (*v. 5*). What had happened to the psalmist was another 'wonder' done by the LORD. A 'wonder' was a supernatural act of deliverance that God alone could perform (Ps. 72:18: 'who alone does marvellous deeds'). Just as the deliverance of Israel from Egypt was a 'wonder', so also was the recent deliverance of the psalmist. The NIV translation of the middle clause is dubious. The Hebrew verb (*'ārak*) can often mean 'to set in order' (cf. Ps. 23:5), but it can also be used in the sense of 'compare'. It is best to follow two standard Hebrew dictionaries and accept that the translation involves an exclamation: 'Many, O LORD my God, are the wonders you have done, the things you planned for us. There is none to be compared to you!'[8] No one could recount all the divine acts of salvation, for they were so numerous.[9]

---

[6] As accepted by M. Dahood, *Psalms I:1-50*, p. 243.

[7] Cf. Dahood's translation, ibid., 'who turns not to pagan idols, or to fraudulent images'.

[8] See *BDB*, p. 789; *HALOT*, 2, p. 885.

[9] It is hard to be sure that the final verb (*sāfar*, Pi.) means recount, as the Pi. form can at times have the same meaning as the Qal, namely, 'to count', rather than 'recount', 'declare'.

The section that follows (vv. 6-10) has often been taken as messianic because of its use in Hebrews 10:5-7. However, in the setting here in Psalm 40 the psalm is not primarily messianic, for among other things David confesses his own sinfulness (v. 12). It is taken over and applied to Jesus, who as the greater David fulfils the spirit of these words. The quotation is made from the Greek Septuagint, whose variations from the Hebrew text made its use easier in Hebrews 10. **Sacrifice and offering you did not desire, but my ears you have pierced; burnt offerings and sin offerings you did not require** (*v. 6*). These words should not be interpreted as if they were denying the validity of the Old Testament sacrificial system. Rather they are to be understood, as in 1 Samuel 15:22, as stressing that obedience was more essential than sacrifice. Such practices were ineffective when not accompanied by a humble and obedient spirit. Four of the common sacrifices are designated. The first two are more general terms, while the last two are the terms for the offering completely consumed on the altar and the expiatory offering. The reference to the piercing of his ears is probably to his readiness to hear the word of the LORD and obey it, as the following verse makes plain. The expression itself is difficult, as a literal rendering is: 'You have dug two ears for me'.[10] The Hebrew verb in question (*kârâh*) normally means 'to excavate' or 'dig', but here it seems to be used to speak of the opening of ears so that they are ready to hear.[11]

Then I said, 'Here I am, I have come – it is written about me in the scroll (*v. 7*). The psalmist showed great readiness to respond in personal commitment to what God required. Like Isaiah (Isa. 6:8) David puts himself totally at the disposal of God. If David is speaking as king he may well be referring to what was written about the king in the law of Deuteronomy

---

[10] This is the translation given by P. C. Craigie, *Psalms 1-50*, p. 312.

[11] Craigie is right in suggesting that we are dealing with 'an ancient idiomatic usage of which the precise sense is no longer clear' (Ibid., p. 313). The LXX is followed in Hebrew 10:5: 'you have prepared (*katêrtisô*) a body for me.'

(Deut. 17:14-20). Otherwise, the scroll would refer to all the written demands of God upon him.[12]

I desire to do your will, O my God; your law is within my heart' (*v. 8*). He longs to do God's will, for within his heart he has God's instruction. 'Heart' is the English idiomatic term, whereas Hebrew uses *mêʿeh* ('bowels', 'intestines') as a metaphorical expression to denote human emotions. The Hebrew figure of speech carries over in the New Testament (cf. Phil. 2:1; Col. 3:12). The idea of internal possession of the law is one that takes a significant place in the later Old Testament teaching regarding the new covenant (Jer. 31:33-34; Ezek. 36:26-27).

I proclaim righteousness in the great assembly; I do not seal my lips, as you know, O LORD (*v. 9*). To the assembled worshipping community David proclaims (or the Hebrew could also be translated 'proclaimed', cf. v. 3) what God had done. The verb to 'proclaim' (*bâsar*, Pi.) is often associated with the idea of joyful proclamation (see Ps. 96:2 and Isa. 52:7 and 61:1). Here 'righteousness' (*tsédek*) is probably not so much a characteristic of God but a term to describe his saving activity. It is virtually a synonym for 'salvation'. David puts the idea both positively and negatively: he proclaims the fact, and does not restrain his lips from taking part in such a proclamation.

I do not hide your righteousness in my heart; I speak of your faithfulness and salvation. I do not conceal your love and your truth from the great assembly (*v. 10*). This continues the same ideas as in the previous verse. What is important is the accumulation of covenant terminology, with a cluster of words relating to God's character and works. 'Righteousness' is the key word, and 'faithfulness', 'salvation', 'love', and 'truth' are all ways of giving further explanation to it. Emphasis is placed on his public proclamation by the repetition of the phrase 'the great assembly', with the adjective 'great' (*râv*)

---

[12] The expression used for the written document is 'a scroll of writing' (*mᵉgillat sêfer*). It is an indication that the papyrus or leather document was in scroll form. For the technical Old Testament expressions for writing and written documents, see A. R. Millard, 'Writing', *NIDOTTE*, 4, pp. 1286-95.

emphasising the quantitative aspect of the gathering of the worshipping community.

2. A Prayer for Fresh Mercy (*vv. 11-17*)

Attention now focuses on the present situation. While there is no express reference to the earlier part of the psalm, yet it forms the foundation for the requests that are made. **Do not withhold your mercy from me, O LORD; may your love and your truth always protect me** (*v. 11*). The repetition of the phrase 'your love and your truth' from the previous verse makes plain the interconnection of the two parts of the psalm. God is the protector of his people, and the appeal is made to him to show his love and truth in this way. The appeal is even more direct than our English versions suggest, as the Hebrew text begins, 'You, O LORD, you do not ...' It is possible to render the verse as a statement, expressing confidence in God's mercy, or (like RSV and NIV) as a prayer.

For troubles without number surround me; my sins have overtaken me, and I cannot see. They are more than the hairs of my head, and my heart fails within me (*v. 12*). The abundance of difficulties is overwhelming for the psalmist, and he feels as if his courage has forsaken him. The verb 'troubled' is used in 2 Samuel 22:5 and Jonah 2:5 of floodwaters. His sight is also affected and his vision has become dim because of the immensity of his troubles (cf. Ps. 69:3-4: 'my eyes fail', 'those who hate me without reason outnumber the hairs of my head'). A repetition of a Hebrew verb ('*âtsam*) that has already occurred in verse 6 is disguised by translation into English (v. 6, 'too many'; v. 12, 'more than'). This is a further indication of the unified nature of this psalm with vocabulary linking both parts together.

The section from here to the end of the psalm reappears in the Psalter as Psalm 70, with slight verbal alteration. **Be pleased, O LORD, to save me; O LORD, come quickly to help me** (*v. 13*). David longs for a speedy resolution for his problem by the LORD, but that resolution has to be in accord with his will. 'Be pleased' (*retsêh*) is an echo of the word 'will' (*râtsôn*) in verse 8, and it is used in other prayers as well as this one (see Deut. 33:11, 24).

May all who seek to take my life be put to shame and confusion; may all who desire my ruin be turned back in disgrace (*v. 14*). This verse is very close in wording and meaning to Psalm 35:4 (see the comment). It makes plain that it was not just his sins which troubled him, but the activities of his enemies. His very life was in danger from them.

May those who say to me, 'Aha! Aha!' be appalled at their own shame (*v. 15*). The cry of 'Aha!' is one of human joy (Isa. 44:16), but here it is malicious joy said over the misery of another. This usage, together with the fact that it is always preceded by the verb 'to say', is the regular one for this expression in the Old Testament.[13] The psalmist wants these enemies to be made desolate. As with other curses in the Psalter, the enemies are not just personal enemies, for David is speaking here as king. It may well be that the enemies were aggressive, neighbouring nations who were ready to attack Israel.

But may all who seek you rejoice and be glad in you; may those who love your salvation always say, 'The LORD be exalted!' (*v. 16*). There is much similarity between this verse and Psalm 35:27. In contrast to the shouts of the enemies, he wants the true worshippers of the LORD ('seek' is often used in this sense) to proclaim his greatness. There is also a contrast between those seeking his life (v. 14) and those seeking the LORD. Nothing can add to God's greatness, but praise is a way of drawing attention to it. Praise for God's salvation is to be a perpetual characteristic of his people.

Yet I am poor and needy; may the Lord think of me. You are my help and my deliverer; O my God, do not delay (*v. 17*). The call to God to 'not delay' balances the call to 'come quickly' in verse 13, and there is still the same reliance upon God as his 'help'. The psalmist pleads for urgent assistance, just as Daniel did using the same words (Dan. 9:19). David

---

[13] This expression (*heʾāh*) is sometimes followed by a phrase (see Ps. 35:25), or it may be used as here without anything following. It is part of a group of particles in Hebrew which, like in English, 'use sounds not ordinarily part of language's sound system' (*IBHS*, p. 683).

knows his own weakness and inability,[14] and expresses the desire that God would think and plan for his salvation. To the God to whom he had looked expectantly in the past, he now looks again for help and rescue.

---

[14] 'Poor and needy' is a standard parallel expression occurring in the Psalms and elsewhere to denote the oppressed righteous believers. Cf. the use of the expression in Job 24:14; Amos 8:4; and Psalms 9:19; 12:5; 70:5; and 74:21.

Psalm 41

For the director of music. A psalm of David.

There are many similarities between this psalm and the ones immediately preceding (Pss. 38-40). In them there is repeated mention of human frailty and sickness, though in each there is confident appeal to God for his mercy and deliverance. A specific link occurs with the preceding psalm in that the opening word here, 'blessed' (Hebrew *'ashᵉrê*), has already been used in verse 6 of Psalm 40. This psalm begins with a general assertion concerning God's character in relation to the righteous. Then follows a prayer for help, with a repeated cry for mercy (vv. 4 and 10). The psalm ends with a doxology, which also concludes the first book of the Psalter.

1. Confidence in the LORD (*vv. 1-3*)
Blessed is he who has regard for the weak; the LORD delivers him in times of trouble (*v. 1*). The opening word recalls the use of the same word (*'ashᵉrê*) in the first verse of Psalm 1 (see comment). It is a word used only of humans, whereas the expression 'praise to …' (*bârûk*) that occurs in verse 13 is only applied to God. The person who looks with favour on the needs of the poor will himself be delivered by the LORD. The verb 'to have regard' (*sâkal*, Hi.) often means to have insight that results in prudent action. The idea of this verse finds its fullest expression in the Sermon on the Mount: 'Blessed are the merciful for they will be shown mercy' (Matt. 5:7).

The LORD will protect him and preserve his life; he will bless him in the land and not surrender him to the desire of his foes (*v. 2*). The theme of the LORD as the keeper of Israel finds fuller development in Psalm 121:7-8. Part of the

343

protection referred to here was preservation in time of serious illness. The phrase 'preserve his life' can also be rendered 'keep him alive'. There are difficulties with the following words. The Hebrew text has: 'he will be blessed in the land and do not *you* give him ...' The NIV follows the Septuagint, the Vulgate, and the Syriac in translating it as active ('he will bless'), but the passive form still yields good sense: 'he will be blessed in the land.' The change to a second person singular form in the final clause is understandable if it is part of the prayer addressed to God: 'May the LORD protect ... and preserve ... and not surrender him into the life of the enemy'.[1] In the good land he will be kept safe (see Ps. 37:22), and his enemies will not see their desire for him fulfilled.

The LORD will sustain him on his sickbed and restore him from his bed of illness (*v. 3*). During illness, strength will be provided by the LORD, with the promise of a radical change to take place. The NIV translation fails to observe the second person singular verb in the final clause ('*you* restore him') and also omits the word 'all' (*kol*) before 'his bed'. The same switch from third to second person occurs as in the previous verse, and while such rapid changes trouble us in English, many can be found in Hebrew poetry. Again, it is best to take the verb here as part of direct address to God: '*you* restore him.' 'All his bed' does not denote his constant lying down, but rather the full extent of his illness. Restoration is possible for those who cry to the LORD for help so that their illness can be turned around. The idea of preservation in the first three verses comes to its climax here. The LORD can so intervene that the situation is totally changed.

2. A Cry for Mercy (*vv. 4-9*)

I said, 'O LORD, have mercy on me; heal me, for I have sinned against you' (*v. 4*). The initial 'I said' may refer to past prayers, though it could also be translated 'I say'. Later in the psalm it becomes clear that he is still sick (v. 10). He makes his plea for

---

[1] 'The life of the enemy' (Hebrew *nefesh 'oyevâv*) is an idiomatic expression (cf. the very similar expression used in Psalm 27:12: *nefesh tsâray*, 'the desire of my foes'). It means to be placed in the control of the enemy, and thus the LXX 'in the hands of his enemy' is a good translation.

mercy and for healing. God had promised through Moses that he was the healer (Exod. 15:26), and the psalmist claims that promise. With his request comes open confession of his sin. All sin is committed against God, as David acknowledges even more specifically in connection with his sin with Bathsheba (Ps. 51:4: 'against you, you only, have I sinned').

My enemies say of me in malice, 'When will he die and his name perish?' Whenever one comes to see me, he speaks falsely, while his heart gathers slander; then he goes out and spreads it abroad (*vv. 5-6*). His enemies are just waiting for his death to take place, so that they can rejoice over it. To have one's name perish meant that there would be no descendants (Ps. 109:13). The importance of having one's name maintained is seen in the provision for levirate marriage (Deut. 25:5, 6). Even when his enemies visit him in his sickness (and this was a normal practice, cf. 2 Kings 8:29), their intent is evil, and they do not speak truthfully. They gossip about him to others and spread false rumours.

All my enemies whisper together against me; they imagine the worst for me, saying, 'A vile disease has beset him; he will never get up from the place where he lies' (*vv. 7-8*). The word used here for 'whisper' is always used of evil whispering, such as when David's servants whispered about his son's death (2 Sam. 12:19). Though the earlier part of the psalm makes mention of 'enemies' (vv. 2, 4), on this occasion they are called 'haters', though the two words appear practically interchangeable in contexts such as this. It is best to allow the alternation of these verbs to show in English translation (cf. AV, RSV, NASB, ESV). Those who hate the psalmist hope that his disease will be fatal,[2] and that where he lies will become his deathbed. They seem to be thinking that

---

[2] The NIV's 'a vile disease' represents the Hebrew *dᵉvar bᵉliyyaʿal*, 'a thing of destructiveness'. The word *bᵉliyyaʿal* is not a proper noun in the Old Testament (cf. the influence of the Vulgate on the AV's use in passages such as in Deut. 13:13 and Judg. 19:22). Though its derivation is not exactly clear, it seems to be an abstract noun meaning 'destructiveness', and 'the sons of Belial are then those whose characters are destructive, harmful, evil' (J. A. Emerton, 'Sheol and the Sons of Belial', pp. 214-18). For further information, see the literature cited in *DCH*, II, pp. 608-09.

his disease is a fitting judgment from God. Hence their actions show that they are not recipients of the ascription 'blessed' as in verse 1 (for the New Testament teaching concerning helping the needy, see James 1:27).
Even my close friend, whom I trusted, he who shared my bread, has lifted up his heel against me (*v. 9*). In this situation even the closest of friends (lit. 'a man of my peace', i.e. with whom I have the friendliest relationship) turns against him. The very friend who shared his food proves to be a traitor to him. The exact phrase, 'to lift up the heel', does not occur elsewhere, but it seems to mark out an aggressive or traitorous action. This is the meaning that is given to the verse when Jesus quotes it of Judas (John 13:18). What was true of David was fulfilled to an even greater degree in Judas' betrayal of Jesus.

3. A Renewed Request (*vv. 10-12*)
But you, O LORD, have mercy on me; raise me up, that I may repay them (*v. 10*). The prayer of verse 4 is now renewed. What he had prayed in the past is fitting for the present, because it represents the urgent cry of a needy sinner. The enemies were saying that he would never get up (v. 8), but the psalmist knows that God is able to lift him up again. He seeks this, not for selfish vengeance upon them, but in order to see God's honour vindicated (see vv. 2-3).

The link with the preceding verse is not made clear in the NIV translation of verse 11, for it fails to translate the first word, 'in this' (*bᵉzo'𝑡*). When the LORD lifts him up, then he will know to a greater extent his love to him. Accordingly he can make the declaration: **I know that you are pleased with me, for my enemy does not triumph over me. In my integrity you uphold me and set me in your presence forever** (*vv. 11-12*). It also follows that if the psalmist is raised up by the LORD, then the enemies would not be able to shout out in triumph. The word translated 'triumph' is often used in situations of great festive joy (cf. 1 Sam. 4:5). No such occasion will be given here, for he can confidently look for God's support. The final phrase is best taken as referring to life in the promised land (v. 2) as

God's servant. Just like Elijah, he shall stand before the LORD (1 Kings 17:1).

4. Doxology (*v. 13*)

Praise be to the LORD, the God of Israel, from everlasting to everlasting. Amen and Amen (*v. 13*). This is the first of the doxologies with which all five books of the Psalter conclude. It is a fitting ascription of praise to the God of Israel. The ascription of 'praise' or 'blessed' to God cannot add to his person, but it tells that he is worthy of praise, and such praise directs attention again to his greatness. The double 'Amen' sets the seal to this declaration.

Book 2

Psalms 42-43

For the director of music. A maskil of the Sons of Korah.

In many Hebrew manuscripts Psalms 42 and 43 are regarded as one psalm. This fact is supported by the observation that Psalm 43 has no title, which is surprising, for all the psalms in Book 2 of the Psalter (with the exception of Psalm 71) have one. Moreover, a question in 42:9b ('Why must I go about mourning, oppressed by the enemy?') is repeated in 43:2b. Also, the two psalms share a common refrain, 'Why are you downcast, O my soul? Why so disturbed within me? Put your hope in God ...' (Pss. 42:5, 11; 43:5). If the two psalms were composed as a single poem, then for liturgical reasons they were separated into two songs.

The transition from Book 1 to Book 2 of the Psalter is marked by the substitution of the word 'God' (*ᵉlohîm*) for the name 'LORD' (*yhwh*). It is possible that originally 'LORD' stood in the text, and was deliberately changed to 'God', perhaps because in a certain area of ancient Israel and at a specific time the name 'God' was more in use than 'LORD'. While 'LORD' still occurs, it is vastly outnumbered by the occurrences of 'God'.[1]

The 'Sons of Korah' were Levites who had special responsibilities in the temple (1 Chron. 6:22; 2 Chron. 20:19). Korah was the great-grandson of Levi. The 'sons of Korah' performed various roles, including being gate-keepers (1 Chron. 9:19). This was clearly an ancient task as the Chronicler says that 'their fathers had been responsible for guarding the

---

[1] 'God' (*ᵉlohîm*) occurs only 15 times in Book 1, but 164 times in Book 2. On the other hand, 'LORD' (*yhwh*) appears 272 times in Book 1, but only 30 times in Book 2.

349

entrance to the dwelling of the LORD'.[2] While they continued this function, under David they also assumed an important role among the musicians and singers, and continued to do so under later kings such as Jehoshaphat. Seven psalms in this second section of the Psalter are attributed to 'the sons of Korah' (Pss. 42-49), while another four occur in the next section (Pss. 84-85, 87-88).

1. Longing for God (*Psalm 42 verses 1-4*)
As the deer pants for streams of water, so my soul pants for you, O God (*v. 1*). Intense longing fills the heart of the psalmist. For some unstated reason he is not able to go and enjoy communal worship. He likens himself, however, to a deer that longs for water. So, from the barrenness of his isolation, he has a similar longing after God.

My soul thirsts for God, for the living God. When can I go and meet with God? (*v. 2*). He repeats his desire for God, and calls him 'the living God'. This phrase is unusual, and it may be connected with the idea that God was the 'living water' (cf. Jer. 2:13; 17:13). It also is a reminder that although other gods may have been worshipped, they had no life in them (Ps. 115:1-8). The psalmist voices his concern as to when he can go and see God's face (NIV 'meet with God'). 'To see the face of God' is the technical expression that the Old Testament uses of appearing before God at the sanctuary (Exod. 23:17; Ps. 84:7).[3] It is an anthropomorphic expression that denotes close fellowship and communion with him.

My tears have been my food day and night, while men say to me all day long, 'Where is your God?' These things I remember as I pour out my soul: how I used to go with the multitude, leading the procession to the house of God, with shouts of joy and thanksgiving among the festive throng (*vv. 3-4*). His enemies taunt him continually,

---

[2] It is hard to be certain which 'dwelling' is referred to in this verse. It could have been the Israelite camp, or, more specifically, the tabernacle.

[3] The MT has the verb 'to see' vocalised as a passive (Ni. *'ērâ'eh*). It is best to follow the active reading (Qal *'er'eh*) that is supported by some Hebrew manuscripts, the LXX, and the Targum.

for it seems as if God has deserted him.[4] Nothing in the context enables the reader to determine whether the enemies are from within the covenantal community or from followers of heathen gods. The doubts he had while absent from the sanctuary were aggravated by these unfeeling comments. In his grief his tears flood down his face and seem to become his food. No answer can be given to the question that is put to him. Instead, his memory recalls the happier times when he led the festive crowd going to the sanctuary.[5] The annual pilgrimages like the Passover, the Feast of Weeks, and the Feast of Tabernacles were meant to be happy occasions as the tribes went up 'to praise the name of the LORD' (Ps. 122:4).

2. The Refrain (*vv. 5-6a*)
For the first time the refrain comes in, and it gives thematic unity to this combined psalm, as well as providing another striking poetic feature. **Why are you downcast, O my soul? Why so disturbed within me? Put your hope in God, for I will yet praise him, my Saviour and my God** (*v. 5*). In the midst of his spiritual barrenness and longing for God, the psalmist encourages himself. Why should he be so troubled in spirit if he has God as his Saviour?[6] The query that points to self-doubt gives way to a speedy exhortation. He calls upon himself to wait for God, and expresses the conviction that he is yet going to praise him. The final part of the verse in the NIV involves a change in verse division, moving 'my God'

---

[4] The NIV's 'while men say' represents the MT 'in saying' (*be'ᵉmor*). It is possible that this should be altered to *bᵉ'omrâm*, 'in their saying', as this form occurs later in v. 11, and is supported by four Hebrew manuscripts and the LXX. Certainly this is the meaning in the context.

[5] The clause 'leading the procession' is difficult because of two factors. First, the word for 'procession' (*sâk*) is a *hapax legomenon*, which, with different vocalisation (*sok*), could mean 'a tent' or 'a booth'. This is the way the LXX took it, using the common word for 'tent' or 'tabernacle' (*skênê*). Secondly, the word translated 'leading' (*'eddaddêm*) also creates a problem. Various emendations have been proposed ('majestic ones', 'exalted one', 'prostrate myself') but none seem more satisfactory than the traditional translation. For some further detail, see *HALOT*, I, p. 241.

[6] The form of the verb translated 'downcast' (*tishtôchᵃchî*) only appears in Psalms 42-43. It has traditionally been taken as derived from *shâchâh*, but it is possible it is from the root *châvâh*, meaning 'to coil'.

from being the first word in verse 6 to being the final word of verse 5. This has some support from Hebrew manuscripts, the LXX and the Syriac version, and is the preferable way to deal with this section. The NIV, however, does not translate the Hebrew word *pânâv* ('his face'). Hence, a translation more like the NKJV is needed: 'I shall yet praise Him for the help of His countenance.' The psalmist earlier had longed to see God's face. Now he knows that God's presence will be his salvation.[7]

3. The Cry of a Troubled Heart (*vv. 6b-10*)

The mood of the psalmist switches back to doubt but he is refreshed by memories of the past. **My soul is downcast within me; therefore I will remember you from the land of Jordan, the heights of Hermon – from Mount Mizar. Deep calls to deep in the roar of your waterfalls; all your waves and breakers have swept over me** (*vv. 6-7*). The geographical expressions here suggest that the psalmist was far off from the sanctuary, perhaps even in exile. He seems to be speaking from the area in which the Jordan River rises, though Mount Mizar (the Hebrew means 'little mountain') is otherwise unknown. Perhaps he is referring to the area from which he himself came, or else the terms he uses amount to a reference to Canaan, the land of promise.[8] The thought of the tumbling waters of the Jordan, such as can still be seen at the waterfall at Banyas, provides the idea of the waves that are presently coming over him. No longer is his mind on the 'living water'

---

[7] Many translators and commentators want to emend 'his face' to 'my face', as the latter form appears in verse 11 and 43:5. But 'his face' is the more difficult reading and should be preserved. S. Terrien, *The Psalms*, p. 353, points out that the alteration to 'my face' does not provide good sense, whereas 'the psalmist crowns the asseveration of the refrain with the expectation of seeing the divine face in intimate communion'.

[8] Nowhere else does a psalmist designate with precision where he himself lived. This in itself may suggest that another interpretation is necessary. Also, the Massoretic punctuation does not link 'the land of Jordan' closely with 'the heights of Hermon', and that latter expression is an unusual one. In Hebrew it is simply 'the Hermons'. Another interpretation that has a lot of merit is that *chermônîm* is from the root *ch-r-m* and means 'holy places, sanctuaries'. In this case 'Mizar' could be a reference to Mount Sion, as many have argued. The view outlined above is found in N. H. Ridderbos, *De Psalmen* (Kampen: Kok, 3rd ed., n.d.), vol. 2 (Psalm 42–60), pp. 23-24.

that God gives (vv. 1-2), but on his own situation in which he has been engulfed.

By day the LORD directs his love, at night his song is with me – a prayer to the God of my life (*v. 8*). In the midst of his distress he is still able to recall God's graciousness to him. In the daytime God commands his steadfast love (*chésed*); at night time he gives a song,[9] that is turned into a prayer.[10] Many Hebrew manuscripts have 'the living God' instead of 'the God of my life'. There is only one letter different in Hebrew, and certainly 'living God' matches well with the same expression in verse 2.

I say to God my Rock, 'Why have you forgotten me? Why must I go about mourning, oppressed by the enemy?' (*v. 9*) The psalmist feels forsaken, yet he is able to call God his 'Rock' (cf. for the use of this description of God, Pss. 18:2; 31:3; 71:3). The use of this metaphor prepares the way for another similar metaphor ('fortress') in 43:2. No fuller explanation is given of the enemies, yet the use of the word 'oppressed' may well be significant. It is most often used of the enemies of the nation of Israel, who attacked and marauded the land.

My bones suffer mortal agony as my foes taunt me, saying to me all day long, 'Where is your God?' (*v. 10*). Illness plagues him, and he has the added pain of opponents who constantly mock him. His present distress is deepened by the attitude and words of others, for they are suggesting that God is unable to help. The continuous nature of their taunts increases his pain.

3. Refrain (*v. 11*)

Why are you downcast, O my soul? Why so disturbed within me? Put your hope in God, for I will yet praise him, my Saviour and my God (*v. 11*). The refrain of verses 5-6a is taken up again, as he expresses confidence in his God. The confident

---

[9] The word *shîroh*, 'his song', has a rare form of 3 masc. sing. suffix. See *GKC* §91.b, p. 256.

[10] Some Hebrew manuscripts have 'praise' instead of 'prayer'. The difference is in one letter only, and in both the old Hebrew script and the square script these two letters (*hê* and *pê*) are not easily confused. Context also favours retaining *tᵉfillâh*, 'prayer'.

call to his God stands in marked contrast to the question that has been flung at the psalmist in verses 3 and 10: 'Where is your God?'

4. A Prayer for Vindication *(Psalm 43, verses 1-4)*
From the mountains of northern Palestine, the scene now moves on to Mount Zion, and the joy of worship there. **Vindicate me, O God, and plead my cause against an ungodly nation; rescue me from deceitful and wicked men** (*v. 1*). Several factors here confirm the impression that the enemies were external ones. They are clearly 'ungodly', an expression that suggests that they are strangers to covenantal love (lit. 'not *châsîd*').[11] His appeal for God to plead his cause is typical of similar passages in the prophets (see, e.g., Micah 6:1; 7:9). He wants deliverance from those who practise deceit and unrighteousness, qualities that must not be characteristic of God's followers (Ps. 119:1-3; Mal. 2:6).

You are God my stronghold. Why have you rejected me? Why must I go about mourning, oppressed by the enemy? (*v. 2*). The psalmist cannot reconcile the truth that God is his stronghold with the fact that he is passing through difficult times and enduring such trouble from his enemies. He wonders why God seems to have rejected him. The second part of the verse repeats a question already asked in Psalm 42:9b.

Send forth your light and your truth, let them guide me; let them bring me to your holy mountain, to the place where you dwell (*v. 3*). He now asks for God's light and God's truth to be his guide, and that they will bring him back to Zion. This, in effect, would be the answer to the question he had asked at the very outset (Ps. 42:2). He wants these two angels ('light' and 'truth') to lead him through the desert and bring him into God's presence.

Then will I go to the altar of God, to God, my joy and my delight. I will praise you with the harp, O God, my God (*v. 4*). He looks ahead and anticipates the joy with which he

---

[11] The Hebrew negative particle *lo'* forms other compounds like 'not *châsîd*'. Cf. 'a no-god', Deuteronomy 32:21; 'a son not wise', Hosea 13:13. These, and other examples, are cited in *DIHG~S*, §116 (d).

will worship his God on Zion. In place of sorrow and grief there will be a fresh realisation of God's character, and he will praise him with the harp.[12] He is the joy and delight of his children, and is worthy of praise from those who can say of him, 'God, my God.'

5. Refrain (*v. 5*)
Why are you downcast, O my soul? Why so disturbed within me? Put your hope in God, for I will yet praise him, my Saviour and my God (*v. 5*). The refrain comes in for the third time, but now the emphasis probably falls on the latter part. The thought of joyful worship at the sanctuary revitalises the psalmist.

---

[12] For an older discussion on the harp, see Sir John Stainer, *The Music of the Bible, with Some Account of the Development of Modern Musical Instruments from Ancient Types* (London: Novello and Co., 1914), pp. 13-27, and for a more recent discussion, with a good bibliography, Robert H. O'Connell in *NIDOTTE*, 2, pp. 666-67.

Psalm 44

For the director of music. Of the Sons of Korah. A maskil.

It was customary in Israel for a song to be sung to the Lord after victory in battle (see Judges 5). It was also commonplace for a song to be sung *after defeat in battle*, and Psalm 44 is such a song. In this psalm the people and the king cry out to God to arise and help them. The language alternates between singular and plural. The singular passages (vv. 4, 6, 15-16) may well have been the words that the king used, while the remainder of the psalm is an appeal from the army or the nation as a whole. However, it may just be a poetic device, used simply to create greater linguistic variation.

A poem like this should not be compared with a string of pearls simply strung together without formal coherence. Rather, it is more like a building in which the upper parts depend on the lower parts. The psalm is composed of four sections (vv. 1-8, 9-16, 17-22, 23-26). 'But when we look at this division from a formal point of view, we are confronted with something striking: the various sections consist, consecutively, of ten, eight, six, and four poetic lines. This could hardly have occurred by chance. The psalm rises up like a *zikkurat*: and only when the poet has come to the topmost flight does he raise up his prayer to God'.[1]

Repetition also plays a part in this poem. In verse 3 mention is made that the people were not saved (*y-sh-ʿ*) by the sword

---

[1] N. H. Ridderbos, 'The Psalms: Style-figures and Structure (certain considerations, with special reference to Pss. xxii, xxv, and xlv)', *OTS* XIII, 1963, p. 50. Note: a *zikkurat* (or *ziggurat*) was a Babylonian temple-tower shaped like a pyramid. Each successive storey was smaller than the one below it.

(*chérev*), while these two words are repeated in verse 6. Then in verse 11, the people are said to have been delivered over by God 'like sheep' (*kᵉtso'n*), while in verse 22 the people are considered 'as sheep' (*kᵉtso'n*) to be slaughtered. Because there is no reference to the destruction of the temple, the psalm is probably from late in the history of Judah, in the time of Hezekiah or Josiah. The language of the psalm has definite similarities to that of Jeremiah (see, e.g., Jer. 11:19; 25:34; 51:40), and that may indicate a date of composition contemporaneous with Jeremiah.

1. Confidence in God's Past Help (*vv. 1-8*)

We have heard with our ears, O God; our fathers have told us what you did in their days, in days long ago (*v. 1*). It was the responsibility of one generation to pass on to the next generation the knowledge of God's actions on behalf of his people. These actions could go back a long way in their history, even 'from days long ago' (*mimê qédem*). Exactly the same phrase is used twice in Isaiah (23:7 and 37:26). They had to 'tell the next generation the praiseworthy deeds of the LORD, his power, and the wonders he has done' (Ps. 78:4). Similarly for the Christian community today, what we receive we are to pass on (1 Cor. 15:1-11; 2 Tim. 2:2).

With your hand you drove out the nations and planted our fathers; you crushed the peoples and made our fathers flourish (*v. 2*). Recognition is made of God's sovereign provision of the land of Canaan for his people. The language used reflects the way in which the Book of Deuteronomy describes the dispossession of Canaan so that Israel could inhabit it (see Deut. 4:38; 11:23; 18:12 and note the usage of the same verb as here, *yârash*, Hi.). God transplanted Israel as a vine (see Ps. 80:8-16) and caused its branches to grow. The NIV rendering at the end of the verse captures the sense well, though it is a very free translation. Literally the Hebrew text has 'you sent them out', i.e. the branches, and this is the same verb (*shâlach*, Pi.) that is used of their growth in Psalm 80:11.

It was not by their sword that they won the land, nor did their arm bring them victory; it was your right hand, your

arm, and the light of your face, for you loved them (*v. 3*). The NIV fails to translate two of the three occurrences of the particle *kî* in this verse. Translating them makes even more forceful the contrast between human weakness and divine power: '*For* not by their own sword did they win the land, nor did their own arm save them, *but* your right hand and your arm, and the light of your face, *for* you loved them' (ESV). This is repeating what Moses had taught the people long before (Deut. 4:34; 7:19; 9:4-6; 11:2; 26:8-9). The victory over the Canaanites was not achieved by human power. It had to be attributed solely to God's intervention on their behalf, based on his love for Israel (Deut. 7:7-9). Reference to 'the light of your face' links in nicely with the reference to God's light in the previous psalm (43:3) and indicates how his loving-kindness lightens all darkness.

You are my King and my God, who decrees victories for Jacob (*v. 4*). Now the king speaks in the first person, and makes a very emphatic declaration. It is quite possible that the first clause should be translated '*Yes*, you are my king', or, '*you alone* are my king'.[2] He confesses that God is both his king and his God. Even the human leader of the people was subject to a higher power. He knew that God alone could bring victory. 'Jacob' became a honourable title for the nation from Numbers 23 onwards, and 'Jacob' is spoken of as the object of God's love (Ps. 47:4; Mal. 1:2).

Through you we push back our enemies; through your name we trample our foes (*v. 5*). The imagery of this verse is taken from the actions of cattle. The victories of the past were like a bull butting its opponents, or trampling on its enemies. Through calling on God's name and seeing his power displayed, Israel's enemies had been subdued before them. This type of imagery was widely used of military activities in the ancient Near East.

Having stated positively the fact that all victories came from the LORD, the psalmist now puts this truth negatively. **I do not trust in my bow, my sword does not bring me victory; but you give us victory over our enemies, you put our adversaries to shame** (*vv. 6-7*). Again, the NIV does not

---
[2] For the grammatical point, see *DIHG~S*, p. 2.

translate two occurrences of the particle *kî* in this verse, and this weakens the contrast: 'For I do not trust ... *but* you give.' Wielding of human weapons of war did not in itself bring salvation in battle. Horses and chariots, bows and swords, would never save. The nation had to know that they should look only to the Holy One of Israel (Isa. 31:1). To shame an adversary was to deprive him of success.

In God we make our boast all day long, and we will praise your name forever. Selah (*v. 8*). At the end of this historical reflection, the psalm rises to a note of joy. The LXX captures the sense when it renders: 'All day long God is praised'. Grateful thanks had always been the hallmark of a rescued people, and there would ever be acknowledgment of God's name.

2. A Lament in the Face of Defeat (*vv. 9-16*)

A sudden change comes into the psalm at this point (for a similar shift using the same verb, 'you have rejected', see Ps. 89:38). After the initial complaint, the psalmist follows on with five more accusations against God, all involving a verbal clause ('you made us plunder for our enemies', v. 10; 'you gave us up', v. 11; 'you sold your people', v. 12; 'you made us a reproach', v. 13; 'you made us a by-word', v. 14). **But now you have rejected and humbled us; you no longer go out with our armies** (*v. 9*). 'But now' (*'af*), with which it opens, marks the transition to complaint. What looked like a victory song in the early verses of the psalm is altered to a national lament. Defeat had taken place on the battlefield, and the people understood this as a rejection by God. They had been shamed in battle, and sensed that God was no longer with them, as, for example, he had been with David when he went against the Philistines (2 Sam. 5:24).

You made us retreat before the enemy, and our adversaries have plundered us. You gave us up to be devoured like sheep and have scattered us among the nations (*vv. 10-11*). They had been beaten in battle and robbed by their enemies. These were neighbouring nations who were filled with spite against Israel.[3] The Israelites accuse God of giving them up to be slaughtered, and of scattering them among the nations. This could be a reference simply to captives taken in battle (cf. the case of Naaman's wife's Israelite slave, 2 Kings 5:2). Captives were often sold off as slaves, further increasing the dispersion. However, the use of the same verb (*zânach*), as in the warning passage in Leviticus 26:33 regarding exile, suggests that the scattering is part of God's judgment against Israel.

You sold your people for a pittance, gaining nothing from their sale (*v. 12*). So worthless were the people, runs their argument, that God had sold them for nothing. He was willing to part with them for no sale price at all. The imagery of sale of Israel to their enemies is common in the Old Testament, especially of defeats suffered during the period of the judges (cf. Deut. 32:30; Judg. 2:14; 3:8; 4:2; 10:7; 1 Sam. 12:9).

You have made us a reproach to our neighbours, the scorn and derision of those around us. You have made us a byword among the nations; the peoples shake their heads at us (*vv. 13-14*). Among the surrounding nations Israel's name had become a laughing matter. The vocabulary used ('reproach', 'scorn', and 'derision') suggests that the neighbours were taunting and ridiculing her. They even had proverbial sayings making fun of her. They scornfully mimic her, and treat her as if she was nothing. Elsewhere shaking the head is also linked with a scornful attitude (Ps. 64:8).

My disgrace is before me all day long, and my face is covered with shame at the taunts of those who reproach and revile me, because of the enemy, who is bent on revenge (*vv. 15-16*). The reproach was not just a national one. Individuals within Israel could feel it deeply too, and now the psalm speaks in personal terms, 'my disgrace', 'my face'. Also, the taunting was done openly and publicly, for the MT speaks of 'the voice (or 'sound') of the reproacher and the reviler'. The enemy wanted more than just the opportunity to

---

[3] The word used here is not the usual word for enemies but 'our haters' (*mᵉsanᵉ'ênû*). Its use reinforces the nature of the animosity that Israel was experiencing.

make fun of Israel. Revenge was the ultimate aim, though the reason that lay behind this desire is not given.

3. Questions in Perplexity (*vv. 17-22*)

Testimony is now presented that Israel had not renounced the covenant. **All this happened to us, though we had not forgotten you or been false to your covenant. Our hearts had not turned back; our feet had not strayed from your path** (*vv. 17-18*). These verses bring us to the heart of the problem that the people faced. They knew that God had said that if his people were disobedient he would bring judgment upon them, including defeat before their enemies (Deut. 28:15-68, and especially vv. 25-26 and 49-52). But here they claim that they have not broken the covenant nor turned from the LORD's ways.[4] This is not to be understood as a self-righteous claim, but a general reference of adherence to the covenant.[5] The thought of verse 17 is expanded in verse 18 by reference to 'hearts' and 'feet'. The claim is that inward thoughts have not resulted in outward actions. God's path is the way of truth and life that he has revealed, and 'path' (*'orach*) can be a synonym for 'law' (*tôrâh*; cf. Ps. 119:115).

But you crushed us and made us a haunt for jackals and covered us over with deep darkness (*v. 19*). The people cannot understand how God has permitted them to be overwhelmed by the enemy, who had turned their land into a terrible wilderness (cf. 'haunt of jackals' with the almost identical expression in Jer. 10:22). They are in despair and feel as though deep darkness has descended upon them. The words 'deep darkness' translate the same Hebrew word (*tsalmâvet*) that appears in Psalm 23:4: 'through the valley of *the shadow of death*.'

If we had forgotten the name of our God or spread out our hands to a foreign god, would not God have discovered it, since he knows the secrets of the heart? (*vv. 20-21*). Again the people profess that they have been faithful to the covenant.

---

[4] The preposition 'from', used here independently, is an unusual lengthened form, *minnî*.

[5] H. C. Leupold, *Exposition of the Psalms* (Welwyn: Evangelical Press, 1977), p. 349, has good comments on this section.

Had they been unfaithful, God would have known that, for he is able to dig into the darkest recesses of the heart. The same verb for 'discover' (*châqar*) occurs in Psalm 139:1, 23 and Jeremiah 17:10 of God's activity in searching the human heart. Nothing is hidden from his all-searching eye (see the whole of Ps. 139).

Yet for your sake we face death all day long; we are considered as sheep to be slaughtered (*v. 22*). The current afflictions of the people are not the result of their turning from God. Rather, they are undergoing oppression because of their faithfulness to him. For *his* sake they face constant persecution, and in their enemies' minds they are reckoned simply as sheep destined for slaughter. Paul quotes these words after he has summed up the tribulations which are endured by the people of God (Rom. 8:36). Terms that are used in this psalm of the Old Testament believing community are rightly applied by Paul to the situation of the New Testament church. There is continuity in the experience of believers.

3. A Prayer for Deliverance (*vv. 23-26*)

Awake, O Lord! Why do you sleep? Rouse yourself! Do not reject us forever. Why do you hide your face and forget our misery and oppression? (*vv. 23-24*). While this call to God is similar in some respects to that in Psalm 7:6 (see the commentary), yet there is a difference. Here the people suggest that God is so uncaring of them in their trouble that it is as if he is asleep. In their despair they think they are rejected *forever*. In situations like this the people felt that God's face was hidden from them (Pss. 10:11; 27:9; 88:14; 143:7; Isa. 8:17). 'Misery' (*'onî*) is used more often than 'oppression' (*lachats*), which is often connected, as here, with enemies or siege situations.

We are brought down to the dust; our bodies cling to the ground (*v. 25*). This is a description of their present distress, but the significance of the expressions are unclear. It describes either their grief which brings them to a prostrate position in prayer, or else their feeling of being so near death that they are almost in the dust of the grave.

Rise up and help us; redeem us because of your unfailing love (*v. 26*). The people have already claimed that they are loyal to the covenant (v. 17), and have asked God to awake. Now they appeal to him to rise up and provide the help they so desperately need. They ask for the continuance of covenantal love (*chésed*, NIV 'unfailing love'), and for this to be expressed in redemption from their present distress. Similarly Paul goes on to assert the unfailing love of Christ Jesus our Lord (Rom. 8:33-39) after he quotes from verse 22.

Psalm 45

For the director of music. To [the tune of] 'Lilies'.
Of the Sons of Korah. A maskil. A wedding song.

It was probably a royal wedding that inspired the composition of this psalm, and it may well have been used repeatedly at later weddings. The greatest difficulty this assessment has is that verses 6-7 appear to be a direct address to God, not to the human monarch who was his vice-regent. Some would then consider the whole psalm as messianic, in view of the use made of verses 6-7 in Hebrews 1:8-9.[1] Preferable is the view that suggests the eyes of the psalmist were lifted up to see the glory of the Davidic ruler as typifying the kingly rule of the Messiah. Accordingly, he addresses him directly, and while this may see a sudden introduction of a messianic element into the psalm, yet it is not without parallel elsewhere (cf. Isa. 9:6-7 and the context).

In support of this change of subject it can be pointed out that change of addressee in psalms is quite frequent. At times the congregation will address God in the third person ('he'), while direct address to him in the second person ('you') may occur in the same psalm. Thus, here a symmetrical structure for the psalm exists with this pattern:

Addressee: The king (v. 2)
            God (vv. 6-7)
            The king (v. 8)
            The bride (v. 10)
            The king (v. 16)[2]

---

[1] For an exposition of the directly messianic view among older commentators, see E. W. Hengstenberg, *Commentary on the Psalms*, II, pp. 118-26, while for modern ones, see H. C. Leupold, *Exposition of the Psalms*, pp. 351-53.

[2] See the discussion by Craig C. Broyles, *Psalms*, p. 207.

1. Introduction (*v. 1*)

My heart is stirred by a noble theme as I recite my verses for the king; my tongue is the pen of a skilful writer (*v. 1*). No other psalm starts in this fashion. The psalmist tells about the great subject matter with which his poem is concerned. His heart is bubbling over with the good things that his verses contain about *a king* (so the Hebrew text, which lacks the definite article 'the'). His tongue is like a skilled writer such as Ezra (cf. Ezra 7:6, which uses the very same phrase as here).[3]

2. Address to the King (*vv. 2-9*)

You are the most excellent of men and your lips have been anointed with grace, since God has blessed you forever (*v. 2*). The king is extolled for qualities that he possesses and for blessings that he has been given. In the Old Testament men are called 'excellent' or 'beautiful', such as the king here, or Absalom in 2 Samuel 14:25. This term refers to their general perfection.[4] Part of God's gift to the king was loveliness of speech, an indication of his blessing. The word 'forever' does not mean 'for eternity' but 'for as long as you live' (cf. its use regarding Moses in Exod. 19:9, and of a slave in 21:6).

Gird your sword upon your side, O mighty one; clothe yourself with splendour and majesty (*v. 3*). The king is thought of as a mighty warrior who needs to buckle on his sword before battle. The second part of the verse is paraphrased by the NIV, as the Hebrew text says simply, 'your splendour, your majesty.' Preferable is the rendering in the RSV and ESV, 'in your splendour and majesty.' These terms may refer to the king's armour, and if this suggestion is correct they may also point to glorious victories in the past achieved because of this armour.

---

[3] It is preferable to render the Hebrew phrase *sôfēr mâhîr* as 'skilled writer' rather than 'quick writer'. The latter translation depends on *mâhîr* being from the root *m-h-r*, 'to hasten'. However, it is more probably connected with a semitic root meaning 'skilled'. Further information is given in J. Barr, *Comparative Philology and the Text of the Old Testament* (London: SCM Press, 1968), p. 295, and the bibliography listed in *DCH*, V, p. 835.

[4] The verbal form is a rare Pealal of *yâfâh*, and while a *hapax legomenon*, no emendation, such as suggested in *BHS*, is necessary.

In your majesty ride forth victoriously in behalf of truth, humility and righteousness; let your right hand display awesome deeds (*v. 4*). The king is pictured as setting out for battle, riding upon his horse.[5] He makes his way through the ranks of the enemy as the champion of truth, humility, and righteousness.[6] The same imagery appears in Revelation of the rider Faithful and True who comes forth on a white horse (Rev. 19:11). These victories will be seen as the victories of God and so inspire awe. Elsewhere, such as in Psalm 65:5, 'awesome deeds' refers to God's own actions.

Let your sharp arrows pierce the hearts of the king's enemies; let the nations fall beneath your feet (*v. 5*). The NIV and many other translations take the phrase 'the hearts of the king's enemies' from the end of the verse (where it comes in the Hebrew text) and link it with the military success spoken of at the start of the verse. The whole verse is difficult to translate, but the essential message of it is clear. From carvings we know that battlefields were littered with slain bodies, shot by arrows. Victory is sure for the king. The fact that the Hebrew text ends with the word 'king' makes the transition to the next verse easier.

Your throne, O God, will last forever and ever; a sceptre of justice will be the sceptre of your kingdom (*v. 6*). Suddenly the psalmist looks beyond the immediate occupant of the throne of David to the kingly glory of the messianic ruler. This is similar to the way in which Isaiah inserts direct address to Immanuel into a passage that is dealing with the impending Assyrian invasion (Isa. 8:8). The divine ruler is not subject to the possibility that his kingdom will be taken from him.[7] Objections have been raised

---

[5] For an illustration of a king setting out, see the picture of Rameses III of Egypt mounting his chariot to go into battle, Othmar Keel, *The Symbolism of the Biblical World: Ancient Near Eastern Iconography and the Book of Psalms* (London: SPCK, 1978), p. 281.

[6] 'Humility and righteousness' translates ʿ*anvâh tsedek*, two nouns placed in apposition. The fact that the MT joins the words together by means of a hyphen called *maqqêf* suggests it was treating them as being in a construct relationship. However, the NIV translation is probably the best way to treat the two words.

[7] My own position on this verse is spelt out more fully in 'The Syntax and Interpretation of Psalm 45:7', John H. Skilton, ed., *The Law and the Prophets: Old Testament Studies Prepared in Honor of Oswald Thompson Allis* (Nutley, NJ: Presbyterian and Reformed Publishing Co., 1974), pp. 337-47.

to the traditional translation and interpretation on syntactical grounds.[8] Thus, it has been claimed that in Hebrew even when the preposition meaning 'like' (k^e) is omitted, though the text may say *a* is *b*, the meaning can be *a* is like *b*.[9] But this claim and its appeal to Psalm 80:11 does not hold up under scrutiny, and hence it cannot be used in support of a translation such as 'Your throne is *like* the throne of God, eternal'.[10] The 'sceptre' stands for the king's rule, and it is depicted as being one of which justice is the hallmark.

In Hebrews 1:8 this verse is quoted in a context that points to the eternal glory of Christ. He is the one who has been given 'the throne of his father David, and he will reign over the house of Jacob for ever; his kingdom will never end' (Luke 1:32-33).

You love righteousness and hate wickedness; therefore God, your God, has set you above your companions by anointing you with the oil of joy (*v. 7*). The person designated as 'God' in the previous verse is now marked off from him by the reference to 'your God'. This passage has to be considered along with other messianic passages in the Old Testament. In the descriptions of the Angel of the LORD he is represented as being God himself, and yet at the same time he is distinguished from God. In verse 6 the king is God, while here in this verse he has been given *by* God an exalted position over his companions. These companions are probably other kings. This king is distinguished from them by the fact that his character is different. He is noted for his love of righteousness and his punishment of evildoers, and consequently God has given him special blessings. The anointing with oil is probably a figurative way of saying that God has blessed him with

---

[8] For summaries of the various views that have and are taken in reference to the translation and interpretation of Psalm 45:6, see Murray J. Harris, 'The Translation of *Elohim* in Psalm 45:7-8', *TB* 35 (1984), pp. 65-89, and Gerard van Groningen, *Messianic Revelation in the Old Testament* (Grand Rapids: Baker Book House, 1990), pp. 362-70.

[9] For this argument, cf. the discussion by J. A. Emerton, 'The Syntactical Problem of Psalm XLV.7', *JSS* 13 (1968), pp. 58-63.

[10] P. C. Craigie, *Psalms 1-50*, p. 337, indicates his support for my discussion on this syntactical question, and upholds the traditional translation, 'Your throne, O God, is for ever and ever.'

happiness. It should not be equated with the anointing at a coronation.

All your robes are fragrant with myrrh and aloes and cassia; from palaces adorned with ivory the music of the strings makes you glad. Daughters of kings are among your honoured women; at your right hand is the royal bride in gold of Ophir (*vv. 8-9*). The scene shifts back to the wedding, and to the robes with which the king is adorned. Myrrh was a fragrant resin and it could be used as a valuable gift (Matt. 2:11). Aloes and cassia are both aromatic resins from the bark of trees. Wealthy homes and royal palaces were decorated with ivory (1 Kings 10:18; 22:39), while ivory could also be used as inlay on furniture (Amos 6:4). Festive music sounds from the palace as the wedding preparations continue.[11] The bride comes adorned in the best gold (cf. Isa. 13:12). Ophir has never been identified with certainty, but it was probably in southern Arabia between Mecca and Medina and was noted for its high-quality gold. The bride is accompanied by women of the royal family as she takes her position at the king's right hand.

3. Address to the Bride (*vv. 10-15*)

Listen, O daughter, consider and give ear: Forget your people and your father's house (*v. 10*). The bride is now addressed and this is shown by the verbal forms and the second person feminine singular suffixes to the nouns. She must give attention to the words of advice, and the command to forget her people and her father's house may imply that she is a foreigner. In the Book of Ruth Naomi speaks of Orpah 'going back to her people and her gods'. Ruth, on the other hand, makes her profession: 'Your people [are] my people and your God [is] my God' (Ruth 1:16).

The king is enthralled by your beauty; honour him, for he is your lord (*v. 11*). The king's attachment to his bride is due to her beauty. The expression 'he is your lord' may indicate that they were already married, as 'lord' is used in this way by Sarah of Abraham (Gen. 18:12; and cf. 1 Pet. 3:6, 'her master', lit. 'lord'). If so, the instruction of the previous verse comes

---

[11] The NIV assumes, and probably rightly, that the Hebrew word *minnî* is a shortened form of *minîm*, 'stringed instruments', as in Psalm 150:4.

after their marriage and reflects the new relationship with her husband's people. She is called on to give homage to him. **The Daughter of Tyre will come with a gift, men of wealth will seek your favour** (*v. 12*). The marriage brings a new relationship to surrounding nations, as gifts are brought by their peoples to the new queen. The word 'gift' (*minchâh*) can imply tribute (2 Sam 8:2, 6; 1 Chron. 18:2, 6). Hence the setting of this psalm may be in a period in which Israel exercised rule over surrounding nations. 'Daughter of Tyre' may indicate the people of Tyre, just as 'Daughter of Zion' and 'Daughter of Jerusalem' are used in a similar way.

All glorious is the princess within [her chamber]; her gown is interwoven with gold. In embroidered garments she is led to the king; her virgin companions follow her and are brought to you. They are led in with joy and gladness; they enter the palace of the king (*vv. 13-15*). Address is made again directly to the king concerning his bride (called here 'the daughter of the king') and her companions. It is clear from these two verses that it is not inward beauty of the princess that is being described, but outward adornment in beautiful garments. She is brought to the king accompanied by her maids of honour. They are brought into the royal palace in a festive procession, something similar to a modern bridal party entering the church.

4. Conclusion (*vv. 16-17*)

Your sons will take the place of your fathers; you will make them princes throughout the land. I will perpetuate your memory through all generations; therefore the nations will praise you forever and ever (*vv. 16-17*). The speaker seems to be the psalmist, as he reflects on the enduring dynasty that the king will have. His sons will be given positions of great responsibility, for 'princes' (*sârîm*) are frequently mentioned as being connected with a royal house (see 2 Chron. 21:9; 31:8; Jer. 26:21). This enduring dynasty would be a matter of praise even among the Gentile nations. Behind the words of the psalmist here lies the promises of the Davidic covenant (2 Sam. 7), but ultimately blessing to the nations will be a fulfilment of God's promises to Abraham (Gen. 12:3; 22:18).

Psalm 46

For the director of music. Of the Sons of Korah.
According to alamoth. A song.

The historical circumstances that lie behind the composition of this psalm cannot be established with absolute precision. Jerusalem has been attacked, but God has intervened on behalf of his people and shattered the enemy. Though it has been argued that the historical background is the deliverance from the Assyrian Sennacherib,[1] yet the situation depicted in 2 Chronicles 20 seems to fit best. The Moabites and Ammonites came against Jehoshaphat. Jahaziel at that time encouraged the people: 'Do not be afraid or discouraged because of this vast army. For the battle is not yours, but God's' (v. 15). Here the psalmist sings of victory won by the LORD Almighty, and of that city in which God dwells.

The psalm is divided by the threefold appearance of 'Selah' and the repeated refrain in verses 7 and 11. Verse 8 appears to be the pivotal verse, with the opening statement of the psalm, 'God is our refuge' (v. 1), being matched at the conclusion of the psalm by 'the LORD Almighty is with us' (v. 11). In addition, verse 8 also serves to conclude the first section and then to introduce the second main division.

The title contains the word *ᵃlâmôt*, which also appears in 1 Chronicles 15:20 as a musical term. The word itself means 'young women'. Hence, it could refer to the type of voices that were to sing the specified song, perhaps tenor or soprano.

This psalm and the two following ones (Pss. 46-48) share many themes in common with Psalm 87. The land of promise (Canaan) was important, but the place of Jerusalem within

---

[1] See the sustained attempt by N. H. Snaith, *Hymns of the Temple* (London; SCM Press, 1951), pp. 70-77, to argue for that background.

it even more so. The LORD had chosen that 'holy mountain' (Pss. 48:1; 87:1) and when the nations turn to him they will become, as it were, citizens of Jerusalem (Ps. 87:6).

1. A Safe Stronghold (*vv. 1-3*)

God is our refuge and strength, an ever-present help in trouble (*v. 1*). A favourite theme of many of the psalms is the fact that God is the refuge of his people (e.g., 61:3; 62:7-8; 71:7; 142:5). The words 'refuge' (*mach^{a}seh*) and 'strength' ('*oz*) are often used in conjunction to depict God's character and his actions on behalf of his people. The confession here is communal (for the Hebrew text has 'for *us*'; and also in vv. 7 and 11). The people acknowledge that when in trouble God is near to help. The translation 'an ever-present help' is a traditional one, but the MT simply says 'in trouble he will be found a help – exceedingly.' The emphasis should rather fall on how great a help the LORD is, rather than trying to describe its continuous nature.

Therefore we will not fear, though the earth give way and the mountains fall into the heart of the sea, though its waters roar and foam and the mountains quake with their surging. Selah (*vv. 2-3*). The troubles they had faced (including the most recent battles) are described as if there was a tremendous upheaval of nature. A mighty earthquake has taken place, but amidst everything the people can say: 'We will not fear.' This is based on what has been asserted about God in verse 1. The sea may be used as a symbol for the world as it is agitated by sinful desires of kings and empires. Insufficient detail is given to locate the psalm in a specific historical context.

There is a river whose streams make glad the city of God, the holy place where the Most High dwells. God is within her, she will not fall; God will help her at break of day (*vv. 4-5*). While the term 'Zion' is not used, the psalmist now describes how secure the people are because God has his dwelling in Jerusalem. In other Old Testament passages we also have the picture of Jerusalem, with water streaming from her (cf. Isa. 33:21). God's sanctuary was in Jerusalem, and as long as the people trusted his provision for them, then his help would never fail. When they despised the softly flowing waters of Siloam, then God would abandon them (Isa. 8:5-8). God 'had pity on his people and his dwelling place' until the people mocked his messengers and ultimately the sanctuary itself was destroyed by the Babylonians (2 Chron. 36:15-19). The psalmist's language about Jerusalem idealises the topographical situation, as no 'river' gladdens the sanctuary. The Kidron only flows for a few weeks in winter, while the spring of Gihon struggles to fill the pool of Siloam.

Nations are in uproar, kingdoms fall; he lifts his voice, the earth melts (*v. 6*). In the midst of turmoil among the nearby nations, God has spoken. Kingdoms 'slip', says the psalmist, using a word he has already used of the mountains (NIV, 'the mountains *fall*,' verse 2). The contrast that is so clear is that God's city will not 'slip' or 'fall' (v. 5). When his voice is heard, the inhabitants of the earth tremble in fear. 'The earth melts' is simply a poetical way of saying that people are terrified.

2. An Affirmation of Confidence (v. 7)

The confession that the people go on to make is that they have God's presence. **The LORD Almighty is with us; the God of Jacob is our fortress. Selah** (*v. 7*). The form of the first clause is reminiscent of 'God is with us', 'Immanuel' (Isa. 7:14; 8:8, 10). Instead of 'God' the psalmist here uses the expression 'the LORD of hosts' (NIV 'the LORD Almighty'; see comment on Psalm 24:10). The covenantal God of the patriarchs is with them as a 'fortress' (*misgâv*). This word signified a fortified height to which one could flee for safety, so symbolising the security of believers in God (cf. its use in 2 Sam. 22:3 and Isa. 33:16). It is definitely a poetic word, being found in the Psalms eleven times out of a total of fifteen in the Old Testament. This is the first occurrence of a refrain that is used again in verse 13 to close the Psalm. It may have been in general use, not just an isolated statement appearing in a context such as this.

3. A Summons from the LORD (*vv. 8-11*)

The invitation goes out to take notice of how God has shattered the enemies that came against his people. **Come and see the works of the LORD, the desolations he has brought on the earth. He makes wars cease to the ends of the earth; he breaks the bow and shatters the spear, he burns the shields with fire** (*vv. 8-9*). The 'works' of God are the distinctive actions he performs, especially in saving and sustaining his people.[2] The word 'desolations' is explained by what follows. He brought peace by destroying the enemies and their weapons. Their military power was broken as if bows and spears were destroyed. In the final clause of verse 9 the NIV renders the Hebrew word 'chariots' by 'shields'. This is following three early translations – the LXX, the Aramaic Targum, and the Latin Vulgate. However, the word 'chariots' makes good sense, especially as we know that chariots were burnt after they were captured (Josh. 11:6, 9).

'Be still, and know that I am God; I will be exalted among the nations, I will be exalted in the earth' (*v. 10*). The call is addressed to the Gentile invaders to withdraw. 'Be still' conveys too much the idea of being quiet, whereas the Hebrew verb means more 'to let alone', 'to abandon'. Because of his actions they should recognise that he is God and submit to his authority. The verb 'know' was used in secular treaties in this sense. He assures them that all nations are going to exalt him, even the whole earth. Quite often this verse is used in encouraging Christians to be calm, but that is a wrong application of it, as it is not addressed to believers but to the Gentile nations.

The LORD Almighty is with us; the God of Jacob is our fortress. Selah (*v. 11*). The refrain from verse 7 is repeated to close the psalm. It is an appropriate way to sum up the gratitude of the people as they again profess their faith in their deliverer.

---

[2] The word used for 'works' (*mifʿālôt*) only occurs three times in the Old Testament (apart from here, in Ps. 66:5 and Prov. 8:22). No indication exists to show that it differs at all from the more common related word, *poʿal*.

Psalm 47

For the director of music. Of the Sons of Korah. A psalm.

Psalms 46 and 47 seem to be positioned together in the Psalter because of their great similarity. Both celebrate God's victories on behalf of his people. This psalm has two calls to praise, followed by explanations. In each case there is a concluding statement. The first one points to God on his throne in Jerusalem (v. 5), while the second one praises him as the universal ruler (v. 9). These explanations are introduced in the Hebrew text in the manner typical of hymns by the presence of 'for' (*kî*) as the introductory word (see comments on Hymns in the Introduction). This is not so apparent from the NIV translation, but is carried over well in the NASB, RSV NKJV, and ESV. In addition to introducing the substance of praise in verses 2 and 7, the word 'for' also prefaces the final declaration of praise in verse 9. The part this word plays in the structure of the psalm is reinforced by the repetition of the words 'king' and 'all the earth' in verses 2 and 7. In fact, the repetition of 'people' (vv. 1, 3, 9), 'king' (vv. 2, 6, 7) and 'earth' (vv. 2, 7, 9) throughout the psalm gives overall unity to it.

1. Call to Praise (*v. 1*)
Clap your hands, all you nations; shout to God with cries of joy (*v. 1*). Clapping hands was a sign of joy, and the call goes out to Gentile nations to share with Israel in praising God. At coronations it was apparently customary to clap the hands and shout, 'Long live the king!' (2 Kings 11:12). Reference to clapping also occurs in a later song of rejoicing over God's

kingship in Psalm 98:8.[1] The content of the shouting could be simply that God is king, or expressed in terms such as we have later in this psalm.

2. God's Rule over Israel (*vv. 2-5*)
How awesome is the LORD Most High, the great King over all the earth! (*v. 2*). The nations are asked to rejoice concerning the LORD, for he is 'the great king'. This term was used frequently by Near Eastern rulers (see 2 Kings 18:19 and Isa. 36:4, 13 in reference to the king of Assyria), but here it is appropriated of the even greater king, the LORD Most High.[2] His territory is not restricted as with earthly rulers, but rather it embraces the whole earth.

He subdued nations under us, peoples under our feet. He chose our inheritance for us, the pride of Jacob, whom he loved. Selah (*vv. 3-4*). The song reflects upon the conquest of Canaan by Israel. It was God who acted sovereignly to dispossess other nations and to make them submissive to Israel's rule.[3] Verse 4 is explaining the conquest and allocation of the land of Canaan in terms that echo statements in the Book of Deuteronomy (see especially Deut. 4:37-38). God's love for the patriarchs and for Jacob in particular (see Mal. 1:2) resulted in his giving them as their inheritance the land of Canaan, called here 'the pride of Jacob'. The conjunction of the verbs 'to choose' and 'to love' both here and in Deuteronomy 4:37 stress the sovereign nature of God's relationship with Israel.

God has ascended amid shouts of joy, the LORD amid the sounding of trumpets (*v. 5*). The verb 'ascended' is used because God is thought of having descended when he came to help his people. The same idea appears in Psalm 68:18: 'When you ascended on high, you led captives in your train ...' The

---

[1] Countries near Israel also practised clapping. For an illustration, see the picture of the Egyptian goddess Mert with hands upraised ready to clap in Othmar Keel, *The Symbolism of the Biblical World*, p. 334.

[2] It is also used of God in Psalms 48:2 and 95:3, and Malachi 1:14. Further comment on its use in Assyrian and extra-biblical sources can be found in M. Cogan and Hayim Tadmor, *II Kings: A New Translation with Introduction and Commentary* (New York: Doubleday & Co., 1988), pp. 230-31.

[3] The verb for 'subdue' is *d-v-r* II, and comment has already been made concerning it in reference to its use in Psalm 18:47.

LORD is pictured as returning to heaven amidst joyful acclaim from his people. The noun used of 'shouts of joy' (*terûʿâh*) links in with the use of the verb from which it comes in verse 1 ('shout'). Blowing of trumpets was specified for certain festive occasions, including New Year (Lev. 23:24; Num. 29:1).

3. Another Call to Praise (*v. 6*)

Sing praises to God, sing praises; sing praises to our King, sing praises (*v. 6*). The second call to praise is notable for its fourfold repetition of the verb 'to sing praises' (*zâmar* Pi.). This adds both emphasis and urgency to the command. The verb is almost exclusively used in the psalms, calling upon individuals and the community to join in praise to God, often in the context of musical accompaniment of song.[4] The people's relationship with God is defined in terms of his lordship over them. They sing to him as their God and as their king.

4. God's Rule over the Nations (*vv. 7-9*)

For God is the king of all the earth; sing to him a psalm of praise. God reigns over the nations; God is seated on his holy throne (*vv. 7-8*). The reason given for this second call to praise is that God's lordship is over all the earth, and this knowledge should result in another psalm of praise. This is the fifth call to praise in two verses, all imperatives from the same verb. The command to praise is followed on this occasion by an object: 'a psalm of praise' (*maskîl*). Apart from its use here, this word appears in the title of thirteen psalms (Pss. 32, 42, 44, 45, 52-55, 74, 78, 88, 89, 142). Hence, the direction could be to sing one of these specific psalms, or, more probably, a song that exemplifies a spirit of wisdom and understanding in accordance with the basic idea of this verb.[5] The Old Testament understands God's kingship to be from eternity (cf. 93:2). From his throne he exercises his rule and judgment over all nations.

---

[4] The verb occurs thirty-nine times in the Psalter, and only four times elsewhere (Judg. 5:3; 2 Sam. 22:50; Isa. 12:5; 1 Chron. 16:9).

[5] The verb is *sâkal*, used seventy-four times of which seventy-two are in the Hi. stem. Quite often it is close in meaning to other Hebrew verbs but it seems frequently to indicate having insight or understanding.

The nobles of the nations assemble as the people of the God of Abraham, for the kings of the earth belong to God; he is greatly exalted (*v. 9*). The word rendered 'nobles' is literally 'willing ones', but the NIV has taken its cue from the parallel word 'kings'.[6] The context here gives a picture of princes of the Gentile nations coming voluntarily and uniting with Jews as 'the people of Abraham'. This is part of the universalistic vision of the psalmists for the ultimate future of God's kingdom (cf. Pss. 67:1-7; 72:8-11). Gentile rulers 'belong to God' in the sense that they have become his servants. The conclusion is that God is indeed 'exalted', using a verbal form connected with 'Most High' (v. 2) and 'has ascended' (v. 5).

---

[6] The NIV is correct in taking the Hebrew word *mâgên* here as suzerain or king. For discussion on this translation, see M. Dahood, *Psalms I:1–50*, p. 17, and also the entries in *DCH*, III, p. 134 and *TWOT*, 1, p. 169. This also obviates any felt need to emend the MT text from *mâgᵉnê* to *sigᵉnê* as suggested in *BHS*.

Psalm 48

A song. A psalm of the Sons of Korah.

This psalm is clearly connected with Psalms 46 and 47. However, it is much more specific in relation to Mount Zion (called simply 'the city of God' in Psalm 46:4) and to matters relating to worship there. Whereas Psalms 46 and 47 speak more of the LORD's victories, Psalm 48 is a song of rejoicing over Zion and the blessings associated with her. It is notable for the collection of phrases used, especially in verses 1-2, to describe Jerusalem. Praise is offered concerning Jerusalem, 'the city of our God' and 'the city of the Great God', of Zion as 'his holy mountain' and especially of the God of Zion.

1. The God of Zion (vv. 1-3)

Great is the LORD, and most worthy of praise, in the city of our God, his holy mountain (v. 1). The initial emphasis is not on Zion, but on the God of Zion. The opening invocation sets the theme for the whole psalm as it directs attention to his greatness, and in particular as it is displayed in the symbolism of Mount Zion. The choice of Zion was the LORD's (Ps. 132:13-14), and from the time that David captured it (2 Sam. 5:6-7) it was central to the theology of the Old Testament. In the wider biblical picture Zion became the model for the New Jerusalem, and in Christian hymnology its imagery is taken over for the church (see John Newton's 'Glorious things of thee are spoken, Zion, city of our God').

It is beautiful in its loftiness, the joy of the whole earth. Like the utmost heights of Zaphon is Mount Zion, the city of the Great King (v. 2). Mount Zion is not actually the highest peak in the area, yet because of its religious significance it is extolled by the psalmist.[1] He pictures it as a place of joy not just to those who live or worship there, but to the whole earth. Zaphon was a mountain in northern Syria known from Canaanite sources, and it was supposed to be the dwelling place of the god Baal. Zion, though like Zaphon, was distinguished by the fact that it is the dwelling place of 'the great king' (see Ps. 47:2). This is an assertion that though others claimed Zaphon as the holy mountain, the *real* mountain of God where divine revelation occurred was Zion.

God is in her citadels; he has shown himself to be her fortress (*v. 3*). God's presence in Zion was shown by the bringing of the ark of the covenant there, and then by the building of the temple. He had taken up his abode in her palaces, and he had proved to be her defender. God's demonstration of his protection for Zion may have been shown just before this psalm was composed, perhaps in some battle situation such as spoken of in Psalm 46.

2. The Glory of Zion (*vv. 4-8*)

When the kings joined forces, when they advanced together, they saw [her] and were astounded; they fled in terror. Trembling seized them there, pain like that of a woman in labour. You destroyed them like ships of Tarshish shattered by an east wind (*vv. 4-7*). In a manner similar to Psalm 2, this psalm describes a gathering together of foreign kings against the LORD and against his chosen dwelling place, Jerusalem. Coalitions could be formed, but they were soon shattered. What the attackers 'saw' is unclear.[2] It could have been the fortified Zion, or, on the other hand, it could have been some visible appearance of God, a theophany. 'There', where they had that vision, they were frightened and panic seized them.[3] The idea of a woman in travail is a frequent Old Testament

---

[1] Zion rises to 743 metres, 66 metres lower than the Mount of Olives. However, from the south end of the walls of ancient Jerusalem, its inhabitants had to climb about 100 metres to reach the top of Zion.

[2] A similar case of the verb 'to see' without an object occurs in the MT of 1 Kings 19:3 in relation to Elijah: 'And when he *saw*, he arose and ran for his life.'

[3] The same idiom occurs here as appears in its fuller form in verse 10. The initial introductory k^e or $ka\,^{\prime a}sher$ is omitted, while the Hebrew word *kên* ('and' in the NIV translation) points to the consequence: 'they saw *so* they feared.'

illustration of pain and anguish (cf. Isa. 21:3; Jer. 4:31; 49:24). Even if the assembled armies are like the mighty ships that trade to Tarshish (see Jonah 1:3), they will be destroyed as easily as an east wind brings them to a watery grave.[4]

As we have heard, so have we seen in the city of the LORD Almighty, in the city of our God: God makes her secure forever. Selah (*v. 8*). These words sum up the experience of the people. They had heard in the past of the wonderful things that the LORD had done for his people (cf. Ps. 44:1: 'we have heard with our ears, O God'; Ps. 78:3: 'things we have heard and known'). The use of the appellation 'the LORD Almighty' (*yhwh ts^evâ'ôt*) is fitting in a context in which God is depicted as the protector and defender of his people.[5] Now, however, their own eyes had seen his saving power right in the midst of Jerusalem. They thought that this experience would make her safe forever, but God's presence was conditional on their continued obedience.

3. The Words of the Worshippers (*vv. 9-11*)

After their deliverance the people address God directly. **Within your temple, O God, we meditate on your unfailing love. Like your name, O God, your praise reaches to the ends of the earth; your right hand is filled with righteousness** (*vv. 9-10*). When the worshippers assemble in the sanctuary they recognise that it is due to covenant love that they have been saved. They now have fresh evidence of the LORD's steadfast love. The expression of this truth is made using a Hebrew idiom ('as is your name … so is your praise') that links God's self-revelation of himself ('his name') with the fact that he is therefore worthy of praise.[6] Worship in the temple had significance for the whole world. What had happened was known far and wide, so that the praise of the LORD was co-extensive with knowledge of his actions. Wherever people

---

[4] Tarshish is linked with Sheba, Seba, and Dedan, and hence its location was probably in Arabia or east Africa. Some port on the Red Sea would satisfy the references to it in the Old Testament. See also the comments on Psalm 72:10.

[5] For discussion on 'the LORD Almighty', cf. the comments on Psalm 24:10.

[6] The Hebrew idiom is dealt with in *DIHG~S*, p. 161.

heard about the events in Jerusalem they would praise the mighty actions of God in giving victory to his people. **Mount Zion rejoices, the villages of Judah are glad because of your judgments** (*v. 11*). On Mount Zion and throughout the villages of Judah there is gladness on account of the recent victory.[7] That victory was called a filling of God's hand with righteousness in the previous verse, and now it is called his 'judgments'. The demonstrations of power shown in overthrowing Israel's enemies were expressions of God's judgments as he established his kingdom. This verse is very similar to Psalm 97:8.

4. An Invitation to View Zion (*vv. 12-14*)

Walk about Zion, go around her, count her towers, consider well her ramparts, view her citadels, that you may tell of them to the next generation (*vv. 12-13*). An invitation is given to view Jerusalem and to see her fortifications. Clearly this was not to take pride in her simply because of her good defences. She was 'the city of the LORD' (v. 8), and as such she was given divine protection. Passing on to the next generation this truth would continue the transmission of knowledge of the LORD. His praiseworthy deeds could not be hidden from the next generation (Ps. 78:4). Each generation of believers has a responsibility to teach the following one.

For this God is our God for ever and ever; he will be our guide even to the end (*v. 14*). The people make confession of the fact that this God who has saved them is indeed their God. They own him as their personal deliverer, and they know that he will shepherd them to the very end. This last clause continues the imagery of God as a shepherd of his people that is frequent in the Old Testament (cf. Pss. 23:1; 77:20; 80:1; Isa. 40:11; 49:9-10; Ezek. 34:11-12).

---

[7] 'Villages of Judah' is literally 'daughters of Judah', but the plural form as here can have the figurative meaning of 'villages', as in Numbers 21:25; Joshua 15:45; Judges 1:27; and Jeremiah 49:2.

Psalm 49

For the director of music. Of the Sons of Korah. A psalm.

The first series of Korahite psalms (Pss. 42-49) ends with a wisdom psalm (see the Introduction). The overriding thought is that the might of those who are rich but godless is not enduring, for all men, rich and poor, must die (see v. 12). In its general form it is like passages in the books of Job and Proverbs, even using the word 'proverb' (v. 4). The reference in that verse to it being sung is the only time in the Old Testament that mention is made of wisdom teaching being accompanied by music. However, many cultures, not only those in the Near East, combine music and instructional poems.

Whereas in another wisdom psalm, Psalm 37, the solution to the problem of the prosperity of the wicked is that God providentially cares for his own, the solution given here is that there is life beyond the grave for those whom God redeems. After an introduction it provides two answers to the problem, each with its own refrain.

No indication occurs in the psalm relating to its date of composition. The inscription 'To the sons of Korah' and also the contents point to a pre-exilic date. Both form and content are similar to other psalms from the time of David, and it is best attributed to that period.

1. Introduction (*vv. 1-4*)
Hear this, all you peoples; listen, all who live in this world, both low and high, rich and poor alike: My mouth will speak words of wisdom; the utterance from my heart will give understanding (*vv. 1-3*). The call (*shim^e û zo't*) is given to all to listen to the words

of wisdom that are going to be spoken.[1] An uncommon Hebrew word is used for 'world' (*chéled*). It not only denotes the physical environment but the whole sphere of transitory life. All classes of society are addressed. The phrase 'low and high' is the translation of an antithetical Hebrew expression (*gam bᵉnê 'âdâm gam bᵉnê 'îsh*) that denotes those of low degree contrasted with those of high degree or influence (cf. the use of the same contrast in Ps. 62:9). The promise is that much (or possibly, profound) wisdom[2] and great understanding will be bestowed. The issues of life and death to be addressed are of interest to all.

I will turn my ear to a proverb; with the harp I will expound my riddle (*v.* 4): 'Proverb' and 'riddle' occur here together as they do in Psalm 78:2, Proverbs 1:6, Ezekiel 17:2, and Habakkuk 2:6. They tell of the ways in which wisdom and understanding are going to be conveyed. A 'proverb' could be much longer than the short saying we think of in English, while 'riddle' has a range of usage from the 'riddles' Samson set his Philistine guests (Judg. 14) to the 'hard questions' which the Queen of Sheba asked Solomon (1 Kings 10:1-3). The usage here is nearer the latter in meaning.

2. Transitory Wealth (*vv. 5-12*)

Why should I fear when evil days come, when wicked deceivers surround me – those who trust in their wealth and boast of their great riches? (*vv.* 5-6). The psalmist already knows the answer to his question, and it will be given later on (see v. 15). He is surrounded by evil men who have put their confidence in their wealth, and he wants to set the record straight concerning them, for no amount of money can buy off death. The MT makes the opposition somewhat more pointed by speaking about '*my* wicked deceivers'.[3]

---

[1] For similar calls to 'listen', compare Deuteronomy 32:1; Psalm 50:7; and Micah 1:2.

[2] The promise is that 'wisdoms' (*chokmôt*) will be proclaimed, the use of the plural giving intensification to the singular *chokmâh*. This usage, sometimes called 'the plural of majesty', is covered in *DIHG~S*, p. 19.

[3] The word rendered in the NIV by 'deceivers' (*ᵃqêvay*) is problematic. The noun 'heel' (*'âqêv*) is well known, but a verb with the same consonants exists and has the meaning 'to deceive'. The word here is probably an adjective from this verb.

No man can redeem the life of another or give to God a ransom for him – the ransom for a life is costly, no payment is ever enough – that he should live on forever and not see decay (*vv. 7-9*). The teaching of these verses is that no one can escape death by paying money. A rich person may live well, and in such a way as to give the impression that he is going to live forever. But there can be no ransom paid to God for him, for such redemption[4] is beyond the ability of men to achieve. Ultimately even the richest person will see decay (lit. 'see the pit'; cf. its use in Ps. 16:10, where it is used in parallelism with 'Sheol', 'the grave').

For all can see that wise men die; the foolish and the senseless alike perish and leave their wealth to others. Their tombs will remain their houses forever, their dwellings for endless generations, though they had named lands after themselves (*vv. 10-11*). The common experience of life is that everyone dies, 'for death is the destiny of every man' (Eccles. 7:2). The reference to 'wise men' and 'foolish' is to the same two groups that Psalm 37 calls 'the righteous' and 'the wicked'. Whatever wealth they have acquired is left to others. The biblical teaching is that we bring nothing into this world and we can take nothing out of it. The real riches consist of 'godliness with contentment', while storing up treasures is achieved by being rich in good deeds and being generous and willing to share (1 Tim. 6:6-7, 17-19). Rich people may build luxurious mansions, trying in this way to perpetuate their memory. Such buildings may last, but they themselves perish, and their eternal home is the grave (Eccles. 12:5).

But man, despite his riches, does not endure; he is like the beasts that perish (*v. 12*). A concluding statement sums up this section of the psalm. Riches cannot bestow eternal life, for man is no different from the animals in this respect. The rich have tried to provide for themselves a lodging place, but they will find no permanent place of abode (the word translated

---

[4] The NIV rendering disguises the fact that the MT speaks of 'redemption' (*pidyôn*), not 'ransom'. The verb 'redeem' (*pâdâh*) has already occurred at the beginning of verse 7, and it appears again in verse 15.

'endure' literally means 'to lodge the night'). The grave will receive both men and animals.

3. Redemption by God (*vv. 13-20*)

The folly of the rich concerning death has been described in the preceding section. Now the teacher goes on to show their folly in life, but he also points to the way in which God can redeem a soul from the grave. **This is the fate of those who trust in themselves, and of their followers, who approve their sayings. Selah** (*v. 13*). Those who have a false confidence,[5] namely in themselves or in their riches, follow a particular way of life (MT, lit. 'their path'). Their followers could either be their descendants or perhaps more likely those who imitate them (Exod. 23:2; 2 Sam. 2:10). They listen to their teachers and adopt their instruction as their own way of life.

Like sheep they are destined for the grave, and death will feed on them. The upright will rule over them in the morning; their forms will decay in the grave, far from their princely mansions (*v. 14*). The Hebrew text of this verse is difficult to translate, as is shown by the variations of it in the English versions, and also by the footnote in the NIV. The proud rich are 'like sheep shipped to Sheol',[6] a translation that attempts to bring out the alliteration in the Hebrew text.[7] They are ready for the slaughter. The grave will swallow them,[8] and the distance between their place of burial and their former mansions will be great. On the other hand, the righteous will come through their suffering and enter a new day. That 'day' is not the morning of the resurrection, but the morning that dawns after the destruction of the ungodly.

---

[5] The MT has 'This is their way, their folly (*kêsel*)'. Elsewhere the word is noted as an evil thing (Eccles. 7:25). To live for this world and what it affords is indeed folly.

[6] The translation is that by Craigie, *Psalms 1-50*, p. 358.

[7] MT *katstso'n lishᵉ'ôl shattû*, with a doubled consonant *ts* being followed by a double *sh*.

[8] The word that the NIV renders as 'decay' (*lᵉvallôt*) could mean 'for consumption'. This is the interpretation followed by Craigie, *Psalms 1-50*, pp. 356-7, and based on Dahood, *Psalms I: 1–50*, p. 301, and J. C. L. Gibson, *Canaanite Myths and Legends*, pp. 68, 143.

But God will redeem my life from the grave; he will surely take me to himself. Selah (*v. 15*). One man cannot redeem another (see v. 7), but God is able to do so. Resurrection of the body will be God's ultimate redemption of his saints. The use of the verb 'take' (*lâqach*) is important for it is used of the translation of both Enoch (Gen. 5:24) and Elijah (2 Kings 2:5), and here too it seems to be used specifically to denote the way in which God will snatch from the grave. Redemption and bringing into God's own presence are divine works. It is God alone who takes us to glory (Ps. 73:24).

Do not be overawed when a man grows rich, when the splendour of his house increases; for he will take nothing with him when he dies, his splendour will not descend with him (*vv. 16-17*). A word of advice is now offered to all the readers of the psalm. After what has been said already about the position of the rich it is clear that they should not be envied nor feared. Their wealth may be real, but a time comes when they have to leave it behind. Paul expands on this Old Testament teaching in 1 Timothy 6:3-10, noting that 'we brought nothing into the world, and we can take nothing out of it' (v. 7).

Though while he lived he counted himself blessed – and men praise you when you prosper – he will join the generation of his fathers, who will never see the light [of life] (*vv. 18-19*). Two characteristics mark out the unrighteous person. First of all, instead of praising God, he blesses himself. Then, secondly, he enjoys the flattery of other people, who see his prosperity and assess him accordingly. But these experiences will not gain him any lasting benefits, for when he joins the dead there is no prospect of life with God.[9] 'To see the light [of life]' implies resurrection from the dead (cf. Isa. 53:11 and the Servant of the LORD).

A man who has riches without understanding is like the beasts that perish (*v. 20*). The refrain is picked up from verse 12, with the change of 'does not endure' to 'without

---

[9] At the beginning of verse 19, the verb is *tâvô'*, 'she will go'. If the MT is retained then the feminine form of the verb must have *néfesh*, 'soul', as its antecedent, even though it is rather remote. The other alternative is to follow the LXX and change to the masculine form *yâvô'*, 'he will go.'

understanding'. That change is intentional to stress that riches, when spiritual understanding is absent, make a man no better than the animals that die. The question of verse 5, 'Why should I fear when evil days come?', finds its answer in this verse.

Psalm 50

A psalm of Asaph.

The covenant relationship comes to the fore in this psalm, with it being expressly mentioned in verses 5 and 16. It has strong resemblances to covenant lawsuit passages such as Deuteronomy 32, Isaiah 1, Micah 6, and Jeremiah 2 in which heaven and earth are summoned to listen to God's judgment against his people. It also has strong affinities with Psalm 81, especially in the call to the people to listen, followed by the opening words of the Decalogue (cf. 50:7-8 with 81:8-10). It should also be compared with Psalm 95, where the divine speech is in the first person ('tested *me*', '*I* was angry', '*I* said', '*I* declared'). The psalm may have been written for a ceremony renewing the covenant, such as was carried out every seven years at the Feast of Tabernacles (Deut. 31:10-11). The opening of the psalm, in the form of a theophany, recalls the manner in which God revealed himself at Sinai to his people. The two further sections declare the true meaning of sacrifice (vv. 7-15) and a warning to those who despise the demands of the covenant (vv. 16-23).

This is the first of the psalms that are specifically linked with Asaph, though the other eleven are all in a single block (Pss. 73-83). In 2 Chronicles 29:30 it is noted that King Hezekiah commanded the people 'to praise the LORD with the words of David and of Asaph the seer'. While no group is ever called 'the sons of Asaph' (cf. 'the sons of Korah'), the phrase does occur in the narrative about David's appointment of singers ('some of the sons of Asaph', 'from the sons of Asaph', 1 Chron. 25:1-2). Clearly Asaph was an important figure in the musical history of the tabernacle/temple. Among those who returned from exile were singers who were the descendants of Asaph (Ezra 2:41). He is again linked with David in Nehemiah 12:46 as being part of a line of temple singers.

1. God Comes to Judge (*vv. 1-6*)

The Mighty One, God, the LORD, speaks and summons the earth from the rising of the sun to the place where it sets. From Zion, perfect in beauty, God shines forth (*vv. 1-2*). God is not described by a single title, but by a cluster of them. The words 'the Mighty One' and 'God' seem to draw attention to the position of God as the judge over all, while 'LORD' identifies him as the covenant God of Israel. If the covenant renewal ceremony was carried out at dawn, the significance of the ceremony would be emphasised by the sun's rays striking Zion. He summons the earth, not for judgment, but to witness his accusations against his own people. Because of God's choice of Zion it is regarded as a place of beauty (Ps. 48:1-2), from which the LORD 'shines forth'. This term is used of his shining from Mount Paran (Deut. 33:2) and from between the cherubim (Ps. 80:1). In the Bible God is pictured as dwelling in light (Exod. 13:21-22; Dan. 2:22; 1 Tim. 6:16).

Our God comes and will not be silent; a fire devours before him, and around him a tempest rages (*v. 3*). The description of God's coming is borrowed from the account of the revelation he made of himself at Sinai. God, who is a consuming fire (Deut. 4:24; 9:3), revealed himself by fire at Sinai, where he spoke 'from out of the fire on the mountain' (Deut. 5:4). The people heard his voice 'while the mountain was ablaze with fire' (Deut. 5:22-23). Elijah was later to have a similar revelation of God at Sinai (1 Kings 19:11-12). Theophanies in the Old Testament involved speech as well as a visionary experience. Hence, God's 'coming' is associated with declaration of his will.

He summons the heavens above, and the earth, that he may judge his people: 'Gather to me my consecrated ones, who made a covenant with me by sacrifice' (*vv. 4-5*). The heavens and the earth are summoned to listen to what God has to say to 'his people'. Those who belong to this category are then defined as God's 'consecrated ones' (Hebrew, *ch^{a}sidîm*; see on Psalm 31:23) and as those who are entering into a covenant by sacrifice. The reference seems to be to the ensuing ceremony which reaffirmed the covenant described in Exodus 24:5-8. The Hebrew text here uses the technical term for making a covenant, 'to cut a covenant' (*kârat b^{e}rît*), which goes back to the common practice of including some cutting ritual as part of a covenant ceremony. The covenant is declared to be God's covenant (*b^{e}rîtî*, 'my covenant'), a term expressing the unilateral nature of his covenantal dealings with men.

And the heavens proclaim his righteousness, for God himself is judge. Selah (*v. 6*). The very heavens seem as if they are announcing God's righteousness, as he comes to enter into judgment with his covenant people. What is left indefinite in verse 4 (namely, who is doing the judging) is now clarified. The judge of the people is none other than the God of the covenant himself.

2. The True Sacrifices (*vv. 7-15*)

At this point the change is made to first person singular, as divine speech is addressed to the assembled congregation. **Hear, O my people, and I will speak, O Israel, and I will testify against you: I am God, your God** (*v. 7*). The opening words of the LORD echo the formula that appears frequently in the Book of Deuteronomy (4:1; 6:4; 9:1; 20:3; 27:9), while the words 'I am God, your God' recall the opening words of the Decalogue (Exod. 20:2; Deut. 5:6). God is now ready to provide the evidence against his people. The use of the word 'testify' provides a link with the prophetic ministry of warning the people of their sins (2 Chron. 24:19; Neh. 9:26). Psalm 81:8 is very similar to this verse, though the NIV translation does not make this clear.[1]

---

[1] When set out in parallel with an alternative translation the similarity becomes apparent:
Psalm 50:7, 'Hear, O my people, ..., O Israel, and I will testify against you.'
Psalm 81:8, 'Hear, O my people,   and I will testify against you, O Israel.'

I do not rebuke you for your sacrifices or your burnt offerings, which are ever before me (*v. 8*). There is no intended rejection of sacrifice in itself in the accusation of the Lord. The people were observing the law regarding the offering of sacrifices, and they were constantly coming to the place of sacrifice with the required offerings. What was wrong, as succeeding verses show, was that a wrong spirit motivated them.

I have no need of a bull from your stall or of goats from your pens, for every animal of the forest is mine, and the cattle on a thousand hills. I know every bird in the mountains, and the creatures of the field are mine (*vv. 9-11*). God makes the declaration that he is the creator of all things. Hence, he does not need the small offerings presented to him as sacrifices. All the animals in the world, both wild and domestic, are his possession, so he does not require a few more gifts to supplement his vast empire. The declaration does not say that God will refuse to accept sacrifices. Rather, even if the people do not voluntarily bring one, he will not come and forcefully remove one from their houses (*lo' 'eqqach mibbêtᵉkâ*). A young steer was a valuable possession, and would often be kept in a stall forming part of the house. 'Creatures of the field' (*zîz sâday*) is a rare expression, only occurring here and in Psalm 80:13.

If I were hungry I would not tell you, for the world is mine, and all that is in it. Do I eat the flesh of bulls or drink the blood of goats? (*vv. 12-13*). Even within Israel there were false views of God. Some thought that their sacrificial offerings were a form of food for him, as happened in other religions in the Near East (see Deut. 32:38). Here God disabuses them of these ideas, for he is already the owner of the whole world and everything in it (Deut. 10:14; Ps. 24:1). He did not need food of this kind to be provided as his meat and drink.

Sacrifice thank-offerings to God, fulfil your vows to the Most High, and call upon me in the day of trouble; I will deliver you, and you will honour me' (*vv. 14-15*). What was needed was sacrifices offered in a true spirit of thanksgiving. Both 'thank-offerings' and 'vows' were sacrifices in which the worshippers shared in a meal, partaking of what they themselves had brought (Lev. 7:12; 22:29-30). The LORD did not *need* such sacrifices, but they were a means of expressing gratitude to him. A promise is added to the command. In difficult times prayer to God will result in deliverance. He does not need to be bribed by offerings, but will respond readily to the heartfelt cry of his people. Then in turn fresh honour will be given him for his answer.

3. True Obedience to the Law (*vv. 16-23*)
The first part of God's speech was directed against those who were trusting in the formal offering of sacrifices. Now attention is paid to those who, though offering sacrifices, were offending against the standards of God's covenant. **But to the wicked, God says: 'What right have you to recite my laws or take my covenant on your lips? You hate my instruction and cast my words behind you** (*vv. 16-17*). There were those within the covenant community whose life was a lie. They were transgressors, yet outwardly acknowledged their obedience to God's demands. They even recited the covenant regulations, but yet in reality they hated God's discipline (*mûsâr*, NIV 'instruction'). This word 'discipline' in its Old Testament usage suggests the fatherly correction that a son receives (cf. Deut. 11:2-7; Jer. 31:18). The reference to God's 'words' may well be specifically to the Decalogue, which is called 'the Ten Words' in the Hebrew text (Exod. 34:28; Deut. 4:13; 10:4). They were even prepared to reject the core of the covenant. The fact that the transgression was against God himself is stressed by repetition: '*my* statutes, *my* covenant, *my* words.' Paul develops the ideas present here more fully in Romans 2:17-29, where he distinguishes between external observance of the law and internal change of heart. The real Jew is one inwardly (2:29).

When you see a thief, you join with him; you throw in your lot with adulterers. You use your mouth for evil and harness your tongue to deceit. You speak continually against your brother and slander your own mother's son (*vv. 18-20*). The Seventh, Eighth, and Ninth Commandments were openly flouted. Theft and adultery were encouraged,[2] while the sins of the tongue were very evident. The closeness of family relationships did not prevent slander and lying, nor did belonging to a circle of friends. While the NIV translation of the beginning of verse 20 is possible,[3] it is better to take the Hebrew verb 'sit' literally. The imagery, then, is of a circle of friends conversing together with the bonds between them broken by false accusations. While the final word in the verse in the MT (*dofi*) only occurs here in the Old Testament, yet the parallelism in the verse points to a translation like that given in the NIV.[4] The sins of the tongue, as compared with other breaches of the Ten Commandments, take up an important place in the warnings of both the Old Testament and the New Testament (Col. 3:9; James 3:1-12). Just as with physical assault, slander is an attack on the image of God (James 3:9).

These things you have done and I kept silent; you thought I was altogether like you. But I will rebuke you and accuse you to your face (*v. 21*). God's silence was being misunderstood by the people. They were thinking that silence was acquiescence in their sin. This was not the only time in the Old Testament when this took place (see Mal. 2:17 and 3:14-15). One of the greatest mistakes humans can make is to think that God is like themselves. Sinners constantly want to exchange '"the glory of the immortal God for images made to look like mortal man and birds and animals and reptiles" (Rom. 1:23). The earlier assertion that God will not keep silent (*v. 3*) is now both reaffirmed and acted upon, as he rebukes and sets out the case against his people. The verb 'accuse'

---

[2] In the first clause the MT has 'and you were delighted with him' (*vattirets*) while the second clause lacks a verb, 'and with adulterers [is] your portion'. The LXX clearly accepted different vocalisation of the verb, reading it as *vatârâts*, 'and you ran along with him', while it added a verb to the second clause, 'and with adulterers *you set* your portion.' The first change is possible, though it does not alter the meaning to any extent, while the second is probably an attempt to render the phrase into Greek idiom rather than implying that there was an alternative Hebrew text available to the LXX translators.

[3] It is followed by Craigie, *Psalms 1-50*, p. 363, though he recognises that Dahood's rendering, 'you sit speaking,' is quite feasible.

[4] The literal rendering is 'you give fault'.

('*ārak*), while basically meaning 'to arrange in order', appears in forensic contexts such as this in the sense of stating one's case in a legal way (Job 13:18; 32:14; Ps. 5:3). At last God speaks, and he now reproves his erring covenant children. **Consider this, you who forget God, or I will tear you to pieces, with none to rescue: He who sacrifices thank-offerings honours me, and he prepares the way so that I may show him the salvation of God'** (*vv. 22-23*). As many as God loves he rebukes and chastens (Rev. 3:19). Those who forget God and despise his instruction are warned that he will come like a lion and tear them. Amos also uses the analogy of a lion to describe God's activities (Amos 3:8). Saying that there is 'none to rescue' is simply acknowledging that salvation was from God alone. In their usage of this phrase, the psalmists and prophets were probably following on from the words of Deuteronomy 32:39, 'no one delivers from his hand' (cf. in addition to Ps. 50:22, Ps. 71:11 and Isa. 42:22 and 43:13). What God wants is heartfelt worship from his people. The theme of the thanksgiving offerings is picked up again (see verse 14). While other sacrifices could be misunderstood as making God in some way obliged to the offerers, the thank-offerings were a response to grace. This was a way of honouring him, just as God requires of Christian people that they 'continually offer to God a sacrifice of praise – the fruit of lips that confess his name' (Heb. 13:15). As he thus prepares his way aright, he will know indeed that salvation is of God alone.

Psalm 51

To the director of music. A psalm of David. When the prophet Nathan came to him after David had committed adultery with Bathsheba.

This is the second of Luther's 'Pauline Psalms' (see Introduction), which declares the same way of forgiveness proclaimed in the New Testament. Traditionally, this psalm was one of the seven penitential psalms (6, 32, 38, 51, 102, 130, 143), a collection known to Augustine, and mentioned by Cassiodorus (AD c. 584). It was often known by its opening word in Latin, *miserere* ('have pity').

The title links it with David, and specifically the incidents concerning his adultery with Bathsheba and his arranging the death of her husband Uriah. This psalm should be read in conjunction with the historical account in 2 Samuel 11:2-12:24. While David received forgiveness from God, he still had to face the consequences of his sin, and this included the death of the child that Bathsheba bore (2 Sam. 12:18). Forgiveness does not free us from responsibility for our actions.

It is a psalm of confession before the LORD and of assurance of his pardon. Redeemed sinners know the reality of God's pardon, and they also share with David in his desire to tell others of the way back to him (see v. 13).

The intensity of David's intercession is marked by the number of imperatives in the text, especially in verses 6-15. The range of requests shows the great variety of different ways that appeal for pardon can take.

The closing verses of this psalm may have been added by a later poet, probably after the fall of Jerusalem in 586 BC, as they imply that the walls of the city have been broken down.[1] If this is so, then these verses form a lament by the community who want the LORD to respond to their need in a way similar to his response to David at his time of great personal need. King and people alike needed God's blessing and could respond with appropriate sacrifices (see vv. 17, 19).

1. A Cry for Mercy (*vv. 1-2*)

David cries for mercy out of the anguish of his heart. **Have mercy on me, O God, according to your unfailing love; according to your great compassion, blot out my transgressions** (*v. 1*). Realising his own great need, he calls for God's gracious act of mercy towards him. This is a prayer that David uses on various other occasions at the beginning of psalms (see Pss. 56, 57, and 86). The basis for his cry is God's unfailing love (Hebrew, *chésed*). This word carries with it the idea of absolute commitment. God had revealed himself to Moses as: 'The LORD, the LORD, the compassionate and gracious God, slow to anger, abounding in love and faithfulness' (Exod. 34:6). He would not go back on that word, and David accordingly pleads for a fresh visitation of mercy for himself. The second part of verse 1 parallels 'great compassion' with 'unfailing love', and 'blot out my transgressions' with 'have mercy'. Because he was conscious of his 'great' sin, he recognises that he needs 'great' compassion. The verb 'blot out' has the idea of wiping a dish clean, or removing something completely.

The next verse repeats the call for mercy but uses other terms: **Wash away all my iniquity and cleanse me from my sin** (*v. 2*). The verb 'wash' is preceded in Hebrew by a form of the verb 'to be many', which some think means that David is praying for repeated cleansings. This goes contrary to the context, which suggests a once-for-all act on God's part, and the verb 'wash' is used elsewhere in the Old Testament for the removal of sin (Isa. 1:16; Jer. 2:22; 4:14). Similarly, the word

---

[1] Cf. Psalm 89:38-51, which appears to be another instance of later words being added to an earlier song. It is clear from the quotations in the historical books that parts of songs were often blended together. See, for example, 1 Chronicles 16:8-36, where sections of Psalms 105, 96, and 107 form the song that David first committed to Asaph and his fellow singers.

'cleanse' is used of a declaration that the priest made over the cleansed leper (Lev. 13:6, 34). Only God can declare the sinner clean.

The cluster of words in these first two verses is remarkable. It contains a rich vocabulary of language relating to sin and forgiveness. To describe his (and our) relationship to God, David uses:

> *transgression*: rebellious actions against authority;
> *iniquity*: what is crooked or bent;
> *sin*: missing the mark;
> *have mercy*: a request that speaks of graciousness beyond expectation;
> *unfailing love*: the term of covenantal commitment;
> *compassion*: the word describing the tenderest love;
> *blot out*: complete removal;
> *wash away*: used of scrubbing clothes and removing all stains;
> *cleanse*: a ritual term for pronouncing someone clean.

2. Confession of Sin (*vv. 3-6*)

David cannot escape from his sin. He says: **For I know my transgressions and my sin is always before me** (*v. 3*; cf. Ps. 32:3, 4). Luther puts this truth in this way: 'My sin plagues me, gives me no rest, no peace; whether I eat or drink, sleep or wake, I am always in terror of God's wrath and judgment.' The psalmist is ready to acknowledge his wayward actions, and he is unable to escape from the consciousness of guilt. For no matter how much he had sinned against others (and specifically against Bathsheba and Uriah), yet the reality of the situation is that his sin was primarily against God.

Against you, you only, have I sinned and done what is evil in your sight (*v. 4a*). This translation brings out well the force of the Hebrew word order here. The primary focus of sin is against God. Though men might have acquitted David, yet he knows that before God he is guilty of adultery and murder. The words that follow, **so that you are proved right when you speak and justified when you judge** (*v. 4b*), have created considerable discussion, because how can God be justified in his speaking? Probably, it is best to think of God being true to his pledged word (see comments on v. 1). He is 'justified' when he hears the cry for mercy and acts in accordance with his covenantal promise. These words are quoted by Paul in Romans 3:4.

David's sin, in this case, is not his first sin, for he has been a sinner from the very beginning. Having looked back to the immediate past, he now focuses on the distant past, even to his birth. As he has owned up to his repeated sins (note the fivefold use of 'my' in vv. 1-3), so he acknowledges the bias in his nature. **Surely** (Hebrew, *hên, behold*) **I was sinful at birth, sinful from the time my mother conceived me** (*v. 5*). He is speaking of the inborn bias that affects all of us by nature. Sin inevitably appears in each new life because it is now part of human nature as a result of Adam's sin ('sin entered the world through one man, and death through sin, and in this way death came to all men', Rom. 5:12). The only one to escape this taint of sin was Jesus (Heb. 4:15), and that was because he was conceived in Mary's womb by the Holy Spirit (Matt. 1:20-21; Luke 1:35-37).[2]

Even as a sinner David knows the standard that God requires. **Surely you desire truth in the inner parts; you teach me wisdom in the inmost place** (*v. 6*). God demands integrity and uprightness, characteristics that David now knew that he lacked. The way of God's wisdom has been forsaken for the way that seems right to a man, but which in the end brings death (Prov. 14:12).

3. Prayer for Forgiveness (*vv. 7-9*)

With deep intensity of heart David prays for cleansing and forgiveness. **Cleanse me with hyssop, and I will be clean; wash me and I will be whiter than snow** (*v. 7*). Hyssop, a common plant, was used at the Passover (Exod. 12:22), and in various procedures carried out by the priests (see Lev. 14:4, 6, 49, 51, 52). Now David asks for God to sprinkle him so that he will become even whiter than snow. This analogy is

---

[2] The *Westminster Shorter Catechism* Q. 16 carefully notes that all mankind descending from Adam 'by ordinary generation' are sinners, thus excluding Jesus.

taken up later in the Old Testament, seemingly in conscious dependence upon this verse. To the sinful people in Isaiah's day, whose hands were full of blood, the LORD says: 'Though your sins are like scarlet, they shall be as white as snow' (Isa. 1:18). In both Psalm 51 and Isaiah 1 it is clear that God's forgiveness can be experienced, provided that true repentance is shown.

To this petition for cleansing David adds: **Let me hear joy and gladness; let the bones you have crushed rejoice** (*v. 8*). Under God's chastening hand, he feels crushed and bruised, and longs for festive joy to be given to him. This is part of God's forgiveness, as his children rejoice in his mercy and love to them. The compound phrase 'joy and gladness' (*sâsôn v°simchâh*) occurs thirteen times in the Old Testament,[3] and with the addition of 'gladness' (or another cognate noun such as 'shout of joy', *rinnâh*) it denotes an enthusiastic expression of joy. Isaiah uses the phrase when speaking of great redemptive acts of God (Isa. 35:10; 51:3, 11), while Jeremiah uses it five times (Jer. 7:34; 15:16; 16:9; 25:10; 33:11). The expression, 'crushed bones', represents the ultimate in physical or psychological distress.[4]

Hide your face from my sins and blot out all my iniquity (*v. 9*). At other times in the Old Testament the people cry out to God because he has hidden his face from them (see e.g. Pss. 10:1; 44:24; 88:14; 104:29; Isa. 8:17). Here David desires that God will not look on his sin, covering his eyes, as it were, so that he would not see his evil deeds. The thought of verse 1 ('blot out my transgressions') reappears with the appeal to 'blot out' completely his iniquities. As the following verses show, David recognised that what was needed was a new creative act by God.

---

[3] Of these occurrences all but two of them (Esther 8:16-17: 'gladness and joy') have the order of the words as here. However, the alteration of order with fixed pairs (see Glossary) is not uncommon, without any discernible difference in meaning.

[4] The verbal form *dikkîtâ* in this verse and the participle *nidkeh* in verse 17 come from the root *d-k-h*, but it is unsure whether this is a discrete verbal root or merely a by-form of the root *d-k-'*. The best discussion on this question is in *TDOT*, III, pp. 195-98.

4. A Call for a Renewed Heart (*vv. 10-12*)

Create in me a pure heart, O God, and renew a steadfast spirit within me (v. 10). The Hebrew verb used for 'create' (*bârâ'*) is exclusively employed in the Old Testament with God as the subject, and here it is paralleled with 'renew'. It is also linked with the word 'steadfast', which comes from a Hebrew word that is often associated with God's creative activity (Ps. 24:2: 'established it upon the waters'; Isa. 45:18). Purification from sin is a work of God alone.

> Not the labours of my hands
> Can fulfil thy laws demands;
> Could my zeal no respite know,
> Could my tears for ever flow,
> All for sin could not atone;
> Thou must save and thou alone.
> (Augustus Toplady, 1740-1778)

When confronted with our sin, there is a feeling that we are to be banished from God's presence because of it. Hence David prays: **Do not cast me from your presence or take your Holy Spirit from me. Restore to me the joy of your salvation and grant me a willing spirit, to sustain me** (*vv. 11-12*). The Holy Spirit was operative in the Old Testament period, though a new phase of the Spirit's ministry began with the death and resurrection of Jesus and the Day of Pentecost. Old Testament believers had the same indwelling Spirit as Christians today, and David pleads that he will not experience the withdrawal of that Spirit. The presence of sin also causes absence of joy, because peace has gone. With the coming of forgiveness there can be a restoration of the joy of salvation. In addition to 'a pure heart' and 'the Holy Spirit' the psalmist also wants 'a willing spirit'. This term carries echoes of freewill offerings such as the voluntary sacrifices that were made, not out of command but as an act of religious devotion.[5]

---

[5] The verb *nâdav* is used to express uncompelled willingness to worship or sacrifice to God. The associated noun *nᵉdâvâh* describes acts that are free. What is typical of the person who is voluntarily sacrificing or worshipping is denoted by the term used here in Psalm 51:12, *nᵉdîvâh*.

4. A Thankful Heart (*vv. 13-17*)

The response of a purified sinner is to seek to make known the good news of God's grace, just as Isaiah later offered himself so willingly as the LORD's messenger (Isa. 6:8). The psalmist had a similar experience. **Then I will teach transgressors your ways, and sinners will turn back to you. Save me from bloodguilt, O God, the God who saves me** (*vv. 13-14a*). An experience of redeeming grace creates an urge to tell others of the LORD's forgiveness and a desire to teach them his ways. The ultimate aim is to see other sinners coming back to God in repentance and faith. The verb 'turn back' (Hebrew, *shûv*) is often used of repentance and of a return to God (Isa. 44:22; Hos. 6:1). David has just asked that God will restore to him the joy of salvation (*shûv* Hi.) and now uses the same verb of his action towards other sinners (*shûv* Qal). The one to whom joy has been restored will himself be the means of restoring others to God. David's sin weighs heavily upon him, and he seems to fear especially the result of his murder of Uriah. The word 'bloodguilt' is literally 'bloods', and by comparison with Genesis 4:10 it denotes bloodshed, murder. Rather than thinking of protection of David from vengeance from Uriah's family, it is preferable to see it as a prayer for deliverance from the guilt of his crime, by the God who saves him. In this way the ideas fit in best with the whole context in the psalm.

A forgiven sinner also wants to praise God for what he has done. **And my tongue will sing of your righteousness. O Lord, open my lips, and my mouth will declare your praise** (*vv. 14b-15*). Here David shows the spirit of thanksgiving that filled him after God heard his cry. The word of pardon came through the prophet Nathan who said to him: 'The LORD has taken away your sin' (2 Sam. 12:13b). His desire is that God will open his lips, and that his mouth will be filled with God's righteousness and praise. This commitment to praise is one of the firstfruits of salvation. Under the Mosaic law various sacrifices were appointed, but there was none for premeditated murder. David's action came under the category of sins of a high hand (see Num. 15:30), for he had acted defiantly and in rebellion against God's law.[6]

But even if a sacrifice could be offered, David rightly recognises that the spirit in which it is offered is primarily important. The Old Testament sacrificial system was never meant to operate without consideration of the heart of the offerer. **You do not delight in sacrifice, or I would bring it; you do not take pleasure in burnt offerings. The sacrifices of God are** (or NIV margin, **My sacrifice, O God, is ...**) **a broken spirit; a broken and contrite heart, O God, you will not despise** (*vv. 16-17*). Mere formal ceremony could never result in forgiveness. Rather, there had to be a heart touched by the Holy Spirit, the one who convicts of sin (John 16:8). The NIV margin represents a very slight change in vocalisation of the MT (*zivkî* instead of *zivchê*), but, as no manuscript support is available, it is best retain the MT and hence the translation 'the sacrifices of'. Brokenness in this case is a sign of deep distress of heart over sin. The word 'contrite' is from the same verb used in verse 8, '*crushed* bones', and it would be best to use the word 'crushed' here as well. 'Contrite' is almost exclusively a theological term, whereas the Hebrew verb in question corresponds exactly to both literal and figurative usages of 'crushed'.

5. Prayer for Zion (*vv. 18-19*)

If these words are those of David, he could be acknowledging that his sin has serious consequences for the whole nation, using concrete illustrations ('Zion', 'walls of Jerusalem') to depict spiritual realities. However, it is preferable to view them as words added during the period between the fall of Jerusalem in 586 BC and the commencement of the rebuilding in 536 BC. The community wants the LORD to respond to their need, just as he did when David cried to him out of his grief of heart. **In your good pleasure make Zion prosper; build up the walls of Jerusalem. Then there will be righteous**

---

[6] An excellent summary of the law relating to 'a high hand' is given by R. K. Harrison, *Numbers*, Wycliffe Bible Commentary (Chicago: Moody Press, 1990), p. 227.

sacrifices, whole burnt offerings to delight you; then bulls will be offered on your altar (*vv. 18-19*). These words show that the preceding reference to sacrifices was not to disparage the whole sacrificial system as such. God had set his choice upon Jerusalem, and the prayer is that God's blessing on, and protection of, his people will continue. Then the people will be able to continue with their sacrifices, and bring offerings with which God will be well pleased. When the rebuilding of the walls of Jerusalem was completed, the fulfillment of this prayer took place: 'And on that day they offered great sacrifices, rejoicing because God had given them great joy. The women and the children also rejoiced. The sound of rejoicing in Jerusalem could be heard far away' (Neh. 12:43).

Psalm 52

For the director of music. A maskil of David. When Doeg the Edomite had gone to Saul and told him: 'David has gone to the house of Ahimelech.'

Psalms 51 and 52, though placed in adjoining positions, are in marked contrast with one another. Psalm 51 deals with David's deep need for God's forgiveness, whereas Psalm 52 contains an extended description of David's enemies, with curses having divine authority being expressed against them. In this respect the psalmist is acting very similarly to the prophets who also proclaimed divine punishment on the ungodly. Though not of the same type as Psalm 49 (a wisdom psalm), yet there are many similarities between the two.

This is one of eight psalms (Pss. 7, 34, 52, 54, 56, 57, 59, 142) whose titles link them with the period in which David was pursued by Saul. The historical note in this title alludes to the incident in David's life when Doeg betrayed the priests who had helped David. When the king's officials were not prepared to kill the priests, Doeg carried out the executions (1 Sam. 22:6-18). Though the title mentions Doeg, it does not necessarily mean that Doeg is the subject of the psalm. It makes better sense to understand it as referring to Saul. The description of the enemy throughout does not match with what is known about Doeg, the servant, but with Saul, 'the mighty man'.[1] While complaining about his enemy at the

---

[1] Older commentators took this position. See, for example, E. W. Hengstenberg, *Psalms*, II, pp. 211-12; J. A. Alexander, *The Psalms Translated and Explained*, p. 236. In more recent times it has been common to reject the superscription as being inaccurate. However, H. C. Leupold, *Exposition of the Psalms*, pp. 409-11, accepts that Saul is in view, a view shared with J. Barton Payne, *TWOT*, 1, p. 210.

beginning of the psalm, by the end the psalmist is expressing confident trust in God.

1. A Complaint against the Evildoer (vv. 1-4)

Why do you boast of evil, you mighty man? Why do you boast all day long, you who are a disgrace in the eyes of God? (v. 1). It is very unusual to find a psalm that does not begin by addressing God, but this one is first directed to an evil man. He is described as a 'mighty man' or 'noble', and because 'nobles' had the privilege of bearing arms for the king (cf. Ruth 2:1; 1 Sam. 9:1) the term then became applied to warriors or soldiers. It is possible that the word comes near to meaning 'tyrant',[2] though he uses words, not the sword, as his weapon. The last part of the verse is difficult and the NIV translation follows the LXX. The Hebrew text says: 'covenant love (*chésed*) of God all the day', which makes sense in the context and was supported by older commentators.[3] It also gives a striking contrast between the animosity of the mighty man and the abiding love of the LORD. Another possibility is to follow the Syriac version and take this as the Hebrew word *châsîd*, which denotes a loyal covenant servant. It would then be a description of the psalmist: 'Why do you boast all day long against God's loyal servant?'[4]

Your tongue plots destruction; it is like a sharpened razor, you who practise deceit (v. 2). The warrior is not described by exploits in battle, but by his ability to use his tongue as his weapon to cause harm. The comparison of the tongue with a sharp razor is not common, whereas linking it with 'deceit' (*r^emiyyâh*) and 'falsehood' (*shéqer*) is (note the use of 'deceit' again in v. 4, and 'falsehood' in v. 5). The phrase, who 'practises deceit', is literally 'one who does deceit' and a good modern English equivalent is 'con-man'.[5] The exact phrase appears again in Psalm 101:7,

---

[2] The cognate word in Arabic has this meaning.
[3] For example, J. A. Alexander, *The Psalms Translated and Explained*, p. 236; F. Delitzsch, *Psalms*, II, pp. 143-44.
[4] For more details and other possibilities, see M. Tate, *Psalms 51-100*, p. 33.
[5] This is the translation of M. Tate, ibid., p. 32. For other synonymous phrases involving the tongue, see Eugene H. Merrill, *NIDOTTE*, 2, p. 821.

while the expression 'a deceitful tongue' occurs twice in Psalm 120, in verses 2 and 3.

You love evil rather than good, falsehood rather than speaking the truth. Selah (*v. 3*). It adds to the accusation when the psalmist speaks directly to the tongue itself (cf. a similar usage in Ps. 120:2). Deceit and destruction that are the hallmarks of the enemy proceed from a heart that is set on evil ways. The preference for evil is an ingrained characteristic, and thus falsehood takes the place of righteousness (NIV 'truth'). 'Selah' occurs at the end of this verse and also of verse 7. These occurrences conform to a common pattern of dividing psalms into three sections by the use of the Hebrew word *sélâh*, but still do not explain whether it is a musical term or serves some other function (see the comments on 3:3).

You love every harmful word, O you deceitful tongue! (*v. 4*). The repetition of 'you love' at the beginning of two consecutive verses serves to reinforce the directness of the accusations. The words that bring destruction are what he treasures. A 'harmful word' (*bâlaʻ*) is one that devours or swallows (cf. Jer. 51:44, which has the only other instance of this word in the Old Testament).

2. God's Judgment Announced (*v. 5*)

Surely God will bring you down to everlasting ruin: He will snatch you up and tear you from your tent; he will uproot you from the land of the living. Selah (*v. 5*). The opening word could also be rendered 'therefore', introducing the concept of judgment on those who lead ungodly lives.[6] The contrast is presented of God's righteous judgment, and the words used to describe it suggest the suddenness with which it comes: 'snatch', 'tear', 'uproot'. 'Everlasting ruin' is a rather free rendering of the MT (*lânétsach*), which only indicates everlastingness. A suitable translation is by a phrase like 'for ever', or, if taken as a superlative, a word such as 'utterly' (cf. NLT, 'But God will strike you down once and for all'). The

---

[6] M. Tate, *Psalms 51-100*, pp. 32, 34, correctly notes this usage of the Hebrew word *gam*. See also the range of meanings listed in *DCH*, II, p. 357, including 'therefore'.

reference to the 'tent' does not seem to be to the tabernacle, but rather to the individual dwelling of the unrighteous person. To be taken from the land of the living is synonymous with death (cf. the same phrase used of the Servant of the Lord in Isa. 53:8). Again *Selah* marks the conclusion of another section of the psalm (see comment on verse 3).

3. The Blessing of the Righteous (*vv. 6-9*)

The righteous will see and fear; they will laugh at him, saying, 'Here now is the man who did not make God his stronghold but trusted in his great wealth and grew strong by destroying others!' (*vv. 6-7*). When the righteous see the judgment of God they stand in awe, for in this way God has displayed his righteous wrath. They also understand that this judgment is meant to be an encouragement to them, and so they rejoice in it. Their laughter is not so much derision as joyful recognition of the just nature of God's actions. They point, in effect, to the unrighteous person, 'See there ...' (Hebrew lit. 'behold the man'). If a man fails to make God his refuge, and trusts in his own riches, isn't it right then if he is uprooted? The pride of the unrighteous is displayed in his boasting and his arrogant attacks on others, seeking to destroy them.[7]

But I am like an olive tree flourishing in the house of God; I trust in God's unfailing love for ever and ever (*v. 8*). The same sort of contrast is drawn between the righteous and the wicked as is made in Psalm 1. Whereas the wicked are like trees that will be uprooted, the righteous are like a flourishing olive tree. The comparison with an olive tree is probably because of its long life and its productive nature. The psalmist expresses the constancy of his trust in God's covenantal love,

---

[7] The MT is difficult in verse 7d, and this explains some variation in English versions (cf. ESV: 'and sought refuge in his own destruction'). The first problem is the verb *yāʿoz*, which could be either from the verb ʿ-z-z, 'be strong', or from ʿûz, 'to take refuge'. As vocalised, it is the former verb, and the meaning fits the context. The second problem is that the final word could be 'in his desire', but as the word 'destruction' has already occurred in verse 2, it seems best to retain it here. An emendation, followed by the RSV translators ('in his wealth'), is unnecessary.

that trust being in marked contrast to the false trust of the unrighteous in his own wealth (v. 7).[8]

I will praise you forever for what you have done; in your name I will hope, for your name is good. I will praise you in the presence of your saints (*v. 9*). God's actions on behalf of his people call forth praise, and this also involves offering praise in an assembly of God's people. His goodness has been displayed to the psalmist who now wants to acknowledge that fact. With the acknowledgment comes a further expression of confident trust in God's character ('your name'), which has been shown to be both good and loving. Much of the language of this verse was clearly part of the common formulae used in praising God for past actions ('what you have done', cf. Ps. 22:31, 'that he has done [it]'; for 'I will wait for your name, for it is good', cf. Pss. 54:6; 100:5; 106:1; 107:1; 135:3; and 136:1).

---

[8] The same verb (*bâtach*) is used in both verses.

Psalm 53

For the director of music. According to mahalath.
A maskil of David.

For comments on the comparison between this psalm and Psalm 14, see commentary on Psalm 14. Repetition of the words from other psalms is a regular feature in the Psalter. Thus Psalm 70 is virtually the same as Psalm 40:13-17, while Psalm 108 repeats the words of Psalm 57:7-11 and Psalm 60:5-12. When earlier words are taken up and used again, there is often some variation in the text to accord with the new situation in which it is used. This is definitely so in this case.

Psalm 53 has a longer title than Psalm 14, including two technical terms, *mâchᵃlat* and *maskîl*. The former occurs elsewhere only in the title of Psalm 88, where it may mean 'sickness', 'suffering', but such a meaning is not particularly appropriate for this psalm.[1] It has also been suggested that it may denote a mournful tune of that name, which certainly fits fairly well in both settings. *Maskîl* is probably a skilfully constructed song or tune, though here the presence of the word in verse 2 may have prompted its use in the title.

In the early part of the psalm, in addition to the alteration of the divine name ('God' replaces 'Lord'), 'iniquity' replaces 'deeds' in verse 1. The expression, 'doing abominable iniquity', strengthens the condemnation and also points further to the narrative in Genesis 6:5-12 forming the background for the description here (see comment on Ps. 14:1-2). The NIV appears to regard the changed term as meaning 'ways'. Then in

---

[1] The suggestion that *mâchᵃlat* could mean 'sickness' stems largely from its similarity to the word *machᵃlâh* that means 'sickness' or 'disease'. However, no proof exists that *mâchᵃlat* comes from the root *ch-l-h*.

verse 3 there is a slight change concerning 'all', and in place of 'turned aside' in Psalm 14:3, the verb is 'turned back' (Hebrew *sûg* in place of *sûr*). Sinful man turns away from God and the only restorative for apostates, including Israel, is the grace and power of God (see the use of *sûg* in Ps. 80:17-18). The more important change is in connection with verses 5-6 in Psalm 14: **There they are overwhelmed with dread, for God is present in the company of the righteous. You evildoers frustrate the plans of the poor, but the LORD is their refuge.** In place of that, Psalm 53:5 has: **There they were, overwhelmed with dread, where there was nothing to dread. God scattered the bones of those who attacked you; you put them to shame, for God despised them.** This verse seems to have been altered to this form to make specific reference to a great historical occasion. The most probable one would have been the destruction of Sennacherib's army by the angel of the LORD (2 Kings 19:35; Isa. 37:36). The meaning would be that God's people were greatly afraid, when there was nothing to fear. The bones of the Assyrian army were scattered on the field, and God had shown how he despised those who were classed with the fools and those who did not know him. For comment on the other verses, see the notes on Psalm 14.

Psalm 54

For the director of music. With stringed instruments. A maskil of David. When the Ziphites had gone to Saul and said, 'Is not David hiding among us?'

The title of this psalm is similar to that of Psalm 52, in that an incident from David's life, when fleeing from Saul, forms its basis (cf. 1 Sam. 23:19; 26:1), though coupled with directions for its use in the tabernacle/temple. The Ziphites seemed to have antipathy to David, perhaps because they did not want a roving band in their territory, led by such a gifted leader. They wanted to be rid of David, and went twice to Saul seeking action against him (1 Sam. 23:19-24; 26:1-5). However, the contents of the psalm do not explain how it ties in with that incident. Its scope is sufficiently wide to allow any persecuted believer to use it as a request for divine intervention.

1. Petition for Deliverance (*vv. 1-3*)
Save me, O God, by your name; vindicate me by your might (*v. 1*). The psalm starts with a reference to God's name, and it ends with praise of it (v. 6). The psalmist calls to God because he knows God's character, and therefore he can confidently cry for help. He seeks deliverance from his present distress, which went beyond the slanderous attacks being made on him. Murder was also part of the scheme (v. 3). The call is to his Saviour and to his Judge. 'Vindicate' (*dîn*) has practically the same meaning as 'judge' (*shâfat*), though it is more common in the poetical books and may well be the more archaic term.[1] It also is used practically exclusively of divine activity, with its occurrence in Ezra 7:25 being the only time it is used of human judges.

---
[1] This is the view of R. D. Culver in *TWOT*, 1, p. 188, who provides a concise summary of the usage of *dîn*.

Hear my prayer, O God; listen to the words of my mouth (*v. 2*). The opening words of the verse seem to have been a standard way of requesting help: 'Hear my prayer, listen to ...' (Pss. 4:1; 84:8; 143:1). At times, customary expressions take on a new urgency, when circumstances drive us to seek God's immediate help. This prayer is a request for God to hear and answer, with no great difference between the verbs 'hear' (*shāmaʿ*) and 'listen' (*'āzan* Hi.), though the latter is predominantly a poetic word. **Strangers are attacking me; ruthless men seek my life – men without regard for God. Selah** (*v. 3*). The word 'strangers' (*zārîm*) is replaced by the word 'proud' (*zēdîm*) in many Hebrew manuscripts and in the Targum. These two words are very similar and the letters *dālet* and *rêsh* can be confused, though in the older form of the Hebrew script they are quite distinct. When this verse reappears in Psalm 86:14 the word is certainly 'proud, arrogant'. These facts explain the variation in some English translations here (cf. NEB 'insolent men'), and though 'proud' fits the context well, the manuscript evidence is not strong enough to compel an emendation here. These violent men are coming against the psalmist with murderous intent. They do not give God the pre-eminence in their lives, and consequently they do not live by his commands (Ps. 119:30). Both terms, 'strangers' and 'violent men', could have been applied to Saul and his men, while the Ziphites could be designated as 'strangers' because of their unneighbourly behaviour.

2. Confidence in God (*vv. 4-5*)
Surely God is my help; the Lord is the one who sustains me. Let evil recoil on those who slander me; in your faithfulness destroy them (*vv. 4-5*). The psalmist turns to the one source of assistance. He certainly knows that the Lord is his only helper.[2] The wish for judgment to come

---

[2] The statement is introduced, as the one in Psalm 52:7, with the word *hinnêh*. While this word normally means 'behold', 'when introducing asseveration or strong affirmation' it can be translated by 'indeed' or 'surely'. See *DCH*, 2, p. 574. An excellent discussion on *hinnêh* can be found in T. O. Lambdin, *Introduction to Biblical Hebrew* (New York: Charles Scribner, 1971), pp. 169-70. A discussion on the role this particle plays in emphasis is in T. Muraoka, *Emphatic Words and Structures in Biblical Hebrew* (Leiden: E. J. Brill, 1985), pp. 137-40.

upon his slanderers has to be understood in the light of the broader question of cursing in the Psalms (see section on the Imprecatory Psalms in the Introduction). Because the slanderers are indeed opponents of God himself, the psalmist prays for their destruction.[3] He knows that God acts in accordance with his faithfulness, and protection to his people is but a tangible expression of it.

3. Spontaneous Thanksgiving (*vv. 6-7*)
I will sacrifice a freewill offering to you; I will praise your name, O LORD, for it is good. For he has delivered me from all my troubles, and my eyes have looked in triumph on my foes (*vv. 5-6*). The offer is made of a voluntary sacrifice. Such a sacrifice could be made at any time by a thankful Israelite (see Lev. 22:18-30; Num. 15:1-10). Praise is to be given to God because he has shown his goodness, expressed in a standard formula (see comment on Ps. 52:9). The psalmist anticipates the LORD's deliverance from all his troubles, and he acquiesces in God's judgment. The final clause has nothing in the MT corresponding to 'in triumph', which is added to many English translations. Without this addition the verse indicates that the psalmist can look on his enemies without any fear or alarm; for he knows that he is protected by God's power.

---

[3] The consonants in the MT for 'let recoil' point to a Qal form of the verb 'to return' (*shûv*), vocalised either as *yâshûv* ('it will return') or *yâshov* ('let it return'), though the Jewish Massoretes vocalised it as *yâshîv* (Hi.).

Psalm 55

For the director of music. With stringed instruments. A maskil of David.

Older Jewish interpreters linked this psalm with the betrayal of David by his counsellor Ahithophel (2 Sam. 16:15-23; 1 Chron. 27:33). Modern writers have often drawn a comparison between the experience of the psalmist and that of the prophet Jeremiah. He too wished to be far off in a desert (vv. 6-7, cf. Jer. 9:2), he suffered at the hands of his own family (Jer. 12:6), and a fellow priest, Pashur, had him beaten and placed in stocks (Jer. 20:1-2). There is an ancient tradition in the Latin church that the psalmist's experience points to the betrayal of Jesus by Judas.

This is a psalm of complaint, as the writer speaks about the terrors that have come to him (v. 5). He also is suffering from a severe reversal of friendship with one who was previously his close companion (vv. 20-21). In all these experiences, though, he learns how to cast his burden on the LORD (v. 22).

Certainly our Lord's betrayal gives us the highest example of the pattern of suffering described here by the psalmist. It is of great encouragement to us that because Jesus 'suffered when he was tempted, he is able to help those who are being tempted' (Heb. 2:18).

1. A Call for Help (*vv. 1-3*)

The psalm opens with a despairing cry. **Listen to my prayer, O God, do not ignore my plea; hear me and answer me** (*v. 1*). From his distress the psalmist appeals for help. His request, that God should not ignore his plea, recalls the passage in Deuteronomy 22:1-4 where the same verb is used (*'ālam*). When a person saw a neighbour's ox or sheep in trouble, they

419

were not to ignore it. Here the psalmist feels as if he is being ignored by God, as if he is unwilling to help. The parallel phrases take the request a stage further, for he wants God not merely to hear but to respond. **My thoughts trouble me and I am distraught at the voice of the enemy, at the stares of the wicked; for they bring down suffering upon me and revile me in their anger** (*vv. 2-3*). He not only has trouble from outside himself, but his own thoughts cause him distress. The MT is difficult because three of the phrases involve problematic words, though the NIV captures the general meaning.[1] The psalmist is humiliated, and the sound of the approaching enemy overwhelms him. That enemy is not identified, except by the description of being 'wicked'. What the wicked do to him is the result of hatred and it is intended to cause him distress. This is aggravated by the fact that the wicked bring verbal accusations against him. They act as court adversaries.[2]

2. Anguish of Heart (*vv. 4-8*)

A succession of words descriptive of the deep trouble of his heart flow from the psalmist's mouth. **My heart is in anguish within me; the terrors of death assail me. Fear and trembling have beset me; horror has overwhelmed me** (*vv. 4-5*). He is under intolerable strain as he faces the attacks of his enemy. He even compares himself to a woman in childbirth (NIV 'in anguish'). The fear he has is that death is near at hand, and the

---

[1] The problems of translation and interpretation here are well set out by Marvin Tate, *Psalms 51–100*, p. 51. NIV 'my thoughts' (*sîchî*) is probably a little weak, as this noun generally has the connotation of a spoken complaint. 'Trouble' represents a verbal form '*ârîd*, but it could be derived from several different roots. The LXX rendering *elupêthên*, 'to give pain to someone', is helpful and supports the NIV translation. 'Distraught' renders a verb that is cohortative 1 sing. in form, though again the root is uncertain. However, the LXX helps by using the verb *tarassô*, pass. 'to be disturbed'. This verb is descriptive 'of mental and spiritual agitation and confusion': W. F. Arndt and F. W. Gingrich, *A Greek-Lexicon of the New Testament* (Chicago: University of Chicago Press,1957), p. 813. The word '*âqâh* (NIV 'stares') is a *hapax legomenon*, and the meaning may possibly be from a Semitic root meaning 'to apply pressure'.

[2] The verb here (*sâtan*) is the root from which the noun *sâtân*, 'accuser', comes.

great anxiety he is experiencing produces physical symptoms of trembling and shuddering.[3] **I said, 'Oh, that I had the wings of a dove! I would fly away and be at rest – I would flee far away and stay in the desert. Selah. I would hurry to my place of shelter, far from the tempest and storm'** (*vv. 6-8*). Another way of describing his despair is to wish that he was far off in some desert location.[4] He wants to fly like a dove and find a safe dwelling place (NIV 'be at rest'). Some additional word is needed in the opening of verse 7 as the MT has *hinnêh*. NASB has the more traditional 'behold', while the ESV has 'yes, I would flee away'. Lodging in the desert[5] would mean that there would be escape from his persecutors as he would find a hiding place there, while 'place of shelter' or 'haven' is one of the synonyms for 'refuge'.[6] Imagery such as that employed here may well reflect military campaigns in the rocky hills of Judah. Jeremiah uses the same imagery of a place in the desert (Jer. 9:2) and of the dove finding a safe nest (Jer. 48:28). 'Tempest and storm' tell of the reality of his present distress.

3. A Lament over Betrayal (*vv. 9-15*)

The psalmist lodges his complaint with God. **Confuse the wicked, O Lord, confound their speech, for I see violence and strife in the city** (*v. 9*). 'Confuse' is literally 'swallow', and it is used to ask for destruction of the oppressors. The idea of confounding the speech is probably intended to recall what

---

[3] NIV 'horror' is the translation of a rare word only occurring three times in addition to this verse (Isa. 21:4; Job 7:18. 21:6). Etymology and context suggest a translation such as 'shuddering'. See M. Dahood, 'Hebrew-Ugaritic Lexicography VIII', *Biblica* 51 (1970), pp. 397-98.

[4] The wish is expressed in a common Hebrew form, 'Who will give to me …' (*mî yittên lî*). Other good examples in the Psalms are found in 14:7 and 53:7. For discussion on this idiom see *DIHG~S*, pp. 185-86, and R. J. Williams, *Hebrew Syntax: An Outline*, 2nd ed. (Toronto: University of Toronto Press, 1984), pp. 21, 91-92.

[5] 'Lodge' represents the Hebrew verb *lîn* which usually means 'to spend the night', but it does seem to have a wider connotation, and so NIV 'stay' is acceptable (cf. the use of this verb in Ruth 1:16 and Prov. 15:31). Marvin Tate, *Psalms 51-100*, p. 52, suggests the translation 'bivouac in the wilderness'.

[6] This word, *miflât*, only occurs here, but the verb from which it comes (*pâlat*, 'escape') is quite frequent.

happened at Babel, when God thwarted the sinful plans of men by confusing their language (Gen. 11:1-9). There is no way of identifying the city, as the Hebrew word (*'ir*) denotes a settlement with fortifications, irrespective of its size. It is a place where the psalmist had experienced violence and strife. **Day and night they prowl about on its walls; malice and abuse are within it. Destructive forces are at work in the city; threats and lies never leave its streets** (*vv. 10-11*). His expressions depict both the character of the city, and the constancy with which the forces of evil show themselves in it. The MT does not identify the subject of the verb 'prowl' (lit. 'go around'). It could be the evildoers, or else, with an ironic twist, 'malice' and 'abuse' are the watchmen on the walls. They are the appointed 'protectors'! 'Abuse' (Hebrew *tok*) is a rare word only occurring four times (in addition to this verse, Pss. 10:7; 72:14; and Prov. 29:13). In this context it is descriptive of a violent, strife-torn city, and since the other instances link it with oppression of the poor, it probably also connotes exploitation of the weak. The city's market area (NIV 'streets') is no longer a place for peaceful trading but distinguished by deceitful practices and danger.

If an enemy were insulting me, I could endure it; if a foe were raising himself against me, I could hide from him. But it is you, a man like myself, my companion, my close friend, with whom I once enjoyed sweet fellowship as we walked with the throng at the house of God (*vv. 12-14*). The opening clauses of verse 12 have problems. The NIV follows the LXX that alters the MT, 'For it is not an enemy that insults me', by a change of one word (MT *lo'*, 'not', changed to *lû*, '*if*'), 'For if an enemy ...' This is not sufficient evidence to warrant emending the MT, and a translation such as, 'For it is not an enemy who taunts me – I could bear [that]', makes good sense.[7] If the opponent was already an enemy, the psalmist could deal with the situation. However, the person is close to him, someone of like mind, though we are not provided

---

[7] This is the translation by Marvin Tate, *Psalms 51-100*, pp. 50, 52.

with enough information to enable identification of David's friend. Within his own close circle of friends, one proved to be a traitor, and that makes the pain of the incident all the more intense. A friend of equal rank with himself, and with whom he had been closely associated in worship or other festive occasions, had turned against him.[8] It is not 'an enemy' or 'a foe' who was insulting him, but one of his own companions. The tragedy of David's words here is that they apply to his own treachery against Uriah, who is reckoned among David's closest associates (2 Sam. 23:39). In applying the truth of God to others, we must also apply it relentlessly to our own lives.

Let death take my enemies by surprise; let them go down alive to the grave, for evil finds lodging among them (*v. 15*). David asks for God's sudden judgment to come on his enemies.[9] It is not just the one former friend who is spoken about, but a group of enemies ('let them ...'). A sudden shift is made from the singular subject in verses 12-14 to the plural in verse 15. This is a typical occurrence in imprecatory psalms. The reference to going down alive into the grave seems to be an allusion to the incident concerning Korah, Dathan, and Abiram (Num. 16:31-40). Just as those who had treated the LORD with contempt in Moses' day were destroyed, so David wants his enemies (who were also God's enemies) to have a similar fate. The final clause is rendered very freely in the NIV, though a more literal translation such as that in the NASB may

---

[8] I am taking the Hebrew word *sôd* to mean the talk between a group, possibly a group of elders at the gate of the city, or a group on a special worship occasion. It is clearly a word with various nuances, as its twenty-one uses in the MT require twelve different words in the LXX translation. See *TDOT*, II, p. 147.

[9] The opening clause is difficult, though not impossible. The MT has 'Desolations [be] on them' (*yassîmâvet ʿâlêmô*). The Qᵉre reading is *yshy mut*, which is followed by ASV, RSV, NIV, ESV, and other translations ('Let death ...'). However, this presumes that the verb in the Qᵉre form was a defective writing of *yashî'* with a final *alef*. I think it is better to retain the MT without emendation. It makes good sense, for, as J. E. Hartley wrote, 'there is no place more desolate than Sheol' (*TWOT*, I, p. 414). A fuller discussion of the suggested emendations is given in Marvin Tate, *Psalms 51-100*, p. 53.

be a better rendering, 'For evil is in their dwelling, in their midst'.[10]

4. Justice with God (vv. 16-21)
But I call to God, and the LORD saves me. Evening, morning, and noon I cry out in distress, and he hears my voice (*vv. 16-17*). As is typical in psalms of complaint, David tells of his approach to God in prayer, and his believing trust in him. 'Evening, morning, and noon' are probably not meant to be taken as the only times in the day when he prayed. Rather, these expressions speak of the constancy of his requests to God. His actions stand in sharp contrast to his former friend, this being marked out in the Hebrew text by an emphatic 'And you' at the start of verse 13, and an emphatic 'I' at the commencement of verse 16. He is assured that God both listens to his plea and acts upon it.

He ransoms me unharmed from the battle waged against me, even though many oppose me (*v. 18*). The confidence the psalmist has is that God is his deliverer. 'Ransom' is used here in this general sense of deliverance from trouble. God is able to bring his people into a peaceful situation (NIV 'unharmed'), even when the opponents are so many and their attacks so hostile. The word used for 'battle' (*qᵉrāv*) is a rare poetic word denoting a hostile approach. Though the verbal form 'ransoms' (*pâdâh*) should normally be translated 'he redeemed', it probably indicates here the intention to redeem.[11]

God, who is enthroned forever, will hear them and afflict them, *Selah* **men who never change their ways and have no fear of God** (*v. 19*). It is to the creator God that the psalmist calls, for the NIV 'forever' is an attempt to translate a Hebrew word (*qédem*) which points backwards, not forwards. Hence a translation such

---
[10] Various opinions have been expressed about this clause. Some suggest the final phrase, 'in their midst' should be deleted, but no manuscript evidence supports this, while the LXX clearly upholds it (*en mesô autôn*). The RSV 'their graves' is only achieved by transposing consonants. '[Their] lodging' (*megûrâm*) has also been interpreted in different ways, and this is the only Old Testament occurrence of the word *mâgôr* (See *DCH*, V, p. 133). While other possible translations have been suggested, it seems most probable that it is from the common root *gûr*, 'to sojourn', 'to lodge'.
[11] The perfect of resolve is noted in *IBHS*, p. 489.

as 'enthroned from of old' is preferable.[12] The verse speaks of God as being enthroned from creation itself (cf. the use of *qedem* twice in the same chapter in Deut. 33:15, 'the *ancient* mountains', and 33:27, 'the *eternal* God'). The eternal God is the one who hears not only his people, but who also takes notice of the wicked. They are described using a term that is normally used of changing a garment (Gen. 45:22; Ps. 102:26). Their characteristics are that they do not change from their ungodliness and they lack the fundamental mark of godliness, the fear of God. The position of *Selah* is most unusual, in that it comes in the middle of the verse (for discussion on *Selah*, see comments on Ps. 3:2). If *Selah* was a musical term denoting loud song or music, then it would be fitting for it to point to exuberant praise of the eternal king.

My companion attacks his friends; he violates his covenant. His speech is smooth as butter, yet war is in his heart; his words are more soothing than oil, yet they are drawn swords (*vv. 20-21*). Another aspect of the attack by his so-called friend comes out in these verses. The Hebrew text lacks a subject for the verb, and from the context 'my companion' is added. Even 'his friends' have to bear the brunt of his antagonism.[13] He is in a covenant bond with someone, as covenants were often made between people (cf. the one between David and Jonathan, 1 Sam. 20:16). But this 'friend' has no regard for such solemn commitments. On the surface he speaks smoothly, but underneath he is plotting treachery.[14]

---

[12] The MT has *v^eyoshêv qédem*, 'and sits [from of] old'. The clause is an explanatory one concerning God, who is the subject of the first two verbs in the verse. The introductory 'and' is equivalent to 'and he ...' The verb *yâshav* is often used with God as the subject, and describes his enthronement. A close parallel to the expression here is Psalm 9:11, 'enthroned [in] Zion' (*yoshêv tsiyyôn*).

[13] The expression for 'his friends' is unusual, as the noun *shâlôm* is used in the plural as an adjective, 'his friendly ones'. Probably the expression here is equivalent to *sh^elêmîm 'ittô*, 'his friends' (see this idiomatic expression in Gen. 34:21).

[14] The MT has 'the curds of his mouth are smooth'. Various emendations have been proposed, changing the verb to the singular ('*his* mouth is smooth[er] ...') and altering 'curds of his mouth' to 'than curdled milk'. Examples of proposed emendations can be found in *DCH*, III, p. 242, and V, p. 221. J. J. S. Perowne, *The Psalms*, I, p. 459, while retaining the MT, explained the rare form by comparison to the formation of other Hebrew nouns.

His words are deceptive, for 'war' is in his heart, with the same word (*qᵉrâv*) being used here that has already occurred in verse 18. In stabbing his covenant allies in the back, he violates a sacred bond to which God is witness.

5. A Divine Burden-Bearer (*vv. 22-23*)

Cast your cares on the LORD and he will sustain you; he will never let the righteous fall (*v. 22*). The 'cares' are all that God gives to us, and the invitation is to throw them on the LORD. The word used for 'cares' (*yᵉhâv*) only occurs here, and it seems to mean a matter of concern, or one's circumstances in life. The promise is not that he will carry *them*, but rather that 'he will sustain *you*'. The word 'sustain' is used of the action of Joseph in providing for his family in Egypt (Gen. 45:11), and especially of God's gracious provision for his people in the wilderness (Neh. 9:21). That sustaining mercy will be given to ensure that there is no final disaster awaiting the righteous. The first part of the verse is echoed in the New Testament in 1 Peter 5:7, while the general theme is amplified in Jesus' teaching (Matt. 6:25-34; 10:19; Luke 12:22-31; 21:34).

But you, O God, will bring down the wicked into the pit of corruption; bloodthirsty and deceitful men will not live out half their days. But as for me, I trust in you (*v. 23*). The relationship between the psalmist and his God is what matters most. The words 'But you, O God' and 'But as for me' highlight this. God may indeed deal with the wicked, bringing them to a premature death, though he does not always act in this way.[15] However, the psalmist's trust is in his God. He clearly has cast *his* cares on the LORD; already he enjoys being sustained by him. These final words are a summary of the whole psalm, for throughout the psalmist has expressed his confident trust in God.

---

[15] The expression 'deceitful men will not live out half their days' is literally 'they shall not halve their days', which seems to be saying the opposite. In the context the meaning is clearly that the normal length of life will be shortened by direct divine intervention.

Psalm 56

For the director of music. To [the tune of] 'A Dove on Distant Oaks.' Of David. A miktam. When the Philistines had seized him in Gath.

While 'For the director of music' is common in the Psalms, occurring fifty-five times, the designation 'To [the tune of] "A Dove on Distant Oaks"' appears only in the title of this psalm. Its translation and significance is uncertain.[1] The use of the word *miktam* in the title links Psalms 56-60 together (for explanation of the term see the introduction to Psalm 16).The historical note in the title refers to an incident in David's life when he was seemingly held captive in Gath. The biblical text in 1 Samuel does not actually say he was captured, but the comment, in 1 Samuel 22:1, that he escaped to the cave of Adullam, leaves no doubt about it. The Philistines came from, or via, Crete (referred to as Caphtor in Jer. 47:4 and Amos 9:7), and they settled on the coast of Palestine. Their major cities were Ashdod, Ashkelon, Ekron, Gath, and Gaza. They were troublesome to Israel from the period of the Judges, until David drove them out of the hill country and even attacked Philistia itself (2 Sam. 5:25). During the divided monarchy they were still a problem, and the last mention of them in the Bible is from the post-exilic period (Zech. 9:6).

The psalm moves from appeal in the opening, through lament in the central part, to joyful thanksgiving at the conclusion. The imprecation in verse 7 links it with the two previous psalms that both include imprecations (Pss. 54:5; 55:9, 15, 23). The mood of the psalmist changes from the early declaration 'I fear' (*'îrâ'*, verse 3) to 'I will not fear' (*lo' 'îrâ*, v. 11). The repeated refrain in verses 4 and 11 indicates abiding confidence in the LORD, giving to the whole psalm the note of trust.

---

[1] Good summaries of the various views are contained in Marvin Tate, *Psalms 51–100*, pp. 65-66, and Samuel Terrien, *The Psalms*, p. 431.

1. A Plea for Mercy (*vv. 1-2*)

Be merciful to me, O God, for men hotly pursue me; all day long they press their attack (*v. 1*). This and the following psalm begin with the identical plea, though NIV varies the translation.[2] It occurs frequently in the Psalter (cf. 4:2; 6:2; 27:7; 51:1; 86:3; 123:3). The description of relentless pursuit certainly fits the experience of David. He cries to God because his enemies are breathing down his neck, and he has no relief from their oppression. The NIV renders the final clause very colloquially, while the MT has 'all day long a fighter presses me'. More literal translations are given, for example, by NASB ('Fighting all day long he oppresses me') and ESV ('all day long an attacker oppresses me').

My slanderers pursue me all day long; many are attacking me in their pride (*v. 2*). There is an emphasis, in this psalm, on the role of the enemies in using bitter words against the psalmist (see also verse 5), though he clearly felt in deadly peril (v. 6). The repetition of 'all day long' in successive verses speaks of the feeling that there was no let up in the attacks upon him. The conclusion of the verse has caused considerable discussion going back centuries. The problem is the final word in the MT, *mârôm*. The NIV follows a commonly accepted view that it is a noun, 'height', used adverbially to mean 'haughtily = with pride'. However, the AV translators took it as a divine title, 'O thou most high', a view reinforced by some modern scholars,[3] and which may be coupled with the suggestion that it should be transferred to become the first word in the next verse (cf. NRSV).[4] An exegetical decision is hard to make, though the easiest choice appears to be to follow the NIV translators.

2. Refrain: Trust in God (*vv. 3-4*)

When I am afraid, I will trust in you. In God, whose word I praise, in God I trust; I will not be afraid. What can mortal

---

[2] Quite a few English translations share the NIV's inconsistency in the translation of a Hebrew word (*chonnênî*, 'be merciful to me').The NKJV is consistent in rendering both opening expressions by 'Be merciful to me.'

[3] See especially M. Dahood, *Psalms I:1-50*, pp. 44-45. This view, though reinforced by modern linguistic arguments, goes back to the Aramaic Targum, Aquila, and Jerome.

[4] For a summary of different viewpoints, see *DCH*, V, pp. 483-84.

man do to me? (vv. 3-4). Striking alliteration draws attention to the confident assertion in verse 3. The statement opens with the Hebrew word 'day' (*yôm*) used adverbially to indicate 'when'.[5] It is followed by four consecutive words starting with the letter *alef* (represented by ʾ in transliteration); *yôm ʾîrâ ʾᵃnî êlekâ ʾevtach*: 'When I fear, in you I trust.' There is no doubt that David knows fear, but he claims that trust in God robs it of terror.[6] He is afraid, yet not afraid! At the time when he fears, he will trust in God, and at the moment of speaking he is confidently placing his reliance on God's word of promise. Other psalms contain similar references to God's word (cf. 107:20; 130:5), without indication of how that word came to the psalmists. It is possible that a 'word' such as Eli spoke to Hannah could be in mind (1 Sam. 1:17). Verse 4 ends with a challenge to mortal man (Hebrew, *bâsâr*, 'flesh'). Human power is nothing compared to God's might, as King Hezekiah said to his officers when Jerusalem was faced with an attack by King Sennacherib of Assyria (2 Chron. 32:8).

3. Complaints against the Enemies (vv. 5-9a)
The evil designs of the enemies are now spelt out in greater detail. **All day long they twist my words; they are always plotting to harm me** (v. 5). The words of David were distorted by his enemies, presumably Saul and his supporters. Another possible rendering is 'they injure my cause', as in Hebrew the 'word' (*dâvâr*) can have a wider connotation than is normal in English. All their endeavours are directed with evil intent.

They conspire, they lurk, they watch my steps, eager to take my life (v. 6). In every possible way the enemies are seeking to harm the psalmist, even to the extent of taking his life. The first verb may have the idea that they troop together to plot an ambush,[7] and while the second verb can have varied meanings, 'lurk' seems appropriate here. Rather than 'steps', the more literal 'heels' is to be preferred as it fits in with the idea of enemies hiding in ambush. What they may have in

---
[5] *DCH*, IV, pp. 171-72.
[6] For the verb 'trust' (*bâtach*), see comment on Psalm 9:10.
[7] This is how Jerome understood it, and hence rendered it in Latin as *congregabuntur*.

mind is some kind of murder by abuse of the legal system, such as happened in the case of Naboth (1 Kings 21:1-14). They treat the psalmist unjustly and are on the look-out for any opportunity to injure him.

On no account let them escape; in your anger, O God, bring down the nations (*v. 7*). The great variation in the English versions of this verse points to difficulty in understanding the Hebrew text. Some have suggested there was an early copying mistake, because, with the change of one letter, the verb 'escape' (*pâlat*) could be 'requite' (*pâlas*). However, leaving the Hebrew text unchanged can still provide the basis for a translation that forms a question: 'On account of their evil, will there be escape for them?' The answer is clearly 'No', for God will show his anger against the nations.[8] The use of the plural 'nations' suggests that it is the Philistines who are in view. David set himself, after he became king, to subdue the power of the Philistines (2 Sam. 5:17-25; 8:1).[9]

Record my lament; list my tears on your scroll – are they not in your record? Then my enemies will turn back when I call for help (*vv. 8-9a*). David knows that God administers justice in his time, not ours. Hence he asks for a record to be kept of his grief,[10] his request being stated in a very emphatic way. He even asks that his tears be kept in a bottle or wineskin (following the footnote

---

[8] No interrogative particle is used, but in biblical Hebrew a simple *Yes–No* question can be asked without one. Presumably the tone of voice could indicate that it was a question, just as can happen in English (cf. the statement, 'You're going home!' which can often be in effect a question). On the grammatical point in Hebrew, see *DIHG~S*, p. 183; *IBHS*, p. 316 n.1.

[9] The use of the word 'peoples' ('*ammîm*) is unusual in this context, as it most commonly denotes foreign nations attacking Israel. To regard it here as having the narrower meaning of the Philistines makes good sense. Another possibility is to suggest that the appeal 'for a particular judgement is absorbed in the desire for a general judgement of the world' (A. F. Kirkpatrick, *The Book of Psalms*, p. 318).

[10] The word translated 'lament' is the first of three rare words used in verse 9. The AV translation 'wanderings' has been followed by the NASB and NKJV. While it could be from the verb *nûd*, 'to wander', the context suggests a meaning in keeping with 'tears'. *DCH*, V, p. 618 is ambivalent.

reading in the NIV).[11] The verse ends with a question that expects a positive response: 'Yes, they are indeed recorded in God's scroll'.[12] God does not need a written record to remember his people and their needs, but the idea is used in the Old Testament as a reassuring way of speaking of God's knowledge of, and care for, his people (Exod. 32:32; Pss. 69:28; 139:16; Mal. 3:16). The following statement (v. 9a) gives proof of the psalmist's confidence. Whenever he calls to God, asking for his intervention, then the enemies will be put to flight.

4. Refrain: Trust in God (*vv. 9b-11*)
By this I will know that God is for me. In God, whose word I praise, in the LORD, whose word I praise – in God I trust; I will not be afraid. What can man do to me? (*vv. 9b-11*). The essential parts of the refrain of verses 3-4 are repeated here. Instead of the opening reference to trusting in God when he is afraid, the psalmist expresses absolute certainty that God is for him. The introductory 'by this', as well as the verb 'know', draws attention to his conviction that God's actions are proof of his continuing care and justice. The following phrases also differ slightly. The first one ('In God whose word I praise') is given twice,[13] while 'his word' in verse 4 is simply 'word'

---

[11] This is the second difficult word in the verse. The Hebrew word (*no'd*) is used of 'skins of milk' or 'skins of wine'. Because parchment made of skins was used as a writing material, and since the final clause contains the word 'scroll', some have thought that the psalmist is asking for a written record. However, the concept of tears in a skin bottle better suits the expression. The LXX rendering (*enôpion sou*) suggests that the translators were reading the Hebrew as *b^enegd^ekâ*, 'before you', but as the LXX gives a very free translation of the whole verse, this is insufficient evidence to justify any possible emendation.

[12] This word is the third problem in the same verse. Some have suggested that 'record' should be translated as 'bag' to carry on the idiom from the preceding clause. The word used (*sifrâh*) is a *hapax legomenon*, but no convincing argument has been given for not connecting it with the root *s-f-r* already used in the first clause. CHAL, p. 260, gives the meaning as '(heavenly memorandum) book'.

[13] The use of refrains in which the second or final occurrence is lengthier than the original is a feature that also occurs in Psalm 99:3, 5 , 9: 'for he is holy ... for he is holy ... for the LORD our God is holy.'

in verse 10, though in the context no confusion arises as to whose word is being mentioned. Also the repeated phrase has LORD [*yhwh*] instead of God. Verse 11 repeats verse 4b, only altering 'mortal flesh' (*bâsâr*) to 'man' (*'âdâm*). The New Testament passage which presents the same message is Romans 8:28-39, and it may be based on this refrain. Paul starts with the certainty of knowledge ('we know', v. 28), and ends with the ringing affirmation that nothing 'will be able to separate us from the love of God that is in Christ Jesus our Lord' (Rom. 8:39).

5. A Vow of Thanksgiving (*vv. 12-13*)

I am under vows to you, O God; I will present my thank-offerings to you. For you have delivered me from death and my feet from stumbling, that I may walk before God in the light of life (*vv. 12-13*). Seemingly David had made special commitments to God which he now says he will pay. He actually calls them God's vows (MT *n^edârekâ*, 'your vows'), which strengthens the idea of his obligation to keep them. Both 'vows' and 'thank-offerings' can refer to sacrificial offerings. He looks back on the reality of deliverance from the danger of death, and though his enemies had watched his every step (v. 6), yet God had also delivered his feet from stumbling. The NIV translation should be emended to make this a question as it is in the MT: 'Haven't [you kept] my feet from stumbling?'[14] The identical phrase, 'my feet from stumbling', occurs again in Psalm 116:8, also in a context in which mention is made of vows (Ps. 116:14). The final clause expresses the confidence of walking joyfully before God in his light (cf. Ps. 36:9). The Old Testament expressions relating to God as light come to fulfilment in the Gospel (John 1:3-5). Jesus declared: 'I am the light of the world. Whoever follows me will never walk in darkness, but will have the light of life' (John 8:12). His subsequent debate with the Pharisees added weight to the declaration.

---

[14] The form of the question is identical to the one at the end of verse 8. They both commence with the interrogative marker (*h^a*-) and lack a verb.

Psalm 57

For the director of music. [To the tune of] 'Do not Destroy.'
Of David. A miktam. When he had fled from Saul into the cave.

There are close links between Psalms 56 and 57, and the titles locate both psalms in the period of David's flight from Saul. They are similar in style, with both beginning with a cry for mercy and ending on a strong note of thanksgiving. Also, both contain a repeated refrain (56:3-4, 10-11; 57:5, 11). Links also exist among Psalms 57, 58, and 59, in that part of their title is common to all three. In addition, they share the words 'Do Not Destroy' in their titles (as does Psalm 75), and it probably represents the first words of a popular song.

Psalm 57:7-11 is repeated in Psalm 108:1-5. This may suggest that the two parts of Psalm 57 were originally separate compositions. God's covenantal love and faithfulness resound in both sections of the psalm, while the opening verse suggests David's presence at the central worship centre of the covenant, the tabernacle.

1. Lament and Refrain (*vv. 1-5*)

Have mercy on me, O God, have mercy on me, for in you my soul takes refuge. I will take refuge in the shadow of your wings until the disaster has passed (*v. 1*). The psalm begins with a call for God to be merciful, along with a repeated assertion of trust in him. The reference to taking refuge under the shadow of God's wings could be either a general allusion to God's protective care,[1] or it

---

[1] The same idiom is found in Boaz's reference to Ruth: 'May you be richly rewarded by the LORD, the God of Israel, under whose wings you have come to take refuge' (Ruth 2:12). This description has to be set alongside Ruth's profession of conversion: 'Your people [are] my people, and your God [is] my God' (Ruth 1:16).

could relate to his presence at the tabernacle. In Exodus 25:20 the wings of the cherubim are said to overshadow the cover (the mercy-seat) of the ark of the covenant. Hence it is possible that 'your wings' is a way of saying that the psalmist will go to the tabernacle to meet with his God and to find refuge there until the present distress passes by. The word 'disaster' has been translated 'destructive forces' in 55:11. It is a rare word but the parallels of 'malice' and 'abuse' in that context help to define its meaning. In this context, the psalmist professes confident trust in God's ability to protect him until the present destruction is past.

I cry out to God Most High, to God, who fulfils [his purpose] for me. He sends from heaven and saves me, rebuking those who hotly pursue me; Selah God sends his love and his faithfulness (*vv. 2-3*). He calls to 'God Most High',[2] using a double name for God which also occurs in Psalm 78:56 (cf. 'LORD Most High' in Ps. 7:17). The verb 'fulfils' is a rare one, only occurring five times in the whole of the Old Testament, all of them in the Psalms. Here, and in Psalm 138:8, it speaks of the way in which God brings to completion what he undertakes for his saints. The Most High God, the ruler over all, brings blessing to his people while visiting his enemies in judgment. He 'sends' salvation to those who are in deep distress, showing in this way his continuing covenant commitment. He is the God who is 'abounding in love and faithfulness' (Exod. 34:6). 'Selah' appears in the middle of a verse in English versions, but at the conclusion of a clause, not, as in Psalm 55:19, in the middle of a sentence.

I am in the midst of lions; I lie among ravenous beasts – men whose teeth are spears and arrows, whose tongues are sharp swords (*v. 4*). The enemies are described as if they were wild animals. The expressions used ('in the midst of lions', 'I lie among ravenous beasts') suggest the constant hostility with which the enemies attacked, while use of the comparison with spears, arrows, and swords depict their cruelty and their venom. The words 'spears', 'arrows', 'sharp', and 'swords'

---

[2] On the use of the word *'elyôn* ('Most High') as a title for God, see the comments on Psalm 7:17.

all commence with the same letter in Hebrew (*chêt*), the alliteration drawing attention to the danger that confronts the suppliant.

Be exalted, O God, above the heavens; let your glory be over all the earth (*v. 5*). The psalmist knows that God is not an idle onlooker. His words in this verse are both a declaration concerning God's glory and an indirect appeal for his help. He longs for the full expression of God's rule to be manifest, because that would mean that deliverance would come for him. One of the ways in which God gets glory is by displaying his power over his enemies (cf. Exod. 14:4, 17, 18). This invocation is repeated exactly as the final verse of the psalm.

2. Transition – The Wicked Trap Themselves (*v. 6*)

They spread a net for my feet – I was bowed down in distress. They dug a pit in my path – but they have fallen into it themselves. *Selah* (*v. 6*). This verse serves as a bridge between the earlier section of the psalm, with its cry to a faithful God, and the later section with its confident praising of him. The truth is that the wicked often fall prey to their own schemes. They prepare a trap for the righteous, but God so overrules in his providence that they fall into it themselves. The song which follows rejoices in this event, which is not brought about simply by the folly of the wicked, but by the direct intervention of God. 'Selah' marks the end of the second section of the psalm.

3. Thanksgiving and Refrain (*vv. 7-11*)

My heart is steadfast, O God, my heart is steadfast; I will sing and make music (*v. 7*). The Hebrew word rendered 'steadfast' is the same word translated as 'willing' in Psalm 51:12. It could also be rendered 'prepared' or 'set'. Its use here describes the fixed trust that the psalmist has in God, and the repetition emphasises that still further. No indication is given in the text to whom the praise is rendered, but it is clear from the context that it is to be sung to God. Faith and praise are very closely linked together. Both the repetition of phrases and the use of parallel expressions in the verse are characteristic of the whole of the psalm.

Awake, my soul! Awake, harp and lyre! I will awaken the dawn (*v. 8*). The psalmist calls on himself[3] and his instruments to wake up and to prepare for praise. Praise often helps to dispel darkness and despair (cf. the experience of Paul and Silas in gaol, Acts 16:25). Harps and lyres refer to stringed instruments that were used in both formal and informal worship situations, and there is little information to make a distinction between them. Before the dawn signalled a new day, praise would be given to the LORD.

I will praise you, O Lord, among the nations; I will sing of you among the peoples. For great is your love, reaching to the heavens; your faithfulness reaches to the skies (*vv. 9-10*). The gratitude of the psalmist is so great that he wants even the Gentile nations to hear his praise of God, in accordance with God's promise to Abraham (Gen. 12:3). The use of the word 'nations' is not a restricted use of the word to mean 'the Philistines' (as in Ps. 56:7), but in the same way that Psalm 67 uses it. The focus is on the nations of the world, as the context and the use of the word 'peoples' (*'ummîm*) makes clear. The subject matter of David's praise relates to God's covenant love and faithfulness (see v. 3). God has sent his love and faithfulness, and the psalmist wants others to know their dimensions. They cannot be measured for they reach to the heavens.

Be exalted, O God, above the heavens; let your glory be over all the earth (*v. 11*). The statement of verse 5 is used as a refrain to conclude the psalm. It fittingly continues the theme of verse 10 and again focuses on the prayer for the manifestation of God's glory.

---

[3] The word translated 'soul' is *kāwôd*, that often means 'glory'. It can also be used as a means of self-reference, as it is here. For further discussion, see Robert Chisholm in *NIDOTTE*, 2, p. 583.

Psalm 58

For the director of music. [To the tune of] 'Do not Destroy.' Of David. A miktam.

This psalm is directed against prominent officials who misuse their office, and so fail to administer justice rightly. It is unique in that the opening words are not addressed to God but to rulers. After they are charged and a description given of their sin, a sevenfold curse is expressed against them. At the close of the psalm the righteous are depicted as rejoicing in the fact that God, the judge of all the earth, will avenge them. This is one of the imprecatory psalms (see the Introduction) and has close affinity with others in this group, but also with those that deal with the seeming triumph of the wicked (see Pss. 37, 49, 73, and 94).

The psalm is carefully crafted. Verse 1 mentions speaking righteously (NIV 'justly') and judging uprightly. The same two Hebrew roots (*ts-d-k* and *sh-f-t*) appear in the closing verse. A declaration is made concerning the righteous, coupled with the assurance that God is indeed the universal judge. Other repetitions within the psalm are the words 'earth' (vv. 2 and 11) and 'the wicked' (vv. 3 and 11).

1. Leaders Charged (*vv. 1-2*)

Do rulers indeed speak justly? Do you judge uprightly among men? No, in your heart you devise injustice, and your hands mete out violence on the earth (*vv. 1-2*). The various English versions show great variety in verse 1. The problem is the Hebrew word rendered 'rulers' in the NIV. The AV took it as meaning 'congregation', but this has no real basis. The Hebrew word in question (*'ēlem*) is best taken as being the word 'gods' (*'ēlîm*), and having the meaning of 'judges', 'rulers', just as a related Hebrew word (*'elôhîm*) has this meaning in Exodus 22:7-8 and Psalm 82:1 (cf. John 10:34-36).[1] The charge is that the rulers neither speak justly nor judge uprightly. The very people who should have represented God's concern for justice instead conjure up evil plans in their hearts, and then act them out. The sequence of 'heart' and then 'hands' is important, for this is the way in which sin works (cf. Jesus' words in Matt. 15:16-20). The close of the psalm shows that the true model for judges is God himself (v. 11).

2. The Sins of the Leaders Described (*vv. 3-5*)

Even from birth the wicked go astray; from the womb they are wayward and speak lies (*v. 3*). While the context is not dealing with universal sinfulness, yet the comparison with David's confession in Psalm 51:5 should be made. What was happening with the judges should not have been thought surprising, because the judges were only displaying their true character. From birth they have been estranged from God and his ways. This is how the Bible constantly pictures sinful men and women. 'They are darkened in their understanding and separated from the life of God because of the ignorance that is in them due to the hardening of their hearts' (Eph. 4:18).

Their venom is like the venom of a snake, like that of a cobra that has stopped its ears, that will not heed the tune of the charmer, however skilful the enchanter may be (*vv. 4-5*). The wicked are compared to a poisonous snake that will not even obey its trainer. It will turn against the person who has carefully trained it and will not listen. The reason for this, as is now known, is that the cobra is deaf, and it only responds to its trainer's movements, not to the sound of the music. Hence the NIV interpretation 'tune' should be replaced with the more literal 'voice'. The final clause in verse 5 employs one of the

---

[1] The translation of *'elôhîm* in Exodus 21 and 22 is discussed by J. R. Vannoy, 'The Use of the Word *hâ'elôhîm* in Exodus 21:6 and 22:7, 8', in J. H. Skilton, ed., *The Law and the Prophets: Old Testament Studies in Honor of Oswald T. Allis* (Nutley, NJ: Presbyterian and Reformed, 1974), pp. 225-41. He concludes that the translation 'God' should be retained in Exodus 21:6, but 'judges' used in 22:7, 8.

technical terms for weaving spells,[2] and the ESV captures the meaning well with 'cunning enchanter'. The point here is that wicked rulers are just as insensitive as the cobra, in that they do not hear the cry for justice from the poor and needy.

3. Prayer for Judgment (vv. 6-9)

The cry goes out for God to intervene in the situation and bring judgment upon these ungodly people (for curses in the Psalms, see the Introduction). This sevenfold curse is very difficult in the Hebrew text, and this causes the great variety in the English translations of it. The prayer for judgment increases in intensity until it reaches its climax in verse 9. **Break the teeth in their mouths, O God; tear out, O LORD, the fangs of the lions!** (v. 6). Instead of being likened to a cobra, the wicked judges are now compared to lions. They are all ready to attack with their teeth, unless God intervenes and breaks them.[3] In the MT the two words for deity frame the content with one beginning the verse (*'elohîm*) and the other (*yhwh*) concluding it. This is brought out in translation by the ESV translation: 'O God, break the teeth in their mouths; tear out the fangs of the young lions, O LORD.'

Let them vanish like water that flows away; when they draw the bow, let their arrows be blunted (v. 7). Two different comparisons are made to suggest taking away the power of the enemies. The psalmist wants them to become 'like water spilled on the ground, which cannot be recovered' (2 Sam. 14:14). This is symbolism for death. If they do persist in their attacks, then he wants their arrows to be blunted so that they cannot harm him.

Like a slug melting away as it moves along, like a stillborn child, may they not see the sun (v. 8). The word rendered 'slug' (*shabbelûl*) only occurs here. It is preferable to take it as parallel to 'stillborn' in the following clause: 'Like the miscarriage that melts away, like the stillborn that never

---

[2] Cf. the use of the same phrase, *chôvêr chavârîm*, in the list of forbidden Canaanite sorcery practices in Deuteronomy 18:11.

[3] The word translated 'fangs' (*malte'ôt*) only occurs here, though a similar word (*metal'âh*) meaning 'tooth' is more common. In the context it is either means the jaws or the teeth of young lions.

sees the sun'.[4] The same imagery is used in Job 3:16 and Ecclesiastes 6:3. The miscarried foetus or the stillborn child never sees the light of day. So the psalmist wishes his wicked enemies to become as if they had never existed.

Before your pots can feel [the heat of] the thorns – whether they be green or dry – the wicked will be swept away (*v. 9*). The NIV footnote rightly says: 'The meaning of the Hebrew for this verse is uncertain.' However, the introductory word 'before' is sometimes used to introduce prophetic speech that is depicting something going to happen (cf. Isa. 7:16; 8:4), while the last clause gives the expectation that God's judgment is going to be final. This is the climax to the whole prayer.

4. Assurance for the Righteous (*vv. 10-11*)
The righteous will be glad when they are avenged, when they bathe their feet in the blood of the wicked (*v. 10*). The righteous delight in justice, and when God vindicates his own people in victory, then they can rejoice all the more. Vengeance belongs to God, and he vindicates them (Deut. 32:35-36; Ps. 94:1-2).[5] Without that vengeance there can be no justice. Bathing feet in blood is a biblical imagery for victory (Ps. 68:23; Isa. 63:1-6; Rev. 14:19-20; 19:13-14).

Then men will say, 'Surely the righteous still are rewarded; surely there is a God who judges the earth' (*v. 11*). Men in general will ultimately make the declaration that the righteous receive the fruit of their lives from the God who judges the whole earth (cf. Ps. 94:2 where God is called 'judge of the earth'). The psalmist is confident that a day is coming when even the heathen will acknowledge this fact. Believers know that God, the righteous judge, is going to reward them at the last day (2 Tim. 4:8) and they must wait patiently for the day of reckoning (James 5:1-11).

---

[4] This is the interpretation of A. A. Anderson, *Psalms 1-72*, p. 433, and is based on a discussion by G. R. Driver that he cites.

[5] For discussion on the biblical concept of God's vengeance, see H. G. L. Peels, *The Vengeance of God: The Meaning of the Root NQM and the Function of the NQM-Texts in the Context of Divine Revelation in the Old Testament* (Leiden: OTS 31, 1995), and his summary in *NIDOTTE*, 3, pp. 154-56.

Psalm 59

For the director of music. [To the tune of] 'Do not Destroy.' Of David. A miktam. When Saul had sent men to watch David's house in order to kill him.

Two sets of enemies seem to be in view in this psalm. On the one hand, wicked men within the nation attack the psalmist like a pack of wild dogs (vv. 6 and 14). On the other hand, surrounding nations are in view (vv. 5-8). It seems, then, to be a psalm appealing for help from both local and foreign enemies. The manner of deliverance is expressed in terms of God's judgments falling on the wicked. This puts this psalm into the same category of imprecatory psalms as the previous one (for the imprecatory psalms, see the Introduction).

Within the psalm there are features that are unusual, in that there are repeated refrains (vv. 6 and 14) and repeated affirmations of confident trust in the LORD (vv. 9 and 17). The second time the refrain occurs a change of a single letter alters 'O my Strength, I watch for you' to 'O my Strength, I sing praise to you'.[1] The use of three cognate words also helps to bind the whole psalm together. In verse 3 the evil adversaries are called 'fierce men' (*'azîm*), while in the refrain (vv. 9 and 17) God is addressed as 'my strength' (*'uzzî*). Also, the psalmist sings to God and uses the expression 'your might' (*'uzzekâ*). These three words all come from the word 'strength' or 'power' (*'oz*). In addition, the psalm is framed by the use of the same Hebrew root in verse 1 (*sâgav*, 'to protect') and in verse 17 (*misgâv*, 'fortress'). There are some interesting word parallels between this psalm and the

---

[1] In Hebrew the change is from *'eshmorâh*, 'I will keep', to *'azammêrâh*, 'I will sing praise.'

441

account in 1 Samuel 19 and 24 of David's flight from Saul (including the reference to wild dogs, cf. vv. 6-7, 14-15, with 1 Sam. 24:14).

1. A Cry for Deliverance, and a Refrain (*vv. 1-10a*)
Deliver me from my enemies, O God; protect me from those who rise up against me (*v. 1*). From the psalmist's heart comes this cry of distress. He longs for the deliverance that comes only from God. The word 'protect' means 'to set on high' or 'defend'. God takes the afflicted and he lifts them up (Ps. 107:41). This is what David asks here, as he acknowledges the fierce opposition he is facing. He appeals for help from his 'enemies', those who 'rise up' against him.

Deliver me from evildoers and save me from bloodthirsty men. See how they lie in wait for me! Fierce men conspire against me for no offence or sin of mine, O LORD (*vv. 2-3*). He repeats his plea for deliverance, and in so doing uses two more terms to describe his opponents ('evildoers', 'bloodthirsty men'). These four terms are all practically synonymous in this context. The people have planned their attacks with military precision,[2] and they are busy stirring up strife against the psalmist. He protests that he has done them no hurt to cause such spite, and the words he uses recall David's words in 1 Samuel 20:1 and 24:11.

I have done no wrong, yet they are ready to attack me. Arise to help me; look on my plight! (*v. 4*). So strong is his protestation of innocence that he uses still another term ('no wrong') to speak of his lack of offence to either God or man.[3] To him it looks as if God is asleep, and therefore he calls on him to stir himself and come to his rescue. The call to God to 'arise' is a standard expression in the Psalter (see comment on 3:7).

O LORD God Almighty, the God of Israel, rouse yourself to punish all the nations; show no mercy to wicked traitors. Selah (*v. 5*). The combination of divine names, 'LORD God

---

[2] The verb translated 'conspire' is *gûr* II, not *gûr* I. See *DCH*, I, p. 336.

[3] The Hebrew has *bᵉlî-'âwôn*, a compound expression created from the negative particle *bᵉlî* and a noun: 'without iniquity'. Cf. 'without water' (Job 8:11); 'without clothing' (Job 24:10).

Almighty,' recurs in Psalms 80:4, 19 and 84:8.[4] It points to the power of God, while the addition of 'the God of Israel' is suggestive of his loving concern for his people. The psalmist appeals to God to deal with the nations around Israel and also with those within the nation who are disloyal to God's covenant (cf. Psalm 78:57 for the use of the same verb, *bâgad*, of covenant unfaithfulness). It is rare to have the verb 'show mercy' used negatively, for almost always it is used positively of a plea for God to be gracious. The only other place in the Psalms where it is used negatively is in another imprecatory one ('May no one take pity on his fatherless children', Ps. 109:12).

They return at evening, snarling like dogs, and prowl about the city. See what they spew from their mouths – they spew out swords from their lips, and they say, 'Who can hear us?' (*vv. 6-7*). The opponents are compared with wild dogs, which hunt for their prey around the city at night. They habitually look for ways to attack and, if possible, to destroy him. They speak so sharply that their words are like swords. The expression is unusual, though other psalms speak of the cutting effect of the tongue (Pss. 52:2; 57:4; 64:3). In their arrogance they claim that no one, including God, hears them, or will take any action to curtail their activities.[5]

But you, O LORD, laugh at them; you scoff at all those nations (*v. 8*). This seems to be a standard way of describing God's derision of the ungodly (cf. the use of the same two verbs in Ps. 2:4 and Prov. 1:26). The contrast is very marked. Wicked men express their blasphemies, but God in heaven knows that his rule will be vindicated. His enemies will in the end become his footstool (Ps. 110:1; 1 Cor. 15:24-25).

---

[4] The Hebrew expression is unusual in that it has *ʾelōhîm tseʿvāʾôt*, 'God, hosts' instead of the expected *ʾelōhê tseʿvāʾôt*, 'God of hosts'. Possibly the phrase in the MT is an example of enclitic *mem*, where the letter *mem* was added to words but with no discernible meaning. For explanation of this phenomenon, see *DIHG~S*, pp. 24-25; *IBHS*, pp. 158-60; M. Dahood, *The Psalms III:101–50*, Anchor Bible: Garden City, NY: Doubleday, 1970) pp. 408-09.

[5] 'They say' is not represented in the MT, but a verb of thinking or saying is needed to make sense in the context.

O my Strength, I watch for you; you, O God, are my fortress, my loving God (*vv. 9-10a*). While the enemies coming against David are strong (v. 3, 'fierce'), yet his trust is in even greater strength. The NIV and other translations emend the first word in the MT (*'uzzô*) to make it a divine epithet, 'my strength' (*'uzzî*).[6] They watch for him (see the title), but he watches for God. He has asked that God will protect him (v. 1), and he now confesses that his place of protection is indeed God himself ('protect' and 'fortress' come from the same Hebrew root). He looks expectantly to his gracious God. In the expression 'my loving God', the word 'loving' represents the Hebrew word *chésed*, and another rendering could be 'my God of covenant love'.

2. A Description of the Enemies and a Refrain (*vv. 10b-17*)

David prays for God's judgments to be made known, not immediately, but progressively, and he wants this to be a testimony to the surrounding nations. **God will go before me and will let me gloat over those who slander me** (*v. 10b*). The NIV translation glosses over a difficulty with the simple translation 'God'. The consonantal text has 'God of his lovingkindness' (*'ĕlohê chasdô*), and while this is awkward grammatically, yet it can be regarded as a regular construction.[7] The psalmist knows that God will meet him (cf. the use of the same Hebrew verb in Psalm 21:3, NIV 'welcomed'), and he will allow him to gaze on the victory he is providing. The

---

[6] This emendation is fairly strongly supported by the Hebrew manuscripts and the early versions. Without emendation it is hard to construe the sentence. The AV adds words to make some sense: '*Because of his strength ...*', and this procedure could be followed with a more modern translation such as 'Because he is so strong'.

[7] By a slight change of vocalisation 'God of' (*'ĕlohê*) becomes 'my God' (*'ĕlohay*) and this translation is supported by the LXX and a few Hebrew manuscripts. Jewish Massoretes noted in the margin (the Q^ere reading) that the vocalisation of the second word in the phrase should be changed (*chasdô* altered to *chasdî*). This enables a translation like 'my loving God' (cf. the identical phrase in verse 17). Most English translations opt for one or other of these emendations. The first is followed by the RSV, NASB, NEB, NKJV, and the ESV, while the second is represented in the AV, NASB margin, and ESV margin. REB alters 'God of' to 'my God' but retains the MT of the following word: 'My God, in his unfailing love ...'

demonstration of God's judgment will be satisfying to him as he sees God vindicated (cf. Psalm 54:7).

But do not kill them, O Lord our shield, or my people will forget. In your might make them wander about, and bring them down (*v. 11*). Appeal is made to God[8] that his judgment should not be a speedy one, lest it be over and done with so quickly that the lesson will not be learned by the people. Instead, the prayer is that the people will wander about aimlessly and thus be seen as a living example of God's judgments. Another interpretation of the verse could be that the psalmist is asking that God should not kill his enemies as this would only be a short-term solution to the problem.

For the sins of their mouths, for the words of their lips, let them be caught in their pride. For the curses and lies they utter, consume them in wrath, consume them till they are no more. Then it will be known to the ends of the earth that God rules over Jacob. *Selah* (*vv. 12-13*). The sins of the enemies are again spelt out as involving vicious words of cursing and lying. The idea of being caught by their own pride is rather like the idea of Psalm 57:6. The wicked are often too clever for themselves, and their own sin rebounds on them. The repeated cry of 'consume them' emphasises the prayer for utter destruction of the enemies. The end result will not only be satisfying to the psalmist (v. 10b) but glorifying to God as well. Judgment is a demonstration of his sovereign rule over his people, and this serves as a witness to the ends of the earth.

They return at evening, snarling like dogs, and prowl about the city (*v. 14*). The words of verse 6 are repeated in this fresh description of the characteristics of the enemies. The use of this refrain draws attention to the pack of roaming dogs that are always ready to attack.

They wander about for food and howl if not satisfied (*v. 15*). The imagery of roaming dogs is continued (cf. verse 11). They are always on the lookout for food, and if they do not find it they whine. Some English versions take the verb translated in the NIV as 'howl' (*lûn*) to be the verb 'to spend the night' (see AV margin and RV), but it is best to assume that

---

[8] For the word 'shield' applied to God, see the note on 3:5.

the verb means 'to murmur', and hence descriptive of the whimpering of hungry dogs.

But I will sing of your strength, in the morning I will sing of your love; for you are my fortress, my refuge in times of trouble (*v. 16*). While the mention of singing is new, all the other ideas are already found earlier in the psalm (for 'strength', see verse 9; for 'love', see verse 10a; for 'fortress', see verse 9). These ideas form the subject matter of song and praise. The psalmist's approach to God in this way stands in marked contrast to the arrogance of his oppressors. The expressions 'in the morning' and 'in the day of' (NIV 'in times of') are parallel and simply denote the constancy with which the psalmist will proclaim God's favour.

O my Strength, I sing praise to you; you, O God, are my fortress, my loving God (*v. 17*). The words of verses 9-10a are picked up as a concluding refrain. The main alteration is the replacement of 'I watch [for you]' (*'eshmorâh*) with 'I sing [to you]' (*'azammêrâh*). In the last two verses of the psalm there are three synonyms in the Hebrew text, all rendered by 'sing' in English (*shîr, rânan* Pi., *zâmar* Pi.). In spite of all his circumstances the psalmist ends on a note of praise, with the very last word in Hebrew being the word *chésed*, 'covenant love'.

Psalm 60

For the director of music. To [the tune of] 'The Lily of the Covenant.' A miktam of David. For teaching. When he fought Aram Naharaim and Aram Zobah, and when Joab returned and struck down twelve thousand Edomites in the Valley of Salt.

The title of the psalm links it with David's victories against Aram Naharaim, Aram Zobah, and Edom (see 2 Sam. 8:1-4, 13; 10:6-19; 1 Chron. 18:1-13; 19:6-19), but the psalm itself is not commemorating any victory. It is a lament of the people when they were defeated and apparently lost some of the southern part of the land. Twice in the psalm they challenge God's rejection of them (see vv. 1 and 10). The difficulty of reconciling God's sure promises to his people with the reality of military defeat and even loss of some of their territory is faced in other psalms as well (see Pss. 44:19-26 and 89:38-51). Part of this psalm (vv. 5-12) is combined with Psalm 57:7-11 to make up Psalm 108.

The title is the longest in the whole psalter. Several of the terms are used elsewhere ('For the director of music' occurs in the title of fifty-five psalms and in Hab. 3:19; 'To [the tune of] "The Lily of the Covenant"' occurs only here though with the plural 'lilies' it is found in the title of Ps. 80; 'miktam' appears in Pss. 16 and 56-60). It is impossible to be certain whether the historical reference is to the same battle(s) as recorded in 2 Samuel 8:13. The number of the slain is different (in 2 Sam. it is 18,000, here it is 12,000) and also the commander is Joab, not David as in 2 Samuel. The latter difference is not of great concern, as victories can be attributed to a king or his commander (1 Sam. 13:3-4).[1]

---

[1] Discussion on the connection between 2 Samuel 8:13 and the title of Psalm 60 is found in commentaries such as Ronald Youngblood, '1, 2 Samuel', *EBC*, vol. 3, p. 908.

1. A Complaint over Rejection (*vv. 1-3*)

You have rejected us, O God, and burst forth upon us; you have been angry – now restore us! (*v. 1*). God's anger is spoken of as the primary cause of the present distress. The people complain that he has made a breach in their defences (NIV 'burst forth'), and they feel that this is a sign that God has rejected them.[2] The same Hebrew verb for 'reject' occurs in other laments (cf. Pss. 44:9, 23; 74:1; 88:14; 89:38; Lam. 3:17). What the people want is action by God to change the situation, for it is beyond their power to remedy it. While the NIV rendering 'restore us' is feasible, yet the verb (*shûv*, Pol.) is used at times of God's action in turning back from executing punishment (see Exod. 32:12; Num. 10:35; 2 Kings 23:26). Hence, a translation such as 'return [from your anger] to us' is also possible.

You have shaken the land and torn it open; mend its fractures, for it is quaking. You have shown your people desperate times; you have given us wine that makes us stagger (*vv. 2-3*). A metaphorical description is given of the trouble as if it was an earthquake that had occurred. Deep fissures have appeared in the land and God is appealed to as the one who alone can heal and restore. The people are going through bitter experiences that have left them dazed as if they were drunk. The use of the word *qâsheh* (NIV, 'desperate times') may well have conjured up recollections of the bitter experiences of Israel in Egypt (cf. its use in Exod. 1:14).

2. Confident of Victory (*v. 4*)

But for those who fear you, you have raised a banner to be unfurled against the bow. *Selah* (*v. 4*). The banner mentioned here is not calling for a military campaign but rather to show where protection is to be found. Against the attacking armies (called here 'the bow'), God is providing a place of refuge for those who fear him. Jeremiah 4:6 illustrates this same use of the word for 'banner', where the signal is for *flight* instead of

---

[2] The Hebrew verb *pârats* can be used of God's punitive action against Israel (Isa. 5:5; Ps. 80:12), just as it can be employed to describe his judgments upon Israel's enemies (2 Sam. 5:20; 1 Chron. 14:11).

fight. The verb 'unfurled' may have been used deliberately as it seems to echo the word 'banner'.[3]

3. An Appeal for Salvation (*vv.* 5-8)

Save us and help us with your right hand, that those you love may be delivered (*v.* 5). In spite of all the troubles, the psalmist still sees the nation as God's people (NIV 'those you love'). He wants God's might to be shown in saving them. The appeal is stated even more urgently than our English versions suggest. He asks: 'Save by your right hand, and answer us!'[4]

God has spoken from his sanctuary: 'In triumph I will parcel out Shechem and measure off the Valley of Succoth (*v.* 6). The assurance which the psalmist has about ultimate victory comes from a declaration which God has made. The word 'sanctuary' in the NIV could also be rendered 'holiness', which would make the expression like that in Psalm 89:35: 'I have sworn by my holiness.' The declaration refers to all the major areas of David's kingdom, both on the west bank of the Jordan and in Transjordania. Occupation of these areas is by the sovereign determination of God. Shechem is north of Jerusalem, near the mountains Ebal and Gerizim. Succoth is east of the Jordan near the brook Jabbok.

Gilead is mine, and Manasseh is mine; Ephraim is my helmet, Judah my sceptre. Moab is my washbasin, upon Edom I toss my sandal; over Philistia I shout in triumph' (*vv.* 7-8). God's sovereignty embraces all the territory occupied by Israel, but also that of the surrounding nations Moab, Edom, and Philistia. Gilead and Manasseh represent the territory captured on the east bank of the Jordan before the main conquest took place. Ephraim and Judah, in turn, represent the territory on the west bank of the Jordan, and they are the LORD's helmet and the commander's staff (for Judah, as the sceptre, see Gen. 49:10 and Num. 24:17). The

---

[3] The word 'banner', *nês*, is followed by the verb *lᵉhitnôsês*, though the verb could be either a denominative verb created from *nês* and meaning 'to rally [around a banner]', or from the verb *nûs* meaning 'to flee'.

[4] The Qᵉre has 'save me', but it is better to follow the Kᵉtiv and read 'save us'.

references to Moab, Edom, and Philistia imply that they are totally subservient to God.

4. A Further Complaint over Rejection (vv. 9-11)
Who will bring me to the fortified city? Who will lead me to Edom? Is it not you, O God, you who have rejected us and no longer go out with our armies? Give us aid against the enemy, for the help of man is worthless (vv. 9-11). In the midst of the seeming alienation from God, the psalmist still knows that help only comes from him. He asks to be brought against a fortified city (possibly an allusion to Tyre, see 2 Sam. 24:7), and for leadership in battle against Edom. In spite of defeats that they had endured, the people recognise that if victory is to come, it will only be by God's leadership in battle. Hence they appeal to God to intervene with divine help. They know that they cannot gain assistance from other human sources, for the strength of man is a delusion (1 Sam. 17:47; Jer. 17:5). In verse 12 the MT has the word 'God' (*'elohîm*) twice, whereas the NIV only translates it once. The double usage gives a further sense of urgency to the prayer for help.

5. A Song of Victory (v. 12)
With God we will gain the victory, and he will trample down our enemies (v. 12). The psalm begins with God's rejection of his people. It ends with a note of assurance. Strength for battle is the LORD's, and he is able to subdue his enemies, who are also the enemies of his people. God, who had allocated the land to Israel (vv. 6-7), and who controlled the destinies of the surrounding nations (v. 8), is able to bring deliverance to his people.

Psalm 61

For the director of music. With stringed instruments. Of David.

Psalms 60 and 61 share some common features. Both have as their background military situations, with the call to God to provide defence and safety (60:9-12; 61:1-4). They also refer to his people in similar terms (60:4: 'those who fear you'; 61:5: 'those who fear your name'). Both psalms also mention the tabernacle, 60:6 calling it 'his holy place' (*qodshô*), whereas 61:4 uses the common expression of 'tent' (*'ôhel*). While Psalm 60 is specific in its reference to enemies, Psalm 61 alludes to them in non-specific terms. This fact, and the generous use of metaphorical language, makes the psalm applicable to many different situations, and so enhances its usefulness to contemporary believers.

The central plea for help contained in this psalm is typical of many other psalms, yet the prayer for the king (vv. 5-7) raises various questions. Is this psalm composed *by* the king, or is it written by someone else who includes the petition *on behalf of* the king? While no definitive answer can be given to these questions, yet it is most probable that the prayer is on behalf of the king by some other Israelite.ABrupt prayers for the king occur in others psalms as well (cf. Ps. 63:11). The prayer for the king reached its fullest answer in the provision of Christ as the one to whom is given the throne of his father David and who will reign for ever and ever (Luke 1:32-33).

1. A Prayer for Protection (*vv. 1-5*)
Hear my cry, O God; listen to my prayer (*v. 1*). The nature of the distress is not spelled out, but the psalmist asks for God to pay attention to his cry. This word 'cry' is used in the Old

Testament both of cries of joy (cf. Isa. 14:7, NIV 'singing') as well as of cries of sorrow (cf. 1 Kings 8:28). Here it is clearly used of sorrow, as the following verses show. The request is for God to hear, and by implication, to answer his call. The vocabulary, especially the use of synonyms, is typical of cries of distress in the Psalter (cf. among other instances, Ps. 17:1, cry/prayer; Pss. 39:12 and 102:1, prayer/cry for help; Ps. 143:1, prayer/cry for mercy).

From the ends of the earth I call to you, I call as my heart grows faint; lead me to the rock that is higher than I *(v. 2)*. The opening of verse 2 has suggested to some commentators that the psalm was composed when David was fleeing from Saul and therefore when he was literally far away. However, the expression need not be pressed in this geographical way. It may well be expressing the conviction that wherever he is, and in whatever distressing circumstances, he will call on God. In his weakness he calls out, and desires to find a sure place of refuge with his God.[1] In the Old Testament God is often called a rock (*tsûr*, cf. 1 Sam. 2:2), and some personal names also reflect this concept (cf. Zuriel [Num. 3:35, 'my Rock is El']; Zurishaddai [Num. 1:6, 'my Rock is Shaddai']). The thought is the same as Psalm 27:5, 'he will ... set me high upon a rock', though there is no need to follow the LXX here and render 'you lifted me up on a rock' which conforms the text closer to that earlier psalm.

For you have been my refuge, a strong tower against the foe *(v. 3)*. The psalmist looks back at past deliverances, and he makes these the basis for confidence for the future. He had found in God a true shelter when he was attacked by enemies.[2] The phrase 'a strong tower' (*migdal 'oz*) occurs in other places in the Old Testament (Judg. 9:51; Prov. 18:10) as well as in documents from Qumran.[3] It can be regarded

---

[1] The NIV inserts a second 'I call' that does not appear in the MT. This is unnecessary as the phrase can be rendered 'when my heart grows faint (or, is faint)'.

[2] The MT has simply 'a foe', not 'the foe'. This suggests the psalmist was not thinking of a specific event, but rather indicating that whenever a threat appeared he had a secure place of refuge.

[3] *DCH*, V, p. 131.

as a compound noun,[4] and may even warrant the translation 'impregnable tower'.

I long to dwell in your tent forever and take refuge in the shelter of your wings. Selah (*v. 4*). Refuge may well have been found at the tabernacle in Jerusalem (see, in addition to this verse, Isa. 14:32). This was an extension of the custom that in certain circumstances a fleeing criminal could find safety by seizing the horns of the altar (1 Kings 1:50). To take refuge under God's wings may be an allusion to the wings of the cherubim over the ark of the covenant, or else as a general allusion to the protective care of God which resembled a bird's care of its young. Isaiah 14:32 utilises the idea of finding refuge under the wings of the LORD to make the point that diplomacy will never save. What is required is finding safety with the LORD (for other passages using the same idiom, see also Ruth 2:12; Pss. 17:8; 36:7; 57:1; and 91:4). The use of the verb 'to take refuge' (*châsâh*) reinforces the idea already made in the previous verse with the occurrence of the derived noun 'refuge' (*machseh*).

In times of past distress the psalmist had made vows to God, and his prayers had been answered. **You have heard my vows, O God; you have given me the heritage of those who fear your name** (*v. 5*). The 'heritage' normally refers to the life in the promised land, which was a possession belonging to those who fear the LORD (Ps. 25:12-14). In more general terms, 'heritage' refers to the benefits of covenant life. The idea is carried over in the New Testament in the words of Jesus: 'Blessed are the meek, for they will inherit the earth' (Matt. 5:5).

2. A Prayer for the King (*vv. 6-7*)

Increase the days of the king's life, his years for many generations. May he be enthroned in God's presence forever; appoint your love and faithfulness to protect him (*vv. 6-7*). The focus switches from personal petition to a prayer

---

[4] As Dahood, *The Psalms II: 51-100*, p. 85, takes the words as a composite noun, arguing that composite words in Ugaritic 'are sufficient to indicate that Hebrew lexicographers have underestimated their number in the OT'. He renders it 'towered fortress'.

for the divinely established monarchy. To ask for 'days' for the king is equivalent to requesting prosperity for him, and this is strengthened by reference to 'years' and 'generations'.[5] The psalmist wants the king to remain for ever,[6] supported and upheld by God's love and faithfulness. The Davidic dynasty had been promised an enduring existence (cf. Ps. 89:36), and ultimately Christ would come of this line. The Aramaic Targum on this psalm (dating from post-Christian times) refers to 'the King Messiah', showing how Jewish understanding of this psalm interpreted it after the seeming end of the Davidic line. The second part of verse 7 is awkward for two reasons. First, the verb 'appoint' (*man*) is omitted in two manuscripts and by Jerome, but that is not sufficient reason to delete it. It appears to be an abbreviated imperative from the verb 'to appoint' (*mânâh*).[7] Secondly, the verb 'to protect' is strictly an imperfect form, 'they will protect', and it lacks the expected 'and' before it. However, it makes good sense to see it as designating the consequence of God's appointment of 'love and faithfulness' as the king's guardian angels.[8]

3. A Vow to God (*v. 8*)

Then will I ever sing praise to your name and fulfil my vows day after day (*v. 8*). The subject in the closing verse is again the psalmist himself. The psalm, which begins with an appeal for help, closes on a note of confidence. Praise shall constantly be made to God's name, and vows will be fulfilled as an expression of gratitude. The emphasis is on continual

---

[5] The literal rendering of the MT is 'days on the days of the king you will add'. This idiom with the preposition ʿ*al*, used in the sense of 'in addition to', is also found in Deuteronomy 19:9 with the same verb (*yâsaf*, Hi.). The form of the verb is imperfect in Hebrew ('you will increase'), but in the context the NIV translation ('Increase') can be defended, even though it is not absolutely required.

[6] The use of the verb 'sit' in the sense of 'sit enthroned' is well attested in regal contexts. Many of the references are given in *TDOT*, VI, pp. 430-31, and in *DCH*, IV, p. 318.

[7] This was noted long ago by F. Delitzsch, *Psalms*, I, p. 204, who cites other similar abbreviated imperatives (*has, nas, tsav*).

[8] *DIHG~S*, p. 107, notes this passage as an example where the *vav* is sometimes omitted in a clause indicating purpose or consequence.

praise, rather than eternal praise. This is made clear by the parallelism between 'ever sing' and 'day after day' (Hebrew, *yôm yôm*, lit. 'day, day'). The vows have previously been referred to as having been heard by God (*v.* 5); now there is an additional commitment to keep them.

Psalm 62

For the director of music. For Jeduthun.[1] *A psalm of David.*

This psalm is unusual in that it does not contain prayer or address to God. However, it does contain repeated assertions concerning his character, especially as saviour and defender. In this respect it is similar to the preceding psalm in the range of metaphors it uses to depict God's might. He is called 'a rock' (*tsûr*), 'a fortress' (*misgâv*), 'my mighty rock' (*tsûr 'uzzî*), and 'my refuge' (*machsî*). These metaphors reach a climax with the declaration in verse 11 that 'might belongs to God' (*kî 'oz lê'lohîm*, NIV 'that you, O God, are mighty'). Another link with Psalm 61 is the fact that both psalms make reference to God's covenantal love (*chésed*) near their conclusion (61:7; 62:12).

There is a refrain in verses 1-2 and 5-6, though this comes at the beginning of sections, rather than at the end of them as is more common. The term *Selah* appears twice (vv. 4 and 8), and in these cases it does seem to designate an end of a specific division of the psalm. Six times in the psalm the same Hebrew particle occurs (*'ack*), always at the beginning of verses. It is very noticeable in the refrain, where in the NIV it is rendered 'alone' in verses 1-2 and 5-6.

Another striking feature of the psalm is the alternation that occurs regarding who is being addressed. In verses 1-2 the psalmist is talking with himself, a conversation amplified in verses 5-7. He also has some opponents in mind in verses 3-4,

---

[1] The word 'Jeduthun' appears in the titles of three psalms (39, 62, and 77). While it may be a reference to a man by that name whom David appointed to be the director of music at the temple (1 Chron. 16:41-42), yet here and in Psalm 77 the fact that it is preceded by the preposition *'al* ('according to') suggests that is the name of a tune.

and the shift to the plural in verses 8-10 ('*our* refuge') implies that he is addressing an assembly of God's people. At the end of the psalm, after ascribing strength to God (v. 11), he directly addresses the Lord (v. 12).

1. Confidence in God (*vv. 1-4*)

My soul finds rest in God alone; my salvation comes from him. He alone is my rock and my salvation; he is my fortress, I will never be shaken (*vv. 1-2*). The concept of rest in the Lord is found in other psalms as well (see 37:7; 131:2; and cf. Lam. 3:26). It denotes a quiet waiting for salvation that comes exclusively from him. The word 'rest' (*dûmiyâh*) is actually from a Hebrew root that means 'to be silent' (*dâmâh* III). The psalmist waits silently and in confidence before his Saviour, and he mounts up expressions to point to his utter confidence in God. He is a rock and fortress, able to give sure defence to those who trust in him. The promise was given that God would never let the righteous be shaken (Ps. 55:22; NIV 'never fall'). The psalmist appropriates that promise for himself and rests in that knowledge.

How long will you assault a man? Would all of you throw him down – this leaning wall, this tottering fence? They fully intend to topple him from his lofty place; they take delight in lies. With their mouths they bless, but in their hearts they curse. *Selah* (*vv. 3-4*). From speaking of his refuge in God, the psalmist turns to the enemies who have been coming against him and addresses them directly. There is much similarity to the words and situation in Psalms 4:2 and 5:9. The words 'how long' imply that they have been opposing him for some time. They are attacking him as if he is a rickety fence, which can be pushed over easily.[2] Even though he is a person who occupies a high position in society, the plan is to remove him. They want to remove him from his lofty place and to bring him low. Hypocrisy is involved, as outwardly these people speak words of encouragement, but inwardly they curse. It

---

[2] This may be a way of speaking of his weakness, or even of the way in which his enemies view him, 'a pushover' (following J. H. Stek in the NIV *Study Bible*, [Grand Rapids: Zondervan, 1985], p. 848).

is significant that the word 'heart' is not used of these people. Instead the expression 'in their inside' (*bᵉqérev*) is employed, as though they had no heart. Later in the psalm the righteous are described as those 'with hearts' (v. 8).

2. Salvation in God Alone (*vv. 5-8*)

Find rest, O my soul, in God alone; my hope comes from him. He alone is my rock and my salvation; he is my fortress, I will not be shaken (*vv. 5-6*). The refrain of verses 1-2 recurs with slight alterations. 'My soul finds rest' gives way to an imperative, 'Find rest', while 'salvation' in verse 1 is replaced by 'hope' in verse 5. The final word of the Hebrew text in verse 2 is omitted in verse 6, and this accounts for the variation in the NIV: 'I will *never* be shaken,' compared with 'I will not be shaken'. The new section starts with a familiar affirmation that salvation is found in God alone.

My salvation and my honour depend on God; he is my mighty rock, my refuge (*v. 7*). This verse carries on the theme of the refrain, repeating some of the terms already used of God ('salvation', 'rock'). The opening descriptive terms ('salvation' and 'honour') are linked by the conjunction 'and'. This combined phrase asserts the single idea, 'my glorious salvation'.[3] It is an assertion that the psalmist's whole hope is to be found in God alone, and the accumulation of so many expressions forms a tremendous climax to his reaffirmation of trust in his sure refuge.

Trust in him at all times, O people; pour out your hearts to him, for God is our refuge. Selah (*v. 8*). An assurance of salvation for himself impels a call to others to share in the same experience of God. He wants the people as a whole to trust God at all times, for he is their refuge as well as his (cf. 'my refuge' in v. 7 with 'our refuge' here). The verb 'pour out', while a common verb, appears only rarely in

---

[3] This is following the suggestion by Marvin Tate, *Psalms 51-100*, p. 118, who also draws attention to the chiasm in the verse:
on God
    my salvation and my honour
    my mighty rock, my refuge
in God.

this expression, 'pour out your hearts' (see Lam. 2:19, 'pour out your heart like water'). It seems to imply prayer to God, openly acknowledging all the needs of the heart and life.

3. A Call to Trust in God, not Man (vv. 9-12)

Lowborn men are but a breath, the highborn are but a lie; if weighed on a balance, they are nothing; together they are only a breath (v. 9). The last division of this psalm is introduced by a statement that speaks of the futility of trusting in men, whether rich or poor. It follows the positive call to trust in God in verse 8 and the negative call of verse 10 not to trust in riches. The Hebrew text uses two different words for man (*'îsh* and *'âdâm*), represented in the NIV by 'lowborn men' and 'the highborn'.[4] It does not matter what status or wealth a person has, for he is nothing[5] and he provides no lasting support.

Do not trust in extortion or take pride in stolen goods; though your riches increase, do not set your heart on them (v. 10). To the sins of lies and cursing, mentioned in verse 4, are added extortion and robbery. Those who have enriched themselves in this way may think that they have acquired lasting wealth and power. However, the psalmist rightly instructs his readers not to trust in these things. The verb 'take pride' (*hâvâl*) is another use of the same Hebrew root from which 'breath' (*hével*) comes. It conveys the idea of acting vainly.[6] 1 Timothy 6:17 could be a commentary on this section of the psalm: 'Command those who are rich in this present

---

[4] The same antithetical expression (*b^enê 'âdâm b^enê 'îsh*), denoting those of low degree contrasted with those of high degree, has already been used in Psalm 49:2. It is used as a term for all humanity.

[5] Twice the Hebrew word *hével* occurs in this verse. It signifies 'a breath of air', and is placed in parallel with *kâzâv*, 'a lie', that has already been used in verse 4.

[6] The translation of the Hebrew word *hével* is not easy. It has been made more difficult because of the English word 'vanity'. It comes from the Latin word ('vanitas') that Jerome used in the Latin Vulgate Bible, taking a concrete Hebrew word and translating it by an abstract term. Contextual translation is required. Good discussions of the word will be found in Tremper Longman III, *The Book of Ecclesiastes* (NICOT; Grand Rapids: Eerdmans, 1998), pp. 61-65, and Roy B. Zuck, ed., *Reflecting with Solomon: Selected Studies on the Book of Ecclesiastes* (Grand Rapids: Baker Book House, 1994), pp. 224-25, 227-31.

world not to be arrogant nor to put their hope in wealth, which is so uncertain, but to put their hope in God, who richly provides us with everything for our enjoyment.'

One thing God has spoken, two things have I heard: that you, O God, are strong, and that you, O Lord, are loving. Surely you will reward each person according to what he has done (*vv. 11-12*). These concluding verses provide the basis for the disparagement of trusting in men given in the preceding verses. Verse 11 opens with a numerical saying of which the Old Testament has several examples (Prov. 6:16-19; 30:18-31). However, here there is no precise enumeration such as in Proverbs 6, for *three*, not *two*, statements follow. Rather than follow the NIV ('two things'), it is preferable to take the Hebrew numerals as meaning 'once, twice', in a similar way to the English use of 'two or three' to indicate an indefinite number.[7] The affirmation of God's strength and his covenantal love may have come through a recital of his great deeds for his people (cf. Ps. 136). The opening assertions of the psalm are now repeated in an alternative form. Rest and salvation are found alone with God who is both strong and loving. The concluding statement gives the subsidiary truth that God deals justly with his creatures, a truth reaffirmed several times in the New Testament (Rom. 2:6; 1 Cor. 3:8; 2 Tim. 4:14; Rev. 22:12).

---

[7] This usage is noted in *DIHG~S*, p. 48. The interpretation ('Once God spoke, twice that I heard it') was held in the nineteenth century by J. A. Alexander, *The Psalms Translated and Explained*, p. 270, and more recently by Marvin Tate, *Psalms 51-100*, p. 119, and Samuel Terrien, *The Psalms*, pp. 457, 459. I am assuming that the word *zû* following 'twice' is not the demonstrative 'this', but the relative 'that'.

Psalm 63

A psalm of David. When he was in the Desert of Judah.

The desire for God, which this psalm expresses, is similar to that in Psalms 42-43 and 84. While it contains some elements similar to the psalms of complaint, yet it is better seen as a song of rejoicing in God. Since it contains references to 'early' (v. 1; the AV, NKJV, and the NEB follow the Latin text in this regard) and to 'night' (v. 6), this psalm was used as a morning prayer from early Christian times.[1] The title sets the psalm in a period when David was a fugitive, and because of the reference to 'the king' in verse 11, the period is probably that of Absalom's rebellion rather than that of Saul's persecution.

Clear links exist between this psalm and the previous one. Words such as 'strength' (62:7, 11), 'glory' (62:7; 63:2), and 'covenant love' (62:12; 63:3) appear in each. Links also exist with Psalm 61, for in addition to the thought of 'covenant love' (61:7; 63:3), mention of the 'king' is prominent in both psalms (61:6; 63:11). The three psalms are tied together by confident trust in God and expressions of commitment to him.

In another respect, however, a contrast exists between Psalm 62 and Psalm 63. In the former the psalmist speaks of God in the third person ('he', 'him'), only changing to direct address in the final verse: '... you, O Lord, are loving.' In this psalm the direct address commences from the outset and continues through to the end of verse 8, while the final verses refer in the third person to God (cf. 'God's name' in v. 11). The abundant use of the personal pronouns 'I' and 'you' highlights

---

[1] The LXX also takes the reference to 'watches' in verse 7 as being the morning by its rendering *en tois orthrois*, 'in the mornings'.

the closeness of the relationship between the psalmist and his God. The repetition of 'I' and 'my' point to the personal nature of the appeals, while the use of 'you' or 'your' direct attention to his source of help and salvation.

1. Longing for God (*vv. 1-5*)

The psalm begins with a confession of absolute confidence in God. **O God, you are my God, earnestly I seek you; my soul thirsts for you, my body longs for you, in a dry and weary land where there is no water** (*v. 1*). Faith always lays hold of the personal relationship with the living God. The verb rendered 'seek' (*shâchar*) may come from a noun meaning 'dawn' (*shachar*), and because of this connection many versions have translated it by 'to seek early'. In the other usages of this verb in the Old Testament the idea of seeking God *early* is not present, and hence the NIV translation ('earnestly seek') seems close to the mark. As in Psalm 42:1-2, the psalmist compares himself to dry land which longs for water, and so does his soul long for his God.[2] The same thought appears in Psalm 143:6: 'My souls thirsts for you like a parched land.' The expression of longing for God is heightened by the parallel statements 'my soul thirsts for you, my body longs for you', even though the verb translated 'longs' only occurs here.[3] Gregory of Nazianzus (*c.* 330-389) expressed it well: 'God thirsts, to be thirsted for' (*Deus sitit, sitiri*). He longs to see his people ardently desiring him.

I have seen you in the sanctuary and beheld your power and your glory. Because your love is better than life, my lips will glorify you (*vv. 2-3*). The NIV does not translate the opening word of this verse (*kên*), which has long been a

---

[2] The Hebrew noun 'land' (*'érets*), being feminine, should be followed by feminine adjectives, but while 'dry' (*tsiyyâh*) is feminine, 'weary' (*'âyêf*) is masculine. This usage reflects the priority of the masculine gender in biblical Hebrew. For general comment on this, see *IBHS*, pp. 108-09, and for this particular example, p. 258.

[3] The verb is *k-m-h*, and the translation of it must depend on the context here. The parallelism is very clear in the Hebrew text: *tsâmᵉ'âh lᵉkâ nafshî/ kâmah lᵉkâ bᵉsârî*. The root may also appear in the personal name Chimham in 2 Samuel 19:37, 38, 40, and in the place name Geruth Chimham in Jeremiah 41:17.

discussion point.[4] Past experience of God vitalises his present relationship. He looks back to times when, at the tabernacle, he has had a vision of God. This could have been similar to Isaiah's vision (Isa. 6:1-3). The thought of 'seeing God' is used elsewhere as a metaphor for worshipping him at the tabernacle/temple (Pss. 11:7; 17:15). The content of the vision is summed up in the words: 'your power', 'your glory', 'your love'. 'Your power' may be a reference to the ark of the covenant, as the word 'power' (Hebrew, *ʿoz*) is used virtually as a synonym for 'the ark'.[5] The love that the psalmist has already experienced is preferable to any kind of life without God's favour, and it causes the psalmist to sing his praise. The verb translated 'glorify' is normally used of praising God for his mighty acts of triumph (Pss. 106:47; 117:1; 145:4; 147:12), and the NIV uses a variety of English verbs to convey the meaning ('glory', 'extol', 'commend').

I will praise you as long as I live, and in your name I will lift up my hands. My soul will be satisfied as with the richest of foods; with singing lips my mouth will praise you (*vv. 4-5*). Constant praise of the Lord is his pledge, as he directs his prayer to him. The lifting up of the hands was an outward expression of the uplifted heart (Pss. 28:2; 141:2; 1 Tim. 2:8). The fact that it was the palms or open hands that are referred to may suggest waiting on God in order to receive his blessings. He has indeed received abundantly, being filled with 'the richest of foods' (lit. 'marrow and fat'). The language may be borrowed from the ritual of sacrifice, but the fat of sacrifices was never eaten (see Lev. 3:16-17). The idea is that God's presence is

---

[4] J. J. S. Perowne, *The Psalms*, I, pp. 509-10, has a note setting out five different attempts to explain the word. His own view is that it means 'so' in the sense that it is referring back to the expressions of longing for God's presence. This is the way that the AV and NASB take it ('thus') and the RSV, NRSV, and the ESV ('so'). A similar usage of the Hebrew word is found in Psalm 127:2.

[5] This is discussed by G. Henton Davies, 'The Ark in the Psalms', in F. F. Bruce, ed., *Promise and Fulfilment: Essays Presented to Professor S. H. Hooke in celebration of his ninetieth birthday 21st January 1964* (Edinburgh: T. & T. Clark, 1964), pp. 51-61. The actual Hebrew word for 'ark' (*ʾarôn*) only occurs in the Psalter in Psalm 132:8.

like the richest of foods, and a satisfied heart will overflow in praise. The psalmist's whole being will be engaged in adoration and thanksgiving ('my soul', vv. 1 and 5; 'my body', v. 1; 'my lips', vv. 3 and 5; 'my hands', v. 4). For Christians today the New Testament direction is that through Jesus we 'continually offer to God a sacrifice of praise – the fruit of lips that confess his name' (Heb. 13:15).

2. Confidence in God's Protection (*vv. 6-10*)
On my bed I remember you; I think of you through the watches of the night (*v. 6*). The thought of verse 1 is expanded to describe a longing for God even during the hours of darkness. In Old Testament times, for civic and military purposes, the night was divided into three watches. The word 'remember' is used in the sense of 'meditate', as it parallels another Hebrew word (*hâgâh*, NIV 'think of') which is used elsewhere of meditation (see Ps. 1:2).[6]

Because you are my help, I sing in the shadow of your wings (*v. 7*). 'Help' in this context means 'deliverance'. Assurance of divine protection gives ground for joyful songs. 'Sing' (*rânan*, Pi.) picks up the element of joyful song already mentioned in verse 5, where a noun from this same root has been used (*siftê rᵉnânôtî*, NIV 'singing lips'). Many other believers have passed through similar experiences to the psalmist, including Paul and Silas (Acts 16:25). 'Shadow of your wings' refers in general to God's protective care of his servant (see comment on Ps. 57:1).

My soul clings to you; your right hand upholds me (*v. 8*). God had invited his covenant people to cling to him (see especially Deut. 10:20; 11:22; 13:4; 30:20; Josh. 22:5; 23:8), and the psalmist acknowledges that he is responding in this way. He is a loyal servant who is walking in God's way and fearing him. Consequently he is held in the sure grip of his God (for the same thought and using the same verb [*tâmak*], see Ps. 41:12 and Isa. 41:10). The promise in the gospel is of a

---

[6] The same parallelism involving *zâkar* and *hâgâh* appears again in Psalm 143:5. For other passages where *zâkar* has a broader meaning than just 'remember', see *DCH*, III, p. 108.

Saviour who holds his people so that no one can snatch them out of his hand (John 10:28).

They who seek my life will be destroyed; they will go down to the depths of the earth. They will be given over to the sword and become food for jackals (*vv. 9-10*). Ultimate vindication lay ahead of the psalmist, when his enemies will come under divine judgment. Those who now seek his life will find that their own lives will be taken. The language of verse 10 describes a military battle and its aftermath, with dead bodies being left in the field as carrion for wild animals.

3. Joy in God (*v. 11*)
But the king will rejoice in God; all who swear by God's name will praise him, while the mouths of liars will be silenced. The psalm ends on a note of joyful confidence. David refers to himself as 'the king', for even when fleeing from Jerusalem he still knows that he is the divinely appointed king. In his rejoicing he will be joined by 'all who swear by God's name' (Hebrew, 'by him'). This is a reference to the practice of taking oaths in God's name (Deut. 6:13; 10:20; 1 Kings 8:31). In the MT no object follows the verb 'praise'. Either 'him' can be inserted as the NIV does, or else an alternative choice of verb that does not need an object can be used (e.g. 'boast'). The liars are those enemies whose destruction has just been described (vv. 8-9). Their voices will be stilled, while those of the faithful will rise in joyful song.

Psalm 64

For the director of music. A psalm of David.

Once more evident links occur with the preceding psalms. Both Psalms 63 and 64 end on the same note of praise and with the same verbs ('rejoice', *sâmach*; 'praise', *hâlal*, Hitp.). While Psalm 63 is expressive of confidence in God who protects and covers his saints, Psalms 61, 62, and 64 all use either the verb 'to trust' (*mâchâh*) or the derived noun, 'refuge' (*machseh*) to describe the relationship with God (see 61:3, 4; 62:8; 64:10).

Many of David's psalms of complaint are similar in tone to this one. They tell of enemies who wound with words, though they are not named. There is a sharp contrast in this psalm between two kinds of attacks. On the one hand, the enemies attack with their deadly arrows (v. 3), but on the other hand God attacks them with his arrows (v. 7). What is striking is the fact that both sections, dealing with the enemies' attacks and God's response, use almost identical language in Hebrew.[1]

evildoers (v. 3, Hebrew, root *p-ʿ-l*)	God's doing (v. 9, Hebrew, root *p-ʿ-l*)
their tongue (v. 3)	their tongue (v. 8a)
arrows (v. 3b)	his arrow (v. 7a)
suddenly (v. 4b)	suddenly (v. 7b)
without fear (v. 4b)	everyone will fear (v. 9a)
who can see (v. 5b)	all who see (v. 8b)
heart (v. 6b)	upright in heart (v. 10b)

This pattern serves to emphasise the fact that the evil actions of the enemies are repaid to them by God, a theme that is

---

[1] This is set out well by Konrad Schaefer, *Psalms* (Collegeville: Liturgical Press, 2001), p. 155.

dealt with in Psalms 7:6 and 37:14-15 (see the commentary on these passages).

The psalm rises to its climax in the final verse, with the thought of God's protective care of his people, and the resultant praise that the upright render to him. This praise is not just from a few who have observed what has happened, but from 'all mankind'. The thought that all will see the great works of God and many will find salvation in him, is developed further in both the Psalms and the prophets (Pss. 67:7; 98:1-3; Isa. 45:20-25).

1. The Opening Call to God (*v. 1*)
Hear me, O God, as I voice my complaint; protect my life from the threat of the enemy (*v. 1*). From a troubled heart the psalmist cries out to God. The more common form of request is 'Hear my prayer' (cf. 4:1; 39:12; 54:2; 84:8), though 'Hear my voice' also occurs elsewhere in the Psalms (cf. 27:7; 119:149), and the two expressions are practically synonymous. He prays for protection 'from the threat (lit. 'fear') of the enemy', for he knows that God has the power to keep his people safe. His love and faithfulness will ever protect them (see the same verb in Ps. 61:7, another link with the preceding psalms).

2. The Description of the Enemies (*vv. 2-6*)
Hide me from the conspiracy of the wicked, from that noisy crowd of evildoers. They sharpen their tongues like swords and aim their words like deadly arrows (*vv. 2-3*). The battle is not fought with physical weapons but with sharp words that wound as if they are swords or arrows. The tongue is 'restless evil, full of deadly poison' (James 3:8). These bitter words (Hebrew, *mar*, 'bitter', 'poisonous') come after the wicked have taken counsel together, and from this noisy crowd there come attacks from which the psalmist needs God's protection.[2] God is able to keep the psalmist and hide him from mortal enemies (see Ps. 17:8-9).

---

[2] NIV's 'noisy crowd' translates *rigshâh*, a word that only occurs here in the OT. In the context this seems close to the mark, as it continues and probably surpasses the idea of evildoers taking counsel together. The rabble are out to take their revenge.

They shoot from ambush at the innocent man; they shoot at him suddenly, without fear (*v. 4*). The enemies act in deceptive ways in that they wait in hiding places (NIV 'ambush').[3] From these they launch their attacks without warning, and they do so brazenly. The psalmist again protests his innocence, not in the sense of sinlessness, but in that he is clear in conscience before God, an upright man (Hebrew, *tâm*). The word occurs thirteen times in the Old Testament, many of these in reference to Job (see, e.g., Job 1:8; 2:3).

They encourage each other in evil plans, they talk about hiding their snares; they say, 'Who will see them?' They plot injustice and say, 'We have devised a perfect plan!' Surely the mind and heart of man are cunning (*vv. 5-6*). The threat of the enemy is further defined.[4] Those who are plotting evil against the psalmist take mutual encouragement in their schemes. They plan 'an evil matter' (*dâvâr raʿ*), a phrase that matches the earlier expression 'a deadly matter' (*dâvâr mar*) in verse 2. The enemies also boast that this is hidden from others, and that they have devised the ideal plot. This displays the innate sinfulness of mankind. In addition, it is a triumphal expression that betrays the pride that sinners take in their own wickedness. The final statement in verse 6, 'Surely the mind and heart of man are cunning', is best taken as an expression of the psalmist, and should be marked off in some way, perhaps with parentheses: ('The inward nature and the human heart – how deep they are!')[5] It should be set beside

---

[3] The word 'ambush' (*mistâr*) is from the same root as the verb 'hide' (*sâtar*) in verse 2.

[4] The translation of the first part of verse 7 is difficult for several reasons: 1. Three words from the same Hebrew root (*ch-f-s*) appear: the verbal form 'they plot' (*yachpᵉsû*), the noun 'plot' (*chêpes*), and the participle 'searched out', 'plotted' (*mᵉchupâs*). 2. The noun *ʿôlot* is most probably the plural of *ʿavlâh*, 'perversity'. 3. The verbal form *tamᵉnû* could be the qal pf. 1 pl. of *t-m-m*, with it being an unusual form instead of the expected *tammônû*, as was suggested by GKC §67.e. Alternatively, it could be from the root *t-m-n*, 'to hide', that has already been used in verse 5 (though the initial letter of this verb is *tet*, not *tav*). In view of the uncertainty, the NIV is an acceptable attempt at translation. Tate, *The Psalms 51-100*, p. 131, goes so far as to say that 'no translation should be treated with confidence'.

[5] This is Tate's translation, ibid., p. 130.

that of Psalm 14:3, as a description of the depth of human sinfulness: 'All have turned aside, they have together become corrupt; there is no one who does good, not even one.'

3. God's Impending Judgment (vv. 7-9)

But God will shoot them with arrows; suddenly they will be struck down. He will turn their own tongues against them and bring them to ruin; all who see them will shake their heads in scorn (vv. 7-8). Earlier the psalmist has spoken of the suddenness with which the enemies shoot at him (v. 4). Now he says it is God who is going to shoot suddenly! This is a presentation of the teaching given elsewhere in the Psalms that the sins of people often turn back against themselves (Pss. 37:14-15; 54:5; 59:12). The NIV is paraphrastic in verse 8. The MT has: 'They will make him stumble, their tongue [being] against them; all who see them will nod their heads' (or, 'will flee from them').[6] A more literal translation than the NIV is: 'And they are confounded, their tongue comes upon themselves, all their admirers flee away'.[7] Despite the uncertainty the general message is clear. God will bring judgment upon these wicked people, and this will be greeted with the recognition by others that this is indeed a just penalty for them. What form the judgment will take is not specified.

All mankind will fear; they will proclaim the works of God and ponder what he has done (v. 9). Those who once showed no fear (see v. 4) will now, along with everyone, show fear. God's judgment will be seen by men in general and cause them to acknowledge the fitness of what has happened. Those who were doers of evil (*poʿᵃlê ʾāven*, v. 2) will discover that what God has done (*poʿal ʾᵉlōhîm*) has made their plans ineffective. Being an eyewitness of God's mighty hand at work should cause men to 'know that the LORD is God; besides him

---

[6] The translation differs according to the view taken on the verb in question. Standard dictionaries take varied positions as to whether the verb is *nâdad* Hitp., 'to flee', or *nûd* Hitp., 'to shake the head'.

[7] This is the translation of E. W. Hengstenberg, *Commentary on the Psalms*, II, p. 308, and similar translations can be found in J. A. Alexander, *The Psalms Translated and Explained*, p. 284; F. Delitzsch, *The Psalms*, II, p. 220; and A. F. Kirkpatrick, *The Psalms*, p. 359.

there is no other' (Deut. 4:35). True acknowledgment of God's actions should lead to proclamation to others of his actions, and meditation on the wonder of his works.

4. A Call to Rejoice (v. 10)

Let the righteous rejoice in the LORD and take refuge in him; let all the upright in heart praise him! (v. 10). The righteous should take encouragement for the future from the promise of God's judgment. We are not to take revenge ourselves on enemies, but to 'leave room for God's wrath, for it is written: "It is mine to avenge; I will repay," says the Lord' (Rom. 12:19). Meanwhile, those who belong to the LORD take refuge in him and extol his name in praise and adoration. Quiet confidence in him has to replace fear of scheming enemies. The contrast between the wicked and the righteous is made clear – the former have pursued their evil plots, while the latter have displayed uprightness of heart.[8]

---

[8] R. Davidson, *The Vitality of Worship: A Commentary on the Book of Psalms*, Grand Rapids: Eerdmans, 1998), p. 202, makes a link between this psalm and Psalm 1, pointing also to Paul's words in Philippians 4:4-9 which call for rejoicing, but then describe the character of the righteous (vv. 8-9).

Psalm 65

For the director of music. A psalm of David. A song.

This psalm is the first of a quartet of psalms that share common themes. While mention is made of the temple in Jerusalem (65:4; 66:13; 68:24, 29), yet the note of universalism pervades them (65:2, 5; 66:1, 4, 8; 67:3-5; 68:28-33). These songs constitute a call to the nations to acknowledge the God of Israel as the mighty saviour and to join in praise to him.

While the latter part of this psalm could easily be called simply a harvest song, yet the clear framework of the psalm shows that it had a much wider setting. Its structure is clear. It begins with a declaration that God is the one who answers prayer, and then shows three ways in which this prayer is answered. There is a meeting with God in his temple (v. 4), a revelation of his power in the created world (vv. 5-8), and finally attention is drawn to the bounty of God in providing so liberally for his creatures (vv. 9-13). There are no indications in the psalm of any specific setting for its use. Hence, it can be assumed to be a thanksgiving song appropriate on many occasions throughout the year.[1]

1. A Prayer-Hearing God (*vv. 1-4*)

Praise awaits you, O God, in Zion; to you our vows will be fulfilled (*v. 1*). The opening phrase is difficult, for literally it says, 'To you, praise is silence.' The AV margin notes that literally its rendering 'waiteth' is 'silent', while the NIV margin

---

[1] Craig Broyles, *Psalms*, pp. 266-67, argues that the psalm points to various specific times throughout the agricultural year (Feast of Tabernacles, Feast of Unleavened Bread, Day of Atonement). The phraseology in the psalm is too indefinite to allow precise identification to take place.

says: 'Or, *befits*; the meaning of the Hebrew for this word is uncertain'.[2] Perhaps the picture is a personification of praise that waits to be stirred up by the worshippers (cf. Ps. 57:8, and see the comments on Ps. 62-1-2). Most English versions follow the AV in suggesting the meaning is that praise waits for God. The psalmist seems to be concentrating on Jerusalem[3] and the temple (see v. 4) as the places where praise is specially dedicated to God, though the following verse shows that he is not restricting it to these locations. The vows could have been made during a time of trouble, or else may reflect a promise to God at the time of planting of the crops.

O you who hear prayer, to you all men will come (*v. 2*). The psalmist is confident that men everywhere will see evidences of God's goodness, and they will turn to him. The words imply that they will come to him as the prayer-hearing God, and make their requests. 'All flesh' (NIV 'all men') elsewhere denotes all mankind (see Ps. 145:21, NIV 'every living creature'). The choice of 'all *flesh*' (*kol bâsâr*) throws emphasis on the frailty of humans as they make their approach to the mighty God (cf. the contrast in Isaiah 31:3 between God/spirit and men/flesh).

When we were overwhelmed by sins, you forgave our transgressions (*v. 3*). In the past the psalmist and his people were in a position in which there seemed to be no answer to the problem of their sin and guilt. The NIV rendering of verse 3 emends the MT, altering 'various kinds of iniquities have overwhelmed *me*' to 'overwhelmed *us*'.[4] However, the MT can be explained without this change. The psalmist thinks first of his own sins in all their variety,[5] and then says to God:

---

[2] The early versions, such as the LXX, interpret the word rendered 'silence' as 'fitting', 'what is due'. This needs an emendation of the MT text so that the word is from *dâmâh*, 'to be like'. Modern versions that adopt this approach include the RSV, JB, REB, and the ESV.

[3] The LXX makes the location of Zion explicit by adding 'in Jerusalem' at the end of the verse.

[4] The alteration involves changing the MT *mennî*, 'from me', to *mennû*, 'from us', which does appear in some Hebrew manuscripts.

[5] The Hebrew expression is *div̂rê ʿᵃvonot*, lit. 'words (or, deeds) of iniquities'. It is a very unusual phrase, and I am taking it as meaning the many kinds of iniquities that the psalmist had committed.

'Our sins – you atone for them!' Where sin abounded, grace abounded all the more (Rom. 5:20)! God provided atonement for their sins, just as he did when he declared to Isaiah: 'Your guilt is taken away and your sin atoned for' (Isa. 6:7).[6]

Blessed are those you choose and bring near to live in your courts! We are filled with the good things of your house, of your holy temple (*v. 4*). How blessed is the person on whom God sets his love (cf. the use of the verb 'choose' of Israel in Deut. 7:7, and of the choice of Zion in Ps. 132:13), and whom he invites into his sanctuary! The emphasis is on God's work – '*you* choose', '*you* bring near'. This is the answer to the questions of Psalms 15:1 and 24:3. Because of God's free grace, he atones for the sins of the penitent and brings them into close and abiding fellowship with himself. What is received at the sanctuary is not only material blessings (i.e. a share in the fellowship offerings), but also the spiritual blessings that are given in full measure to forgiven sinners. The expression 'the good things' (*tûv*) is a collective one denoting the fullness of blessings that God provides.

2. A Creator God (*vv. 5-8*)

You answer us with awesome deeds of righteousness, O God our Saviour, the hope of all the ends of the earth and of the farthest seas, who formed the mountains by your power, having armed yourself with strength, who stilled the roaring of the seas, the roaring of their waves, and the turmoil of the nations (*vv. 5-7*). The great creator God answers the prayers of his people by deeds that inspire awe. The phrase 'awesome deeds' can refer to the events of the Exodus (see Exod. 34:10; Deut. 10:21; and Ps. 106:21-22), but here it refers to some more recent demonstrations of God's saving power. The thought of 'deeds of righteousness' is similar to the use of the word 'righteousness' (*tsédek*) in Isaiah in particular to denote 'victory' or 'triumph' (Isa. 41:2, 10; 46:13; 51:5-6). Here God has shown his saving power on behalf of his people. Three things are then said about this Saviour. First, he is the object of the hope of all the world. Even those of the farthest seas will come

---

[6] The same Hebrew verb *kâfar*, Pi., 'to atone', is used in both Isaiah 6:7 and here in verse 5.

to trust in him. The psalms show us that the missionary vision flowing from Genesis 12:3 was very real for some Old Testament believers (cf. Ps. 67 also). Secondly, he is the creator of the mighty mountains, which stresses how powerful he is as Saviour. Thirdly, he is the controller of his world, in that he stills both the roaring of the mighty oceans and also the turmoils of human society.

Those living far away fear your wonders; where morning dawns and evening fades you call forth songs of joy (*v. 8*). The vision of the psalmist is still on the ends of the earth. Even to the remotest place, knowledge of God's wonders will reach, and there people will come to fear him. The word 'wonders' is literally 'signs', which most commonly points to miraculous acts of God's power such as the plagues at the time of the Exodus (Exod. 7:3; Deut. 4:34). 'Morning' and 'evening' are used here to denote 'east' and 'west'. All over the world God is going to call forth songs of joy from creation itself, a theme developed later in the Psalter (see 96:11-13; 97:1, 6; and 98:4-9).[7]

3. A Bountiful God (*vv. 9-13*)

The switch to the third section of the psalm takes place here. The subject is the fruitfulness that God grants to the land. Because of his gracious providence, there is bountiful provision for his world. **You care for the land and water it; you enrich it abundantly. The streams of God are filled with water to provide the people with grain, for so you have ordained it. You drench its furrows and level its ridges; you soften it with showers and bless its crops** (*vv. 9-10*). While this part could be a harvest song, yet its use is far wider, as it appears to be stating general principles.[8] One of the promises of God to the children of Israel was that the land of

---

[7] Craig Broyles, *Psalms*, p. 271, is right in pointing out that whereas the NIV translates the final verb without an object, it should have 'the going forth of the morning' (east) and 'the evening' ('west') as the object, so that the picture is of creation, not only its inhabitants, rejoicing.

[8] It is difficult to decide on the best tenses for the English translation of verses 10-13. Some want to see verses 10-12a as being in the past, while verses 12b-13 are in the present. Others want to take some of the verbs as imperatives – 'drench', 'soak', 'bless'. I agree with the NIV translators that the passage is describing God's characteristic actions towards his creation.

Canaan was going to be a land 'that drinks rain from heaven. It is a land the LORD your God cares for; the eyes of the LORD your God are continually on it from the beginning of the year to its end' (Deut. 11:11-12). Here that promise is put into poetic language. 'The streams of God' may be equivalent to the expression 'the floodgates of the heavens' (Gen. 7:11; 8:2). The preparation of the land (see NIV margin) is described in greater detail in verse 10. The early rains prepare the ground for sowing, while later rains in mid-winter soften it and allow the crops to grow.

You crown the year with your bounty, and your carts overflow with abundance (*v. 11*). The climax of the whole process is that God gives the harvest, he provides the bounty (*tôvâh*, lit. 'goodness'; cf. its use in Pss. 31:19 and 68:10).The NIV presents one interpretation of the second half of the verse. God is pictured driving through the land in his chariots, which are so richly laden that they drop some of their abundance. However, the word rendered 'carts' is a rare word, and it is preferable to take it as meaning 'pastures' as in Psalm 23:3, as this fits the context admirably.[9]

The grasslands of the desert overflow; the hills are clothed with gladness. The meadows are covered with flocks and the valleys are mantled with grain; they shout for joy and sing (*vv. 12-13*). Nature herself is personified, as in Psalms 96:11-12 and 98:7-8 and Isaiah 44:23 and 49:13. She sings for joy at the bountiful harvest that God has given. Even the deserts will blossom, overflowing with new growth. Grasslands, hills, meadows, and valleys have all experienced his bountiful provision, and together they rejoice at such evidence of his love and care.

---

[9] The difficulty of translating this word is highlighted by the fact that the *DCH*, V, pp. 379-80 gives four possibilities for it. One of these is followed in the NLT ('even the hard pathways overflow') and this also makes good sense in the context, as it forms a parallel with the expression 'grasslands of the desert' in the next verse.

Psalm 66

For the director of music. A song. A psalm.

There are obvious links between Psalms 65 and 66. Both have the vision of all the earth praising God (65:2, 8; 66:1, 4), and specific reference to his awesome deeds in both is a further connecting idea (65:5; 66:3). No precise historical setting can be given for Psalm 66. It seems to be a song of thanksgiving after some victory by the nation, such as when Sennacherib of Assyria was defeated (2 Kings 19:35-36). The sudden switch from the use of the first person plural in verses 1-12 to the first person singular in verses 13-20 has suggested to many that two earlier psalms were joined together. However, the 'I' of verses 13-20 could be the king speaking on behalf of the people, or a personification of the nation as an individual (cf. a similar situation in Lam. 1). The latter suggestion, though, seems unacceptable, as the speaker appears to be a real person who can appeal to his fellow-believers (v. 16). Also, the content of verses 13-20 flow on from the historical references in verses 8-12.[1] The use of similar phrases, 'Come and see' (*l^ekû ûr^e'û*, v. 5), and 'Come and hear' (*l^ekû shim^{e'}û*, v. 16) link the two major sections of the psalm together.

1. Universal Praise of the King (*vv. 1-4*)
Shout with joy to God, all the earth! Sing to the glory of his name; make his praise glorious! (*vv. 1-2*). The opening call is repeated in Psalms 98:4 and 100:1 (with the substitution of 'Lord' for 'God'). A series of imperatives ('shout', 'sing',

---

[1] The personification view was advanced, among others, by E. W. Hengstenberg, *Commentary on the Psalms*, II, pp. 328-29, and followed by J. A. Alexander, *The Psalms Translated and Explained*, p. 280.

'make') call for praise to be given in song to God. Because of his greatness, glory is to be ascribed to his name. His character surpasses all others, and while human praise does not add to his glory, it is rightful recognition of his majesty and kingly rule.

Say to God, 'How awesome are your deeds! So great is your power that your enemies cringe before you. All the earth bows down to you; they sing praise to you, they sing praise to your name.' *Selah* (*vv. 3-4*). When the people look on God's actions, both those in the distant past and those more recently, they acknowledge that they are demonstrations of his great power. Onlookers stand in awe of them, and enemies will submit before him. The Hebrew word translated 'cringe' (*kâchash*) is not a common word, and it has an unusually large range of meanings. Basically it seems to mean 'deny' or 'deceive' and this may well lie behind this and other similar passages in which 'cringe' or 'submit' seems best in English (Deut. 33:29; Pss. 18:44; 81:15). This would suggest that the submission takes place, but without true belief on the part of the enemies. It is only feigned submission. In verse 4 the thought is probably that *in the future* all the earth will worship the Lord, rather than that it is doing so now. It is a picture of universal adoration and praise as the nations bow in worship before him. Ultimately all God's enemies will bow in subjection to him (Phil. 2:10-11; 1 Cor. 15:25), and they will worship him (Rev. 15:4).

2. Praise for God's Deliverances (*vv. 5-12*)

Come and see what God has done, how awesome his works in man's behalf! (*v. 5*). The invitation goes out (presumably to 'all the earth') to take notice of God's works, with this expression being practically the same as that in Psalm 46:8. In particular, his awesome deeds as he intervened on behalf of his people, are to be the object of admiration and awe. The two following verses illustrate this by appealing to the events of the Exodus.

He turned the sea into dry land, they passed through the waters on foot – come, let us rejoice in him. He rules

forever by his power, his eyes watch the nations – let not the rebellious rise up against him. Selah (*vv. 6-7*). Part of God's miraculous provision for his people was that he dried up the Red Sea. 'The waters' is 'river' in Hebrew, but nowhere is this particular word used of the Jordan. Hence, rather than see here a reference to the Red Sea *and* the Jordan, it is better to take it as alluding to the former only. The clause, 'Come, let us rejoice in him,' has been interpreted as an invitation to join in praise, but it is best to take it as a past tense.[2] The NIV 'come' translates the Hebrew word *shâm*, which normally means 'there', but at times it can mean 'then'.[3] The expression points to the rendering of praise to God for what he did at the time of the Exodus. While this may include the Song of the Sea (Exod. 15:1-18), it is a general comment on the response of the people to God's intervention on their behalf. The recollection of past divine actions is meant to form the basis of continuing praise. The reference to God's kingly rule in verse 7 is interesting, because the Song of the Sea concludes with the words: 'The LORD will reign for ever and ever' (Exod. 15:18). It is as if the psalmist is making a conscious allusion to the Book of Exodus. God's eyes are on all the nations, for he oversees all and yet overlooks none. The warning follows that the rebellious person should not vaunt himself against such a sovereign. The first of two occurrences of 'Selah' in this psalm indicates a break at the end of verse 7.

Praise our God, O peoples, let the sound of his praise be heard; he has preserved our lives and kept our feet from slipping (*vv. 8-9*). Attention switches to more recent displays of God's power, and the nations are again asked to participate in praise of what God has done. Whatever the precise details were of the recent events, it was a difficult time for the people, for their lives were in danger. God had preserved them, and he had been their keeper. When the verb 'slip' is used with 'foot' or 'feet', it denotes slipping in a time of trouble. The Lord is the one who is immovable and who gives stability to

---

[2] Though the form of the verb here is cohortative, 'let us rejoice', yet it can be translated as a past indicative, 'we rejoiced'. See *DIHG~S*, p. 83, rem. 3.

[3] *IBHS*, p. 658. Another example in the psalms occurs in Psalm 36:12.

believers (Pss. 30:6; 62:2; 112:6). He holds his children so that their feet do not slip (Pss. 17:5; 94:18).

For you, O God, tested us; you refined us like silver. You brought us into prison and laid burdens on our backs (*vv. 10-11*). The experiences the people had just undergone were intended by God to purify them. This may have meant refining the people so that the ungodly among the nation were removed (Jer. 6:29), or that the people were better prepared for service. The idea of refining of metals becomes a common Old Testament metaphor for the testing and refining of God's people (Pss. 17:3; 26:2; Isa. 1:25; Zech. 13:9). The word translated 'prison' may mean a net or a fortress, and so it serves as a metaphor for imprisonment. The word 'burdens' only occurs here in the Old Testament, and seems to indicate the afflictions associated with prison.

You let men ride over our heads; we went through fire and water, but you brought us to a place of abundance (*v. 12*). The imagery is of conquered people being forced to lie down and to be trampled underfoot, a practice widely attested in the ancient Near East. 'Fire and water' speak of the great dangers that the people endured (cf. Isa. 43:2), before they were finally brought through them and into God's generous provision. The ancient translations of the Old Testament (Greek LXX, Latin Vulgate, and the Aramaic Targum) all render the last phrase 'place of liberty' (*rᵉvâyâh*), which fits well with the picture of prison in verse 11. However, the comparison with its use in Psalm 23:5 ('my cup *overflows*') suggests that it is used here to express God's overflowing goodness to them, perhaps with the idea in mind of the provision of the land flowing with milk and honey.

3. Personal Thanksgiving (*vv. 13-20*)
I will come to your temple with burnt offerings and fulfil my vows to you – vows my lips promised and my mouth spoke when I was in trouble (*vv. 13-14*). During times of troubles vows were made to God. Some of these could be like the sinful vow Jephthah made when he went to fight the Ammonites (Judg. 11:30-40; the same verb 'promised' (*pâtsâh*) is used in

vv. 35-36 as here in Ps. 66). What had been spoken to God as a promise by the king (cf. Ps. 65:1 for reference to vows) is now to be paid. Vows were made for a variety of reasons, including, as here, for deliverance in a time of trouble. Usually thanksgiving offerings were partially consumed on the altar and the remainder was used in a communal meal. In this case the whole offering is dedicated to the LORD, which indicates a sombre mood on the part of the people as they reflect on the gravity of the danger through which they have come.

I will sacrifice fat animals to you and an offering of rams; I will offer bulls and goats. Selah (*v. 15*). The variety of animals offered in sacrifice helps to emphasise the spirit of thanksgiving. Not content with one kind, the psalmist pledges himself to present several kinds as a reflection of his total dedication to the LORD. The word used for 'offering' (*qᵉtoret*) is strictly 'smoke' or 'incense', but it is also employed in a more general way for offerings.[4] 'Selah' introduces another pause before the final song of thanksgiving.

Come and listen, all you who fear God; let me tell you what he has done for me. I cried out to him with my mouth; his praise was on my tongue (*vv. 16-17*). The final section of the psalm starts with a double command: 'Come; listen.' While it is conceivable that 'all you who fear God' is a reference to the God-fearing Gentiles (cf. the use of the term God-fearers in the New Testament, Acts 2:5), yet in the context it is more likely that devout believers within Israel are intended. The psalmist gives his own personal testimony concerning the things God has done for him. With his mouth he both called to God, and with it he extolled him. The same lips that prayed were ready to praise. The final clause, 'his praise was on my tongue', translates the MT that says 'praise was *under* my tongue'. The word 'praise' (*rômam*) is a *hapax legomenon*, and is often emended. It appears to be an unusual form from a common Hebrew root (*rûm*) that is used to express 'exaltation' or 'praise'. The idiom, 'under the tongue', may be similar to the English one, 'on the tip of the tongue'. The point is that the

---

[4] L. C. Allen, *Psalms 101-150* (Waco: Word Books, 1983), p. 272, n. 2.b, discusses the meaning of the word.

psalmist experienced a speedy response from God and he was ready immediately to give him praise.

If I had cherished sin in my heart, the Lord would not have listened; but God has surely listened and heard my voice in prayer (*vv. 18-19*). The verb 'listen' binds verses 16-19 together. 'Come, *listen,*' says the psalmist, for 'God has surely *listened.*' He proclaims his innocence before God, announcing the truth that if a person looks with satisfaction on his sin (the Hebrew text says 'if I had *looked* on'), then God will not hear him. It is to the godly man who does God's will that the LORD will listen (John 9:31; cf. 1 John 3:21-22).

Praise be to God, who has not rejected my prayer or withheld his love from me! (*v. 20*). The concluding verse is an expression of adoration of God. It probably goes back to Exodus 18:10, when Jethro, on hearing of what had happened to Israel, said: 'Praise be to the LORD, who rescued you from the hand of the Egyptians and of Pharaoh …' The psalmist praises the Lord for answering prayer and for bestowing covenant love upon him. God has not proved false to his own declared character (Exod. 34:6-7). He who was Israel's God ('*our* God', verse 8) is also the God of the individual believer ('*my* prayer', verse 20).

Psalm 67

For the director of music. With stringed instruments. A psalm. A song.

Psalms 65-67 are all linked together because of their universalism. The expression 'all [the ends of] the earth' occurs in each one (65:5; 66:4; 67:7). The link with Psalm 66 is even more patent, as it ends with the phrase 'blessed be God' (*bârûch ᵉlohîm*), while Psalm 67 begins and ends with the thought of God's blessing on his people ('may he bless us', *vîvârᵉkênû*, v. 1, and 'may God bless us', *yᵉvârᵉkênû*, vv. 6 and 7).

This psalm goes further than the previous ones as it includes a prayer for double blessing – first on Israel, and then on the Gentiles. The repetition of the refrain in verses 3 and 5 highlights the vision of the Gentiles sharing in the saving mercy of God, and it also divides the psalm into three parts. The beginning and the end invoke God's blessing (vv. 1-2 and 6-7), while in verses 3-5 God is addressed directly. Such a switch in address is not unusual in Hebrew poetry.

1. A Prayer for Blessing (*vv. 1-3*)
May God be gracious to us and bless us and make his face shine upon us, *Selah* that your ways may be known on earth, your salvation among all nations (*vv. 1-2*). The opening verse is an echo of the priestly benediction of Numbers 6:24-26. This is one of six occurrences of this expression in the psalms (the others are in 31:16; 80:3, 7, 19; 119:135). The use of well-known words forms a link with the past history of Israel as the psalmist seeks a fresh demonstration of God's mercy upon the people. 'Selah' comes at a most unusual place, though it

may well be positioned to emphasise the opening petition.[1] What follows is a desire for Israel's saving knowledge of God and his ways to be manifest to all nations. The thought here may be similar to Isaiah 43:10-13, where Israel is declared to be a witness that the LORD is God, and that there is no saviour apart from him. After being blessed, Israel becomes a blessing to the nations.[2]

May the peoples praise you, O God; may all the peoples praise you (*v. 3*). The desire of verses 1-2 is now turned into a direct prayer, which is repeated exactly in verse 5. Knowledge of God should flow into acknowledgment and praise of him. Hence, the psalmist prays that when the nations have come into knowledge of the one true God, they lift their voices in thankful song.[3] The reference to 'all the peoples' comes at the end of the clause in Hebrew and accentuates the thought: 'May the peoples praise you – all of them!'

2. A Prayer for the Nations (*vv. 4-5*)

May the nations be glad and sing for joy, for you rule the peoples justly and guide the nations of the earth. *Selah* (*v. 4*). The thought of the preceding verses is taken a step further with the idea of exuberant praise being given by the nations. God's saving power (v. 2) is also seen in his just rule, for there is a standard of equity that governs his acts of judgment.[4] Though in operation now, this rule will come to full expression at the return of Christ, when he 'will judge the

---

[1] A number of commentators suggest moving 'Selah' to the end of the verse. However, the Hebrew manuscripts uniformly have it in its present position, and the LXX is testimony to this being so at the time when it was translated.

[2] The word here for 'nations' is *gôyîm*. While it is sometimes used of Israel (Deut. 4:6; Josh. 3:17), yet much more often it is used of the Gentile nations. Two other Hebrew words for 'nation' occur in this same psalm, *'am* and *le'um*, all virtually interchangeable in a context like this.

[3] The verb translated 'praise' is not one of the usual ones (*h-l-l*, *z-m-r*, *sh-v-ch*) but *y-d-h*, that has more the meaning of 'acknowledge' or 'thank'.

[4] The word for 'justly' is *mîshôr*, which has the basic meaning of a 'plain' or 'flat land', but takes on a wider meaning of what is 'right' or 'just'. It is also used in Isaiah 11:4 conjoined with the verb 'to judge' (*shâfat*) as here in this verse (cf. Ps. 72:12-14).

world in righteousness and the peoples with equity' (Ps. 98:9). Just as God leads his own people, so the prayer is that he will bring blessing and salvation to the Gentiles. The Christian's prayer is:

> Let Zion's time of favour come;
> O bring the tribes of Israel home;
> And let our wondering eyes behold
> Gentiles and Jews in Jesus' fold.
>
> Almighty God, Thy grace proclaim
> In every clime of every name;
> Let adverse powers before Thee fall,
> And crown the Saviour Lord of all.
> (William Shrubsole, 1759-1829)

May the peoples praise you, O God; may all the peoples praise you (*v. 5*). The use of the recurring refrain (see comment on v. 3) serves to draw attention to the theme of universal praise that dominates throughout this psalm. The vision is of a world falling down in praise to God the Saviour. Ultimately the Lord Jesus will be the object of praise as depicted in Revelation 5:12: 'Worthy is the Lamb, who was slain, to receive power and wealth and wisdom and strength, and honour and glory and praise!'

3. A Prayer for Universal Blessing (vv. 6-7)
Then the land will yield its harvest, and God, our God, will bless us. God will bless us, and all the ends of the earth will fear him (*vv. 6-7*). One of the opening petitions is made the focal point of these final verses. The psalmist is confident that God, whom faith claims as 'our God', will indeed bless his people with abundant harvest in the land he has given them.[5] The wording of the first clause is almost exactly the same as Leviticus 26:4. Material and spiritual blessings seem to be joined together, for blessing of Israel is linked with the idea that the ends of the earth will come to fear the Lord. The

---

[5] While the Hebrew word *'érets* is translated as 'earth' earlier in the psalm (vv. 2 and 4), yet here when the reference is to 'our God', 'land' is necessary.

opening and close of the psalm strike the same note. Blessing of Israel brings God's knowledge to the nations so that they will revere him. Through the fall of Israel riches indeed came to the Gentiles, and how much greater riches will the ingathering of Israel bring (Rom. 11:11-12)!

Psalm 68

For the director of music. Of David. A psalm. A song.

There is no more triumphant song in the whole of the Psalter than Psalm 68. It begins with an echo of Moses' prayer when the ark of the covenant led the people in the wilderness (Num. 10:35). It moves on to a description of the journey from Sinai to the promised land, with the procession of the ark into Jerusalem in David's time. This was seen as God's coming there. It closes with a song of praise to the Lord who rules over all the kingdoms of the earth.

There are many textual difficulties in this psalm, including the fact that fifteen words or expressions in it occur nowhere else in the Old Testament. At times a sudden change of ideas occurs that is difficult to fit into the overall unity of the psalm. The emphasis on God is maintained throughout, and a great variety of names for God is employed (*ᵉlohîm*, 23×; *ᵃdonay*, 6×; *ʾêl*, 2×; and *shaddai*, *Yahweh*, *Yâh*, *Yahweh ᵃdonay*, and *Yahweh ᵉlohîm* once each). In the centre of the psalm (vv. 19-20) a cluster of references to God is an emphatic declaration concerning his saving activity. Alternation in the use of the third and second person forms which is seen in Psalms 66 and 67 appears here also ('May God arise ... God sets the lonely in families ... You went out ... The Lord announced the word ... When you ascended on high ... Praise be to the Lord ... Your procession has come into view ... Summon your power, O God ... Sing to God, O kingdoms of the earth ... You are awesome, O God ... Praise be to God!').

1. A Prayer for the Coming of the Lord (*vv. 1-6*)
May God arise, may his enemies be scattered; may his foes flee before him. As smoke is blown away by the wind, may

you blow them away; as wax melts before the fire, may the wicked perish before God (*vv. 1-2*). The call to God is given in the language that Moses used whenever the ark set out: 'Rise up, O LORD! May your enemies be scattered; may your foes flee before you' (Num. 10:35). This processional hymn starts with the request for God's intervention on behalf of his people, just as he intervened in times past. The enemies are compared to smoke and wax to illustrate how feeble they are to stand against the power of the LORD. Four verbs are used to describe the reaction of the wicked to God's presence – 'scatter', 'flee', 'blown away', and 'perish'. As the metaphors change, a varied picture is given of God's ability to overcome his enemies.

But may the righteous be glad and rejoice before God; may they be happy and joyful (*v. 3*). Whereas the wicked flee before God (v. 1), the righteous are joyful before him. The initial 'but' marks the sharp contrast that is going to be stated.[1] Just as four terms were used of the wicked's reaction, so here four terms are employed to describe the way in which the godly respond – 'be glad', 'rejoice', 'be happy', 'joyful'. Relationship with God determines conduct in his presence. At the final coming of the LORD, the wicked will be shut out from his presence, while the righteous believers will glorify him in that day (2 Thess. 1:9-10).

Sing to God, sing praise to his name, extol him who rides on the clouds – his name is the LORD – and rejoice before him (*v. 4*). The invitation is to sing to God, whose name is the LORD. In the Hebrew text the word 'LORD' is an abbreviated form of the divine name (*Yâh*), and it occurs most commonly in poetic passages such as this, in names like Elijah or Uzziah, and in the expression 'Hallelujah' ('Praise the LORD!'). Another three words relating to praise appear in this verse ('sing', 'sing praise', 'extol him'). The last of these (*sâlal*) is quite common, but with the meaning of building a highway. Because it comes here in parallel with two well-known verbs denoting praise (*shîr* and *zâmar*, Pi.) the context requires a translation

---

[1] 'But' is represented by the conjunction (*vᵉ*), which is used here in an adversative way, and the normal word order in such cases (conjunction + subject) is followed. For this usage, see *IBHS*, p. 129, 8.3b.

that carries on this idea. It is quite possible that a verb that originally meant 'to lift up [stones]' could be extended to mean 'lift up a song'.[2] The translation of the description of the LORD as the one 'who rides on the clouds' is difficult. It is better to follow the NIV footnote, 'who rides through the deserts', which then would agree with verses 7-8. The ESV also accepts this interpretation.[3]

A father to the fatherless, a defender of widows, is God in his holy dwelling. God sets the lonely in families, he leads forth the prisoners with singing; but the rebellious live in a sun-scorched land (*vv. 5-6*). Though God is so powerful, yet he has a concern for the needy. The three groups most likely to suffer injustice were the orphans, the widows and the strangers (Deut. 10:18-19; 24:17). Here, and in Psalm 146:9, the fatherless and the widows are said to be the special objects of God's interest. It is unclear whether God's holy dwelling is heaven or the temple. The strangers and other lonely ones are brought under his protection, while even the foreign prisoners (the word usually means this, cf. Ps. 69:33; Isa. 14:17; and Zech. 9:11) experience his redemption, and consequently his joy. The rebellious within Israel, however, have none of this joy, and they are depicted as if they live in a barren place.

2. From the Exodus to Jerusalem (*vv. 7-18*)

A poetic description is now given of the way in which God led his people through the wilderness to Canaan (vv. 7-10), his gift

---

[2] I discuss the root and its derivatives in *NIDOTTE*, 3, pp. 264-67. No noun from the root *s-l-l* means 'praise'. They are all related to road building or construction of siege ramps. Articles relating to this root are listed in *DCH*, VI, p. 834. For this passage *CHAL*, p. 257, offers the translation 'prepare a road (while singing)'.

[3] The Hebrew word in question is *ʿărāvôt*, 'wildernesses'. While it can refer to specific geographical areas (see its use for the rift valley along the Jordan in Num. 22:1 and Josh. 4:13; and for the shore area south-west of the Dead Sea in 1 Sam. 23:24 and Isa. 51:3), it also designates, in general, sparsely vegetated areas (as in Isa. 33:9 and Jer. 51:43). The translation 'clouds' derives from equating it with the Ugaritic epithet for Baal, 'rider of the clouds' (*rkb ʿrpt*). This assumes that the Hebrew consonant *b* has replaced the Ugaritic *p*. The *DCH*, VI, pp. 552-53, gives it as meaning 'steppe, desert', and then tentatively points to the possibility that it means 'cloud'.

to them of the land (vv. 11-14), and how he then took up his abode on Mount Zion (vv. 15-18). There is a change from the use of the third person to direct address to God himself.

When you went out before your people, O God, when you marched through the wasteland, – *Selah* – the earth shook, the heavens poured down rain, before God, the One of Sinai, before God, the God of Israel (*vv. 7-8*). This account of the Exodus draws upon the Song of Deborah (Judg. 5:4-5). God went ahead of his people (Exod. 13:21), after the events at the Red Sea had demonstrated his great power. The reference to 'wastelands' uses a word (*yᵉshîmôn*) that can denote a specific area, either in the Negev (1 Sam. 23:19, 24; 26:1, 3) or in Transjordan (Num. 21:20; 23:28). It can also have a wider meaning much like the regular word for 'desert' (*midbâr*), as is shown by the use of these two words in parallel (cf. Isa. 43:19, 20). Earthquake and storm were symbolic of God's presence and power. He was the one who had displayed his greatness at Sinai when he entered into a covenant with his people Israel.[4] The use of 'Selah' here and in verses 19 and 32 in the middle of a stanza appears to give special emphasis to the preceding expression.

You gave abundant showers, O God; you refreshed your weary inheritance. Your people settled in it, and from your bounty, O God, you provided for the poor (*vv. 9-10*). The land of Canaan was a gracious provision of God for his people. He gave them a land 'that drinks rain from heaven' (Deut. 11:11). Several of the phrases in verse 9 are difficult to translate. NIV 'gave' is a verb (*nûf*) that may mean 'sprinkle' or 'deliver in large measure', the latter matching the context well.[5] 'Abundant showers' (*géshem nᵉdâvâh*) uses the regular word for 'rain' but qualifies it with an adjective that is often used of the freewill offerings or contributions for building the tabernacle and the temple (Exod. 35:29;

---

[4] NIV's 'the One of Sinai' is the translation of *zeh sînai*, lit. 'this Sinai'. When compared with other expressions like *zeh ʿonî*, 'this poor one' (Ps. 34:6), the NIV translation makes good sense. It is the equivalent of 'the God of Sinai'.

[5] *DCH*, V, pp. 645-47, lists six homonyms for *nûf*, preferring the alternatives given above for this passage.

2 Chron. 31:14; Ezra 1:4). It denotes 'rain of generosity', hence 'abundant rain'. 'Refresh' (*kûn*, Pol.) conveys the idea of sustaining God's 'inheritance' (*nachᵃlâh*), one of the distinctive terms for the gift of the land. It is described as being 'weary' (*nil'âh*), a land impoverished because of drought.[6] The beginning of verse 10 is rather cryptic, and both the early versions and modern translations differ widely. The opening word (*chayyâh*) is normally used to denote animals, not humans. The LXX understood it to mean 'living creatures' (*ta zôa sou*, cf. Revelation 4:6-9), though the context demands a reference to people. Hence, the NIV translation 'your people', or 'your troop' fits the passage.[7] The mention of the 'poor' is significant, for this word ('*onî*) is translated as 'afflicted' in other places, and it is used to describe the condition of Israel in Egypt (see Exod. 3:7, 17 [NIV 'misery']). While these verses draw attention to material blessings in Canaan, most probably they also speak of all the bountiful and varied ways in which God blessed Israel.

The Lord announced the word, and great was the company of those who proclaimed it: 'Kings and armies flee in haste; in the camps men divide the plunder. Even while you sleep among the campfires, the wings of [my] dove are sheathed with silver, its feathers with shining gold' (*vv. 11-13*). Comparison with other translations shows how difficult all translators have found these and the following verses.[8] There seem to be allusions to Deborah's Song (Judg. 5), but perhaps also to other songs not recorded in Scripture. The general picture is that God gave his message concerning the conquest of Canaan, and the women proclaimed it ('those who proclaimed it' is

---

[6] The Hebrew phrase is 'your inheritance and weary' (*nachᵃlâtᵉkâ vᵉnil'âh*), a grammatical construction (*hendiadys*) in which the one idea is presented in two expressions. Cf. the English phrase, 'with might and main'.

[7] *DCH*, III, pp. 207-09, gives four possible meanings for *chayyâh*, and prefers the translation of the clause as 'Your dwelling place, they dwelt in it'. Some Hebrew manuscripts have a different verb, 'they return' (*yâshûvû*), but the LXX translators clearly read it as the verb 'to dwell' (*katoikousin*).

[8] Very helpful notes on verses 12-13 can be found in VanGemeren, 'Psalms', p. 448, and in *NIDOTTE*, 2, pp. 269-70.

feminine in Hebrew). The verb used (*bâsar*, Pi.), while it can be neutral, yet significantly is used to depict the servant of the LORD's mission of proclaiming 'good news' (Isa. 61:1; cf. also Isa. 40:9 in connection with proclamation of salvation). Armies were forced to flee before Israel (the RSV stays close to the Hebrew, and depicts the vividness of the action, 'they flee, they flee'!), leaving their spoils behind them. 'In the camps' is a possible interpretation of an obscure phrase (*nᵉvat báyit*),[9] though, since the following verb (*tᵉchallêq*, 'she divides') is feminine singular, another interpretation is preferable. This expression may be rendered 'the beauty of the house' and be a collective expression for 'the women'.[10] 'In the campfires' lacks credible support. The word rendered 'campfires' (*shᵉfatâyim*) only appears here and in Ezekiel 40:43 in the Old Testament, and some consider it means 'pack saddles'.[11] The verse is best taken as describing the women who wait at home and then are given spoils won in battle. The exact nature and significance of the 'dove' is unclear. It may have been some special cultic object taken after victory over Canaanites.

When the Almighty scattered the kings in the land, it was like snow fallen on Zalmon (*v. 14*). Similarly, this verse is perplexing, because we cannot be sure of the location of Zalmon, nor of the significance of the snow. It could mean that God sent a snowstorm to rout the enemy forces at Zalmon. This could be a location either near Shechem (see Judg. 9:48), or on the east bank of the Jordan, as suggested by the mention of Bashan in the next verse. An alternative interpretation is that the bleached bones of fallen warriors looked like snow on the hillside.

The mountains of Bashan are majestic mountains; rugged are the mountains of Bashan. Why gaze in envy, O rugged mountains, at the mountain where God chooses to reign, where the LORD himself will dwell forever? (*vv. 15-16*). God did not choose the highest of mountains within the land of

---

[9] For the various possible translations, see M. Tate, *Psalms 51–100*, p.164-65.

[10] This interpretation is the one preferred by Tate, ibid., pp. 160, 165.

[11] So *KB*, p. 1006.

promise. Rather, he chose Zion (see Ps. 132:13-18).[12] Bashan may well have been Mount Hermon, and it represented what was powerful and rich (Deut. 32:14; Amos 4:1; Ps. 22:12).[13] It is rebuked for being envious of Zion, which is the seat of God's kingdom. Zion was the mountain of God's inheritance, and from there the LORD would reign (Exod. 15:17-18).

The chariots of God are tens of thousands and thousands of thousands; the Lord [has come] from Sinai into his sanctuary. When you ascended on high, you led captives in your train; you received gifts from men, even from the rebellious – that you, O LORD God, might dwell there (*vv. 17-18*). On the march into Canaan God is accompanied by his mighty forces. The expressions for the numbers are unusual (lit. 'two countless hosts, thousands of repetition'), but NIV captures well the general sense.[14] These are his heavenly servants (Deut. 33:2; 2 Kings 6:15-17). Jesus could have called for such heavenly assistants and his Father would have sent more than twelve legions of angels (Matt. 26:53). The revelation at Sinai was a revelation of God's holiness (Hebrew has 'in holiness', which the NIV interprets to mean 'in the holy place', 'in the sanctuary'). This revelation left the people fearful (Deut. 5:23-27). God's holiness was shown in so many incidents on the way to Canaan. When Zion was finally reached it was like a victory procession, with captives being led there, along with their tribute gifts (2 Sam. 8:11; 1 Kings 4:21). Verse 18 is quoted by Paul with some variation in Ephesians 4:8, and in particular he has 'he *gave* gifts to men' in place of 'he *took* gifts'. The exegetical problem in Ephesians has been noted as far back as the early church fathers, with Chrysostom (AD 345-407) commenting that the words 'took' and 'gave' convey the same meaning. Many explanations have

---

[12] The verb used here for 'choose' is *châmad*, which often means 'desire'. However, in Isaiah 1:29 it is paralleled with *bâchar*, the much more common verb meaning 'choose'.

[13] The NIV rendering 'majestic mountains' is probably correct, though the MT has *har ʾelohîm*, 'the hill of God'. The use of a divine name in connection with a noun is a Hebrew way of giving a superlative sense. For details on this usage, see *DIHG~S*, p. 46, rem. 5; *IBHS*, p. 268, including bibliography in f.n. 26.

[14] The word 'repetition' (*shinʾân*) is a *hapax legomenon*, and presumably it is a by-form from the verb *shânâh*, 'to repeat'.

been offered for the change.[15] The parallel with God's action in taking the Levites and giving them back to Israel as a gift (see Num. 8 and 18) fits well the context in Ephesians. Paul's stress lies on the fact of Christ's ascension and his bestowal of gifts on his people, just as the psalm goes on to speak of the blessings that God dispenses (vv. 19-30).

3. Praise for the Saviour (vv. 19-23)

The account of the triumphal procession is broken off (not resumed until v. 24) for an ascription of praise to the Saviour. **Praise be to the Lord, to God our Saviour, who daily bears our burdens.** *Selah (v. 19).* Recollection of God's great acts of deliverance and redemption call forth a song of praise. He is extolled as the Saviour and as the burden bearer. The wonderful thing is that the mighty God stoops to his people, and daily carries their burdens (or possibly it could be rendered, 'who daily carries *us*', i.e. like a shepherd).[16] The New Testament still encourages us to cast all our anxiety on the Lord because he cares for us (1 Pet. 5:7).

Our God is a God who saves; from the Sovereign LORD comes escape from death *(v. 20).* A more literal translation is 'Our God is a God of *deliverances,* to the Sovereign LORD belong *escapes* from death'. The plurals may be used deliberately, as Calvin suggested, to show that although numerous threats of death may come against us, yet God has innumerable ways of delivering us.[17] The emphasis is on the bounteous provision that God makes for his people, in displaying his abundant grace and power in deliverance.

Surely God will crush the heads of his enemies, the hairy crowns of those who go on in their sins *(v. 21).* The reverse is also certain. God is pledged to destroy those who oppose

---

[15] An excellent summary of the various viewpoints can be found in Peter O'Brien, *The Letter to the Ephesians,* pp. 288-93. Two important journal articles are G. V. Smith, 'Paul's Use of Psalm 68:18 in Ephesians', *JETS* 18 (1975), pp. 181-89, and R. A. Taylor, 'The Use of Psalm 68:18 in Ephesians 4:8 in Light of the Ancient Versions', *BS* 148 (1991), pp. 319-36.

[16] 'Daily' is represented in the MT, not by the common word *yômām,* but by the repetition of the word 'day', *yôm yôm.* It, and similar forms (*yôm vâyôm* and *yôm b^eyôm*), signify 'day after day'.

[17] John Calvin, *A Commentary on the Psalms of David,* II, p. 210.

him. The same verb 'to crush' is used in Psalm 110:5-6 of God's activity in judging kings and rulers. 'The hairy crowns' seem to refer to the pride of the enemies as they go on in their sinful ways.

The Lord says, 'I will bring them from Bashan; I will bring them from the depths of the sea, that you may plunge your feet in the blood of your foes, while the tongues of your dogs have their share' (*vv. 22-23*). In the Hebrew text the object of the verb 'bring' in verse 22 is not expressed.[18] While it could be 'you', i.e. the people of Israel, yet the context suggests it is 'them', i.e. the enemies. No place is so remote that God's enemies can find a hiding place from him. Both from inaccessible places on land (Bashan, east of the Jordan) and sea (the depths) God will bring his enemies for judgment. The graphic imagery of battle may be too strong for modern Westerners, but it certainly is in agreement with other Old Testament descriptions, including the account of the deaths of Ahab and Jezebel (1 Kings 21:19; 22:38; 2 Kings 9:36). The reference to dogs licking the blood may have been a proverbial expression for retribution.

4. Praise of God in the Congregation (*vv. 24-27*)

Your procession has come into view, O God, the procession of my God and King into the sanctuary (*v. 24*). Attention comes back to the procession after victory in battle.[19] Whereas previously God was called 'our God', the psalmist now speaks in more personal terms still, calling him '*my* God and King'. The procession continues until it arrives in the sanctuary, already mentioned earlier in verse 17. True faith appropriates this type of language as it responds to the close relationship with God. New Testament parallels are

---

[18] The verb is actually 'bring back' (*shûv*, Hi.). Though it is used more often of the return of Israel to Palestine, yet here the context requires 'the enemies' to be the subject.

[19] The NIV translation of the opening clause is rather free but captures the sense. The MT has simply 'they saw' (*râ'û*), an impersonal use of the 3rd pers. pl. form of the verb. No need exists for emendation in order to agree with the LXX, 'they were seen'.

Thomas's words, 'My Lord and *my* God' (John 20:28), and Paul's, 'the Son of God, who loved *me* and gave himself for *me*' (Gal. 2:20).

In front are the singers, after them the musicians; with them are the maidens playing tambourines (*v. 25*). This scene recalls what happened after the deliverance at the Red Sea, when Miriam led the women in singing and dancing (Exod. 15:19-21). The singers and musicians are going before the main procession, rejoicing in the deliverances that resemble the Exodus. The NIV translation suggests that the maidens are simply 'with' the singers and musicians. The MT requires the translation 'in the midst of girls [playing] tambourines'.

Praise God in the great congregation; praise the LORD in the assembly of Israel (*v. 26*). Either these words form what the women said in praise, or else they are a call to everyone to extol him in the midst of the congregation of Israel. Israel was made up of many companies (NIV 'great congregation'), which all stemmed from the one source, 'the fountain of Israel' (following the Hebrew text).[20]

There is the little tribe of Benjamin, leading them, there the great throng of Judah's princes, and there the princes of Zebulun and of Naphtali (*v. 27*). The four tribes mentioned seem to represent the whole of Israel. North and south are together, as they were at the time of the conquest. Even in the New Testament these tribes were important, as our Lord and some of his apostles came from Judah, while Paul, 'the least of the apostles' (1 Cor. 15:9), came from Benjamin (Phil. 3:5). Various suggestions have been made as to why Paul draws attention to his Benjamite background, but it is probably simply to make the point that he was truly an authentic Jew.[21]

---

[20] The evidence is not conclusive that the word *mâqôr* should be rendered 'assembly' or 'convocation'. No need exists here, or in Proverbs 18:4, for this translation, the two passages claimed as supporting the alteration (see *DCH*, V, p. 466). 'Source' or 'well-spring' fits well in this context: '[You who are] from the source of Israel' (so Marvin Tate, *Psalms 51-100*, pp. 161, 167-68).

[21] A good survey of the various interpretations of Paul's use of the phrase 'from the tribe of Benjamin' is given by W. Hendriksen, *A Commentary on the Epistle of Paul to the Philippians* (London: Banner of Truth, 1963), pp. 156-58.

The remainder of the apostles were from the territory of Zebulun and Naphtali.

5. Praise of God in all the World (*vv. 28-35*)
Summon your power, O God; show us your strength, O God, as you have done before. Because of your temple at Jerusalem kings will bring you gifts (*vv. 28-29*). The NIV interpretation is that God is enthroned, and now he is asked for a fresh demonstration of his great power. The problem is that the MT has '*Your* God has commanded *your* strength' (NKJV, following the AV, NASB; the ESV margin has 'Your God has commanded your power').The reference is to the way in which God had in the past strengthened his people. The psalmist goes on to request a fresh demonstration of God's power, seen in the Exodus and in many later deliverances (v. 20). However, now the demonstration is to all the kingdoms of the earth, and foreign kings will come to do homage before the Lord in Jerusalem. The eschatological picture here is amplified in the Book of Revelation. Into the New Jerusalem, which has the Lord God Almighty and the Lamb as its temple, 'the kings of the earth will bring their splendour' (Rev. 21:24).

Rebuke the beast among the reeds, the herd of bulls among the calves of the nations. Humbled, may it bring bars of silver. Scatter the nations who delight in war. Envoys will come from Egypt; Cush will submit herself to God (*vv. 30-31*). 'The beast' is probably an allusion to an historical enemy, most probably Egypt. Elsewhere Leviathan (apparently either the crocodile or the hippopotamus) stands for Egypt (Ps. 74:14; Isa. 27:1). 'The herd of bulls' (*ᵃdat 'âbbîrîm*) is probably intended as a reference to the leaders or kings,[22] while the calves seem to be less powerful nations who follow their leaders.[23] The second half of verse 30 is uncertain. The verb 'humbled'

---

[22] Cf. the expression 'a band of ruthless men' (*ᵃdat 'ârîtsîm*) in Psalm 86:14.
[23] The expression 'among the calves of the people' (*bᵉ eglê 'ammîm*) is very unusual, and it is difficult to ascertain its significance. To translate it 'calf-people' (see M. E. Tate, *Psalms 51-100*, p. 168) does not elucidate it any further. I am presuming that it depicts smaller nations that follow leaders, just as calves follow a bull.

(*mitrappês*) may come from a root meaning 'to make oneself polluted by trampling' and hence be equivalent to humbling oneself.[24] 'May it bring bars of silver' is one interpretation of the following words, though the RSV rendering 'those who lust for silver' is probably closer to the mark.[25] Nations that delight in war find that God's hand comes against them, and they are dispersed. Egypt will come[26] and do homage to the Lord by sending ambassadors.[27] This is part of the prophetical picture of the events on the great day of the LORD (Isa. 19:18-25). Even ancient foes of Israel such as Egypt will come in submission, while her tributary Cush (upper Egypt or Ethiopia) will also display her allegiance (cf. Isa. 45:14).

Sing to God, O kingdoms of the earth, sing praise to the Lord, Selah – to him who rides the ancient skies above, who thunders with mighty voice (*vv. 32-33*). A song of rejoicing is needed from all the kingdoms of the earth as a fitting acknowledgment of the universal sway of God. 'Selah', inserted in the middle of the stanza, stresses this call. The song itself is an expansion of verse 4, using again two of the verbs already employed (*shîr* and *zâmar*, Pi.). The thought of riding through the skies is probably based on Deuteronomy 33:26, while 'the ancient skies' (*sh*e*mê qédem*) recalls Moses' assertion that 'to the LORD your God belong the heavens, even the highest heavens' (Deut. 10:14). The heavens are ancient in the sense that no one knows their beginning. God is pictured as riding through them like a king in his chariot traversing his territory. The God of eternity, who had already made his proclamation (see v. 12), now speaks in mighty power (cf. Ps. 29:3-5).

---

[24] See the discussion of this word by Bruce Waltke, *Proverbs 1-15*, p. 333, f.n. 53.

[25] The RSV takes the verb to be *râtsâh*, 'to be pleased with'.

[26] The verb for 'come' is *'âtâh*, found only in poetical passages in Hebrew, but much more common in Aramaic. It appears in the standard formula, 'Come, O Lord' (*maran-atha*, 1 Cor. 16:22).

[27] The word for 'ambassadors' (*chashmannîm*) only occurs here in the MT. If we follow the LXX translation of *presbeis*, 'envoys', this does not preclude the possibility that such envoys were marked out by the wearing of red cloth, as W. F. Albright suggested. See M. E. Tate, *Psalms 51-100*, p. 169, f.n. 32.a.

Proclaim the power of God, whose majesty is over Israel, whose power is in the skies. You are awesome, O God, in your sanctuary; the God of Israel gives power and strength to his people. Praise be to God! (*vv. 34-35*). The wording here seems to continue echoing Deuteronomy 33:26. God's majesty is displayed in two ways. First, he shows his power in creation and providence, as he rules over the earth and skies. Secondly, his majesty is seen in a special way as it is revealed to his people Israel. The psalmist addresses God directly, declaring that he is there in the midst of them in the sanctuary or holy place ('from *your* sanctuary'), and he is to be feared (*nôrâ'*). The great God condescends to meet his people, and as they worship him he imparts strength to them. Then a switch back to the third person takes place in the final declarations. Earlier the psalmist has spoken a doxology on behalf of Israel (v. 19). Now he concludes with one that is to be spoken both by Israel and by the kingdoms of the world: 'Praise be to God!' The psalm concludes on the note of fulness of praise being ascribed to Israel's God. The New Testament points to a day when the kingdoms of this world will become the kingdoms of our Lord and of his Christ (Rev. 11:15).

Psalm 69

For the director of music. To [the tune of] 'Lilies.' Of David.

This is one of the most quoted psalms in the New Testament. The following list shows how widely it is utilised: verse 4 (John 15:25); verse 9 (John 2:17); verse 21 (Matt. 27:34, 48); verses 22-24 (Rom. 11:9-10); verse 24 (Rev. 16:1); verse 25 (Acts 1:20). The psalm deals with sin and its consequences, and the extended use of it in the New Testament shows that even Christians today cannot evade the issues it raises. There is no separation of sin from the sinner in the Bible, in the way in which people often wish to divorce a sinner (who is loved) from his sin (which is hated). This is another psalm that has many curses in it (see Introduction), but the very fact that Jesus takes part of it on his lips should cause us to look carefully at it. Originally it referred to the bitter experiences of David, and then typically it is applied to Christ. The similarities between David's experience and those of Jesus are not exhausted by the quotations. The mockery mentioned in verse 12 is reflected in the mockery of Jesus recorded in Matthew 27:27-30, while the offer of vinegar to drink (v. 21) has its parallel in the wine mixed with myrrh that the soldiers offered to Jesus (Mark 15:23).

Interesting connections also exist between Psalm 69 and Psalm 40, so much so that they have been called 'twin-Psalms'.[1] The description of need as sinking into water or mire occurs in both psalms (69:2 and 40:2), while the expression 'more than the hairs of my head' also appears in both (69:4 and 40:12). Very similar statements are made about

---

[1] The phrase is that of F. Delitzsch, *Psalms*, I, p. 275.

505

ceremonial acts (69:31 and 40:6) and the indication is given that the righteous will extol the Lord's deeds (69:32 and 40:16). No dependence can be shown, but certainly the vocabulary indicates that expressions common in Israel were being used in both psalms. The link between Psalms 40 and 69 is made explicit by the fact that Psalm 70 is composed of a slightly altered version of Psalm 40:13-17.

1. A Personal Cry (*vv. 1-4*)
Save me, O God, for the waters have come up to my neck. I sink in the miry depths, where there is no foothold. I have come into the deep waters; the floods engulf me (*vv. 1-2*). The psalm commences with a general cry, and it is not until a few verses later that the nature of his need is specified. The psalmist compares himself to a drowning man, who is desperately trying to keep his head above the water. Sudden floods in Palestine made very realistic the idea of water reaching up to the neck (see Isa. 8:8). Though the MT simply says 'water up to neck' the context requires '*my* neck', a translation that goes back as far as the LXX.[2]

I am worn out calling for help; my throat is parched. My eyes fail, looking for my God (*v. 3*). The psalmist's distress has been going on for some time, for he is wearied by his attempts to attract God's attention. His throat is sore and, as he waits for God to intervene, his eyes are like those of a sick person who has wept copiously.[3]

Those who hate me without reason outnumber the hairs of my head; many are my enemies without cause, those who seek to destroy me. I am forced to restore what I did not steal (*v. 4*). This verse presents difficulties of translation and interpretation. The first two clauses are clearly parallel:

'[More] numerous than the hairs of my head [are] those who hate me without cause'

---

[2] I am taking the Hebrew word *néfesh* as meaning 'neck'. For the wide range uses of this word in the Old Testament, see *DCH*, V, pp. 724-34.

[3] The word for 'looking [for God]' (*yâchal*, Pi.) conveys the idea of 'expectant waiting', and hence of 'hoping'. Cf. its use in Psalm 31:24.

'[More] numerous [are] my destroyers [than] those who are
my enemies without reason'

The verbs are to be taken as synonyms (*râvâh*//*ʿâtsam*),[4] while
the final phrases are also synonymous, having exactly the
same Hebrew construction.[5] The full parallelism breaks
down in reference to the middle words ('from the hairs of my
head', 'my destroyers'). Emendation has been proposed by
various scholars so that 'my destroyers' becomes 'my locks',
so matching the reference to hair.[6] But the MT makes sense in
that his enemies, without any legitimate reason, are dedicated
to his destruction. This first part of the verse is quoted partially
in John 15:25 when Jesus is speaking about the world's hatred
of his disciples. The final clause declares that there is no truth
in the false accusation that he is stealing from others. It may
well be a proverbial saying in question form: 'What I did not
steal must I now restore?'[7]

2. An Explanation of His Suffering (*vv. 5-12*)

**You know my folly, O God; my guilt is not hidden from
you** (*v. 5*). Before going on to describe further his suffering,
the psalmist makes an open confession to God. He has done
foolish things in God's sight,[8] and he knows that he cannot
hold anything back from him. His very nature is under the
scrutiny of God (Ps. 139:15). Later in the psalm (v. 26) mention

---

[4] It is correct that the verb *ʿâtsam* can refer to strength, but the context here is about the large number of foes, not their physical capabilities.

[5] Both have a Hebrew participle + an adverb: 'my haters without cause' (*sonᵉʾay chinnâm*) and 'my enemies without reason' (*ʾoyᵉvay shéqer*). For these constructions, see *DIHG~S*, pp. 41-42. They have the same word order: verb + prepositional phrase + subject.

[6] See, e.g., M. Dahood, *Psalms II:51–100*, p. 157. However, no manuscript support can be cited, and apart from the Syriac, which has 'from my bones', the early versions support the MT.

[7] This is an interpretation suggested by M. E. Tate, *Psalms 51–100*, p. 189, n. 5. c.

[8] The expression 'my folly' (*ʾivvaltî*) is preceded by *lᵉ*. This is an example of the use of *lᵉ* in a non-prepositional way. Here it serves a function rather like *ʾêt* to mark a direct object of a transitive verb. For discussion of this usage, see *DIHG~S*, pp. 108, 115-18, and *IBHS*, p. 165.

is made of God's 'wounding', probably a reference to the consequences of his sin spoken of here.

May those who hope in you not be disgraced because of me, O Lord, the LORD Almighty; may those who seek you not be put to shame because of me, O God of Israel (*v. 6*). The cluster of names for God is highly appropriate in this setting. Appeal to him as LORD Almighty (i.e. over all things) is made, yet he is also the covenant God of Israel who is near his people to help them in times such as this. The thought of not being disgraced has already been presented in Psalm 25:3, and the two roots denoting disgrace or shame (*bûsh* and *k-l-m*) occur several times in parallel in other psalms (cf. Pss. 44:15; 70:2; 71:13; 109:28-29). The psalmist does not want those who are truly God's (lit. 'your hopers' and 'your seekers') to suffer because of anything he does.

For I endure scorn for your sake, and shame covers my face. I am a stranger to my brothers, an alien to my own mother's sons; for zeal for your house consumes me, and the insults of those who insult you fall on me (*vv. 7-9*). It is not for his own sake that the psalmist suffers reproach or mocking (lit. 'carrying reproach', *nâsâh cherpâh*). The description adds to the use of the verb 'put to shame' (*kâlam*) in the previous verse by the employment now of the related noun 'shame' (*kᵉlimmâh*). He is cut off from his closest family members for God's sake (cf. the communal acknowledgment of suffering for God's sake in Ps. 44:22). He is so identified with the temple, for which he has the deepest longing, that he becomes the object of taunting from God's enemies. The manner in which the longing for the temple is displayed is not stated. The NIV rendering, 'the insults of those who insult you', fails to bring out the fact that the Hebrew root for 'insults' and 'insult' (with verb and noun from the same root being used together) has already been employed in verse 7. As the theme of reproach is central to this psalm, consistency of translation helps focus on this aspect. The word 'reproach' (*cherpâh*) occurs in verses 7, 9, 10, 19, 20, for which the NIV has 'scorn(ed)' in all but verse 9, where it uses 'insults'. The first part of verse 9 is quoted in

John 2:17 in reference to Jesus' cleansing of the temple. What Jesus did was evidence of consuming zeal for God's house.

When I weep and fast, I must endure scorn; when I put on sackcloth, people make sport of me. Those who sit at the gate mock me, and I am the song of the drunkards (*vv. 10-12*). The taunting is made more bitter by being directed at him when he is clearly in mourning. Even when it is evident that he is suffering, he has to endure reproach. Instead of joining him in his expressions of grief, his enemies 'make fun of him'.[9] Just as people gather in a town mall today, in ancient Israel they gathered at the city gate (Ruth 4:1-4; 2 Sam. 15:2). The assembled community, as they gossip together, talk disparagingly of the afflicted sufferer, while even the drunkards join in with rowdy songs. When he longs for the worship of the temple (v. 9), all he hears is a totally different kind of singing.

3. A Prayer for Help (*vv. 13-18*)

But I pray to you, O LORD, in the time of your favour; in your great love, O God, answer me with your sure salvation (*v. 13*). Out of his pressing need, the psalmist makes his cry to God. He knows, that in God's good and favourable time, help will come for him. The expression 'time of favour' (*'êt râtsôn*) points to the anticipated activity of God that involves his gracious deliverance (cf. the same use in Isa. 49:8). There seems to be an echo here and in the following verses of Exodus 34:6, where God declared his own character as 'abounding in love and faithfulness'. Because of God's revelation of himself, the psalmist can appeal for a sure answer.

Rescue me from the mire, do not let me sink; deliver me from those who hate me, from the deep waters. Do not let the floodwaters engulf me or the depths swallow me up or the pit close its mouth over me (*vv. 14-15*). Reference to 'mire' (*tît*) recalls the opening of Psalm 40: 'He lifted me out of the

---

[9] The expression is lit. 'I became a *mâshâl* to them'. This word *mâshâl* has a range of meanings, from 'pithy saying' through to 'parable'. Sometimes, as here, the word is used when there is an intention to make the hearer or reader pass judgment on himself/herself. Cf. also its use in Isaiah 14:4, where the NIV has 'taunt'.

slimy pit, out of the mud and mire' (v. 2). The imagery of flood waters is still to the fore (cf. the opening verses), with the word for 'floodwaters' (*shibbolet*) being repeated from verse 2.[10] The picture is of grievous trouble surrounding him, possibly even death, for the word 'pit' (*b^e'êr*) seems to be a synonym for 'Sheol', 'the grave'. He appeals with great intensity for God to intervene and save him.

Answer me, O LORD, out of the goodness of your love; in your great mercy turn to me (*v. 16*). It is for covenant mercy that the psalmist prays, as he picks up the theme of verse 13 and rephrases it. The same expression, 'out of the goodness of your love' (*kî tôv chasdékâ*) occurs in Psalm 109:21, and there too it is associated with the appeal, 'Rescue me' (*nâtsal*, Hi. imper.), as here in verse 14. The use of the phrase, 'in your great mercy', recalls its use in David's appeal for forgiveness in Psalm 51:1: 'According to your great mercy blot out my transgressions.' He wants God to let his gaze be set on him, and so see his need and send deliverance.

Do not hide your face from your servant; answer me quickly, for I am in trouble (*v. 17*). The opening petition is an appeal to God not to withdraw his favour. It became almost a standard expression for seeking God's forgiveness or forbearance (see the use of it in Pss. 27:9; 102:2; 119:19; and 143:7). Someone in a covenantal relationship with God, like the psalmist, could plead as a servant. The use of this term 'servant' recognises that relationship and uses it as a basis for prayer. Speedy help is needed, and divine assistance is the only way of escape from trouble.

---

[10] Two homonyms exist in biblical Hebrew. *Shibbolet* I means 'an ear of grain', while *shibbolet* II is used in contexts such as this to indicate 'a stream' or 'a flood'. In both verse 2 and verse 14 *shibbolet* is used with the verb *shâtaf*, 'flood, overflow'. Good discussion on these homonyms, with accompanying bibliography, can be found in *NIDOTTE*, 4, pp. 30-32. The word *shibbolet* was pronounced differently by the Israelites east of the Jordan than by those in Canaan, who gave the initial letter a softer 's' sound and hence said *sibbolet*. In Judges 12:1-6 the men of Ephraim were marked out by their pronunciation of this word, and from this passage 'Shibboleth' came into English to denote a peculiarity of speech or the catchword of a group.

Come near and rescue me; redeem me because of my foes (*v. 18*). In this psalm many different expressions are used as the psalmist pleads with his God. He has already said 'save' (*yâshaʿ*, Hi.), 'answer' (*ʿânâh*), and 'rescue' (*nâtsal*, Hi.). Now he adds 'come near' (*qârav*, Hi.), 'rescue' (*gâʾal*, a different word than that in v. 14), and 'redeem' (*pâdâh*). The multiplicity of terms adds intensity to his requests, but there is little advantage in trying to distinguish sharply among them.[11]

4. The Psalmist's Enemies (*vv. 19-21*)

You know how I am scorned, disgraced and shamed; all my enemies are before you. Scorn has broken my heart and has left me helpless; I looked for sympathy, but there was none, for comforters, but I found none. They put gall in my food and gave me vinegar for my thirst (*vv. 19-21*). The psalmist makes his renewed appeal to God, repeating the account of his experience of derision and shame (see v. 7). The description is intensified by the repetition of 'scorn/reproach' (2×) and 'shame', and the introduction of 'helpless' (*ʾânûsh*).[12] Those whom he expected to provide comfort failed to stand by him, and he waited in vain for them to offer support. Another addition here is the reference to gall and vinegar in verse 21. 'Gall' (*roʾsh*) was derived from a poisonous herb, and the word may be a Babylonian name for a specific plant. The idea is that the comforters went so far as to betray him by application of poison to his food. In his agony Jesus was offered wine mixed with gall, but he refused to drink it (Matt. 27:34), as it

---

[11] This applies particularly to any attempt to distinguish sharply between 'rescue' (*gâʾal*) and 'redeem' (*pâdâh*). Both verbs mean 'redeem', as is shown by the fact that the same range of Greek words are used in the LXX to translate them. In this passage the LXX uses 'redeem' (*lutróomai*) for the first one, and 'rescue' (*rúomai*) for the second. For discussion on these two Hebrew verbs, see B. B. Warfield, *The Person and Work of Christ* (Philadelphia: Presbyterian and Reformed Publishing Company, 1950), pp. 429-75, and Leon Morris, *The Apostolic Preaching of the Cross* (London: Tyndale Press, 1955), pp. 9-17.

[12] This is the only occurrence of this verb in the Old Testament. The NIV translation seems close, especially when *DCH*, V, p. 648, is very indeterminate, offering several possibilities: 'be sick', 'incurable', or 'tremble'.

could have affected his self-control at this crucial stage of his suffering. He did not want his senses dulled as he offered up himself as a sacrifice for the sins of his people (Heb. 7:27).

5. A Call for God's Judgment (*vv. 22-28*)

May the table set before them become a snare; may it become retribution and a trap. May their eyes be darkened so they cannot see, and their backs be bent forever (*vv. 22-23*). The psalmist appeals for God's direct intervention in the situation, and for his judgment to be visited on his enemies (for the wider problem presented by these passages, see the Introduction). Those who had tried to poison him will find their own table will become a trap for them. The NIV marginal note on verse 22 follows the Aramaic Targum, which suggests that instead of 'retribution' the Hebrew word should be read as meaning 'peace offerings'.[13] This provides a good parallel with 'table' in the first part of the verse. Verse 23 refers to physical changes that would be a sign of God's disfavour. The psalmist has undergone physical changes (cf. v. 3), and now he prays that the health of his enemies will be affected. He wants them to be afflicted with blindness, and their loins to be trembling.

Pour out your wrath on them; let your fierce anger overtake them. May their place be deserted; let there be no one to dwell in their tents (*vv. 24-25*). The petitions continue to ask for the reversal of all the good things of life. In place of mercy the request is for wrath; in place of joyful family life a deserted dwelling place. Peter quotes the words of verse 25 in reference to the reward that Judas Iscariot received for his wickedness (Acts 1:18-20). He illustrated the same antagonism

---

[13] The word that gives the difficulty is *sh^elômîm*, the plural of *shâlôm*, 'peace'. The only other time the plural occurs is in Jeremiah 13:19. The LXX points to a translation like 'recompense' or 'vengeance', while the Syriac probably supports this. The AV understood it as referring to 'welfare', an interpretation followed in the NKJV, 'well-being'. The evidence does not point strongly in one direction, and so I prefer to take it as being the plural of *shélem*, this in my judgment best suiting the context. Cf. RSV 'their sacrificial feasts'. More detail can be found in the note in M. E. Tate, *Psalms 51-100*, p. 190, n. 23.a.

that had been displayed by the psalmist's enemies, and he came under a similar judgment.[14]

For they persecute those you wound and talk about the pain of those you hurt. Charge them with crime upon crime; do not let them share in your salvation (*vv. 26-27*). The opening words of verse 26 are simply 'For you', which do not fit easily with the words that follow: 'whom you have struck, they persecute'. Likely, after the opening words, 'As for you', the psalmist breaks off to speak about those like himself who have been wounded by God: 'As for you – they persecute whomever you have struck'.[15] The psalmist was willing to accept God's chastisements, but when he was under the afflicting hand of God, enemies visited him with even greater hurts. The talking about him was clearly a form of mockery (cf. v. 12), as they rejoiced over his suffering. He asks that they be given what they deserve – punishment corresponding to their sins, and exclusion from God's saving activity. This means additional guilt (the lit. translation is 'Give them iniquity upon iniquity'), and absence of any vindication by God.

May they be blotted out of the book of life and not be listed with the righteous (*v. 28*). The idea of the book of life comes from Exodus 32:32, where Moses prays that if God does not forgive his people, then let his name be blotted out of God's book. For the wicked, the request of the psalmist is that they perish, and that their names not be written alongside those of the righteous. The same concept of a book appears also in Daniel 12:1 and Revelation 3:5; 13:8; 17:8; and 20:15. Clearly this is an anthropomorphic expression, as God does not need a written list of the names of his people.

---

[14] The NIV marks off Acts 1:18-20 as a parenthesis, implying, probably correctly that the words are not part of Peter's speech, but form a commentary by Luke, the author of Acts. The primary references of the two psalms quoted (Pss. 69 and 109) were connected to enemies of David, but as Judas' character matched the enemies in those psalms, the words are applied to him. For commentary on the passage in Acts, see F. F. Bruce, *The Acts of the Apostles: The Greek Text with Introduction and Commentary*, 3rd ed., (Leicester: Apollos, 1990), pp. 109-10.

[15] This is the explanation offered by M. E. Tate, *Psalms 51-100*, pp. 188, 190-91.

6. A Song of Praise (*vv. 29-33*)

I am in pain and distress; may your salvation, O God, protect me (*v. 29*). The focus now shifts back to the psalmist himself a little more emphatically than the NIV rendering suggests: '*But as for me*, I am afflicted …' He is concerned, not only for the punishment of evil enemies, but for his own salvation. The verb 'to protect' (*sâgav*, Pi.) has the idea of setting on high, and therefore of putting in a position of safety.

I will praise God's name in song and glorify him with thanksgiving. This will please the LORD more than an ox, more than a bull with its horns and hoofs (*vv. 30-31*). In anticipation of God's salvation the psalmist declares his intention of praising him in song. The 'thanksgiving' could be a sacrifice (cf. Lev. 7:12; 22:29) which formed a thank-offering, or a song of praise, which seems to be the meaning here. Such heart-felt praise is more acceptable to God than the mere offering of animal sacrifice, even if it was complete with horns and hoofs! Like Psalm 51:16-17, there is recognition that the sacrificial system did not work automatically. The heart of the worshipper was also very important.

The poor will see and be glad – you who seek God, may your hearts live! (*v. 32*). When the humble (defined further by the expression 'who seek God') see what is happening and hear this praise, they too will rejoice. An individual response will translate into a communal one. In turn the worshippers will find that reviving comes through this experience of seeing and acknowledging the salvation of the LORD. The expression 'May your hearts live' is equivalent to saying 'Do not lose heart'.

The LORD hears the needy and does not despise his captive people (*v. 33*). This is the statement of an abiding truth. It is characteristic of God that he listens to the cry of the needy. The 'needy' are shown elsewhere in the Psalms to be those whose distress is caused by their enemies, but whose trust is in the LORD. 'His captive people' is a rendering of the Hebrew 'his bound ones', which is either a reference to binding in sin before the LORD brings release, or else to those who are bound in service to him as devoted captives.

7. Universal Adoration (vv. 34-36)

Let heaven and earth praise him, the seas and all that move in them, for God will save Zion and rebuild the cities of Judah. Then people will settle there and possess it; the children of his servants will inherit it, and those who love his name will dwell there (vv. 34-36). Earlier (in verse 2) the waters were engulfing the psalmist. Now they are subdued. Along with all of inanimate nature they should praise the Lord, for he makes himself known as the saviour of his people. Earlier in the psalm there has not been any mention of the need of the nation, or of distress that has come upon Zion and Judah. While it is possible that the psalmist's great need was but a microcosm of the need of the nation as a whole, these verses may well be an addition to adapt the psalm for use at a time much later than that of David. Reference is made to Judah, not Israel. This ending would fit in with the period of Hezekiah (see 2 Kings 18-20; 2 Chron. 29-32), or with the Babylonian exile, if the captives were being encouraged to look for the restoration of Zion (see Jer. 30:18-31:14; cf. Ps. 51:18). God is able to provide help for Zion, and to bring his people back to settle again in the land. The lesson is clear from this psalm that, even in times of great distress, the eye of faith has to look to the full demonstration of God's restoring mercy. There is 'a home of righteousness' awaiting the people of God (2 Pet. 3:13).

Psalm 70

For the director of music. Of David. A petition.

This sung prayer is almost the same as Psalm 40:13-17 (see the fuller comments on that psalm). There are, however, several variations. The first two terms of the title are the same as those in Psalm 40, but the word 'psalm' is replaced here by 'petition' (*lᵉhazkîr*).[1] There are also changes in respect to the use of the divine name, but not in a uniform manner, for twice *ᵉlohîm* replaces *yhwh* (Lord), but then Lord is used in place of both *ᵃdonay* and *ᵉlohîm* and retained in verse 1b. Other changes include the absence of 'be pleased' (v. 1), the absence of 'to take' (v. 2), the change of 'be appalled' to 'turn back' (v. 3), and the alteration of 'think on me' to 'come quickly to me' (v. 5). These verses may have been taken over from Psalm 40 and used at some time of great distress. The fact that the Aramaic Targum has 'Make haste to deliver *us*' in verse 1 points to a use of the psalm with an application to the nation as a whole. The changes of cognate nouns ('salvation' and 'help') could have been for dialectal reasons.

No indication is given in the text as to why this part of Psalm 40 has been repeated here in a slightly altered fashion. A psalm that was composed for another occasion has been adapted for a new set of circumstances.

---

[1] As a term used in the titles of Psalms, *lᵉhazkîr* only occurs here and in Psalm 38. It could relate to singing while bringing an *ʾazkârâh*, 'a token offering', a word that occurs in Leviticus and Numbers to denote a handful taken from a grain offering (Lev. 2:2, 9, 16). See *DCH*, I, p.169, and note the variety of meanings listed in *CHAL*, p. 8.

Psalm 70 forms a bridge between Psalms 69 and 71. Corresponding ideas occur in Psalms 70 and 71.[2] In this second book of the Psalter, where nearly every psalm has a title, the absence of one for Psalm 71 suggests that it may be reckoned as almost a continuation of Psalm 70. In this way these two psalms correspond essentially to the way in which Psalms 42 and 43 function as a single unit.

Hasten, O God, to save me; O Lord, come quickly to help me (*v. 1*). The opening word in Psalm 40:14, 'be pleased' (*retsêh*) is omitted. This makes the commencement of the psalm more abrupt. The LXX translators realised the problem that now 'to save me' lacked a prior verb, and so they added the first clause to the title, 'that the Lord may save me'.

May those who seek my life be put to shame and confusion; may all who desire my ruin be turned back in disgrace (*v. 2*). Two changes are made to the text. The word 'together' has been omitted after 'May they be put to shame and confusion', and 'to snatch away' at the end of the first colon has also been omitted.

May those who say to me, 'Aha! Aha!' turn back because of their shame (*v. 3*). 'Turn back' (*yâshûvû*) replaces 'be appalled/made desolate' (*yâshommû*) in Psalm 40:15, a somewhat softer expression. Also, 'to me', is not represented in the MT of this verse, and hence the translation should only be 'who say, "Aha! Aha!"'

But may all who seek you rejoice and be glad in you; may those who love your salvation always say, 'Let God be exalted!' (*v. 4*). In addition to the alteration of the divine name ('God' for 'Lord'), 'and' is put before 'say', and one word for 'salvation' (*t^eshu'â*) is replaced by another from the same root and with identical meaning (*y^eshû'â*).

Yet I am poor and needy; come quickly to me, O God. You are my help and my deliverer; O Lord, do not delay (*v. 5*). In this final verse there are several changes as compared with Psalm 40. Instead of 'O Lord, take account of me', Psalm 70

---

[2] Cf. 70:1, 5 with 71:12; 70:2 with 71:13, 24; 70:4 with 71:6, 8, 14-16, 24. Also, 71:24 expresses confidence in the Lord in a way that is the fulfilment of the request of 70:1.

has 'O God, hasten to me', repeating the cry for speedy intervention already used in verse 1. Then, like the change for the words for 'salvation' in verse 4, one word for 'help' (*'ezrâh*) is replaced by another from the same root (*'êzer*).

Psalm 71

This is a psalm of old age (see vv. 9 and 18), written by a believer who, even near the end of life, is still being tormented by enemies. There is no heading to help set the psalm in a particular historical setting, or to note any ascription of authorship. It is to be taken as being linked inseparably with Psalm 70 (see comments on that psalm), and forms part of a trilogy of psalms (Pss. 69-71). These three psalms have many themes in common – the need of the psalmist, the cry for rescue, the declaration of praise to God the redeemer. God's righteousness is again to the forefront, while the psalmist's shame is mentioned at the beginning (v. 1), in the middle (v. 13), and at the end (v. 24). Like the previous two psalms, this one ends on a strong note of praise.

Persecution is a fact of life for committed believers (2 Tim. 3:12), and there is no stage of life when they are exempt from it. Here the psalmist blends together phrases from other psalms, which shows how deeply ingrained in his mind and heart were the words of other singers of Israel. Yet the psalm is a song of hope, as he looks expectantly to the LORD.

1. A Confident Prayer (*vv. 1-4*)
In you, O LORD, I have taken refuge; let me never be put to shame. Rescue me and deliver me in your righteousness; turn your ear to me and save me. Be my rock of refuge, to which I can always go; give the command to save me, for you are my rock and my fortress. Deliver me, O my God,

from the hand of the wicked, from the grasp of evil and cruel men (*vv. 1-4*). These opening verses are very similar to the start of Psalm 31 (see commentary on that psalm). They express the sure confidence that his abiding refuge ever since his youth (see v. 5) has been the LORD. He continues to appeal to God to be attentive to his cry and to save him in his present trouble. The NIV translation 'rock of refuge' (*tsûr mâʿôz*) in verse 3 follows a few Hebrew manuscripts and makes this verse conform to Psalm 31:2. However, it is better to retain the reading in the majority of manuscripts, 'rock of habitation' (*tsûr mâʿôn*).[1] Clearly, from early times, Israel had thought of the LORD as being the dwelling place of his people (see Moses' words in Ps. 90:1). Even in his old age the psalmist is still surrounded by wicked men, from whose grip he seeks release. Whereas Psalm 31:4 refers to deliverance from a snare, here the thought is release 'from the grasp of evil (*mᵉʿavvêl*, Pi. ptc.) and cruel men' (*chômêts*, Qal ptc.), using two rare words to create the parallel with 'from the hand of the wicked'. Words like 'rescue', 'deliver', and 'save' stress the urgency of the situation, and the need for God's speedy intervention.

2. A Declaration of Praise (*vv. 5-8*)

For you have been my hope, O Sovereign LORD, my confidence since my youth. From birth I have relied on you; you brought me forth from my mother's womb. I will ever praise you (*vv. 5-6*). Several times Jeremiah calls God 'the hope of Israel' (Jer. 14:8; 17:13), which is one reason why it has been suggested that he may be the author of this psalm. The words also seem to echo Psalm 22:9-10. The psalmist's confidence in the LORD is no newly found trust, but one which goes back to the very commencement of his life. Right from birth when

---

[1] The number of other differences between Psalms 71 and 31 suggest that the alteration of 'habitation' to 'refuge' is deliberate. While the first verse is identical in both psalms, Psalm 71 is not just a duplication of the earlier song. Some other phrases are repeated ('Turn to me your ear', 'Be my rock of ...', 'For you are my rock and my fortress'), while certain words occur in both (such as 'righteousness', 'rescue', 'deliver', 'save'). However, the changes look like deliberate alteration and expansion.

he was taken from his mother's womb,[2] he has set his hope on the LORD. Hence, it is not his own faith that is the object of his praise, but the grace of God that he has known since childhood. Constant praise is a way of indicating his response to God's keeping power. **I have become like a portent to many, but you are my strong refuge. My mouth is filled with your praise, declaring your splendour all day long** (*vv. 7-8*). To many of his contemporaries he has become a sign or wonder. The word 'portent' (*môfēt*) is used in the section of Deuteronomy dealing with the curses that will come on Israel because of disobedience, and it is in parallel with the more common word 'sign' (*'ôt*, Deut. 28:46). Here it seems to indicate that the psalmist feels himself to be the object of God's chastisement, so that he becomes an example to others. However, in spite of this, he does not hesitate to commit himself to his sure place of refuge. He picks up on the thought of praise already mentioned in verse 6, with stress on how continual was his adoration (v. 6, 'ever praise'; v. 8, 'all day long'). God's splendour or glory was what he wanted to proclaim constantly.

3. Prayer in Old Age (*vv. 9-13*)

Do not cast me away when I am old; do not forsake me when my strength is gone. For my enemies speak against me; those who wait to kill me conspire together (*vv. 9-10*). From reflection upon his commitment to the LORD from his youth, the psalmist now turns to his present old age.[3] In his increasing weakness he pleads that God will not cast him off (the same expression as David uses in Ps. 51:11). 'Casting off' is the equivalent of being abandoned. Even at this stage of his earthly pilgrimage there are those who plot against him,

---

[2] The translation 'you brought me forth' (*gôzî*) certainly fits the context, though the derivation of the verb is uncertain. It is best taken as the Qal part. of *gâzâh* and means 'the one who severed me [from the womb]'. Various emendations have been proposed but they lack manuscript confirmation. See *DCH*, II, p. 339.

[3] The word for 'old age' (*ziqnâh*) only occurs six times in the Old Testament, two of which are in this psalm (vv. 9, 18). It points more to bodily weakness, rather than to great age. The suffix 'my' is not added, as often it is omitted if the context supplies it. See *DIHG~S*, pp. 4-5.

watching to see if they can take his life.[4] Evil men combine together as they plan their attacks on believers (cf. Ps. 83:3). **They say, 'God has forsaken him; pursue him and seize him, for no one will rescue him'** (*v. 11*). The opening words, 'they say', picks up on the use of the same verb in the previous verse (NIV 'speak'), and then gives the content of what they say.[5] Similar speeches of enemies are given in Psalm 3:2 and 41:6. One of the hardest taunts for believers to face is the one that in their distress God has forsaken them. But the reality is that God will not forsake his faithful ones (Ps. 37:28), and so the taunt is a lie. While the enemies claim that there is no deliverer, the psalmist knows full well that this is untrue, as the following petitions show.

Be not far from me, O God; come quickly, O my God, to help me (*v. 12*). This verse seems to be an echo of Psalms 22:11, 19; 38:21-22; 40:13; and 70:1. It is a help in times of distress to use words that others have used before us in their urgent situations. Others have passed the same way and have made their plea for speedy assistance. The change from 'O God' to 'O my God' in the second clause stresses the covenantal relationship between the needy servant and the powerful deliverer.

May my accusers perish in shame; may those who want to harm me be covered with scorn and disgrace (*v. 13*). These words are close to Psalms 35:4, 26; 40:15; 70:3, and 109:29.[6] His appeal is for God to vindicate him and he awaits divine judgment upon his enemies.

---

[4] The expression 'those who wait to kill me' is literally 'the watchers of my soul'. The thought of 'waiting to kill' is implied in the context, especially with the use of the verb 'to take counsel' (cf. Ps. 2:2).

[5] 'They say' is a translation of *lê'mor* ('to say, saying'). It often occurs in Hebrew prose following a finite form of the same verb, 'say, saying ...' but rarely in poetry. In prose passages it is frequently omitted in English translation, and could be here without any alteration of meaning as the inverted commas mark the speech content.

[6] All of these passages use either the verb *kâlam* (Ni. 'be ashamed') or the related noun *k^elimmâh* ('shame', 'disgrace'). They also use similar constructions to denote the enemies: 'seekers of my life' (35:4), 'gloaters over my distress' (35:26), 'seekers of my life' (40:14; 70:2), 'my accusers' (109:29), and 'condemners of his soul' (109:31). This common phraseology suggests a standard way of denoting enemies in petitionary prayers.

4. Confidence in Old Age (vv. 14-18)

But as for me, I will always have hope; I will praise you more and more. My mouth will tell of your righteousness, of your salvation all day long, though I know not its measure (vv. 14-15). The contrast is very clear between the fate of the enemies and the future of the psalmist.[7] He is confident that even in his old age he will proclaim God's salvation, and do so to an increasing degree. 'Righteousness' is used in the sense of God's saving acts, as is shown by the parallel 'salvation'. The word 'measure' (s^eforôt) is connected to the Hebrew word for 'tell' (sâfar, Pi.), and it only occurs here in the whole of the Old Testament. It probably means he is unable to count the 'number' of God's saving acts.[8]

I will come and proclaim your mighty acts, O Sovereign LORD; I will proclaim your righteousness, yours alone. Since my youth, O God, you have taught me, and to this day I declare your marvellous deeds (vv. 16-17). The opening clause of verse 16 has given difficulty, as the variety in English versions shows. The AV rendering, 'I will go in the strength of the LORD God' is hard to sustain, as the 'strength' (g^evurôt) is the LORD's, not the speaker's.[9] The NIV rendering is also without support, for it inserts 'and proclaim' without any textual evidence. An attractive possibility is that the verb 'come' (bô') can mean to commence or begin an action. This makes good sense here as the psalmist is asserting that he will begin with the mighty acts of the LORD.[10] Several words are used to describe God's actions. The psalmist will make mention of

---

[7] The contrast is marked in the Hebrew text by the way the verse opens: 'But I continually, I will hope ...' The NIV translation captures the meaning, as does the NLT: 'But I will keep on hoping ...'

[8] Because of the rarity of this word it is difficult to make a decision regarding its meaning. Another suggested translation is 'the art of writing': 'My mouth shall declare your victories, your salvation all the day, for I do not know the art of writing.' However, that hardly fits the context for the psalmist *is* writing. See the various possibilities listed in *DCH*, VI, pp. 193-94.

[9] The suffix 'your' attached to 'righteousness' also applies to 'mighty acts'.

[10] For this interpretation, see *DCH*, II, p. 102; G. R. Driver, 'Hebrew Notes', *VT* 1 (1951), p. 249.

those actions which are God's alone,[11] his royal power which has been displayed in victories. He is also declared to be a God of faithfulness who does things that are beyond human capability (*niflâ'ôt*, 'marvellous deeds'; cf. its use in Pss. 72:18 and 86:10). All that he has learned of the LORD's actions on behalf of his people forms part of his songs of praise. This learning has been from his early days right up to the present, for God not only teaches his people in general but individuals like the psalmist also.

Even when I am old and grey, do not forsake me, O God, till I declare your power to the next generation, your might to all who are to come (*v. 18*). As he nears the end of life the psalmist still wants to declare to the coming generation the great things that God has done. Not only the nation but he himself has experienced the power of God (Hebrew, *z^erô'^akâ*, 'your arm'), and this forms a further testimony to God's saving might. Having already prayed that God would not abandon him (v. 9), he again prays for his sustaining presence and help.

5. A Confident Song (*vv. 19-24*)
Your righteousness reaches to the skies, O God, you who have done great things. Who, O God, is like you? (*v. 19*). The psalm moves to a conclusion with a strong note of confidence. The early part of this verse echoes Psalm 36:5-6, while the rhetorical question, 'Who is like you?', is paralleled in Psalm 89:8. Both the latter passage and this verse in Psalm 71 may be echoing the words of the Song of the Sea in Exodus 15:11. 'To do great things' is a standard expression for demonstrations of God's power. The whole verse is an emphatic assertion of the fact that God's righteousness is beyond human comprehension, and that no one can be compared to the LORD.

Though you have made me see troubles, many and bitter, you will restore my life again; from the depths of the earth you will again bring me up (*v. 20*). Just as the psalmist has declared that God's righteousness extends to the heavens, he now speaks of the experiences he and others have been

---

[11] 'Make mention' is the translation of the Hebrew verb *zâkar* Hi. that means 'to cause to be remembered', hence mention in praise.

through.[12] The experiences of the individual blend into those of the nation. They have seen many distressing situations (perhaps even the exile) when they seemed as good as dead (cf. Ps. 30:3). From the grave or the depths of the earth they can appeal to God to restore them again.[13] This is a confessional response by the believing community, which, having been afflicted, can cry for restoration. The psalmist is sure that God will not forsake them, and this must always remain the confidence of believers.

> Though troubles assail and danger affright,
> Though friends should all fail and foes unite,
> Yet one thing secures us, whatever betide,
> The Scripture assures us the Lord will provide.
>
> No strength of our own or goodness we claim;
> Yet, since we have known the Saviour's great Name,
> In this our strong tower for safety we hide,
> The Lord is our power, the Lord will provide.
>
> (John Newton, 1725-1807)

You will increase my honour and comfort me once again (*v. 21*). The psalmist switches to speak of his own condition, and he appeals for restoration to a place of dignity. He wants to know the comforting presence of his God once again.[14]

I will praise you with the harp for your faithfulness, O my God; I will sing praise to you with the lyre, O Holy One of

---

[12] While in the NIV the objects of the verbs are singular in this verse ('you have made *me* see troubles', 'you will restore *my* life again', 'you will again bring *me* up'), the K^etiv reading in the MT definitely has plural objects for the first two, while many manuscripts, the Targum, and Jerome have a plural for the third one as well.

[13] The idea of 'again' is conveyed twice by the use of the Hebrew verb *shûv*, which by itself normally means 'return', 'go back'. Hebrew lacks the adverbs that occur in English and other European languages. Instead it often uses two verbs, whereas these other languages use a verb + an adverb. Information on this Hebrew usage can be found in *IBHS*, pp. 75-76, 656; *DIHG~S*, p. 139; with good examples listed in *BDB*, p. 998.

[14] 'Again' represents the Hebrew verb *sâvav*, 'to turn', used here in the same way as *shûv* was in the previous verse.

Israel. My lips will shout for joy when I sing praise to you – I, whom you have redeemed (*vv. 22-23*). The NIV translation fails to render the very first word in verse 22 (*gam*). While it often means 'also', in some situations it signifies 'therefore' as here and in Psalm 52:5 (see comment on that verse).[15] God's faithfulness and holiness form the subject of praise. The expression 'Holy One of Israel' is most frequently used as a title for God in the prophecy of Isaiah (see, e.g., Isa. 1:4; 5:19, 24; 29:19; 47:4; 60:14).[16] God's holiness is seen in the way in which he redeems his people, and it will always be mentioned in the songs of the redeemed (cf. Exod. 15:11; Rev. 15:3-4).

My tongue will tell of your righteous acts all day long, for those who wanted to harm me have been put to shame and confusion (*v. 24*). The Hebrew text opens with the word *gam* (see comment on v. 22). The NIV omits it, while many translations render it by 'and' or 'also'. However, rendering it 'therefore' makes good sense in the context. Praise follows redemption. The psalmist knows, too, that God will not desert him. The judgment of God upon his enemies is a demonstration of his righteousness, and as such it forms the subject of his continuous song of praise.

---

[15] This same usage can be seen in prophetic passages (such as Isa. 66:4, Ezek. 16:43 and Mal. 2:9) where *gam* = *lâkên*.

[16] 'Holy one of Israel' (*qᵉdôsh yisrâêl*) occurs twenty-nine times in the Book of Isaiah, and only six times elsewhere. Three of these other occurrences are in the Psalms (71:22; 78:41; 89:18).

Psalm 72

Of Solomon.

Jesus shall reign where'er the sun
Does his successive journeys run;
His kingdom stretch from shore to shore,
Till moons shall wax and wane no more.

With these words Isaac Watts (1674-1748) captured the spirit of this psalm. The promises that are given concerning the king go far beyond anything that could be promised to an ordinary descendant of David. The psalm is devoted to celebration of the Davidic kingship, seeking gifts for him that are going also to come upon his people. Thus, for example, endowed with righteousness (v. 1), he will be able to judge righteously (v. 2). The vision presented of the Davidic king far transcends any other description. *All* kings are going to bow before him (v. 11), and the extension of his kingdom is described in terms identical to the messianic passage in Zechariah 9:9-13. Early Jewish thinking took the same viewpoint, as the Targum adds after the word 'king' in verse 1, 'Messiah'. The background of the psalm is the covenant with David in 2 Samuel 7, but the vision is of the ultimate Davidic ruler, Jesus Christ. The Hebrew title is ambiguous, as it can mean either 'by Solomon', or 'for Solomon'.

1. A Prayer for the King (*vv. 1-4*)
Endow the king with your justice, O God, the royal son with your righteousness (*v. 1*). In terms of the covenant with David, the Davidic king was adopted as God's son (2 Sam. 7:14; cf. also Ps. 89:26-27). Hence he can be called either 'the king' or 'the

son of the king' (NIV 'the royal son'). The initial appeal here is for the gift of righteous rule to him, so that his administration will reflect the very character of God himself.

He will judge your people in righteousness, your afflicted ones with justice. The mountains will bring prosperity to the people, the hills the fruit of righteousness (*vv. 2-3*). The idea expressed in verse 1 is carried over into these following verses. The endowment with justice and righteousness will enable the king to rule well. Clearly here and elsewhere (cf. Exod. 22:25) 'your people' (*'amm^{e}kâ*) and 'your afflicted ones' (*'^{a}niyyekâ*) are synonymous, for 'the afflicted' (*'^{a}niyyîm*) are the LORD's people in a special relationship with him.[1] The effective and just rule of the king is stated poetically in the thought that there will be a harvest of peace[2] and righteousness, so that even the mountain ranges will produce the crops that denote prosperity (cf. a similar poetic usage in Joel 3:18).

He will defend the afflicted among the people and save the children of the needy; he will crush the oppressor (*v. 4*). None of the oppressed need to fear during the reign of this king, for they will be defended by him. He will bring vindication to them, and so the thought of verse 2 is enlarged to embody the promise that the defenceless are his special care. The oppressors will find that they are treated in the way in which they themselves treated others, a principle which the New Testament reasserts (James 2:13).

2. An Enduring Kingship (*vv. 5-7*)
He will endure as long as the sun, as long as the moon, through all generations (*v. 5*). In contrast to other dynasties, the promise to David was that his kingdom was going to endure (2 Sam. 7:11b-16), expressed here in comparison with

---

[1] The significance of 'the afflicted' is also shown by the fact that the opposite in biblical terms is not the rich but the wicked. Full discussion on the term is provided by W. J. Dumbrell, *NIDOTTE*, 3, pp. 454-64.

[2] While the word 'peace' (*shalom*) is used, it has its wider meaning here and in verse 7 of 'well-being', 'prosperity'. The English word 'peace' tends to have negative connotations (absence of war or conflict), whereas in Hebrew it is positive. The biblical and modern Hebrew way of enquiring about the well-being of someone is asking whether they have *shalom* (Cf. Gen. 43:27, lit. 'Does your aged father [have] peace?').

the sun and moon. The promise was repeated several times in the Old Testament (Pss. 89:28-29; 132:11-12; Isa. 9:7), and it was renewed in the words of Gabriel to Mary, as he announced the coming birth of Jesus (Luke 1:31-33). **He will be like rain falling on a mown field, like showers watering the earth. In his days the righteous will flourish; prosperity will abound till the moon is no more** (*vv. 6-7*). The opening of verse 6 picks up an idea from David's last words in 2 Samuel 23:3-4: 'when one rules over men in righteousness, ... he is like ... the brightness after rain that brings the grass from the earth.' The prosperity, under the Davidic house, is likened to the effect of rain that stimulates further the growth of newly mown grass. The righteous will have conditions in which they will flourish (for the same expression see Ps. 92:12 and Prov. 11:28), and this will continue until the end of time.

3. A Universal Kingdom (*vv. 8-11*)
He will rule from sea to sea and from the River to the ends of the earth (*v. 8*). The extent of the kingdom of the messianic ruler is stated in terms of the promise to Abraham. It was during the Davidic/Solomonic empire that the boundaries of 'the promised land' reached their fullest extent (1 Kings 4:21, 24). However, there is one notable change here compared with the earlier Old Testament references to the land. The boundary does not extend up to the [Euphrates] River,[3] but from it outwards! No longer will it be the restricted territory allotted as the promised land, but it will consist of a universal kingdom. Psalm 72:8 cannot be considered on its own, as almost identical language is used in Zechariah 9:10: 'I will take away the chariots from Ephraim and the war-horses from Jerusalem, and the battle-bow will be broken. He will proclaim peace to the nations. His rule will extend from sea to sea and from the River to the ends of the earth.' Both in that

---

[3] Hebrew has an amazing number of words denoting 'river', the one used here (*pᵉrât*) designating only the Euphrates. Cf. the NLT of this verse: 'May he reign from sea to sea, and from the Euphrates River to the ends of the earth'.

passage and here in Psalm 72 the contexts are dealing with eschatological events.[4]

The desert tribes will bow before him and his enemies will lick the dust. The kings of Tarshish and of distant shores will bring tribute to him; the kings of Sheba and Seba will present him gifts (*vv. 9-10*). From far-off places people will acknowledge the rule of Messiah, and his enemies will be brought to own his authority over them. 'To bow before' and 'to lick the dust' are synonymous expressions of submission (see Isa. 49:23). The places mentioned (Tarshish, Sheba, and Seba)[5] represent the distant nations, with their rulers coming to present their tribute as a sign of allegiance to this universal king. The New Testament speaks of a day coming when Jesus will have destroyed all other dominions and powers, and all his enemies will be placed under his feet (1 Cor. 15:24-25).

All kings will bow down to him and all nations will serve him (*v. 11*). Though this and the previous verses express the idea of submission in terms alluding to Solomon's kingdom, yet the final fulfilment of this promise will be when Jesus, as the Lamb, overcomes because he is Lord of lords and King of kings (Rev. 17:14; 19:16).

4. Concern for Righteousness and Justice (*vv. 12-14*)

For he will deliver the needy who cry out, the afflicted who have no one to help. He will take pity on the weak and the needy and save the needy from death (*vv. 12-13*). Earlier in verses 2-4 the psalmist spoke about the king's support for those who needed his special care. Now he returns to this theme, with the assurance that he will act in mercy to those who are oppressed. In contrast to other Near Eastern kingdoms, the

---

[4] Cf. the use made of the Zechariah passage in Matthew 21:5, with the opening words being taken from Isaiah. The sort of language used of the kingdom extension 'is extravagant unless heard in an eschatological key', as Christopher Wright expresses it. See *NIDOTTE*, 1, p. 521.

[5] Several references to Tarshish in the Old Testament link it with the sea, but it is unclear whether this is the Mediterranean or the Red Sea (or even the coast of Africa). Sheba was probably located in south-eastern Arabia, while Seba could be near it, or else just another name for Sheba. This would mean taking the 'and' linking the two words here as meaning 'that is'. Cf. *DCH*, II, p. 597 and the literature cited on p. 641; also, *IBHS*, pp. 652-53.

Davidic throne was established in love, and the Davidic king was 'one who in judging seeks justice and speeds the cause of righteousness' (Isa. 16:5).

He will rescue them from oppression and violence, for precious is their blood in his sight (*v. 14*). It was part of the promise to David that the wicked would not oppress any more (2 Sam. 7:10). This verse picks up that theme, declaring that when subjects are faced with violence, the king will rescue them (Hebrew, lit. 'will redeem'). The Hebrew word used for redeem (*gā'al*) often denotes the action of a kinsman in redeeming his kin from difficulty or danger (cf. its use in Ruth 4, where it refers to the redeeming of the land which belonged to Naomi). In the king's sight, the life of even these afflicted ones is very special (cf. the almost identical phrase used of God in Ps. 116:15).

5. Universal Blessing (*vv. 15-17*)

An even more direct reference to the covenant with Abraham occurs in these closing verses, with the psalm ending with a prayer for the fulfilment of that covenant. **Long may he live! May gold from Sheba be given to him. May people ever pray for him and bless him all day long** (*v. 15*). The prayer for the continuing existence of the dynasty is put in terms of the normal salutation of a new king (cf. 1 Sam. 10:24; 2 Sam. 16:16; 1 Kings 1:25, 34).[6] Just as the Queen of Sheba brought gifts to Solomon, including gold (1 Kings 10:10), so the psalmist pictures further tribute being presented to the Davidic king. In addition, prayer is made for his welfare and praise given to him for the prosperity he brings.

Let grain abound throughout the land; on the tops of the hills may it sway. Let its fruit flourish like Lebanon; let it thrive like the grass of the field (*v. 16*). The picture of prosperity is painted in terms of abundant crops, even to the very tops of the mountains! Just as Lebanon was noted for its bountiful forests, so may the land yield an abundant harvest.

---

[6] The form of the prayer is simply 'and let him live' (*vîchî*), but this verb (*châyâh*) quite often has the sense of continuing in life, remaining alive (*BDB*, p. 311), and hence the English phrase 'Long may he live' is quite appropriate as a translation.

The covenantal blessings that promised abundant crops and herds (Deut. 28:3-6) will find their fulfilment through the messianic king. **May his name endure forever; may it continue as long as the sun. All nations will be blessed through him, and they will call him blessed** (*v. 17*). An enduring kingship was going to bring blessing to many more countries than just Israel. In fact, the promise of the covenant with Abraham (Gen. 12:2-3) was going to find its fulfilment through the messianic kingship of Jesus, when the nations would receive the blessing of the Spirit (Gal. 3:14). It is curious that the 'name' is not expressly mentioned either in this verse or verse 19 ('his glorious name'), yet the allusion to the blessing through Abraham seems the obvious reference point.[7] The allusion goes back to what the LORD said to Abraham as recorded in Genesis 12:3 and in Genesis 22:17, and to Isaac in Genesis 26:4. Through the king's/messiah's government the Abrahamic covenant will find fulfilment. What is especially significant here is the link that is made between the Abrahamic and Davidic covenants.[8]

6. Concluding Benediction (*vv. 18-20*)

Praise be to the LORD God, the God of Israel, who alone does marvellous deeds. Praise be to his glorious name forever; may the whole earth be filled with his glory. Amen and Amen (*vv. 18-19*). Like all the five books of the Psalter, this second one concludes with a doxology. The covenant God of Israel is indeed the only one able to do 'marvellous' deeds (see the comment on Ps. 71:17). His name is worthy of praise because of the glory of his actions in redeeming and keeping his people. The desire for the whole earth to be filled with God's glory is an echo of Numbers 14:21. To that desire the people respond with a double 'Amen'. 'Amen' is frequently

---

[7] The form of the verb 'to bless' in this passage is Hitpael imperfect (*yibar^{e}kû*). This follows the use of the same form in Genesis 22:18. One of the advantages of opting for a reflexive or reciprocal meaning for this verbal form here is that it provides a concrete significance to the use of Abraham's name. The meaning will be that people invoke a blessing on themselves. 'May we be blessed just as Abraham was blessed!'

[8] Craig Broyles, *Psalms*, p. 298, makes this point well.

used after prayers and hymns of praise (see 1 Chron. 16:36; Neh. 8:6; Pss. 41:13 and 106:48).

This concludes the prayers of David son of Jesse (*v. 20*). This note does not refer to the whole Psalter, for there are later Davidic psalms (cf. Pss. 86, 108-110, 138-145). It appears to have been added to the collection, that precedes, to mark it off from the psalms of Asaph which follow (Pss. 73-83).

Matthew
A MENTOR COMMENTARY
Volume 1: Chapters 1-13
Knox Chamblin

Matthew
A MENTOR COMMENTARY
Volume 2: Chapters 14-28
Knox Chamblin

Matthew

Volume 1 (chapters 1-13)
Volume 2 (chapters 14-28)

A Mentor Commentary

Knox Chamblin

This thoughtful and thorough commentary on the First Gospel comes from a scholar who has obviously spent many years at the feet of Matthew the teacher, and even more importantly, at the feet of the One to whom Matthew bears witness.

Jonathan Pennington,
Associate Professor of New Testament Interpretation,
The Southern Baptist Theological Seminary, Louisville, Kentucky

What, you might say, am I to do with 2 volumes and 1,400 pages on Matthew? Well, what should you do if given two million pounds? Spend it, of course–but not all at once. So with Chamblin's Matthew. Preach an Advent series – and use Chamblin on chapters 1–2; then preach from the Old Testament and come back to the Sermon on the Mount – and use Chamblin on chapters 5–7; then map out a series on Matthew's passion narrative – and use Chamblin on chapters 26–28. I'm not a hypocrite – I'm using him on Matthew 13 even as I write this!

Dale Ralph Davis,
Well respected author and Bible expositor

Knox Chamblin taught for thirty-four years in Jackson, Mississippi, first at Belhaven College, then at Reformed Theological Seminary until retirement in 2001.

Volume 1 ISBN 978-1-84550-364-2
Volume 2 ISBN 978-1-84550-379-6

Ezra & Nehemiah
A MENTOR COMMENTARY

Tiberius Rata

Ezra & Nehemiah
A Mentor Commentary
Tiberius Rata

Tiberius Rata combines exegetical skill, knowledge of the ancient world, and a pastor's heart in this volume. His explanations of the text are clear, forceful, yet concise. This work will assist the church in understanding its call to godly service to Christ and will motivate its readers to re-consecrate their lives and possessions to the work of the Kingdom.

Kenneth A. Matthews,
Professor of Divinity, Beeson Divinity School, Birmingham, Alabama

Reasoned, researched, and concise, Rata's commentary on Ezra and Nehemiah opens a window on the historical setting for these significant books of the Old Testament. This volume ably addresses the interests of laymen and pastors alike as they study the biblical text of the two books.

William D. Barrick,
Professor of Old Testament, The Master's Seminary, Sun Valley, California

Tiberius Rata's work should be warmly received by pastors and teachers. His commentary is clear and to the point, yet he discusses some problems at length, furnishing thoughtfulness and insight for solutions. His viewpoint is solidly orthodox and reverent. His high view of Scripture and of the God of Scripture is reflected throughout the work. His work demonstrates competent scholarship and conveys a pastor's heart-the work of a pastor scholar. His outlines and comments are helpful for understanding the flow of the historical narrative and are suggestive for sermon preparation.

Russel Fuller,
Professor of Old Testament Interpretation,
The Southern Baptist Theological Seminary, Louisville, Kentucky

Tiberius Rata is the chair of the Biblical Studies Department and professor of Old Testament Studies at Grace College and Theological Seminary, Winona Lake, Indiana.

ISBN 978-1-84550-571-4

Galatians
A MENTOR COMMENTARY

David McWilliams

Galatians

A Mentor Commentary

David McWilliams

...addresses interpretive issues with clarity and cogent discernment, and he engages recent misperceptions of Paul's central concern—which is not merely sociological or ecclesiastical, but soteriological (How may guilty sinners be reconciled to their holy Creator?)—all the while keeping in view the aim of preaching this good news of sovereign grace.

Dennis E. Johnson,
Professor of Practical Theology,
Westminster Seminary in California, Escondido, California

Timely, lucid, and reliable, this is an excellent commentary for preachers, Bible study leaders and others. David McWilliams admirably succeeds in his aim for brevitas and claritas, the two qualities in commentators that Calvin most commended. He distils a great deal of scholarship into uncluttered and readable prose. Paul's message in Galatians has rarely been so urgently needed as today, when justification only by faith is under attack from many sides. McWilliams explains it with judicious care.

Robert Letham,
Senior Tutor, Systematic & Historical Theology,
Wales Evangelical School of Theology, Brigend, Wales

Having had the opportunity of reading this clear and gracefully written book during its production, I commend it most highly. Certainly it is one pastors ought to consider adding to theirs libraries.

Richard Gaffin,
Professor of Biblical and Systematic Theology, Emeritus,
Westminster Theological Seminary, Philadelphia, Pennsylvania

David McWilliams has been the senior pastor at Covenant Presbyterian Church, Lakeland, Florida for 20 years.

ISBN 978-1-84550-452-6

Lamentations
A MENTOR COMMENTARY

John L. Mackay

Lamentations

A Mentor Commentary

John L. MacKay

The five chapters of Lamentations may be easily overlooked. Not only is it brief, but it is also sandwiched between the two giants of Old Testament prophecy, Jeremiah and Ezekiel. Lamentations also deals with realities which we rather wish were not discussed – consequently the book is little studied. However, although there much here to challenge faith, there is much that builds it up. Lamentations was not written in the first instance to serve as warning to others, or to even keep alive the present memory of past suffering, it is the present that dominates the thought of the book.

And in that present are overiding thoughts – 'has God left us?'; 'Have we blown our chance as God's covenant people?' 'Is there a way forward towards the restoration?'

A popular view today is that Lamentations is a dreary book with nothing to say to today's society. The reality is that it could not be more relevant, more authentic.

Mentor combines a high view of Scripture with access to the latest academic theological research. This unique combinations allows the reader to see what recent scholarly research has discovered without losing sight of Scripture.

John L. Mackay is the Principal of the Free Church College, Edinburgh and internationally known as an Old Testament scholar. He is also in demand for church retreats where his skill in the practical exposition and application of doctrine are well respected.

ISBN 978-1-84550-363-5

Christian Focus Publications
publishes books for all ages

Our mission statement –
STAYING FAITHFUL
In dependence upon God we seek to impact the world through literature faithful to His infallible Word, the Bible. Our aim is to ensure that the Lord Jesus Christ is presented as the only hope to obtain forgiveness of sin, live a useful life and look forward to heaven with Him.

REACHING OUT
Christ's last command requires us to reach out to our world with His gospel. We seek to help fulfill that by publishing books that point people towards Jesus and help them develop a Christ-like maturity. We aim to equip all levels of readers for life, work, ministry and mission.

Books in our adult range are published in three imprints.

Christian Focus contains popular works including biographies, commentaries, basic doctrine and Christian living. Our children's books are also published in this imprint.

Mentor focuses on books written at a level suitable for Bible College and seminary students, pastors, and other serious readers. The imprint includes commentaries, doctrinal studies, examination of current issues and church history.

Christian Heritage contains classic writings from the past.

Christian Focus Publications, Ltd
Geanies House, Fearn, Ross-shire,
IV20 1TW, Scotland, United Kingdom
www.christianfocus.com